Susan B. Anthony: A Biography
of a Singular Feminist

KATHLEEN BARRY

Susan B. Anthony: A Biography of a Singular Feminist

New York University Press

NEW YORK AND LONDON

Library of Congress Cataloging-in-Publication Data

Barry, Kathleen.
   Susan B. Anthony: a biography.

   Bibliography: p.
   Includes index.
   1. Anthony, Susan B. (Susan Brownell),
1820–1906. 2. Feminists—United States—
Biography. 3. Biography (as a literary form) I. Title.
HQ1413.A55B36   1988   305.4'2'0924[B] 88-1228
ISBN 0-8147-1105-7 (alk. paper)

Book design by Jennifer Dossin

New York University Press books are Smyth-sewn
and printed on permanent and durable acid-free paper.

Contents

Illustrations

Acknowledgments

THROUGH EIGHT YEARS OF BEING FULLY ENGAGED WITH THE the life of Susan B. Anthony, I am first of all indebted to today's women's movement, particularly radical feminism, for its persistent political presence in championing the cause of women. In offering women a way to know and act on the hidden realities of male domination, it has created a context that has made it possible to more deeply explore Susan B. Anthony's life and her movement's struggle, and it has given me a network of women whose support has often been more like a personal life line. For those moments when the demands of research and writing have taken me out of the field of action, I hope this work gives something back to that movement.

The idea for this book was first conceived fourteen years ago with Joan Hoff-Wilson. While it has taken many twists and turns since then, she has given it its own history with her involvement in the later stages of the manuscript, when she offered critical reading, comments, and new insights which helped to restore to the book some of the vitality that had begun to dissipate in repeated revisions. Christine Delphy's reading of earlier drafts was critical in helping to expand the theoretical scope of this work. Likewise, Sondra Stein, Cynthia Enloe, and Janice Raymond's readings of some chapters helped to keep me on track when I was still finding my way and conceptualizing the work. Throughout, Sandra Elkin has been more than a literary agent as our discussions have given me insights that have enriched this work. But I mean to express more than gratitude for intellectual rigor from these women. Their per-

sonal care and the political commitment that came with these readings and comments is what makes feminism more than politics, but
a way of life—the ultimate lesson I learned from Susan B. Anthony.
Robin Morgan's political insights and support were essential through
a movement crisis, which enabled me to return to this work with
renewed vigor. I am also grateful to Andrea Dworkin, Pat Hynes
and Florence Rush, for being there with ideas, support and the courage of their convictions. Denise Pouillon and Renee Bridel helped
make possible the time I spent in Paris working on this manuscript
and Nicole Revel-MacDonald and Diane Prokopis each provided
support that was essential to seeing this work to its completion.

Jean Pouillon and Francoise Heretier in the Department of Social
Anthropology at the Centre nationale de la recherche scientifique
in Paris honored me with a research appointment, which gave me
the time and a rich intellectual environment in which to develop the
theory of women's biography in this work. Travel and other research expenses were supported by the Sachar International Fellowship from Brandeis University. And I am very grateful for the continuing encouragement for my research from Abram Sachar,
Chancellor of Brandeis University.

Other material support for this work came from the MacDowell
Colony, which provided me with a residence that permitted sustained and concentrated writing for several months. The Radcliffe
Research Fellows Program and the Mazer Fund of Brandeis University each funded travel to archival sources. The Wonder Woman
Foundation's recognition gave me material support and more: Their
award was a real shot in the arm. And I am especially grateful to
Kitty Moore and New York University Press for their faith in my
work.

I am very appreciative of such scholars as Miriam Reed for sharing her research findings with me and of archivists all over the United
States who have made their collections of Anthony papers known
to me. While travel for research was extensive and time consuming
in order to study all the library holdings of Anthony papers, during
this travel my meetings with archivists proved invaluable to this research. I would particularly like to thank Mary Huth at the University of Rochester Library, whose knowledge of the Anthony papers and Rochester history added an important dimension to my
research.

I would like to gratefully acknowledge the institutions and libraries that have allowed me to use materials from their collections:

The Bancroft Library, University of California, Berkeley; the Trustees of the Boston Public Library; the Department of Manuscripts and University Archives, Cornell University; The Huntington Library, San Marino, California; the Massachusetts Historical Society; the Rochester Museum and Science Center; the Local History Division, Rochester Public Library; the Schlesinger Library, Radcliffe College; the Smith Family Papers in the Rare Books and Manuscripts Division of The New York Public Library, Astor, Lenox and Tilden Foundations; the Stowe-Day Foundation, Hartford, Connecticut; the Theodore Stanton Collection of the Elizabeth Cady Stanton Papers at the Mabel Smith Douglas Library, Rutgers University; and Vassar College Library.

I extend my thanks to Helene Wenzel for her assistance with the final editing, and certainly, without the seemingly tireless help of Amy Elman and Michael Blackmore, the tedious work of footnoting and entering revisions would have continued for much longer than it did.

Finally, the less visible but the most personally essential support for this work came from my brothers, Dan and Jim, who were able to care for our father in his last year of life, when geographic distance and the pressures of this book sometimes made it difficult for me to be there. It is to my father James Barry's memory that this book is dedicated, for without his unconditional love perhaps this project and many others would never have been attempted.

Susan B. Anthony as woman's rights activist with her hair bobbed, age thirty-six. (Courtesy of the University of Rochester Library.)

At the end of the Civil War, age forty-five. (Courtesy of the University of Rochester Library.)

Anthony in her fifties. (Courtesy of the Rochester Public Library.)

In the 1890s, in her seventies. (Courtesy of the Rochester Public Library.)

Prologue

SHE SAT THERE ON THE PLATFORM WAITING TO BE INTRODUCED; she was calm and poised, with her hands folded easily in her lap. Every eye in the hall seemed to be riveted upon her. Her charismatic force captured her audience, and they anticipated her words with eagerness. On this trip to St. Louis, throngs were coming out just to catch a glimpse of her; among them were many devoted followers. It was 1895, and suffrage organizations across the country were celebrating the seventy-fifth birthday of Susan B. Anthony. She had become a legend in her own time.

Waiting for the program to begin, she was caught by surprise when seventy-five children—black and white—filed into the packed hall, marched ceremoniously to the platform, and, as they passed by her, each laid a rose in her lap. After the venerable Susan B. Anthony's young niece stepped forward and presented her rose with a kiss for her aunt, the rest of the children did the same.

Two days in St. Louis; next stop Denver. The excitement there was even more dramatic and festive, for the women of Colorado had recently won the vote. Now they heralded Susan B. Anthony as the symbol of their victory. "America's Joan of Arc Shakes Hands with an Army of Women Voters," a newspaper headline proclaimed.

A few days later she was en route to Utah, then on to Idaho. Everywhere honors preceded her; speeches and testimonies told of her courage, her selfless dedication, a life committed to womankind. Her next stop was California. Crossing the Sierra Nevada range, the train stopped on the wind-blown, snow-laden Donner Pass, and Susan stepped out for a moment into the radiant sunshine to take a deep breath of fresh mountain air. The panoramic vista was breathtaking. Since childhood, when she had roamed the Berkshire Hills and sat behind her house looking up at Mount Greylock, the majesty of nature had the effect of a spiritual force upon her.

Finally, she arrived in San Francisco. The adulation that greeted this always-campaigning woman culminated with her entrance into the Woman's Congress. Thousands packed into Golden Gate Hall, while hundreds more pressed at the doors trying to get in. When Susan B. Anthony entered from the wings of the stage, the crowd rose in thunderous applause and cheers. A sea of white handkerchieves waved in the air—a silent tribute from the older women who had learned in their youth that this greeting, the "Chautauqua salute," was more ladylike than loud handclapping. Many could not hold back their tears when Susan B. Anthony began to speak. They were remembering the days when this woman had been one of the most reviled and ridiculed in the nation.

Susan wore her garnet velvet, a dress she disliked packing and one she found cumbersome to travel with as it required its own special trunk. But years before, her younger "coadjutors," as she called them, had insisted that she have one dress for "state occasions" that was not her usual black. They took her to a dressmaker in London where she chose a dress of garnet velvet, her favorite color. Now when groups invited her to speak, they frequently requested that she appear in this special dress.

The gown was heavy and made in two pieces—a fitted "basque" jacket that came neatly to her waist and then a long, full skirt, loosely ruffled at the bottom, that slightly trailed on the floor behind her. The sleeve cuffs and high neck were fitted with her best rose-point lace, a gift from one of the suffrage associations. The lace, which was caught at the neck, was clasped with her cameo and cascaded down the front of her jacket. As always, her thick, silver hair was fastened in a coil at the base of her neck.

Susan was escorted to the stage by an entourage that included San Francisco's mayor and her own dear friend Reverend Anna Howard Shaw. Around her, other speakers were sitting on elegant sofas and richly unholstered armchairs. A lavish array of tropical plants and flowers filled the platform. Eying the throne in the center, which had been draped with a canopy of roses, Susan mumbled, "Oh dear-a-me." But then, she did look radiant sitting in this place of highest honor. The deep reds and subtle pinks of the roses of the canopy set off her garnet velvet dress, and the audience was enraptured. Now, she wondered, what would she do next and how would she handle the adulation this time? A procession started from the rear of the grand auditorium, and one woman after another who had followed her in the cause came forward to present her with a bouquet of flowers.

This kind of honor and awe had always made Susan feel awkward. Once when she entered a hall on the arm of Anna Shaw and the crowd rose in applause, it had puzzled her. Anna explained, "It's for you, Miss Anthony."

"Nonsense, it's not for me. It's for the cause—the Cause!"[1] Susan insisted. Did Anna not know that the two had become one?

She was relieved when the ceremonies were finally concluded, and she could get on to the work of the evening—that was to rouse her admirers and to convince her foes to work in a new campaign for woman's rights. The *San Francisco Chronicle* reported that when she was called upon to speak, "Susan B. Anthony stood like a princess."

Nearly twenty-five years earlier the same newspaper had condemned her as a heretic. This night, even as she came to this festive celebration, she still felt the sting of that ugly night in 1871 when she had defended a San Francisco prostitute who had been convicted and jailed for killing a local dignitary. When word spread through the city that afternoon that Susan B. Anthony had asked to be taken to the prison to visit the condemned Laura Fair, the local citizenry was indignant. Despite the uproar Anthony made the visit and then, satisfied that Laura Fair had acted to protect herself, asserted in her typically straightforward, no-nonsense manner in her speech that evening that "if all men protected women as they would have their own wives and daughters protected, you would have no Laura Fair in your jail tonight."

Back then in 1871, Anthony's audience had become nearly riotous; they hissed, booed, and shouted vile comments at her. They tried to silence her with their menacing behavior. Stomping on the creaky wooden floors, it seemed as if they would rush to the platform at any moment. But Susan B. Anthony stood unshaken before them. They continued their provocations for several minutes, but her poised adamance subdued them. Silence fell over the auditorium. Anthony did not move or say a word. Finally, when she had their undivided attention again, she repeated her statement without drama but in a tone and manner that reflected all the firmness of her convictions—a stance that was called "strident" in those days.

Then, after more hisses and boos, she repeated it yet again and added, "I declare to you that woman must not depend upon the protection of man, but must be taught to protect herself, and there I take my stand."[2] Words of heresy in 1871!

The next day she was resoundingly condemned in every newspaper in northern California. Newspapers across the nation picked up the story and thoroughly castigated her. "Never in all my hard experience have I been under such fire," she remembered. "The shadows of the newspapers hung over me everywhere I went." Even though she had been subjected to this kind of attack numerous times and ridiculed constantly for more than twenty years, that night she admitted, "I never before was so cut down!" But later when the sting of attack had dulled, she worried that she had not been strong enough. Defending Laura Fair without speaking of what prostitution does to women, Anthony claimed, was like going into the South "and failing to illustrate human oppression by negro slavery."[3]

Born in 1820 in a small town in western Massachusetts, Susan Brownell Anthony was the daughter of a principled and plain Quaker father and a loving, committed, but withdrawn mother. Hers was neither a prominent nor an important family. Rather, they were ordinary people who, in Quaker fashion, were hardworking and industrious. Susan's childhood was spent in the midst of her mother's unending domestic chores, and her brief and limited education was designed to cultivate in her the female virtues of piety and humility. She rebelled against neither. When she was young, her family was economically secure and filled with devotion and love. The Anthonys' Quaker faith was so secularized and humane that in the face of the harsh Calvinism inherited by Puritan New England, it would not have been likely to stir a rebellious streak in her either. In this very average family, she did not mingle with great leaders; instead, she spent long hours quilting with her sisters and whole days baking bread for her family and their many boarders.

From this ordinary world, Susan B. Anthony became one of the most unconventional women of the nineteenth century. Her life of confrontational political leadership on behalf of her sex provokes the question: If not from personal anguish and rebellion, if not through political connections, how did a common woman arise and, in Anthony's case, become the most dramatic and charismatic of feminist rebels—known to many as the "Napoleon" of nineteenth-century feminism?

1

The Rise of a Common Woman

1820 WAS A GOOD YEAR TO BE BORN SUSAN B. ANTHONY. IT WAS
from her generation of women, born around the 1820s, that the first
political movement of women in American history would arise thirty
years later. Elizabeth Cady (Stanton), born five years earlier than
Susan B. Anthony, and Lucy Stone, born in 1818, would all meet
one day and together with many other strong-minded women militate on behalf of their sex. Their commitment would mark the beginning of the long-delayed rebellion that Abigail Adams had promised her husband John on the eve of the framing of the Declaration
of Independence. "If particular care and attention is not paid to the
Ladies, we are determined to foment a Rebellion." Adams knew
well that marriage laws put "unlimited power into the hands of
husbands." Like Abigail Adams, Anthony, Stanton, and Stone were
defiant women; but unlike women in colonial America, they were
able to build an organized woman's movement to press for their
demands. Adam's singular voice had been easily silenced. But by
the late 1840s—when women were already breaking out of the private sphere, if only to go to school in the new, advanced female
seminaries and to work in the burgeoning mill industry—a new
generation of women, already freer from the home than their mothers had ever thought of being, dared to act collectively for their sex.

If 1820 promised a future of assertive and defiant action for women,
it was not yet evident when Susan B. Anthony's mother, Lucy Read,
married Daniel Anthony in 1817 and their marriage scandalized the
rural community of Adams, Massachusetts.

.   .   .

Daniel Anthony and Lucy Read had grown up together in this small community. Their families lived on adjoining farms in the hilly but fertile countryside of the Berkshire Hills in Adams, Massachusetts. The Anthony family had migrated to western Massachusetts from Rhode Island as part of a small group of Quakers, at a time when persecution of their sect had waned in the Commonwealth. They became industrious farmers and had lived peacefully alongside the Baptists in the Adams community. Eventually, Daniel went away to the Quakers' Nine Partners Boarding School. When he returned, with too many sophisticated airs to satisfy his father, Lucy Read was no longer a childhood playmate. A romance developed between them, and they were married without official Quaker approval on July 13, 1817.

Now Lucy Read Anthony sat alone in the parlor of her mother's house. Downcast, she listened while in the next room a delegation of the Society of Friends pronounced their verdict to her husband: His marriage "out of meeting" had violated the rules of their society. It was the summer of 1817. Daniel and Lucy had just returned from their honeymoon, a trip by covered wagon over the log-laid corduroy roads of the rugged western frontier of New York State, where they visited some relatives in the barely settled frontier of Rochester, New York. While the Anthonys had been away, the Society of Friends had met in their own village of Adams to consider the unorthodox marriage.

"How unlike my own mother I am now," Lucy must have thought to herself as she withdrew into the pain and embarassment of the moment. Why only a few days before her wedding she had gone out to a party and danced until four in the morning, while Daniel sat against the wall knowing that this partying would soon come to an end. She knew it too. But she did not expect that her marriage to a Quaker would bring her humiliation.

Lucy Read had lived among Quakers all of her life, but as a Baptist she was not practiced in their ways. She loved to dress in lively colors and attend parties. Some days she would go into the fields and sing to her heart's content. But the Quakers were a somber people, who dressed in simple greys and were quiet in their mannerisms. They spoke to each other in "thee" and "thou" to avoid making class distinctions. When the Anthonys went to their Meeting house, which sat on a hill on the other side of the village, instead of singing hymns and praying aloud together like the Baptists who were led by their minister, they sat in silence—a kind of meditation and during which they awaited God's revelation.

The Quakers had actually originated as a religious movement founded in the seventeenth century in England as a reaction against Puritan morality and the Calvinist belief in predestination, which gave the clergy the power to judge who would be saved and what kind of good works would lead to salvation. Instead of following a God who, as the Puritan fathers preached, had already determined who would gain entrance to heaven and a clergy that scrutinized public and private morality, the Quakers followed the Inner Light— the representation of God in theirs and everyone's soul. In their belief, they made no distinction between clergy and laity. But by the nineteenth century, this climate of austere Quaker authority had combined with rigid Calvinistic Puritanism that monitored private thoughts and individual acts for signs of violations of God's will.

Now in Lucy's parents' home a committee of Friends announced to Daniel Anthony that he had been found guilty of violating a basic rule of the Friends by marrying Lucy Read, who was a Baptist. After the judgment was declared against her husband, Lucy spoke not a word about it; and through the long summer months while Daniel's case was being considered by the Adams Society of Friends, she stayed at home and kept her somber posture.

Her husband did not give the Friends satisfaction by renouncing his marriage and abandoning his wife; and the sect, dwindling in numbers and fraught with numerous splits, did not insist. But Daniel was as loyal and dedicated to his society as he was to his wife. He had to find a way to keep both.

Meanwhile, Lucy began to teach herself to bear up under the Quaker scrutiny of her marriage, which, she learned, governed even the smallest aspects of her and her new family's everyday life. After all, she was living in puritanical New England, where evangelical Protestantism with its more liberal interpretation of the Bible was only beginning to wrest itself from the tight grip of Calvinism's severe religious authority over all personal matters.

Originally a doctrine preached by Anne Hutchinson in the Massachusetts Bay Colony in the 1640s and one for which she was condemned and exiled as a heretic, the belief that God dwelled in each human soul had the effect of making individuals responsible for their own salvation. Over the centuries the Protestant clergy, while still considering this belief heretical, had begun to loosen its control over its own faithful and the determination (with God, of course) of who would win salvation. Over the years, the New England Quakers had assimilated much of the religious fervor they had originally opposed—as was evident in their scrutiny of the Anthonys' marriage.

Daniel Anthony was excluded from Meeting until he could "make satisfaction" to the Society. In Meeting, Quakers made all decisions that governed individual and community life. Meeting was the business unit as well as the locus of worship for the Society, and before it came all matters of care for the poor, apprenticing of children, enforcement of discipline, and establishment of schools, as well as requests for permission to marry or to remove to a new location.[1] By the end of the summer, Daniel had decided to apologize to the Society. The committee reported back to Meeting that "he appeared in his disposition to make Friends satisfaction—he having forwarded to this Meeting acknowledgement of his misconduct." The Society did not try to exact any more from him, and once again he was restored to full participation. It had been a trying experience for the young couple but one that Lucy paid more dearly for in the long run than did Daniel. Lucy knew that to question the legitimacy of a young woman's marriage had deeply serious moral implications.

When Daniel explained his apology to his new bride, he told her that the statement he forwarded to the Society said: "I am sorry that in order to marry the woman I love best, I had to violate a rule of the religious society I revered the most." His apology was judicious but not more, and sometimes just and balanced explanation is not enough for the heart. As Lucy remembered the whole affair, she recalled that her husband told the Society that he "was sorry he married her."[2] Perhaps that is one reason she never became a Quaker. All her life Lucy contended that she was not good enough to be a Friend. By refusing to join her husband's society and reacting to their marriage scandal with silent and somber withdrawal, Lucy Anthony had mounted her own, albeit unnoticed, acts of resistance and opposition to accepting her husband's way of life that gave her no context for her own. Women of her generation had little voice at home or in the world around them, but they did have their own private ways of maintaining their sanity and dignity under such circumstances.

Quakerism with its egalitarian ethic held the potential of giving women a fairer status in their communities with its emphasis on the Inner Light, which cultivated self-responsibility that freed them from the rest of society where Protestantism imposed more restrictions or inequality on women. But in the nineteenth century even Quakers began to adopt the evangelical Protestant ethic of true womanhood, which asked women to look into themselves not for self-reliance but with piety and humility. Lucy Anthony had been reared according to the tenets of evangelical Protestantism, in which women were told that they were the guardians of morality. While the clergy remained their spiritual leaders, women looked to themselves and with strict self-regulation internalized what were considered virtues, but what were in reality the limits and confinement—that is, the domination—that society and the clergy had enforced upon them earlier.

The shift from an externally imposed Calvinistic Puritanism to a personalized moralistic piety was essentially a change from being dominated by others to internalizing that domination and passing it on to the female children. By the time of Lucy Anthony's marriage the Quakers had assimilated into the tradition they had originally opposed. Lucy Anthony learned to be pious and humble as a young bride, and soon she would pass these virtues on to her daughters. Lucy was dealt a double blow: the austerity of Quakerism without its liberating qualities and the piety in the religious awakening's idea of the true woman.

In the first months of their marriage Daniel and Lucy lived with Lucy's parents, while Daniel built their home on land given to them by Lucy's mother and with wood his father had given him in return for work he had done. The sturdy, large New England farmhouse rested on a knoll on the first ledge of the Berkshire range. Surrounded by rolling countryside, Mount Greylock, the highest mountain in Massachusetts, loomed in the distance behind the house; before it, less than a mile downhill, the little town of Adams formed along the Hoosic River as it cut its way through the Berkshire Valley. The Anthonys' house was ample but austere. In Quaker fashion, they had what they needed but no more. There were no decorations, musical instruments, or any other distractions that would draw the inhabitants of the house away from their attention to the Inner Light.

Lucy sang no more, not even to her babies. She bore her first child a year after she married and named her Guelma, after Gulielma, the first wife of William Penn who was the Quaker founder of Pennsylvania. The veil of silence and withdrawal that had descended over Lucy at the beginning of her marriage did not lift then and indeed never lifted. Her pregnancies only exacerbated her inwardness. She carried her babies without ever speaking a word of her condition, not even to her own mother. As time went by, Lucy extended her own silence and embarrassment about women's sexual and reproductive functions to her children. In 1830 she bought a book of medical advice called *Domestic Medicine or Treatise on the Prevention and Cure of Diseases*, which was a guide for nursing illnesses and wounds that she would use to protect the health of her growing family. Susan later remembered the book that "for years was kept hidden away from us children . . . to save us from a knowledge of maternity—[Mother] cut out the leaves from page 396 to page 423—and pasted over the Table of Contents—page xxxvii with 'The right to petition from John Quincy Adams letter to his constituents in 1837,' when I was 17 years old—and then blotting out from the Index . . . reference to the expurgated pages of the book. This all shows how carefully our mother watched over us that we might not know the Mysteries of Life."[3]

While Lucy awaited the delivery of her second child, she and her mother sat and sewed together. When Susannah Read finished a layette for her expected grandchild, she quietly laid it out in a drawer. No words were spoken between the two women about the coming childbirth, but silent concern was reflected in a glance here, a gesture there. Infant and maternal mortality were high in those days, and no woman prepared for the delivery of her child without some anxiety about the outcome. But whatever were Lucy's hopes and fears about childbirth and her next baby, she kept them to herself.

It was into this world that Susan B. Anthony, the second of the Anthony children, was born on February 15, 1820. Daniel and Lucy were pleased. Lucy had a safe delivery and Susan was a strong and healthy baby. February 15 was a cold day for this baby girl to come into the world. Susan arrived in the midst of a long winter—when the excitement of December's first snows and the satisfactions of winter's hibernation had passed. The New Englanders anxiously awaited spring with the feel of warmth that would break the long chill in the air and allow windows to be opened to air out the winter's staleness.

Susan B. Anthony was not the first-born of her family; she was not particularly her father's favorite, nor did she become a tomboy or hate being a girl. Moreover, few of the standard male characteristics found in anyone who begins as a path breaker and becomes a charismatic leader can be found in Susan B. Anthony's early life.

Susan was a child of her age. But childhood had taken on new meaning in the early nineteenth century. "The age of the child" discarded the older notion that children were little adults whose workload increased with their age.[4] In its place emerged a romantic view of children, one that sentimentalized them as the human beings closest to nature in their spontaneity, simplicity and straightforwardness.

Lucy Anthony had eight closely spaced pregnancies at a time when family size in the United States was becoming smaller. Hannah was born only nineteen months after Susan. Then came Daniel in 1824, Mary in 1827, Eliza in 1832 and J. Merritt in 1834. The Quakers were dwindling in numbers and expected large families to compensate for the sect's shortcomings. Seven of the Anthony children survived childbirth; but one of the seven, Ann Eliza, born in 1833, died in infancy.

Lucy and Daniel provided a typical Quaker home for their children, which was positive even in its austerity and was characterized by the Quaker maxim:

> All work and no play, makes Jack a dull boy,
> All play and no work, makes Jack a mere toy.[5]

When freed from their daily chores and school work, Susan and her sisters roamed the Berkshire Hills. In winter, they played in the fresh deep snows, sometimes running out to catch snowflakes. In summer, they might set across the open rolling hills for an afternoon of picking wildflowers or just walking. Often Susan sat in the grass behind their house and watched the sunset behind the looming Mount Greylock. She was enchanted with nature and could sit in wonder over the workings of a community of insects or nursing a wounded bird back to flight.

Susan's father was a stern-looking man. His stiff and upright posture and his serious, almost severe countenance suggested a harsh disciplinarian. But this was not the case. True, he was firm, but he believed in guiding his children, not directing them. He excluded the world of childish amusements, such as toys, games, and music, as distractions from the Inner Light. But in their place he introduced self-discipline, principled convictions, and belief in their own self-worth. Lucy remained somber and emotionally withdrawn for the duration of her life. But emotional withdrawal did not mean emotional rejection, and her children knew it. She was devoted to them in her quiet ways, and they felt her warmth and delighted in her occasional efforts to dress them in lively plaids, replacing their somber Quaker grays.

In 1824, when Susan was four, Lucy was pregnant again. As her confinement approached, she sent her three daughters, Guelma, Susan, and Hannah to their Grandmother Anthony for six weeks. Years earlier, Susan's grandfather had organized a school for his own children on the Anthony homestead. Now he wanted his small grandchildren to have the benefit of instruction there. During these six weeks Susan and Guelma learned to read in Grandfather Anthony's school. Their lessons consumed long hours of each day, and the strain was too much for young Susan's eyes. When she returned home, the first thing her mother noticed was that her eyes were crossed.

Lucy was very upset, but she comforted her daughter by telling her that she had the prettiest eyes she had ever seen. Then she put away all the books, hoping that rest would allow the muscles in Susan's eyes to relax and correct their position, which seemed to be impairing her vision. A few weeks of rest almost restored these already intense eyes to their normal position; however, Susan's left eye remained crossed and gave her considerable trouble in reading for the rest of her life.

Susan's was an ordinary, uneventful childhood—one that was not marked with evidence of child prodigy or filled with events that could predict the dramatically different future before her. She was well cared for and loved. Neither she nor her family were unusual. But it must be admitted that, except in the accounts of those who tend to romanticize the ordinariness of working-class life, this kind of childhood is largely uninteresting. Young Susan's daily life does not lend itself to compelling biographical description or psychological probing. It stood for what it was—hard work and some play in an uneventful setting. Only in retrospect, when precisely because of her common origins she rose to become an extraordinary leader of women, can the significance of these early years be fully appreciated. At that time, there was no thought that she would become anything other than a common woman like her mother.

With all of the setbacks Lucy Anthony had experienced with her marriage, probably the most unnoticed—but ultimately the most decisive factor in determining what she and other married women could do with their lives—was the legal status of married American women at this time. In colonial America a few women with property had occasionally been permitted to vote; many married women had been able to make special legal arrangements to protect their own property and inheritance rights; and some actually ran their own businesses.

In fact, in the disruptive years of the Revolution, it was not unusual for women like Susannah Read to manage family farms and conduct essential family business with independence and autonomy. But this did not last. With peace, more formal restrictions of the functions of married women crept into the new United States legal system—some by design; others by default. Consequently, by the time Susannah's daughter Lucy had married, there were even more legal obstacles that prevented wives from managing businesses or family farms. In fact, in Lucy's time there were fewer equity procedures to protect inherited property than had been available to her mother-in-law, Hannah Anthony when she married Humphrey Anthony. By the 1830s, when Susannah Read left her daughter what was then a small fortune of ten thousand dollars, as a married woman Lucy Anthony could not legally accept the money in her own name— only a man or a single woman could do that. Her husband, by that time having declared bankruptcy, agreed that her brother Joshua should hold the money for her so that Daniel's own pursuing creditors could not get access to it. Lucy Read Anthony was an old woman before her daughter, Susan B. Anthony, had begun to champion and win greater property rights for married women.

Such rights had diminished after the American Revolution. As state laws were codified in the early decades of the nineteenth century, married women found that informal and formal procedures allowing them the right to own, manage, or inherit property, or even to obtain custody of their children, were not codified in the new laws. These practices followed Blackstone's *Commentaries On the Laws of England* published in 1765–69, which stipulated that "the very being or legal existence of the woman is suspended during the marriage, or at least is incorporated and consolidated into that of the husband; under whose wing, protection and cover, she performs every thing."[6]

Blackstone's definition of the relation in marriage of wife to husband which Anthony would later compare to slavery as a "blot on civilization,"·made women the legal property of their husbands under essentially the same conditions that had bound serfs or vassals to their lords during the period of European feudalism in the tenth and twelfth centuries.* Under feudalism, vassals were free men in dependence, "the man of another man." The lord held direct power *over the person* of the vassal and required his *self-surrender*. In this highly paternalistic arrangement, the vassal's obligations to the lord (sealed with a kiss) formed a lifetime commitment; in return, the lord of the manor was obligated to provide protection and maintenance to his vassal, like the husband for his wife.[7] Christian marriage was largely shaped by the structure of feudalism. The relations of power between lord and vassal most closely approximated the relations defined between husband and wife under English coverture centuries later which in fact then identified marital partners as "Baron and Feme" thus leaving a woman with no status beyond that of her sex.[8] In many ways, the post-Revolutionary republic drew some of the battle lines of the future woman's rights movement.

Lucy Read Anthony and her generation experienced all of the continuing legal and social limitations of women's condition stemming from the colonial period while they did not enjoy the few possibilities for women's legal and economic independence that could be arranged privately and in special court considerations known as equity jurisprudence. When Lucy's father went off to fight in the Revolutionary War, her mother, Susannah Read, had managed the business affairs of the family farm. She was a strong woman, assured and assertive in handling all facets of the farm business, which she could conduct in her own name. And when her husband returned from the war, they agreed that she should continue to be the real proprietor of their farm. Such family arrangements were possible as long as women were acting for their husbands and on behalf of their families. But in 1876 when Matilda Joslyn Gage, a married woman's rights activist, tried to rent a room as headquarters for a feminist campaign, she was informed that her signature had no authorizing or binding power.

The rise of the common woman had no history; it was not expected to occur. But during Susan's younger years the rise of the common man was a national theme—almost a patriotic duty. The nineteenth century was fond of its common man, that glorified ideal that preoccupied politicians and philosophers of Jacksonian democracy. Andrew Jackson came to the United States presidency in 1828 as a self-made frontiersman—a symbol of what the common man could become. When Susan B. Anthony was growing from girlhood to womanhood, Jacksonian democracy's "self-made man" had become the national ideal. He was endowed with natural rights, which, having been granted to him after a hard-fought war for independence, encouraged him to grow toward his unlimited potential and to join with his fellow man to express the "will of the people." As white and male, secure in his citizenship, and with increased political and economic rights, the self-made man was a part of the foundation of the new, proud, and growing democracy, in which it was believed that any boy, regardless of his class or station in life, could grow up to be president.

While Lucy was confined to her private sphere, Daniel Anthony received the call of the common man to set farm life aside and launch into the age of industry. With the introduction of the power loom in Waltham, Massachusetts, in 1815, mass production of cotton cloth initiated large-scale American industrialization. Young and eager to take advantage of the new opportunities that would come with industrialization, Daniel Anthony built a small mill—the first of many—on a rushing brook across the road from his house in Adams.

Daniel Anthony patterned his mill after the ambitious Waltham project. When he began his operation in Adams in 1822, the Boston Associates, who were the financiers of the early mills, had already enlarged their project from their first small mill in Waltham. They had moved to Lowell and had built an extensive canal system to harness water power from the Merrimac River for a full factory. They had hired thirteen- to sixteen-year-old farm girls, who provided them with the cheapest pool of available labor; the value of their labor reflecting the unpaid labor of women in the home. They earned a meager $1.45 for a six-day work week, which started at 6 A.M. and ended at 6 P.M. each day. But this was more than the girls could ever have earned had they stayed on the family farm. The Boston Associates could probably have found even cheaper labor in children, but they were determined not to replicate in America the deplorable conditions of child labor in England. For one thing, the citizens of the young republic would not have tolerated child labor at that time. Having conceded to and rationalized black slavery within their democratic and egalitarian ideals in the 1820s, they could not tolerate further obvious exploitation as a part of the white American dream. At best, this was only a temporary barrier because accelerated industrialization turned to child labor later in the century.

The Boston Associates housed their young mill girls in boarding-houses that were strictly regulated and guaranteed the girls' families that their daughters' virtue would not be compromised. Daniel Anthony's mill, with its twenty looms, was much smaller. He turned to his home, his wife, and sister for the back-up labor to sustain his mill. Lucy boarded eleven of his workers in their house, and his sister Hannah boarded the other twelve. Susan grew up in a house bustling with many people most of the time. Lucy welcomed the mill girls as if they were family. But in 1822, with their new baby Hannah, she had three daughters under the age of four and her workday was unending. Occasionally she had the help of a thirteen-year-old girl who did chores for her before and after her own school day. Daniel could afford to hire more help for her, but by social custom, which both Lucy and her husband accepted, this was considered inappropriate.

In contrast to all the talk about the aspiring common man in search of his unlimited potential, what could be said of the common woman? Unlike her husband, there was no place for her outside the home, no national themes or grand philosophies to eulogize her. Instead, each day Lucy prepared three meals for sixteen people. The fare was simple in those days before refrigeration. Lucy could get butter and cheese—the only dairy products that would keep—from Grandmother Anthony, whose Berkshire cheese had been marketed in Boston by her husband for years. Usually there were no leafy vegetables as they were difficult to farm and impossible to store for very long. But boiled potatoes and possibly turnips, or beets or carrots in season, were added to the fare, along with some pork and bacon that did not spoil as easily as other meats. Bread was the other staple in their household and baking it, usually twenty loaves at a time, consumed an entire day.[9]

Laundry was a particularly onerous chore for Lucy Anthony, as the water had to be carried by pail from a spring to her kitchen. This was explicitly woman's work: "One wash, one boiling, and one rinse used about fifty gallons of water—or four hundred pounds." When Catharine Beecher began to write on domestic economy, she said the best technique was to "wash each article in the suds bath, rubbing it against the washboard. Wring them out, rub soap on the most soiled spots, then cover them with water on the boiler on the stove and 'boil them up.' "[10]

But at least Lucy no longer had to spin cotton and weave the cloth of that harsh homespun from linen, flax, and cotton. The new fabric, which Daniel produced in abundance from his mill, was soft to the touch yet durable. "Cotton cloth, just coming into use," Susan recalled, "was considered a luxury. Mother had sheets and pillow-cases—half cotton, half linen. She was thought to be very fortunate to have such cloth."[11]

As soon as Guelma, then Susan, and then Hannah became old enough, they began to help Lucy with the household chores. By contrast, the mill girls boarding with them but earning their own wages must have seemed to Susan to have had the better situation. True, they worked long hours. But their hours were set, and when the mill closed at the end of the day, they were finished until the next morning. Their income was small, but they did receive a salary for their work, which many sent home to help support their families or to put an older brother through school. But the longer women remained in the public work force, the more they could use their income to support themselves—or even to put themselves through school. In contrast to the mill girls, married women of Lucy Anthony's generation were total dependents. They had no income of their own and were forced to rely on the beneficence of their wage-earning husbands. This was a subject that feminist writer Charlotte Perkins Gilman would take up later in the century with force in her book *Women and Economics*.[12] Some, like Lucy Anthony, were lucky that their husbands were industrious, that they did not drink up their income, that they were not abusive.

These were the conditions of the common woman of the early nineteenth century that made a women's movement impossible—even to conceive of the idea of it. Living in economic dependency, relying on or hoping for the beneficence of their husbands, and confined within separate homes, these women were robbed of the kind of social space that makes it possible to think and act on one's own behalf, the first step in acting on behalf of women collectively. But by the 1830s, when women constituted sixty-eight percent of all employees in American cotton mills and working outside the home was still considered unladylike,[13] these workers for the first time found themselves in the public world where they could come together and act out of their own independence. This did not lead them directly to feminist organizing. There were many more changes in women's lives that would have to happen before a feminist movement would be possible. But mill work, like the female seminaries, made the first cracks in the private sphere and opened a world beyond the home to the common woman.[14]

. . .

Daniel Anthony's mill was a success, and his Quaker "square deal-ing" won him considerable recognition in the business world. In 1826 a New York judge, John McLean, offered to put up the capital to build a factory system if Daniel would relocate to Battenville in the eastern part of New York State.

Battenville was a tiny village along the rushing Battenkill River, situated about thirty-five miles north of Albany and some ten miles east of the Hudson River in the lower hills of the Adirondack range. An 1824 gazetteer for New York State does not mention Battenville at all. When the Anthonys moved there, it was a very small village populated with only a few houses. By 1836, ten years after Daniel Anthony had built up a small industrial community there, a ga-zetteer noted that it "contains 1 Methodist and 1 Baptist church, a post office, a cotton factory, 1 grist mill and 1 sawmill, 1 tavern, 2 stores and about 40 dwellings," many of which Anthony had built for his employees. Except for the churches and tavern most of the rest of the village was either built by Anthony or was a result of his factory system. In addition, he had opened a satinette factory and some other small mills in nearby Hardscrabble, an ugly little village two miles down river. The Anthony family was thriving in the early 1830s, and Daniel frequently traveled to New York to sell his goods. But life in the household for Lucy and her daughters changed very little. Long hours of cooking and sewing continued to fill their days.

Even in the midst of his own prosperity, Daniel did not raise the wages in his mills. Once, when one of his spoolers was ill, Susan drew the luck of being able to replace her and receive her salary of three dollars for two weeks work. This was less than the salary earned in the 1830s by the mill girls at Lowell, who had worked on a piecework basis and whose salaries had ranged from forty to eighty cents per day. This was still only a small proportion of the wages earned by men in the mills, who by then were able to negotiate their daily wages according to established rates for their crafts, and made from eighty-five cents to two dollars a day.[15]

When Susan was eleven, she asked her father to make one of the girl operatives an overseer. She had observed on several occasions that this operative, Sally Ann Hyatt, knew more about weaving than did her overseer Elijah. Her father firmly replied that "it would never do to have a woman overseer in the mill." The matter was settled, but it rested as a contradiction in the back of Susan's mind for years.

Unlike the Boston Associates, John McLean did not advance Daniel Anthony solid capital for their ambitious enterprise. But

McLean's credit was good, and when it was needed, his credit was extended over and over again. These were years of economic prosperity for the Anthonys and the McLeans alike. Indeed, because of new industries the economy of the whole country was expanding rapidly. Banks extended loans and credit easily, property values rose, goods were plentiful, and consumption was high.

In the spring of 1832, Daniel began to build a new fifteen-room house for his still-growing family. Lucy—pregnant again—boarded the dozen bricklayers Daniel hired to build the house, but she was so ill throughout most of her pregnancy that her daughters Hannah, Susan, and Guelma—ages 10, 12, and 14—had to take over the chores of preparing meals and keeping house. In 1834 the Anthonys' moved into their new house, resplendent with hand-finished plaster walls, light green woodwork, and four fireplaces; but their housewarming was saddened by the death of Eliza, the baby sister. Within a few months Lucy gave birth to a son—her last child—J. Merritt.

Between home and factory Daniel Anthony had constructed his own paternalistic community in which he extended his care for his wife and children to his workers. "Everything about the factory was conducted with perfect system and order. Each man had a little garden around his house," Susan remembered. It was a Quaker practice, which Daniel had inherited from his father, to organize "home schools" to insure a proper education for their children. Initially, Daniel had sent his children to the district school, until one day ,Susan came home upset and reported that her male teacher would not teach her long division because she was a girl.,Quakers were firm in their egalitarian approach to education. When Daniel organized a home school for his children, he also provided an evening school for his employees. Susan recalled that the school was in session "from eight to nine o'clock, and it was considered unpopular not to attend. Half the employees of the factory were there, learning to read and write or spell."[16] At first, Susan's father taught the classes himself, but eventually he hired a full-time teacher who instructed the children during the day and the employees in the evening.

To find a teacher for his own school, Daniel Anthony inquired at the new female seminaries and found a young woman who had been a student of Mary Lyons. In the late 1830s in western Massachusetts, Mary Lyons had made a pioneering advance in women's education when she had founded Mount Holyoke Seminary, then the only school to provide the closest approximation to a male university education. There was no full-fledged university education for women at that time. Not until 1864, when Vassar opened as the first all-women's college, was the same level of undergraduate college education available to young women that had been offered to men since the founding of Harvard in 1636. Mount Holyoke did not begin as a woman's college but it was the first endowed seminary for young women that made it possible for girls from all social classes to take advantage of a higher level of education, as entrance was not dependent on their ability to pay. But before her dream of Mount Holyoke had come to fruition, Mary Lyons had taught at Ipswich Academy in Massachusetts, and one of her students there had been Mary Perkins.

After she finished her studies, Daniel Anthony hired Mary Perkins to teach in his school. The community found it very impressive that he had brought such a "fashionably educated" teacher to their "modern" school. The school "was the first in that neighborhood to have a separate seat for each pupil, and although only a stool without a back, it was a vast improvement on the long bench running around the wall, the same height for big and little."[17] With her advanced teaching techniques, Miss Perkins drew considerable attention in the community when it was learned that she was teaching her young students to "recite poems in concert, introduced books with pictures . . . and gave them their first idea of calisthenics."[18]

Calisthenics were introduced early into American school curriculums as it was patriotically reasoned that part of being a good American was having a healthy body. But there were special reasons why girls were said to need daily physical exercise at school. Many doctors promoted the popular fear that educating girls would strain their brains and mental capacities and consequently impair their reproductive functions. It was widely believed that only one major physical function in the body could develop at a time and that greater exercise of the brain would cause the uterus to atrophy.[19] Partly in response to these arguments, Emma Willard introduced a physical exercise program aimed at developing the health of the whole body when she opened the Troy Female Seminary in 1822. She hoped to calm the fears of her opponents and to assure them that the true womanhood of her students would not be compromised by their education.

In the Anthony "home school," Mary Perkins began to teach the children music and songs. When Daniel heard them singing he stepped in and firmly drew the line, explaining to Miss Perkins that he would have no such worldly distractions in his school. He believed that music acted upon the senses and incited passions; it could be innocent or evil in its effects. To prevent the latter, the children would have to study it for years, and that would distract them from their pursuit of practical knowledge, not to mention the weakened moral condition that would result from a sedentary life. Daniel Anthony, like many of his fellow Quakers, believed that he was protecting his children from the traumatic effects of having their passions incited with toys, music, games, and art; and then, like many of the evangelical Protestants, having to subdue those passions to be holy and righteous.

Mary Perkins offered a new image of womanhood to Susan and her sisters. She was independent and educated; as a teacher, she held a position that had been traditionally reserved to young men graduating from universities and theological seminaries. Guelma and Susan soon began to follow her example and took up small teaching assignments near Battenville. Their father had reared all his children, girls as well as boys, to be self-reliant and through practical work to be self-supporting. Unusual as this approach was at the time, it was possible for girls of Susan and Guelma's age group to get jobs teaching very young children during the summer months, when male teachers and boys abandoned the district schools for farm work. This was the first step toward women taking over elementary school teaching. But this summer school teaching was actually more like babysitting. When young women went off on special assignments to tutor in home schools, they were considered more like governesses in English homes—somewhere between a daughter and an employee or a servant and a teacher. This was the situation when Susan boarded with a family in nearby Easton one winter. She taught the children basic reading and writing skills; and when she put the books away, she helped with daily chores as she did at home.

It was not long before Susan became aware of the limits of her own education in their home school. When her father saw how much she loved school and her eagerness to continue, he began to inquire about an appropriate Quaker boarding school for his daughters. He found a suitable school, Deborah Moulson's Female Seminary, far away in Hamilton, Pennsylvania, outside of Philadelphia. But just as he was ready to enroll his daughters, his business began to plunge during the panic of 1837.

The early 1830s had been a time of rapid economic expansion in the United States. The new mills and factories generated a profitable trade, both foreign and domestic commerce were thriving, the value

of real estate rose, and there was no absence of money in the economy. But this optimistic economy stood on shaky ground. As property values rose, overtrading and restless—if not reckless—invest-
ing threatened the economy. Then President Jackson decided to close
the Bank of the United States, causing a rapid downward spiral in
the economy. This bank, originally chartered in 1816, was to be
rechartered by 1836. But Andrew Jackson, who distrusted banks and
did not understand their function, argued that monied interests,
merchants, financiers, and paper money were the enemies of the
common man. He prevented the bank from being rechartered, dis-
mantled it, and arranged for the federal government's deposits to
be made in state banks. At the same time, the government tried
to institute specie payments and began to accept gold and silver
for the sale of public lands, which was at an all-time high with
the settlement of the West. A wildly fluctuating currency resulted
and forced the withdrawal of specie payments. Coins became rare
and were hoarded, which consequently provoked counterfeit-
ing. These problems, along with overproduction—particularly of
cotton—and high speculation on the market, accelerated the economic crisis and finally brought the country into a deep depression,
the panic of 1837.[20]

Daniel sent Guelma away to the seminary first; but later that year
he told his brother that "there is none to pay her tuition bills.
. . . It seems inevitable now that my business is likely to turn out
most miserably."[21] But Deborah Moulson offered Guelma a position as a teaching assistant, which allowed her to stay in school.
Daniel cautioned his daughter that "cash in this country is scarce,
the best of economy in the use of it will be highly necessary, thy
mother advises nothing but except what stern necessity calls aloud
for."[22]

Caution began to mark all of the Anthony family's life. But in
regard to the children's education, Daniel and Lucy strictly observed
William Penn's advice to "spare no cost for by such parsimony all
is lost that is saved."[23] When Guelma became ambivalent about
staying on at school for a second term, Daniel told her that this
"opportunity for study and improvement in many branches should
be taken seriously, when I consider that this most likely will be the
last opportunity thou will ever have of acquiring information of the
kind much needed by all before commencing life and being absorbed in the cares thereof."[24] By the end of the year, with the few
resources he had left, Daniel enrolled Susan in Deborah Moulson's

seminary, somehow managing to pay the 125-dollar tuition when it became clear that there was no way she could work her way through as a teaching assistant as had Guelma.

Unlike her gifted future friend Elizabeth Cady, Susan B. Anthony could not be particular about her education. Susan did not question at all going to a girls' seminary, nor did she wonder whether her education would be inferior to the education that boys were receiving in college. She was glad to have the opportunity and thought it should be made available to all girls. At her young age she had come to believe that the publicly supported district schools were lax in teaching the feminine morality of humility and piety. She, like her mother before her, had already internalized the most constraining and traditional of womanly values. She once wrote home from Hamilton: "I regret that Brothers and Sisters have not the privilege of attending a school better adapted to improvement, both in Science and Morality; surely a District School (unless they have recently reformed) is not an appropriate place for the cultivation of the latter."[25]

Contrary to Susan's reaction to the female seminary, her future friend Elizabeth Cady was furious when she learned that she could not go off to Union College with her male classmates where she had counted on being able to continue her classical education. But that was reserved for boys. Instead, she was destined for Mrs. Willard's Troy Female Seminary, where she would be seriously educated but not with the rigor of the classics. Even though Troy Female Seminary was the most prestigious education a father could offer his daughter in the 1830s and even though she worshiped Mrs. Willard, Elizabeth Cady was furious and frustrated. By the time Susan B. Anthony began her one and only term at Deborah Moulson's academy, Elizabeth had already graduated from Troy.

Deborah Moulson had advertised her female seminary with a flier in which she declared its purpose. "The inculcation of the principles of Humility, Morality and love of Virtue will receive particular attention."[26] Even though Susan studied "Arithmetic, Algebra, Literature, Chemistry, Philosophy, Physiology and Bookkeeping," Deborah's main emphasis was "improvement in morality." Her discipline was severe and with it she cultivated the most moralistic piety of those times, which was meant to fashion the true woman.

Susan valued highly the opportunity to advance her education— as she put it—but more than anything Susan was a homebound young girl who at fourteen had written:

What so sweet—
So beautiful on earth, and oh! so rare
As kindred love and family repose.

The busy world
With all the tumult and the stir of life,
Pursues its wanton course; on pleasure some,
And some on happiness; while each one loves
One little spot in which her heart unfolds
With nature's holiest feelings; one sweet spot,
And calls it *Home!* If sorrow is felt there
It runs through many bosoms, and a smile
Lights upon in kindred eyes a smile
And if disease intrudes, the sufferer finds
Rest on the breast beloved.[27]

Going to Deborah Moulson's seminary proved to be a wrenching experience for Susan. Her father accompanied her to Hamilton, and took her and Guelma sightseeing in Philadelphia, but when it was time for him to leave, Susan's reaction was intense and a bit dramatic: "O what pangs were felt, it seemed impossible for me to part with him, I could not speak to bid him Farewell."[28]

Daniel was sure that this was childish homesickness and it would pass quickly. He wrote to his daughters while en route to Battenville: "I suppose Susan by this time has lost sight of home having had the whole day to become interested in all absorbing topicks [*sic*] of Hamiltonville."[29] But Susan's anguish did not pass. A few days later, crying even while she was writing to her father, she tried to reassure him that "I was ready on the ensuing morning to commence my studies. Do not suppose I carry a gloomy countenance all the time." But a week later, "300 miles from the beloved spot, separated from all that is dear to me, excepting my elder sister," she still could not shake off her homesickness. Every time she thought of her father's departure, it "cast a gloom over my mind" and "I felt as if I could not contain myself."[30]

Going away to school forced her to separate herself from home, to make new friends, to shoulder new responsibilities, and to enter a different social world which required new loyalties and confidences from her. She resisted! Stubbornly she proclaimed that she was in exile from her "Native Land." With no little amount of drama, she worried that this exile could be permanent. "Home! that inestimable spot is far distant," she confided to her diary. "O may I be permitted to return once and mingle with those dear Friends of my youth."[31]

This was more than a child's usual homesickness. Susan was seventeen, approaching adulthood, and in deep emotional turmoil for probably the first time in her life. She had been a serious child. But now she was intense—deeply so, passionately so. She had no other object for the expression of her feelings than her home and family. So she focused her intensity there. Then she became rigorous with herself; each day she tried to console herself with self-rectifying thoughts. "A few moments of painful separation from friends, is but the improvement of my mind, and I ought to be content."[32] But her emotional reactions still seemed to her to be beyond her control and that alone intensified their effect on her. When she was at home, she had focused her powerful feelings on her family. Now this sensitive and intense young woman, away at school, was lost and without focus.

Sometimes she withdrew herself from her friends at school and walked alone, while other girls played and talked together. Often she spent long hours curled up in the window seat of her room writing long letters home. Susan became depressed, not so much from missing home, although that may have triggered it, but because, like most girls of her time, she had no focus for her energy, her drive, her developing passions. Girls did not think about or plan for their future; but without this kind of self-definition, Susan was lost and for comfort anchored herself emotionally even more insistently in her family life in Battenville.

Ultimately, the practical necessity of study impressed itself upon her.

> This cloud I anticipate will soon be expelled, at least were it to continue I should be able to make but small progress in my literary pursuits. Oft times when in the act of committing lessons to memory, will all the enduring allurements of home rush upon my mind, and surely it required all the fortitude that I can command to overcome such feelings but they must be conquered or otherwise my mind would be wholly unfit for study.[33]

Something of her mother's self-discipline, occasioned by Lucy's own experience of Quaker morality early in her marriage, became evident in Susan. School work became a way to regain emotional control because it drew her out of herself and these depressive moods. This began what would become a life-long emotional strategy for

Susan. At this young age, she was teaching herself to funnel her emotional intensity into her school work. Eventually, her work would become the expression of her intensity and her passion.

Yet there were joyful moments at the seminary. "Nature, how bounteous, how varied are thy works," she exclaimed on a field trip to the Academy of Arts and Sciences. "Numerous specimens of the mineral kingdom were exhibited. Animals and the shell tribes. On beholding them I was ready to exclaim 'O Miracle of Miracles' with the celebrated naturalist when speaking of the metamorphoses of insects."[34] But a short time later she confessed that while studying a physiology lesson, "I indulged a little in my natural unpleasant feelings in the forepart of the evening."[35] The trouble with her eyes compounded all these difficulties. "My eyes held in performing their wanted office. [But] often do their nonconformance mortify this frail heart, when attempting to read in class."[36]

Deborah Moulson did not often appear in school during the classes, but when she did it was a momentous occasion for the girls. One day when she walked into the classroom unexpectedly, Susan rushed to her and in a burst of enthusiastic pride presented her with the exercise she had just completed. Deborah stiffened, scorned Susan's paper, and without looking at the young girl said, "Obviously Susan, you do not know the rule for dotting 'i's.' " Susan was crushed. It took all the self-discipline she had to hold back her tears. She looked down and admitted, "I do not know the rule." Deborah, who obviously was in ill health, looked over the class and then turned to Susan and said, "It is no wonder I have undergone so much distress in both mind and body. I have devoted my time to you in vain." Susan now saw that she was the cause of Deborah's illness and could barely hold back her tears until the end of class, when she ran first to the privy and then to her bed to cry her heart out.

Deborah Moulson's pedagogy, a replication of guilt-laden Puritanism, oriented as it was to cultivating feminine piety, engaged her students in almost endless self-examination over the smallest infraction of her rules and the most trivial displays of pride. Susan took every admonition to heart. Although Deborah's demands for humility diverted Susan from her preoccupation with home, the consequences were often mortifying. One day Deborah reproved the girls for their moral laxity, which she said was apparent in their inattentiveness to housekeeping. In response, Susan decided to clean the schoolroom before class. She took off her shoes, climbed on top of the desks, and began to sweep away the cobwebs from the corners of the ceiling. "After going around the room, I stepped on D's desk, that I might sweep in that part, thoughtlessly, and strained the lock, bent the hinges and how much more damage I do not know." At that moment, the teaching assistant came in followed by the other girls. A tense silence gripped the air. Dutifully, the teaching assistant left the room to inform Deborah.[37]

When Deborah arrived, Susan immediately came forth and made a full confession. "Deborah, see what I have done. I have broken your desk." Deborah ignored her. In Deborah's eyes, the road to piety and humility could not be walked that easily; experiencing humility was more important than merely admitting to an error. Susan must be made to feel it. Deborah walked slowly to her desk, inspected it, and then, as if Susan had said nothing to her, turned away from her and asked the other girls in the room who had broken her desk. Susan knew that she must remain silent; this was to be a lesson in humility. "It was Susan B. Anthony," several of the girls said.

Deborah turned to Susan and glared, "How did you come to step upon it." By this time, Susan was "too full to answer" and holding back the tears was almost impossible. Deborah turned away, leaving Susan with her humiliation. Now Susan knew that she was evil; she worried that she would never succeed in improving in morality, and that she could never overcome her evilness with piety and humility. In her old age, Susan recalled this incident while talking with her original biographer, Ida Harper, and remembered that "not once in all the sixty years that have passed, has the thought of that come to my mind without making me turn cold and sick at heart."[38]

Being pious about small incidents made the girls feel moral or at least that they were trying to be moral. That was the essence of female morality at this time. It focused on the insignificant, the trivial and made them meaningful with heightened emotionality. The girls' conversations with each other at the Seminary were preoccupied with questions about such subjects as "feminine delicacy." In one such discussion, Susan confided to her friend Lydia Mott, Lucretia Mott's niece, "Lydia, sometimes I feel as if I were the worst girl of all being." Lydia hastily assured her that "you are right to think so. But Susan, do not give up in discouragement."[39] These conversations and the reprimands that preceded them stimulated endless self-examination. The less specific the offense the more vague the feelings of wrongdoing and the more personally intense were the girls' self-reflection and efforts to correct the error of their ways.

Personal, private morality was meant to be the all-absorbing work of the private sphere. One day when Deborah reprimanded the girls for "levity and mirthfulness," likening them to the traitor Judas Iscariot, Susan first rejected the charge, but as she thought it over, she finally concluded that "I cannot see my own defects because my heart is hardened."[40]

This was how young girls learned to be true women in the 1830s. Although Deborah's was a Quaker boarding school, it cultivated the same guilt-inducing private piety that the early Puritan fathers had used to rule over the faithful of seventeenth-century New England. Ironically, it was the same piety that George Fox had rejected in founding the Quakers. And like the women who had been subjected to the more severe rigors of Puritanism in Anne Hutchinson's time, the impressionable young girls at Deborah's seminary often became anxious and then depressed with the seeming futility of their search for the correct path to humility and God. Many young girls simply succumbed to this training, absorbed it, and went on with their lives. Susan's sister Guelma seems to have responded in this way. But Susan's reaction was different. First anxious, sometimes depressed, she ultimately took on this code. Her emotional intensity was focused but not subdued by Deborah's discipline.

Unlike most of the other girls, achieving piety was a challenge for Susan, and one she took up with rigor. She struggled with it. She searched within herself, disciplined herself, and eventually began to formulate her own values. It was a rough course. For better or worse, it was capable of cultivating tough—as well as true—women.[41]

Sometime after she had left school, a dream prompted Susan to reprimand her youngest sister, twelve-year-old Mary. In Susan's dream Mary appeared sulky, and when a request was made of her she hesitated to respond. Susan interpreted her dream as an omen that showed her that she was to guide her sister away from evil ways in the manner that Deborah had guided her. She confronted Mary with her dream and asked, "Is not this dream too frequently verified in your daily conduct toward those who ask favors of you?" Mary hung her head. Susan instructed Mary not to use the handkerchief Susan had given her as a gift; until she had corrected this fault,

> Rest assured Dear Sister that we all regard you equally with the rest, but that particular trait in your character, we do so dislike, and sincerely hope you may be enabled to command strength to overpower

it, and thus secure your own happiness as well as those around you. Do not indulge anger toward any one, for that will also make you unhappy. Suffer yourself to think much about serious things and Death, for that will strengthen you in doing well.[42]

Having internalized the values of true womanhood—this personalized moralistic piety—Susan was in a position to impose these values on others. She started with the youngest and weakest. Nevertheless, however negative and moralistic female seminary education was, it did encourage young women to think and act on their own. Even if their actions resulted from values imposed upon them, the point is that they *acted* and did so outside of their family context. That was more than Susan's mother had been able to do. In this fashion, female seminaries actually created a social space outside of the private sphere, where women could experiment—even in limited ways—with creating their own identity. This social space, available to young women collectively for the first time since Emma Willard had initiated her "experiment" in 1821, eventually created some of the conditions that would make it possible for women to originate their own movement.

Not all was moralistic piety at Deborah Moulson's seminary. Lucretia Mott, the famous and controversial Quaker abolitionist, came to the school to speak to the girls on the importance of improving their intellect. A few years earlier, she had organized the Philadelphia Female Anti-Slavery Society when she found that William Lloyd Garrison's newly organized American Anti-Slavery Society was, at best, conflicted over the role women could play in it. Lucretia Mott was a different role model for the young girls, and Susan listened to her with rapt attention.

Lucretia Mott was modest but not self-deprecating; she was wise yet not intellectually ostentatious. She did not indulge herself in the petty attitudes that characterized personal piety. Instead, based on the original spirit of the Quakers, her moral convictions took the form of social and civil responsibility. Yet the distinction between morality based on civil responsibility and morality derived from personal piety was blurred in the girls' seminary training. As a result, these very different kinds of morality were made to appear as if they were the same. Mott's civil responsibility and Moulson's piety would remain undifferentiated for several years for Susan B.

Anthony following her time at Deborah Moulson's academy. She would learn to make these distinctions and transform her morality only with considerable personal struggle. It would be a struggle that was unavoidable once she had embarked on a course of political leadership.

From the time Susan's early childhood, Lucretia Mott's name had been well known in the Anthony household. In 1827, the Society of Friends had suffered a major fissure—the Hicksite separation—of which Lucretia Mott had been one of the most influential leaders and to which Daniel Anthony had been intensely committed. The Hicksite Quakers claimed that the growing orthodoxy of the Society was drawing the Friends away from their original purpose. The Hicksites intended to return the Society to its original spirit, to purify it, and to bring back its original meaning. They rejected the growing domination of elders, which they viewed as a form of clerical power, and they disapproved of the increasing tendency to rely on the Bible as the source of divine revelation—instead of the Inner Light. They also insisted that the Quakers take a firm position against slavery at a time when many Friends equivocated on the subject. The Hicksites committed themselves to boycotting all products of slave labor and especially cotton. Lucretia Mott preached this doctrine, and she herself refused to use cotton cloth or eat cane sugar.

On the other hand, Daniel Anthony had expanded his cotton mills in the 1830s, when his only likely source of raw cotton was from southern plantations. Throughout Susan's childhood, her father's strong antipathy to slavery existed alongside certain unspoken concessions he had made to it. This contradiction was evident when the Anthonys first moved to Battenville in 1826. At that time they were living with Judge McLean, who kept two unmanumitted (or still-enslaved) black servants in his household. Daniel's attitudes toward slavery contradicted some of his practices. It is evident that they were not the formative influences on his daughter who later took on the work of abolition. In many people who became great leaders, contradictions such as those in Daniel's life stimulated a precocious awareness of injustices. But there is no evidence that this was true of the young Susan B. Anthony at this time. Her father's influence was more personal and unconventional—he prepared all of his children to be self-reliant.

Shortly after Lucretia Mott spoke at the seminary at Hamilton on May 15, 1838, a series of antislavery meetings were disrupted in Philadelphia by proslavery forces. Mott's home was threatened but spared, while the new Pennsylvania Hall constructed for abolitionist work was burned to the ground. Susan and Guelma heard reports of the clashes and frenzied mob violence in Philadelphia, but by that time they were back home in Battenville and their own personal losses demanded all of their attention.

During the term, Daniel had confided to his daughters that he was close to bankruptcy. One factory was gone, and so were most of his mills. He had lost their home. Susan was crushed. "Can I ever be reconciled to such a change. The reading it brought tears to my eyes, but I must be resigned to whatever my dear Father thinks proper respecting the temporary affairs of this world . . . can I ever forget that loved residence in Battenville, and no more call it home, it seems impossible."[43]

Not until she arrived home did Susan fully comprehend the extent of her father's losses. An auction was set to sell even their personal belongings.

> Not an article was spared from the inventory. All the mother's wedding presents, the furniture and the silver spoons given her by her parents, the wearing apparel of the family, even the flour, tea, coffee and sugar, the children's school books, the Bible and the dictionary, were carefully noted. On this list, are "underclothes of wife and daughters," "spectacles of Mr. and Mrs. Anthony," pocketknives of the boys," "scraps of old iron"—and the law took all except the bare necessities.[44]

But the Anthonys were saved from the final humiliation of the auction when Joshua Read, Lucy's brother, stepped in and "bid for all the family desired to keep and restored them their possessions, making himself their lenient creditor."

With the recent deaths from old age of Grandmother and Grandfather Read, Susan had written in her diary: "It assuredly seems as if some more appalling judgment will come upon us, on account of not being roused to faithfulness by the afflictions which providence has seen meet [*sic*] to send us."[45] Susan's aunt gloomily forecast that now with all their losses, the Anthony's would be condemned to travel in "low company." Susan was more sure, "Let the future bring what it may, our happiness is far more complete to live an upright life."[46]

However, Susan and her sisters now had to try to find teaching positions, not only for their own practical education but because their self-support was necessary to the family. When Susan went off to one assignment, she pondered, "I again left my home to mingle with strangers, which seems to be my lot," adding that "separation was rendered more trying on account of the embarrassing condition of our business affairs."[47]

She returned home a few months later when her father reopened their home school. But within a month he was forced to close it. The family, having lost their wonderful Battenville house, prepared to move to Hardscrabble, which Susan described as that unpleasant little village of "brown hovels and broken rough appearance" that she "a thousand times abhorred,"[48] where "the scenery was not so beautiful as in Battenville where there were hills and mountains all around."[49]

On the last day of class in home school when Susan was asked to read her composition, she broke down "when my turn came, I, the one whom all thought the most courageous and least liable to feel any of those horrid feeling—but for once they were deceived." She left her class in a pensive mood, wondering what the future would bring. "I probably shall never attend school again . . . all the advancement which we will hereafter make must be by our own exertion and desire to gain useful knowledge."[50] All of this prepared her for but did not guarantee that she would become a most uncommon representative of the common woman.

2

To Marry or Not to Be a Wife

MARRIAGE WAS IN THE AIR SHORTLY AFTER THE ANTHONY family gave up their Battenville home and settled into a rented tavern in Hardscrabble (later renamed Center Falls when Daniel became postmaster there), where they began to take in boarders and travelers to cover the cost of their rent. Aaron McLean, Judge McLean's son who had become a successful businessman in Battenville, had been courting Susan's older sister Guelma since the summer before. Pressing family needs required that the older children find self-support or marry. Guelma and Aaron set a date for their wedding, while Susan took a teaching post in New Rochelle, New York.

In May of 1839, Susan began her assignment as the assistant teacher at Eunice Kenyon's Quaker boarding school, where she was paid thirty dollars for two and a half months work. Here Susan struck up a friendship with Eunice, and for the first time developed a serious relationship with someone outside of her own family. "I am perfectly free with her,"[1] Susan told her mother. She found that Eunice "is not as precise as Deborah was, notwithstanding that, I like her much, she is agreeable and kind, as big as I and weighs one pound more."[2]

She was at ease with Eunice. Often they strolled down to Long Island Sound or walked into town together. Sometimes they took their students strawberrying. On one outing, Eunice helped Susan pick out a new gingham bonnet and afterward they stopped for tea.[3] On another day they went sailing together. Susan shared her love of nature with Eunice. Slipping the boat quietly over the waters and with more silence than conversation, they drank in nature's beauty and Susan noted:

> The first glance of the eye beheld the broad expanse of waters and the far distant village, on Long Island, which seemed like specks in the distance. Shall I say the sight was beautiful or grand? Will that describe it? No it was sublimity itself and to a mind unused to such scenes it seemed like a peep into brighter regions. The sun was passive toward the Western horizon and all seemed calm and tranquil, save the momentary wash of the briny waters against the sandy beach and a gentle breeze from the water soothed our fatigued bodies, for we had walked, I think nearly a mile and a half.[4]

No matter how much she enjoyed her life in New Rochelle, Susan went through the wrenching experience of separating from home all over again. Guelma wrote that "after you left we were quite lonesome, missed you very much," and that she and Hannah had stopped the quilting the three had been doing together. Susan invited Guelma to visit her in New Rochelle, enticing her with a promise to teach her how to swim, which was something she was doing with her students. Guelma did miss her sister, but now she was occupied with her marriage preparations. It was no longer her sisters who were the focus of Guelma's attention, but Aaron. Guelma wrote less frequently now and that hurt Susan. Instead, Aaron struck up a correspondence with Susan. He began telling her about all of the marriage preparations—about how they were reading books on the subject, how Guelma was preparing her trousseau, and the like.

Susan liked Aaron—not as a future brother-in-law but as a friend at least. But now Susan began to get the gnawing feeling that she was about to lose her sister to him. This threw her into an emotional turmoil because she could not resign herself to Guelma's marriage. For some reason that was not entirely clear to her at the moment, she did not trust that Aaron was truly worthy of her sister's society. She believed that if he were she would not resist his marriage to Guelma. "I would as cheerfully give her up to be the companion of another."[5] Susan's loyalty to her sister was a part of her fuller emotional world, which was based on networks of women: her mother, sisters, cousins, and friends. Disrupting any of these relationships would risk emotional havoc for her.

After reading about marriage, Aaron wrote Susan that the subject was fine as long as it was theoretical, "but when one comes to the practical part of the subject, I am doubtful it would prove so fine and nice. . . . I think the practice of single blessedness plenty and good enough, don't you?"[6] Patronizing Susan did not help her, nor did it establish an alliance of "single blessedness" between them, which would have helped him cultivate a complicity with her and hopefully draw her attention away from her sister.

Aaron was acting out the expected male rebellion against the loss of bachelorhood. About the boys of Battenville he wrote: "Several more of us have been exposed to the same fever (which appears to be contagious) and we stand trembling not knowing the day nor the hour when we may be taken."[7] Susan had herself quipped about marriage in similar ways. She told Aaron that "You who have been exposed to this fever ought to be very careful to remember the old saying 'that an ounce of prevention is worth a pound of cure.' I should like to know how deeply and extensively the contagion has spread in your hearts, as it appears to be a heart disease when any of you get so near the brink of ruin." For the young, it was in vogue to humorously protest that which they knew was inevitable for them. Marriage was not inevitable for Susan. "These old Bachelors," she told her sisters, "are nothing but a nuisance to a society but an Old Maid is the cleverest creature I ever saw and I am now living with one of the right sort." On the other hand, she suggested, would it not be better that these boys of Center Falls and Battenville marry, and then "they will be out of the way."[8]

Susan was losing her sister, and Aaron's letters and Guelma's silence seemed to affirm her worst fears of what that would mean to her. Tensions momentarily rose between her and Aaron when it became evident that he had no use for their sisterly affections; he told Susan that "these sisters are always twice as much trouble and bother as they are worth. . . . Kind of necessary evils."[9] He seemed to her to be trying to chip away at her sisterly loyalty. Guelma had promised Susan that she would not set a date for the wedding until she knew when Susan could come home. Aaron wrote that "you better not come home this fall," because the most Guelma cared about "is to have you there to do the work." Fearing he had gone too far, he added that, of course, "you may come down if you choose."[10]

The result was that Susan withdrew and tried to assume an air of detachment. She sent Guelma "a thousand thanks to you for your kindness in putting off the wedding and parties and all the good things until my return home." She then cautioned, "Do not reserve too much happiness or pleasure until that time, for recollect, it may never be realized, & that the most certain time for enjoyment is the present."[11]

Susan was holding out, and for the moment she stubbornly clung to her intense loyalty to Guelma. In the world of marriage, this kind of behavior was considered childish and something that Susan should have outgrown by the time she was old enough to marry. After all, marriage meant that a woman must subordinate all other friendships and relations to the relationship with her husband. But Susan was not prepared to let go of Guelma in this way. Her identity was formed in her family and shaped in her female networks. Her life with her sisters, cousins, and girlfriends psychologically oriented her. These were the reasons why Susan was not seriously concerned about marriage for herself. Her primary loyalty was to her family and to the women in her life; that was the nature of the world of female affection.[12] The problem before Susan was how all of this could be reconciled to her sister's marriage. She did not outrightly reject Aaron; but she sensed that he was taking her sister away from her, so she could not fully accept him either.

Alone with her problem of whether or not to go home for Guelma's wedding, Susan thought about the year before at Hamilton, when she had "one dear Sister, who helped to cheer those lonely hours of separation, but now I have no loved sister to whom I can freely open all my heart and in whom I can confide all my little griefs."[13] Withdrawn, lonely, and sad, she summoned her self-discipline and decided to remain in New Rochelle, for "reason says deny thyself this inestimable pleasure, for it is good . . . to learn and practice self-denial in all things."[14] Besides, she thought, as she had been taught through her exercise in humility and piety at Hamilton, "often I have felt as if I were hardly worthy of a Sister, such an ungrateful being am I that I do not merit such a blessing."[15]

Again Susan reverted to her mother's strategy for dealing with pain and disappointment—silence and withdrawal. With a calm, poised exterior, she closed the subject. "My feelings are inexpressible, therefore I will not try to say any more in reference to them." She cut off correspondence with Aaron for the time being.[16] Over the weeks, she slowly reconciled herself to losing her sister. By the end of the summer, when she had finished her assignment in New Rochelle, to everyone's surprise she returned home in time for the wedding.

It was a difficult time for Susan. The prospect of Guelma's wed-

ding must have stirred some marriage anxieties in her, which came
out in her dreams.

> I dreamed of being married last night, queerly enough too. I imagined
> myself in New York and father with me, it seemed as if I had married
> a Presbyterian minister that I had never seen before that day. . . . I
> repented thoroughly before one day had passed. It appeared to me that
> I had acted rashly. My mind was troubled.[17]

At this point it was not clear to her whether in her dream she had
acted rashly because she had married so quickly or because she had
married at all. Her dream reflected probably as much of the social
pressure on young women of her age to marry as it did her distress
over her sister's marriage.

In her youth, Susan neither forcefully rejected marriage nor felt
compelled to marry. For a short time she enjoyed dating and going
to a few parties. Certainly she was pleased that a young man like
I. Whipple "has found in me a spirit congenial with his own."[18] But
when such attractions came to nothing, it was of little significance
to her. Neither marriage nor the young men in Battenville interested
her very much. Unlike most of her young women friends she was
not interested in marriage for its own sake, and few men in her
village measured up to her intellect or her standards, which, even
at an early age, made an unequal relationship incomprehensible to
her. Choosing a single life would come later, only after she had
chosen her life's work.

Unlike marriage the choice to remain single is one that usually
goes by unnoticed—unmarked as it is by ceremony, gifts, dramatic
announcements, or change of residence. Therefore, more attention
has been paid to proposals she received, such as one from "a real
soft-headed old bachelor" and another from a wealthy widower with
a large Vermont farm,[19] even though they do not reflect her real
choices or the direction of her single life at this time. Later in her
life when she saw inscriptions in graveyards that read: "Sacred to
the Memory of ____, Relict of the Late ____," she defended her
choice to remain unmarried rather than have her existence recorded
simply as that of one left behind—the " 'relict' of some man."[20]
But at this point her choice was not between marriage and being
alone. Her emotional world had become firmly fixed and attached
to the women in her life, such as her sisters and friends like Eunice.

Later, in her political life, Anthony would more strongly affirm
her choice to remain single. As Elizabeth Cady Stanton remem-

bered, Anthony typically responded to the question of why she never married by asserting that "when I am crowned with all the rights, privileges, and immunities of a citizen, I may give some consideration to this social institution; but until then I must concentrate all of my energies on the enfranchisement of my own sex." But even in these responses, being single was always framed in the absence of the possibility of a true marriage. The time had not yet arrived when the choice to be single could be affirmed for itself, without tagging the future possibility of a beau or marriage onto it—even though Anthony did not actively seek that in her own life. Stanton recalled Anthony's caustic answer when someone questioned her on this point. "I would not consent that the man I loved, described in the Constitution as a white male, native born, American citizen, possessed of the right of self government, eligible to the office of president of the Great Republic, should unite his destinies in marriage with a political slave and pariah."[21]

Although it is not known what she would have done if she had received a proposal from someone she loved and considered her equal, there is not much evidence to suggest that this was important to her. And it must be admitted that there was something about Susan B. Anthony even in these early years—which did not have to do with mere beauty—that was singularly unattractive to the bright, promising young men who were considered "the best catches of the day." They were looking for wives to adorn their households with feminine charms and many children. Susan was certainly a good cook and had a good hand for housekeeping, and her teaching revealed her strong feelings for children. And God knows, she was well trained in the outward manifestations of "true womanhood." But she would not make the ideal wife. Already there was an intensity about her. There was a kind of determination in her eyes, an independence in her spirit, and even a rigor in the way she adopted the piety appropriate for women at that time that made her appear unfeminine, according to the standards by which young men were seeking wives. Her young, angular face with its set jaw conveyed the appearance of a personal autonomy that would not slip easily into submission and dependence.

In the 1840s teaching was one of the few professions open to women. The woman teacher could be justified as someone whose work was like that of a mother. But aside from this traditional women's role, teaching permitted women to explore their own independence and create their own identities. At New Rochelle when Eunice Kenyon left Susan with full responsibility for the school and the boarders, Susan admitted that "I feel quite motherly now a days, having the care of a family of 5 children, myself and one domestic."[22] Her growing self-determination and personal autonomy, considered unfeminine at this time, actually mingled easily in her character with the traditional virtues of "feminine morality."

Teaching allowed women to establish their own identities and to gain economic independence; as a result, many of them never married at all.[23] Yet creating one's own independent identity with no models, without prescribed roles such as those writ large for wife and mother, could be awkward and trying. At least Susan had the Quaker tradition behind her, which recognized and valued the single woman. She also had her parents' encouragement to train herself for practical work and self-reliance. Now at Eunice Kenyon's school she had to find her own way with the responsibilities placed on her young shoulders. "Rather a melancholy morning to me, arising from the great responsibility resting on me. Indeed I do feel as if my task were very trying. I have now had the entire charge of the school and house for three weeks and very much fear all has not been done to the satisfaction of E [Eunice]."[24]

But Eunice was not the exacting taskmaster Deborah Moulson had been. She encouraged Susan to try out her own ways of teaching. When Susan compared herself to Eunice, she noted that "many of her ways are different from mine in school, but when she hears a recitation, it is done in her manner, so when I hear one, it is done in my way."[25] Susan was no longer bowing to the authority of others. She was finding her own independent way and creating her own separate identity in her work at a time when other young women, like her sister Guelma, were learning to establish their identities through their husbands. This loss of personal identity became a source of deep anger and rebellion for many of these women later in their lives. Many of them, however, would reclaim a sense of self through the woman's rights movement. But Susan was secure in her family's support and caring and with Eunice found an affectionate and permissive environment where she began to establish her autonomy. She would eventually champion the cause of woman's rights not because she was robbed of her personal identity and independence, but because she had experienced a progression into independence that she came to see as essential for all women.

Personal autonomy had to be won, and it was sometimes an awkward process. For example, Eunice Kenyon's liberal teaching style contrasted with Susan's strict, almost authoritarian method of teaching, which she modeled after Deborah Moulson's methods. She was such a strict disciplinarian that she once had to assure her mother that "no whipping business goes on here." For Susan, strict classroom management was a sign—if not proof—of her adulthood. To some of her students it was a cause for revolt. When one boy complained to his parents about Miss Anthony's harsh discipline, his mother came to the school, confronted the teacher, and stated that "it is not an assistant's business to punish a scholar." Overwhelmed by this challenge to her adult authority, Susan glared at the mother whom she thought was overprotective of her child. "She does not think her children capable of doing wrong because they have a guarded education." What she really worried about was that the mother had tried to deny her the right to punish the student and to her that was tantamount "to informing me of my limited power."[26]

She sat in her room trying to suppress her tears and worried about what Eunice would think about this incident, which had grown out of proportion in her mind precisely because she felt that her autonomy and independence were at stake. She turned the incident over many times in her mind trying to find her defense; she knew but could not fully admit that she had been wrong. Fortunately, Eunice was there to reassure her. "I highly approve of all the reproof you have ever given and if you would not assist me in that part, I would not have you at all."[27] Susan had won the battle but not the war. She worried that evening that "Eunice possesses more independence than I fear I ever shall."[28]

Susan also began to form her own ideas on politics and equality. When President Martin Van Buren came through New Rochelle on a campaign visit and the entire town turned out to see him, Susan remarked with disgust that "one would have thought an angelic being had descended from heaven to have heard and seen the commotion." How absurd that "large crowds of people called to look at him as if he were a puppet-show." She heard that her family had rushed to see the president when he had visited Saratoga Springs and was shocked that they were "possessed of so little sound sense merely to look at a human being who is possessed of nothing more than ordinary men and therefore should not be worshipped more than any mortal being."[29] Here was the germ of what would become her lifelong ethic—radical egalitarianism, a kind of equality that simply meant that no human being was superior to or inferior to any other. у

Susan began to formulate her own convictions out of her personal sense of independence, through new friendships, and as a result of her new professional responsibilities. Nevertheless, she still clung to her pious morality. At a Quaker Yearly Meeting she tried out her temperance muscle on her Uncle Dickenson, whom she had seen drinking cider and ale (not all Quakers were teetotalers). "Even Aunt Hannah partook of those beverages. . . . This did really surprise and shock me to see the wife of a drunkard partake in the least of any stimulus."[30] Her uncle calmly reminded her that he and his wife were temperate drinkers, and then he cajoled her into remembering that "it is a great thing to say what one will not do before having any experience." He laughingly reminded her of her letter-writing style; for when she came to the end of a page, she continued along the margins, then wrote upside-down across the top of the page, and sometimes at an angle over the text already written. Was this a sign of her scrambled ideas about intemperance? "We hope thy cranium will get straightened when the answer to this is penned, so that we may follow thy varied thoughts with less trouble."[31] Being accepted as an independent adult with authority was not as easy as she thought. But Susan rebounded in good spirits. "Such a dressing as he has given me for talking about Wine and cider can't be beat by anybody," she told Aaron. "Such a whipping as I have taken is a caution."[32]

Susan still lacked the experience to express herself clearly on the political issues of the day. On one of her first trips alone on a steamboat down the Hudson River to New York, Susan met the son of a Louisiana slaveholder. "He said his father's family owned 237 slaves. . . . Shocking indeed to tell. O that the hearts of those obdurate men may become softened and they be constrained to loose the bonds of those poor degraded brethen," she thought as she sat and listened for two hours while an "antislavery" man challenged him. "The slave man could but recoil under the cutting remarks which fell from the lips of this truly noble minded man. The guilty man became weary and asked if he could be excused to go to bed."[33]

In her diary she noted that she met some young black women in New Rochelle, a town filled with "hotheaded anti-abolitionists and Anti everything that's good, I believe." She observed with relief that "they eat, walk and associate with white people without reserve."[34] Sitting at tea with a group of young black women from the Oneida

School, she felt personally gratified. "For to show this kind of people respect, I think, in this Heathen land (for such I esteem it) affords me a double portion of happiness."[35] Yes, she thought, "O what a happy state of things is this, to see these poor degraded sons of Africa privileged to walk by our sides."[36] Susan's comments were awkward, they expressed a young woman's moral outrage but in a voice stuck in the piety of "true womanhood." Her sentiments reflected the antislavery thinking of the time. In antislavery circles, the most frequently proposed solution to slavery was to send slaves back to Africa. Very few abolitionists considered full equality between blacks and whites as a viable solution. In the early abolitionist movement of the 1830s, there had been a movement to abolish slavery; but most abolitionists still considered blacks inferior beings. That was not what was on Susan's mind. She was trying to express what an egalitarian world should look like.

In the summer of 1845, Susan's sister Hannah announced her plans to marry Eugene Mosher. At the time Daniel and Lucy Anthony were across the state in Rochester looking for a farm to purchase with the ten thousand dollars Lucy had inherited upon her parents' deaths. At home in Center Falls between teaching assignments Susan took over the wedding preparations for Hannah. When Daniel and Lucy returned home just in time for the wedding, they found "the arrangements cake and all was well got up in a simple, cheap and Friendly style notwithstanding the old folks had not a word to say— The connection as far as we know is agreeable all around."[37]

This marriage wasn't particularly agreeable to Susan however, nor was she ready to give up Hannah to Eugene Mosher. Almost predictably, Hannah stopped writing within a few months and Susan worried, "I fear she will be so changed, she seems so swallowed up in things pertaining to self." After reflecting on her reaction she conceded that, "It is I who am thus selfish, it is I who am unwilling to allow her to love other than those around our own fireside. Yes, here is the conflict, I hope after having seen her and Eugene I shall feel different and give it up."[38]

Few in her family realized the extent of Susan's pain. Mostly they thought she tended to overreact, to take these things too seriously. It was one of her young woman friends, Caroline, who noticed how deeply Susan was affected and tried to console her. "You must miss the society of your sisters, especially Hannah," Caroline observed, "as you were together so much and confided everything to each other."[39] The sisterhood of the three oldest Anthony daughters was broken now. Susan was adrift.

To calm her doubts and rest her fears, she went to Easton, New York, to visit Hannah and Eugene and found them happily situated. The sisters visited while working about the house together. One evening after Eugene went to bed, they picked up their shawls and walked arm in arm into the cool night air. "It was necessary for us to take a walk and we had a good old fashioned chat and cried because we could not all be together."[40] But for the same reasons that she had liked Aaron as a friend but rejected him as a brother-in-law, Susan did not fully accept Eugene. After another visit to Hannah, she reported to her mother that Eugene was indeed a good man, but "no one is good enough for my Hannah." When her sisters' were married, Susan reacted from fears that although real were never spoken in society. She feared that her female world and her emotional networks with women, which had begun with her sisterly society, were being broken.

Susan was right. Her sisters moved further and further away from her emotionally. Meanwhile, Susan became more fully involved in her work. In 1846 while settling into the family farm her parents had bought in Rochester, she was offered the prestigious post of headmistress for the female department of the Canajoharie Academy. The salary was determined by the number of students in her classes. From their tuition, which ranged from three to five dollars per annum, she paid twelve and one-half percent to the school and kept the rest. With a class of twenty to twenty-five girls, she earned ninety to one hundred dollars per year.

Canajoharie was a lovely village built up along the verdant banks of the Mohawk River. Its name came from the language of its first inhabitants, the Mohawks, a tribe of the Iroquois Confederacy. "Canajoharie" meant "pot that washes itself," which described the rushing waters at the foot of the steep falls that dropped from a winding creek into a gorge at the edge of the village. It was a dramatically beautiful spot where Susan sometimes went, either with her students or alone, and stood on the overlook point marveling at nature's wonders.

In Canajoharie Susan first boarded with her Uncle Joshua, who noticed that Susan was more than a little anxious about her new teaching assignment. She was now twenty-six and for the first time in her life, she was on her own in an advanced private school, the academy being roughly equivalent to a private high school at this time. She was no longer teaching only very young children or working as someone else's assistant. Would she have the education and talent to meet this new challenge, she wondered now. Uncle Joshua advised her to put those thoughts out of her mind. "Your success depends very much upon you thinking you know it all."[41]

When her dreaded first day of school came, she mustered as much self-confidence as she could, but she still felt undereducated for this work. That afternoon after school she smiled with satisfaction and reported to Uncle Joshua, "I am most happy to say to you my confidence in my ability to teach the Canajoharie *Misses* has increased tenfold since morning." In the evening she penned a note to her family telling them that her fears that her students would outstrip her own education and abilities were dispelled. "The scholars are not so far advanced as I had anticipated, rather backward if anything."[42]

Her confidence was tested again at the end of the term when, according to custom, the teacher held a public examination of her students before the principal, the trustees, and parents. Everyone knew that it was as much a test of the teacher as it was of her students. Susan approached her first examination day, that "awful day, that day of days" when "I feel my credit as a teacher is at stake," with near terror.

By this time Susan was boarding with her cousin Margaret Caldwell across the river in Palatine Bridge. Margaret knew that Susan was very anxious and that she had been preparing for days for the exam. Susan did not sleep at all the night before. She was up before dawn getting ready. She put on the new gown she had had made especially for this event, a lively plaid of white, blue, purple, and brown that had "two puffs around the skirt and on the sleeves at shoulders and wrists, white linen undersleeves and collarette."[43] The dress was fancier than any she had ever owned, and she thought the occasion so special that she even bought new blue prunella gaiters with patent leather heels and tips.

Margaret helped Susan dress and then began to arrange her hair. Susan sat quietly as Margaret brushed her long hair and then wove it into four braids, sewed the braids together, and wound them around a large shell comb that rested at the back of her head. The style was quite different from the way she usually coiled her hair and fastened it at the nape of her neck. When all was in order, Margaret fastened her own watch with a gold chain and pencil onto Susan's bodice.

The school marm was a different and special person in almost any village at this time. And this day Susan felt very elegant and handsome, more stylishly dressed than she had ever been before. She crossed the bridge and walked up the main street at her usual brisk pace, trying to muster her self-assurance. The villagers watched her pass by. Saying her polite "good mornings" as she went on up the steep hill to the academy, which sat atop the village overlooking the rest of Canajoharie, she overheard some neighbors commenting on her appearance. That day she received more than a few compliments: "All say the school marm looks beautiful and I heard some of the scholars expressing fear that some one might be smitten and they thus deprived of their teacher."[44] She had not yet dismissed the possibility of a beau.

Her students honored their teacher by demonstrating their abilities to the satisfaction of the trustees and parents alike. Susan B. Anthony had established herself as a competent, intelligent, and handsome figure in the Canajoharie community. In her teaching she was still strict but no longer the rigid authoritarian of her first years after leaving Deborah Moulson's academy. She taught reading, spelling, writing, composition, grammar, arithmetic, botany, philosophy, and history. More relaxed and secure with herself, Susan was also more lively with her students and they liked her. She took them on field trips, played games with them, and finally relaxed enough to show her irrepressible humor to them. On one examination day, she had her girls present a play with "a little touch of female oratory." She invented a plot and wrote a script that turned out to be a social commentary on the differences between urban and rural living. She dressed her girls according to their roles, "the country girls plain and city girls ornamented with chains, watches, pencils, splendid hats, trimmed with wreaths, plumes." Susan doted over each one of them as she helped them into their costumes, telling them how they looked like little fairies. The girls were excited. But it was Susan's heart that was pounding. She had never undertaken such a grand and daring venture before. She told her family, "Can you imagine my excitement, the hope and fears that filled my mind are indescribable. *Who ever thought Susan Anthony could get up such an affair.* I am sure I never did but here I was, it was sink or swim, think I. I will make a bold effort and so I did and the victory" (emphasis added).[45] Her family was proud of her.

With her new work Susan's confidence grew. On her twenty-seventh birthday she observed, "I can see in the mirror I grow older but in feelings I know no change unless it be *greater flow of spirits*."[46] She had become comfortable with herself, and was beginning to give up the intense self-examination and self-deprecation of earlier years. Her homesickness had passed by the time she came to Canajoharie. Uncle Joshua worried, "Susan I fear that you are or will be homesick." Susan responded in good spirits, "Never fear Uncle, I am midway between the two places which are dear because they hold the friends I love."[47]

Several times Susan thought about going home for a visit to Rochester but found some reason or another to postpone the trip. Consequently, during her first two years in Canajoharie she did not go home at all. No longer seized with bouts of homesickness, she still missed her family; but now her life was centered in her work, with her new friends, and in herself. She had become independent, emotionally as well as economically. There was almost a tinge of guilt in her voice when she confided to her cousin Margaret, "I really believe Mother would feel bad if she knew how happily my time is passed, how seldom I cried to see her—not more than once this term."[48]

Now secure in her own identity, Susan abandoned many of the prohibitions of her Quaker upbringing, something easily encouraged in Canajoharie living with her non-Quaker relatives. Her gray dresses were replaced with lively plaids, and she abandoned the Quaker custom of using "thee", "thou", and "thine" to insure that her speech would not be marked with hierarchy of class or caste. The occasional gingham bonnet or lace cuffs she had permitted herself in earlier years turned into a veritable shopping spree, and she became a very un-Quakerly clothes-conscious young woman. Her plain bonnets yielded to "a new gypsy hat, pearl shawl, white ribbon with fringe on one edge and a pink satin stripe on the other, with a few white roses and green leaves for inside trimming."[49]

Her mother could hardly have understood what she meant when Susan wrote: "I've got my wardrobe pretty well replaced," and then corrected herself, "no, *placed* for the first time."[50] Lucy had always liked to see her children in lively colors and stylish fashions, but after the last decade of stringent living when it was often difficult to make ends meet, she would undoubtedly have thought Susan a bit extravagant. But Susan's parents were now managing on the farm and with her father's additional jobs, first in teaching and later in the insurance business in Rochester, they no longer needed Susan's salary. For the first time in her working career, she was free to spend her own money on herself. She did not overlook the fact that she earned one-fourth of what her father was paid for teaching in Rochester and one-half of the eighteen dollars a month her younger brother Daniel R. was earning in a district school. Even with her limited income, one winter she was able to buy a new broach, a shawl, a fox muff, and a white, ribbed silk hat. Then she added a new plum-colored merino dress to her wardrobe.

Not surprisingly, the pace of her social life quickened. A certain Mr. Loaux inquired of the Reads about the school marm, asking whether or not she was handsome. Susan's cousin assured him she was and a meeting was arranged. George encouraged Susan, "It does him good to look on a handsome woman." Susan took extra time to dress for their meeting. The evening was pleasant, and the next morning she commented, "Well, I passed the fiery ordeal, no doubt he thought I was *handsome*."[51] She received several visits from Mr. Loaux, and then all of a sudden he disappeared without explanation. Meanwhile a Mr. Wells, who was interested in Susan's younger sister Mary, came to visit with a Mr. Stafford, and Susan "had the unspeakable pleasure of entertaining them with my sprightly answers."[52] After a prolonged absence, Mr. Loaux reappeared. He and Susan had a polite conversation, but after he left Susan dismissed him from her mind rather abruptly with a quip about how the moon was not made of green cheese.

One evening she met a certain Dan S. When he came by unexpectedly the next day to pick her up for a ride in the country, he caught her by surprise. "I was in order in a twinkling, left my hair to dress [until] after the ride." The spontaneity was as exciting to her as the attention she received. When Dan stopped the carriage in front of her friend Sarah's house, she noted that "not a few men on the store steps were watching" as Dan escorted her inside. Word went around town that Dan had taken Susan and Sarah for a ride into the country and then to an inn for dinner. Susan enjoyed seeing him teased for "carrying two such beautiful girls."

Susan lived in Canajoharie for almost three years before she stepped out for her first dance. She found dancing to be fun but awkward as she was unable to identify tunes or pick up their rhythm. But the next day she denounced the whole event on other grounds. She was made "witness to Brandy sipping, [they] had it in a room off the eating room. Oh rum, horrid rum!" When her escort to a military ball a month later had had too much to drink, she decided that "my fancy for attending dances was fully satiated." "I, next time I consent to go, must have a total abstinence man to accompany me. I cannot think of going to a dance with one whose highest delight is to make a fool of himself."[53] By the time Susan had proved to herself that she was attractive and sociable, she lost interest in the enterprise. Her new social life, even when it was not offensive, did not satisfy her that much at all, and she did not feel any pressing obligation to engage in it. Unlike most women of her generation who would champion women's rights by beginning with a personal rebellion against their private lives, Susan B. Anthony was freeing herself from private lifelong obligations and restrictions and more and more locating the emotional center of her life with women.

In 1848 while Susan was still enjoying her new life in Canajoharie, across the state in the small village of Seneca Falls, Elizabeth Cady Stanton, now married for eight years to the energetic abolitionist lawyer Henry Stanton, was becoming increasingly frustrated with the confinement of her own life and that of women generally. She had recently moved from the lively city of Boston to the small village of Seneca Falls, and with three sons under the age of five had little to distract her from her family. This was when she and Lucretia Mott began to correspond about the idea of calling a convention to address the civil, political, and religious liabilities of women.

At the moment Susan B. Anthony knew nothing of Stanton and Mott's activity, which ultimately would so dramatically shape her own life. She had become dissatisfied with schoolteaching and was beginning to wonder about what else she would do with her life. She began to think of her mother frequently. "How often when I am enjoying the sweet hour of twilight, do I think of the sadness that has long o'shadowed her brow." Her thoughts turned into an intense reflection on her mother's life, which foreshadowed and previsioned her own feminist consciousness. She would sometimes sit by herself in the evening and think about her mother, especially when she knew her father was away from home. "Then do my thoughts rest with my dear mother, toiling unremittingly through the long day and at eve, seated in her armchair rapt in solemn stillness, and later reclining on her lonely pillow."[54]

Until now, her mother's long years of selfless toil had been an unquestioned and accepted part of family life. What had been blurred and embedded in the meaning of motherhood now came forward in sharp relief in Susan's mind as a kind of suffering. She reflected on her mother's life and as she did her identification with her mother stirred something inside her which began to be expressed in her dreams. In long letters to her mother, she recounted every detail of her dreams.

In one dream, Lucy was seriously ill and Susan could not get to her. After terrible struggling, she finally reached her mother and "at the first glance upon your emaciated countenance burst into tears and bitterly reproached myself for suffering you to be left alone, while I please another . . . neglecting my own best of 'Mothers.'" Susan awoke from this dream in tears and deeply shaken. She wrote her mother to "live on hope, one child you have that shall return to you. I hope to do something towards happifying your declining days." Until she could return home she encouraged her mother to write often, opening her heart and telling her "all of your feelings while you are alone. Let us have a perfect interchange of feelings."[55]

Lucy probably thought that Susan was overly dramatic. Long ago she had buried her feelings in her own heart, taking her difficulties as they came, largely without question. But her daughter was of another generation, one that attributed much more significance to love and placed more emphasis on feelings than did women of Lucy's generation.[56] Meanwhile, Susan was wholly engrossed in her reflections on her mother's life. "I had imagined all you have had to suffer. I now feel as though I had witnessed the loneliness of those waking midnight hours." Her most ardent desire was to "recall the past, and be at my own home, where I might be of some comfort to [you]." When her father came to visit her in Canajoharie, she sadly bid him farewell at the dock, but she could only think "how sad my mother was feeling now that we are all gone." Yes, she wrote, she missed her father very much, but "I have thought of you the oftener of the two."[57]

These dreams and reflections forged a new bond for Susan with her mother. They elicited in her a propelling desire to go home and to be at her mother's side and attend to her happiness. "I tell you, there must be something more powerful than dollars and cents to induce me, longer than this year to make other than my mother's home my place of abode."[58]

For the first time, Susan's letters and diaries reveal her enveloped by a new kind of reflection—one in which she began to personally feel what her mother's life had been. This was more than a passing identification with her mother. It was the way in which her mother became a subject to her—a subject of her own life, and one that held new meaning for Susan. For the moment, Susan's response was personal. She wanted to go home and be with her mother. Soon her reflections would extend from her mother and become generalized to other women, and as she took women collectively as a subject to her, her response became a political one. This marked the beginnings of her political consciousness.

New consciousness changes the way one views the world by upsetting and undoing old assumptions and patterns of believing about the world and the meaning of life. At first this change may be destabilizing. It left Susan not knowing what she wanted precisely because she was beginning to find that consciousness created new wants and needs in her, a new ordering of her existence.

Susan's moods began to shift from impending depression to agitation and back again. She was weary from teaching, and her work no longer offered any challenge. Her social life held only minimal interest for her, and it was no longer enough for her to be personally independent. "I have a pleasant school of 20 scholars," she admitted, but "I have had to manufacture the interest duty compels me to exhibit . . . energy and something to stimulate is wanting." Even a vacation to Rochester left her dispirited. She wrote to her parents that "a weariness has come over me that the spring vacation did not in the least dispel."[59] Yet she had no plans for her future, which aggravated her depression. "I am out of sorts with the world," Susan admitted. Would a shopping spree solve her problem? "I want a new $5 fancy hat, $15.00 pin, $20.00 mantilla, dresses, shoes, gloves, pocket handkerchief, oh yes, a nice fur."[60] Apparently not. Instead she decided to have her old bonnets retrimmed and to remake her old dresses. Conservation was necessary if she were to leave teaching, especially since she had no future work or life direction in mind.

If teaching drained her, an argument with her uncle and cousins over slavery enlivened her. She was excited when her father visited and was "really glad to have Father express his sentiments with regard to reform. Though the good old folks call us crazy fanatics now, the day will come when they must acknowledge their stupidity."[61] Temperance reform sparked her attention, and she joined the Canajoharie Daughters of Temperance. "Reform must be the watchword," she told her mother. She wanted action now that "commenced at the root of all evil." But she was not focused; she only knew, as she told her mother, "I am tired of theory. I want to hear how we must act to have a happier and more glorious world."[62]

It is not surprising that Susan B. Anthony's first involvement in the world of reform was in the temperance movement. Her father had supported the movement for many years, and the goals of the temperance workers were compatible with her privatized morality. Reform solutions treated temperance as a personal and not a social problem. Nor is it surprising that temperance activism was one of the first expressions of organized feminism in the United States. In the 1840s the major temperance organization, the Sons of Temperance, shifted their platform from reforming the drunkard to halting all alcoholic consumption—by the sober and drunk alike. Independent women's temperance societies began to appear in the early 1840s with the same rallying call. Legally and economically powerless, women found temperance reform and advocating teetotalism to be the only apparent approach to the abuses women and children suffered from alcoholic husbands.

Declaring Canajoharie a "hot bed of vice and drunkenness," Susan B. Anthony, in her first public speech in 1849 for the Daughters of Temperance, issued a special call to women. Since "it is generally conceded that it is our sex that fashions the Social and Moral state of Society," she urged "our sex to cast their United influence into the balance." Calling for a united sisterhood to stamp out the effects of intemperance, she formulated the problem.

> We would that some means were devised, by which our Brothers and Sons shall no longer be allured from the *right* by corrupting influence of the fashionable sippings of wine and brandy, those sure destroyers of Mental and Moral Worth, and by which our Sisters and Daughters shall no longer be exposed to the vile arts of the gentlemanly appearing, gallant but really half-inebriated seducer.[63]

More than anything, Anthony believed in women's ability to assume their moral imperative and bring about a greater good in society.

> How is this great change to be wrought, who are to urge on this vast work of reform? Shall it not be women, who are most aggrieved by the foul destroyer's inroads? Most certainly. Then arises the question, how are we to accomplish the end desired? I answer not by confining our influence to our own home circle, not by centering all our benevolent feelings upon our own kindred, not by caring naught for the culture of any minds, save those of our own darlings. No, no; the gratification of the *selfish* impulses *alone,* can never produce a desirable change in the Moral aspect of Society.[64]

She was speaking as much to herself as she was to her audience. Three weeks after this speech she tendered her resignation to the Canajoharie Academy.

Canajoharie celebrated its new moral leader with a banquet, and each time Susan heard "Miss Anthony was the smartest woman that was now or ever in Canajoharie,"[65] her faith in her own ability was reinforced. Her plans were to return to Rochester, but by now her horizons had been stretched beyond her "own mother's home."

Drained of energy while she was teaching yet excited and engaged when arguing the antislavery cause—agitated to the point of irritation over whether to shop or save, yet passionately committed when giving a temperance speech—these were the contradictions that gripped Susan at that moment. These were also the first signs of political consciousness, defined by the moment when reflection upon women's condition begins, however tentatively, to surely dislodge thinking from the habitual ways in which one approaches daily life. In the past, she had accepted her mother's life as that which came with being a woman and a mother. But her geographic and social distance from home and her security in her own profession enabled her to look with a new eye at what had been accepted and embedded in ordinary daily life.

Shattering the routine of daily life by stepping onto the public platform and letting her intensity flow into her speeches and from there into her organizing, she began to connect her life to the larger world and the causes of social injustice. This life opened new knowledge and consequently brought her to new reflections, which touched with compassion what she would soon extend from her mother to women in general.

It is not accidental that Susan B. Anthony's reflections about her mother coincided with her yearning for the world of reform and represented the first tentative formation of her own political consciousness. Consciousness is not a psychological process. Rather, it is fully *formed* in and through doing and action.[66] Further, as it engages a subject in the public world, in Anthony's time, political consciousness was possible only when a woman was breaking from her assigned private sphere. In this sense political consciousness surpasses morality as it begins with reflections that *reveal* power and domination and develops into a critical understanding of one's place in the world in relation to power and domination.

With these early promptings of political consciousness and her desire for social action Susan was at odds with the concept of private piety. Resolution of this dilemma marked the beginning of the transformation of her morality into an ethic of social responsibility. She no longer saw alcohol as an evil unto itself, as she had when she confronted her Uncle Dickenson for "drinking Cider and ale" ten years before. Instead, she intended to get to "the root of all evil," to "produce a radical change in our Moral Atmosphere." A fuller comprehension of the social, political, and economic dimensions of women's powerlessness that would ultimately form her radical thinking was still ahead of her. Yet her awareness and analysis of woman's condition was opening at this point, and her insistence on action was strong. She called upon the prevailing "idea of progress," a philosophy which flowed from the eighteenth-century Enlightenment and viewed the world as progressing toward a state of human perfectability. As she told her Canajoharie audience: "Now, Ladies, all we would do is to do all in our power, both individually and collectively, to harmonize and happify our Social system."[67]

Susan's emerging political consciousness lodged her in the issues of the world. With issues of temperance, slavery, and women's rights she had neither the time nor inclination to indulge in personal piety. Her work in the world with her reflections over the suffering of others allowed her to abandon her earlier preoccupation with punitive self-evaluation, which had so often led to self-deprecation. As soon as she did, she found a release of her own full spirit, a propelling movement forward as she thought more about "forgetting self." She reminded her brother of their childhood.

> Had we been indulged in the gratification of every imaginary want in those days how illy should we have been fitted to struggle on through the disappointments incident to those who depend upon public patronage for support. Had we never been taught to yield our own wishes, that others might gratify theirs, how incapable would we be to endure with any degree of cheerfulness . . . I believe our happiness is increased by yielding momentary self gratification and doing all in our power to render others happy.[68]

How these words are interpreted depends on the circumstances of a woman's life and the passion in her soul. They may be interpreted as fulfilling the most traditional requirements of female self-effacement, or they may be understood as giving voice to a new sense of self, the first sparks of political consciousness setting the stage for greater things to come. Although one might be tempted to read repressive self-denial in Anthony's words, that interpretation would fail to grasp the new moral commitments that engaged her in the public world that she meant to change. Released from her personalized morality, her growing political consciousness not only engaged her in the world but offered her an emancipation from her personal preoccupation with her ego's needs.

Susan resigned her teaching position and made plans to return to the farm in Rochester. But as her cousin Margaret was about to give birth, Susan decided to continue teaching a little longer to remain with her through the delivery. Margaret had become almost a sister to Susan, supporting and encouraging her in her new public work and comforting her through her disaffection with teaching. They had become loving friends, spending long hours talking together with deep care and concern for each other. Each day when Susan was about to return home from school, Margaret drew near the window to watch and wait until she could see her coming down the lane. Susan reported this to her brother, "to show you how much she esteems my society." And after Susan mentioned to Margaret one day that she might go home for a visit, Margaret "laid awake nights and wept over the thought."[69] Such concern and affection were natural among women of the time, but like most women of her era, Susan accepted marriage as an even deeper and more important relationship. She wondered, "If she could feel thus at the thought of my leaving, judge you of her agony at the thought of parting of her husband."[70]

Gold was discovered in California that year, and Susan's concern for her cousin's "matrimonial bliss" was heightened when Margaret's husband, Joseph Caldwell, announced he was leaving— he had "caught the fever." Susan thought Joseph selfish, frivolous, and self-centered for wanting to leave Margaret behind to go to California. Revealing another view of marriage, she quipped sarcastically to her brother, "How much harder for them who have known such joys supernal thus to be left to depend upon themselves destitute of Lord and Master."[71]

Margaret's pregnancy increasingly disabled her. Joseph finally realized that it would be dangerous to leave her and remained in Canajoharie. But he was hardly supportive. When he complained of a headache one day and Margaret reminded him that she had had one for weeks, he retorted, "Mine is a real head *ache, real* pain, yours is a sort of natural consequence."[72] On March 7, 1849, Margaret delivered a baby girl. Susan was with Margaret and the doctor through the long night assisting in the birth and worrying over the gravity of Margaret's condition. "I never slept a wink," she confided to her mother, "went to school next A.M., everytime one of the girls would speak, I imagined it was Margaret's groan." Susan was completely absorbed with Margaret; she fixed her whole self, body and soul, on Margaret's travail. It was as if she could feel the pain herself. And she knew Margaret was in danger. "I was with her through the whole. . . . It is rather a tough business, is it not Mother. Oh am I glad she is through with it."[73]

Margaret lingered in bed for seven weeks, and her mother worried. "I am afraid you are not having a good getting [on]." Susan attended her day and night, and Margaret was completely wrapped up in her ministrations. "She calls me if I leave the room for five minutes. She don't [sic] know why but she wants Susan at hand." As was traditional for men at the time, Joseph was practically excluded from the sickroom. Susan had to lift Margaret and help her when she needed to get out of bed. "When she got in bed, she put her arms around my neck and kissed me." When Margaret worried that she was a burden for Susan, Susan gently reassured her cousin. "Oh no . . . it is a pleasure to me to be thus privileged, I did not wish you to suffer thus, but since you must I am very happy that I am here." She took Margaret's hand. "Don't you believe Margaret that I love to wait on you." Margaret simply gazed at her, and Susan was a bit overcome. As she thought later, "Oh, with how much affection did she look upon me."[74]

Irritability mounted between Joseph and Susan. Unmarried at the age of twenty-nine and considered the old maid of the house, Susan was left with all of the household chores. "I get her meals once in four hours, clean up the rooms, superintend the kitchen works and it occupies every moment of mine. No one pretends to take any charge of household matters but myself. I am somewhat jaded, and they say look thin but am blessed with health—strength to perform."[75] When Susan went to Joseph with the suggestion that the baby be named after her, he sharply retorted, "I will have no Susie about the house."[76] Susan's resentment mounted. She was selfless in her care of her own dear Margaret, but she was expected to care for everyone else's needs as well. "It seems to be that no one feels that it is any thing out of the common course of things for me to sacrifice my every feeling, almost principle, to gratify those with whom I mingle."[77]

Margaret died, and Susan's grief was profound. Her mother was ill and couldn't come to Canajoharie to mourn the loss of her niece.

Without her mother, her sisters, or her dear friend, Susan was alone in her grief and exhausted. She poured out her heart to Hannah: "Sister, I feel that I have lost the only friend I had (out of our own family circle) who loved me because of union of soul, of sympathy, of spirit, but that friend is gone."[78]

Neither Hannah nor Guelma had written to her in over two months. Susan tried to retrieve her sisterly society. She turned and urged Hannah to "let us while we live, enjoy each other's society all that may be, let us not make a God of this world or its cares."[79] Some of her growing bitterness came out in a letter to Guelma. "I often feel that I have not a disinterested friend, not one who loves me for my very self, but many who endure my presence because they may derive some service from me."[80]

This is not what Susan had meant when she wrote to her brother about "forgetting self," but was surely the tyranny unmarried women faced in becoming old maids. It is no wonder that when she speculated on the California gold fever one day, she proclaimed, "If I were a man, wouldn't I be off."

The problem for Susan at the moment was not that she was not a man but that she had not yet discovered how her intense emotional bonding with women and her new expanding political consciousness would shape her life and her work.

3

"Woman Must Take to Her Soul a Purpose"

Every woman must marry, either with or without love, for the sake of support, or be doomed to a life of utter dependence, living after the death of parents in the home of married brother or sister, the drudge and burdenbearer of the family, without any financial recompense, and usually looked upon with disrespect by the children.[1]

EXHAUSTED AND DISPIRITED, SUSAN BOARDED THE TRAIN FOR Rochester. More than ever, she wanted to be home on the family farm. The past several months in Canajoharie had sapped her spirit and raised some difficult questions for her. For the last ten years, she had taken one teaching assignment after another but without planning for her future. Now when she thought about her "future course," she had to face the fact that she had reached the limit of her career possibilities. In 1849, there were a few women journalists and many more novelists, but there was hardly any profession comparable to teaching that was open to women. The choices before Susan were either to remain a teacher, to marry, or to return home to be an old maid in her family.

Before she returned to Rochester, her father and mother had written offering her the opportunity to take over the family farm as her own business. "Now if you are really tired of school teaching and would like to farm it a while—here's a first rate chance for you. If however you would like a respite from teaching, whether long or short, we think well of your having your choice."[2] Her father's offer was timely in spirit. Only a year before, the New York State legislature had extended some limited property rights to married women (*feme covert*), lifting them somewhat from the legally dead where Blackstone's *Commentaries* had consigned them. But Susan, as a single woman (*feme sole*), had not been robbed of the right to conduct the business of the farm in her own name; she could indeed become its proprietor. Surely this was a good opportunity, she thought to herself as the train rolled along, but she felt agitated for it wasn't only a matter of choosing another form of work.

Susan could not find satisfaction with any of the possibilities she saw before her. Something within her remained unsatisfied. Her parents had already sensed her dilemma and her need for rest, and they tried to be consoling. "We shall all be very happy to welcome you to the little white cottage and should you want to go to teaching again some future day, I have no doubt that some chance would offer to accommodate you and then perhaps without going so far from home."[3]

Susan stared out the train window. There was something else that cast its spell over her thoughts about her future. Perhaps it was only that she was tired, but it did seem that these last trying months in Joseph Caldwell's household were a foreshadowing of what her life as an old maid would be like, whether she taught school or managed the farm. Remembering much later in her life the poignancy of her reflections in 1849, she was able to give words to what at that moment was more of a nagging concern.

> Women might work like galley slaves for their own relatives, receiving only their board and clothes, and hold their social position in the community; but the moment they stepped outside of home and became wage-earners, thus securing pecuniary independence, they lost caste and were rigidly barred from the quilting bees, the apple-parings, and all the society functions of the neighborhood.[4]

So be it! There was a certain challenge in the defiance of not caring what others thought when she was convinced of the appropriateness of her course. Even though her spirits were low at the moment, long ago as a matter of practicality she had trained herself to refuse to indulge them. She was finished with teaching; now she must find her way into the world of reform that had invigorated her and sometimes made her energy seem boundless.

Yet the problem remained: If she were to pursue her reform work, how would she support herself and keep her economic independence? Except for men like William Lloyd Garrison who had wealthy financial backers, there was no obvious way to carry out that work and keep one's independence. Such a course had not been taken and held to by a single, independent woman. At that time, most unmarried women who entered reform work left it after a few years and returned to their families, trading their independence and the strain of being a woman in a "man's world" for the social validation and security that came from being dependent old maids—which although demeaning was at least socially acceptable.[5]

Susan later recalled that in those days, "Politics seemed a great deal farther away than paradise, and the most radical reformer had not the prophetic eye which could discern the woman politician."[6] There was something firm and resolute in Susan's refusal to give up her independence for the life of an old maid and her insistence that she could find her way in the world of reform—indeed even in politics. Later she thought, "Is it any wonder that a sour and crabbed disposition was universally ascribed to spinsterhood, or that those women should be regarded as most unfortunate, doomed to a loveless, aimless, and dependent existence, universally considered as having made a failure of life?"[7]

The train sped through the countryside so familiar to her, and Susan relaxed into knowing that for now she would have some time on the farm to rest. Then Daniel met her at the train depot in Rochester and took her to the farm in nearby Gates in their horse-drawn wagon. She was glad to be back home, where "the house stood on an elevation, and the walk was lined on either side with pinks, and there were roses in the yard, and cherry trees, and currant and gooseberry bushes everywhere, and the driveway was lined with quince bushes."[8] After the panic of 1837, Rochester had turned from grain and wheat production to cultivating fruit orchards and flower beds. So lovely was the transformation that Rochester had earned the title of "Flower City."[9] The saplings that the Anthonys had planted in 1845 were now fruit-bearing orchards.

At first Susan was content to put away her better clothes and don her calico dress to work in the garden. But typically she would become engrossed in a project, such as planting a new bed of raspberries, and then leave it untended to go off to a series of temperance or antislavery meetings. After several failed projects, Susan's sister Mary remarked that she hoped that "when you get a husband and children, you will treat them better than you did your raspberry plants, and not leave them to their fate at the beginning of winter."[10]

Susan was soon spending more time at temperance and antislavery meetings than on the farm. Finally, she decided to try to make it on her own in reform work. She had saved some money while she was teaching in Canajoharie, even while she had been helping her family through the financial crash that had wiped out her father's businesses years earlier. Now her father was able to return some of that money to her as the income from his insurance business and the farm gave him adequate support.

Susan continued her temperance work, which she began to connect to anti-slavery work. At a "Temperance Festival" she organized in 1851, she reminded the Daughters of Temperance that "while they do deeply commiserate the degradation of their sisters who are subjected to the brutal outrages of drunken husbands," they must remember "the woes and sufferings of their own down trodden sisters on Southern Plantations who are under the lash, compelled to submit to the fiendish insults of their more than fiendish masters."[11] This was a big step. Temperance reform provided one of the few legitimate public outlets for women's moral concerns at this time. The campaign to reform drunkards and for teetotalism emphasized individual change; it did not touch the larger social and political questions connected with alcohol abuse, which made temperance compatible with women's personalized morality. But Susan was pushing herself further; her growing consciousness propelled her to make connections between temperance and the political issues of slavery. But soon even that was not enough for her.

Susan decided to school herself in antislavery agitation. Antislavery leaders like William Lloyd Garrison and Wendell Phillips remained distant and courageous luminaries to her. However, she met the Quaker abolitionists Stephen and Abby Foster when they came to Rochester for a series of antislavery lectures. Susan's outspoken temperance views were already known to the Fosters, who invited her to join them on one of their lecture tours through northern New York State. Abby Kelley Foster had been a schoolteacher, who had become a daring, courageous abolitionist. Susan had heard stories of the abuse Abby endured for years from her audience because she was the only woman speaker on the antislavery platform. Susan admired her for this, but when the Fosters recognized the potential of an ardent abolitionist in Susan and asked her to join them in the work, Susan decided that she was not yet ready. She knew that she could not yet speak to the deeper, more complicated political issues of slavery. She knew that it was not enough to approach slavery only from the egalitarian ethic that addressed individual injustice.

Slavery was a deeply entrenched economic institution protected by political alliances and power, which would have to be understood and analyzed to address the issue effectively.

Susan B. Anthony would learn as she worked. She wanted to find her own way to the heart of the movement. She was not one to join in or tag along. In May 1851, she went to Syracuse to a series of antislavery meetings and was moved deeply by the passionate oratory and strong arguments of William Lloyd Garrison and his English counterpart, George Thompson. Garrison and Thompson were the most radical abolitionists, and Susan found in them the commitment and political wisdom with which she could identify.

But it was the even more radical and controversial Elizabeth Cady Stanton whom Susan had wanted to meet for a long time. Stanton had called the 1848 Seneca Falls Woman's Rights Convention to assert a radical analysis of women's condition and to initiate a woman's rights movement organized to champion the rights and self-determination of women. But Mrs. Stanton was not at the Syracuse antislavery meetings, and it was said that she rarely attended conventions. With a growing family of her own, she focused her ebullient personality on creating a social life close to home. She loved the gaiety of parties and a frequency of visitors and kept her door always open to her friends. Susan had heard about her courageous work in calling the 1848 Seneca Falls convention, and she followed the continuing events in the newspapers, where the controversial Mrs. Stanton was frequently lauded or attacked. Mrs. Stanton lived her radicalism and often scandalized her neighbors in Seneca Falls with such daring practices as raising a flag on her flagpole to announce the birth of each of her children, at a time when the subject was not considered appropriate for discussion. Stanton's brilliant articulation of the position of women in society in the Declaration of Sentiments she issued at the Seneca Falls Convention revealed a woman who had transcended the personalized pietistic morality of women's private sphere. Aided by her classical education and the tutoring she received in her father's law office, intellectually she broke ground by offering a new view of the nineteenth-century American woman—one who would ultimately win civil and political identity.

While Susan was still in Canajoharie, her family had attended a meeting Mrs. Stanton had organized in Rochester as a follow-up to the Seneca Falls meeting. Susan listened attentively to her sister's enthusiastic reports, but she was not drawn to the new movement with hearty conviction. Again not being one to merely join in, it was necessary for something more than a report of a meeting to move her into action. The catalyst that would catapult her into her life's work had not yet occurred.

Yet she was moved when her Quaker friend Abigail Bush told her the story of how she was pushed to preside over that first woman's rights meeting in Rochester. Mrs. Stanton and Lucretia Mott had decided that it was necessary to have a man preside over the convention in Seneca Falls, as they feared a woman president would not be taken seriously. But a few weeks later, the militant-minded Quaker women in Rochester decided to change that. "Oh Susan," Abigail later remembered, "in the vestibule before the meeting, my old friends Amy Post, Rhoda DeGarmo and Sarah Fish . . . at once commenced laboring with me to prove the hour had come when a woman could preside and led me into the church. Amy proposed my name as President. It was accepted at once." Abigail's story stirred something in Susan.

Abigail explained that when she took the podium in the 1848 Rochester meeting, Lucretia Mott and Elizabeth Cady Stanton left the platform and took seats in the audience, abandoning her to open the meeting by herself. "But this did not move me from performing all my duties; and at the close of the first session, Lucretia Mott came forward, folded me tenderly in her arms and thanked me for presiding." It took every bit of energy and endurance Abigail had for her to prevail through the entire meeting. When it was over, "my strength seemed to leave me and I cried like a baby."[12] Susan could commiserate with her friend; any woman who dared to step up on a public platform knew that public speaking was a major act of defiance for women, and one not to be taken lightly. Women were doing the unheard of by merely speaking in public, but they paid heavily for such flagrant challenges to their traditional role, particularly in terms of the personal insecurity and self-doubt it raised in them.

Meanwhile, Susan's attention was focused on the antislavery oratory at the Syracuse meeting in 1851. Antislavery agitation was escalating in response to the Fugitive Slave Law, enacted the year before, which made it easier for a slave owner to recapture an escaped slave or even to take a free black into his possession and claim him as his own property. The former escaped slave Frederick Douglass, now one of the most powerful abolitionists in the country and editor of his own antislavery paper, *The North Star,* was the prime mover behind the Underground Railroad. Rochester's Amy Post estimated that in the 1850s one hundred fifty escaped slaves were coming through that strategically located city each year on the Underground Railroad, on their last stop before reaching Canada and freedom. Often during the early 1850s, Susan helped a runaway slave coming through Rochester.

As crucial as this individual aid and support was, it was the American Anti-Slavery Society's political confrontation with the complex economic and institutional underpinnings of slavery that challenged Susan's mind and heart; and she became determined to surpass the social conventions and womanly manners which restrained women's voices and limited their actions to individual change.

While they were in Syracuse Susan's friend Amelia Bloomer, who edited a woman's temperance paper called *The Lily*, invited Susan to come home with her to Seneca Falls, where she could hear more of Garrison and Thompson on the next stop of their lecture tour. Susan accepted the invitation with pleasure, and with some small hope that in Seneca Falls she might finally meet Elizabeth Cady Stanton.

"There she stood," as Mrs. Stanton recalled their first meeting on a street corner after the antislavery lectures, "with her good earnest face and a genial smile, dressed in gray silk hat and all the same color, relieved with pale blue ribbons, the perfection of neatness and sobriety." But with Garrison and Thompson as house guests and worrying about what terrible antics her boys might be up to at home, Mrs. Stanton was preoccupied. The two women exchanged polite formalities, and Mrs. Stanton left abruptly. "I liked her thoroughly," she later recalled, "and why I did not at once invite her home with me to dinner I do not know."[13] Susan was left with Amelia Bloomer standing on the street corner; a bit disappointed that there had not been more.

It was Mrs. Stanton who found the opportunity for their next meeting. She had invited Lucy Stone and the journalist and political leader Horace Greeley to her home to discuss a plan for a coeducational college. Of course, Susan should come and stay with her for several days. The project did not develop any further, but after this visit Susan began to stop by Seneca Falls whenever she had the opportunity.

According to Mrs. Stanton, she and Susan became "fast friends" at once[14] and remained "Mrs. Stanton and Susan" to each other for the next fifty years. As Susan recalled, from their first meeting there was an "intense attraction" between them.[15] Mrs. Stanton's flamboyance, openness, and enthusiasm touched Susan's serious self-discipline, and each found her complement. Susan was drawn by the boldness of Mrs. Stanton's ideas, and Mrs. Stanton found in Susan an independence of mind and spirit that became a compelling attraction. Their converging ideas, quick minds, and sharp wits sparked something between them that was not diminished and was perhaps even augmented by the fact that their lives were going in different directions at that time. While Susan was trying to find her place in the public world, Mrs. Stanton, even though she had been the center of controversy since she had called the Seneca Falls convention, was enclosing herself within her domestic world where she was busy having babies and raising her family. She already had four boys, and before the end of the decade would give birth to two daughters and another son. She enjoyed motherhood, and brought to it her own radical ideas on health and child rearing. Yet as much as she intellectually and philosophically transcended the private sphere assigned to her sex, Stanton wrapped herself in the family life of that private world and often used her husband and children as buffer between her and the world. She herself never fully transcended these limits that marriage placed on women until very late in her life. Then her freedom was celebrated in her famous speech "The Solitude of Self."

Mrs. Stanton's "open door" especially welcomed her new friend. As they spent more and more time together, Susan became one of the family and was almost another mother to Mrs. Stanton's children. Since Henry Stanton's political and legislative work kept him away from home several months a year, Susan and Mrs. Stanton's relationship became a primary bond for both of them. As Mrs. Stanton was not about to leave home, it was up to Susan to bring the world of reform and her own restless spirit—her craving for action—to Mrs. Stanton. As they spent time together, a deep and abiding affection developed between them. Theirs was a friendship of profound loyalty and egalitarian love that neither had known with anyone else and that when mixed with their political visions and daring actions, ultimately made them one of the great couples of nineteenth-century America.

Later in her life, Stanton characterized their complementarity in this now-famous statement.

In writing we did better work together than either could alone. While she is slow and analytical in composition, I am rapid and synthetic. I am the better writer, she the better critic. She supplied the facts and statistics, I the philosophy and rhetoric, and together we have made arguments that have stood unshaken by the storms of thirty long years; arguments that no man has answered.[16]

This famous testimonial, which has been reproduced in many accounts of the woman's rights movement, has suffered from a reductive interpretation over the years that has left us with an image of Stanton as the intellectually superior one, who had neither the skills nor the patience for the important—but less significant—work of the shrewd political organizer, which was Anthony's domain.[17]

Such implicitly hierarchical dichotomies between theory and action inevitably favor the theorists. But this kind of hierarchy was unknown to Mrs. Stanton and Susan. For Susan, theirs was "a most natural union of head and heart." At last she was loved for herself, for her deep convictions, her quick mind, and her energetic work. While at times she may have stirred the pudding or tended the children, she was no old maid in Mrs. Stanton's home. In Susan, Mrs. Stanton found the egalitarian love that her marriage had failed to give her. Yet she kept her marriage as an ever-present emotional wedge between her and Anthony and that would have profound implications later in their lives and for their movement. Both women were charged and excited by their intellectual and emotional compatibility. They needed each other in much more subtle and dynamic ways than a rigid hierarchical categorization of their relationship could ever reveal. That became evident over the long and often difficult half-century during which they worked and loved together.

Something more than reading a tract, studying an abstract theory, or having vivid discussions with Mrs. Stanton was necessary to crystallize Susan's feminism. Brilliant ideas are not enough to form something as profound as political consciousness, which is a powerful force precisely because it is launched from one's direct engagement in the world. Anthony's political consciousness crystallized as she was confronted with the reality of male domination in the world. At this point in time, it was the male temperance leaders, or as Anthony called them "the white orthodox male Saints," who became the foil for her political consciousness.

In January 1852, Anthony attended a meeting called by the Sons of Temperance in Albany. Submitting her credentials as a delegate from the Rochester "Daughters," she joined the other ladies, who, as custom required, quietly took their place in the meeting and held their silence. She soon became impatient. The men's discussions droned on until finally she decided she must speak. But when she rose, she was rebuffed with the booming declaration that "the sisters were not invited there to speak but to listen and learn."[18] Outraged and indignant, Anthony stormed out of the meeting, followed by some other women.

This was her first spontaneous protest action. Next she organized a countermeeting, invited the press, and announced that the protesting women would form their own independent organization. "We are heartily sick and tired of the round of unmeaning encomiums which Gentlemen Temperance lecturers are pleased to lavish upon our sex," Anthony proclaimed repeatedly.[19] To many of the temperance clergymen and their followers, these were the words of "a hybrid species, half man and half woman, belonging to neither sex."[20]

Susan B. Anthony's first organization, the new Woman's State Temperance Society, was thus born. Her next step was to call a convention. Mrs. Stanton wrote, "I will do all in my power to aid you. Work down this way, then you come and stay with me."[21] Susan brought with her a spirited report on the row she had created in Albany. As Mrs. Stanton sat and listened, she could not help but recall the 1840 Anti-Slavery Convention in London, when the right of women to speak was blithely compromised by the Garrisonian abolitionist Wendell Phillips, when he concurred with George Thompson after the convention and agreed to exclude women from the discussion. Phillips stated then, "I have no doubt the women will sit with as much interest behind the bar as though the original proposition had been carried in the affirmative."[22] It was when women were excluded from anti-slavery deliberations, that Mrs. Stanton and Lucretia Mott had first conceived of the idea of calling a woman's rights convention.

Mrs. Stanton agreed with Susan that it was now time to act. "We will get up a meeting here & do what we can to advance the interests of the society."[23] Her anger had not abated. "Men and angels give me patience!" she proclaimed, "I am at the boiling point! If I do not some day use my tongue on this question, I shall die of an intellectual repression, a woman's rights convulsion."[24]

"Shall our society lead or follow public sentiment," Stanton demanded. "I say lead." Her indignation fed Anthony's energy. Stanton's experience was essential to Anthony's organizing. Stanton told her to ignore the "too small namby pamby" pronouncements from some of the conservative women who wanted to avoid issues like suffrage and divorce while many of the other women were still hesitant to speak in public. It was clear to Stanton and Anthony that if they were to move forward they must provide the leadership and direction to their new organization.

Mrs. Stanton counseled Susan on speech making. "Dress loose, take a great deal of exercise & be particular about your diet & sleep sound enough, the body has a great effect on the mind." Good advice, Susan thought, but she had no intention of giving the opening speech at the convention herself. Instead she told Mrs. Stanton that "your radical words will be just the right thing." Mrs. Stanton refused. "I have no doubt a little practice will make you an admirable lecturer. I will go to work at once & write you the best lecture I can."[25]

Mrs. Stanton had recently given birth to her fifth child, her first daughter, and had no intention of giving in to Susan. She would help orchestrate their new plan from her home in Seneca Falls. "Oh, Susan! Susan! Susan! You must manage to spend a week with me before the Rochester Convention, for I am afraid that I cannot attend."[26] Susan, knowing that Mrs. Stanton had two full-time girls assisting her, was adamant.

Elizabeth Cady Stanton did address the Woman's State Temperance Convention at Rochester and she came in style—wearing the new militant woman's rights fashion, which came to be known as "the Bloomer." The year before, at the first meeting of the Women's State Temperance Society, Elizabeth Cady Stanton had appeared for the first time in "the Bloomer dress." This was a Turkish-style costume she had just adopted from her cousin Elizabeth Smith Miller, who had designed a new outfit in this style and wore it when she visited Seneca Falls a few years before in the winter of 1851. She was "dressed somewhat in the Turkish style," recalled Stanton, "short skirt, full trousers of fine black broadcloth, a Spanish cloak, of the same material, reached to the knee." Stanton had watched her cousin move about the house and saw the ease with which she could go up and down the stairs carrying baby, lamp, and all.[27]

Elizabeth Smith Miller, the daughter of the wealthy philanthropist Gerrit Smith, championed many reforms and became a strong proponent of dress reform. It is often the case that the more daring ventures into rebelliously dramatic social statements, such as new costuming that defies all sense of propriety, are initiated in the upper classes, where an implicit social permissiveness frequently exists toward novelty or eccentricity.

In the June 1852 issue of *The Lily,* Amelia Bloomer described Stanton's appearance at the Rochester meeting.

> . . . rich black satin dress, a plain waist after the prevailing style of ladies' dresses, full skirt falling six or eight inches below the knee, plain wide trousers of the same material, and black "congress" gaiters. On her neck, a fine linen cambrick collar, fastened with a gold pin, and cuffs of same material about her wrist.

From then on, Bloomer regularly promoted the new costume in her paper until the dress came to be known as "the Bloomer." But what she failed to mention in this account was that before leaving home for Rochester, Mrs. Stanton had visited James (the barber in Seneca Falls) and had her hair cut into a short bob, which had completed her liberated appearance.

Standing before the first Woman's State Temperance Convention at Rochester in the spring of 1852, Stanton's defiance was not limited to her dress. She wove the issues set forth in her 1848 Declaration of Women's Rights (in which she had demanded full rights, including the vote for women) into the problem of intemperance. "Let no woman remain in the relation of wife with a confirmed drunkard," she preached. And in a daring demand for woman's right to divorce—one of the earliest—she urged, "Let us petition our State government to modify the laws affecting marriage and the custody of children, that the drunkard shall have no claims on wife or child."[28] Her radical words made many of the women present uncomfortable, but she was, nevertheless, elected president of the new society.

The women appointed Anthony their general agent, and she announced that the organization would "place such agents in the lecturing field as shall speak the whole truth to women." Further, she insisted that the women take "the right to the entire control of the funds of the Woman's New York State Temperance Society." They denied men voting power, although they were permitted to attend the meetings. Then Anthony took to the field—lecturing, organizing, petitioning, and raising funds throughout the state as the agent of her own society.

Susan's rapid rise to the heart of the woman's rights movement did not go unnoticed, especially since her drive soon surpassed that of other women. Clarina Howard Nichols, another woman's rights advocate, told Susan, "it is most invigorating to watch the devel-

opment of a woman in the work for humanity: first, anxious for
the cause and depressed with a sense of her own inability; next,
partial success of timid efforts creating a hope; next, a faith; and
then the fruition of complete self-devotion. Such will be your history."[29] A new woman's rights leader was born.

In her speeches, Anthony claimed that women had been wrongly
directed into reforming the drunkard. She criticized the temperance
reformers. "They have done much, very much toward lessening the
evil effects of the abomination, but they have for the most part failed
to strike a *death blow* at the *root* of the evil." She insisted on radical
change and eschewed reform, or "our work is to be done over and
over again."[30]

At this point, temperance workers thought that radical change
would become possible because of a new law that had been recently
passed in Maine, which was directed against the *traffic* in alcohol.
The Maine law closed many of the loopholes of other prohibition
laws: its jurisdiction was statewide, not local; it provided for search-
and-seizure warrants allowing for arrest if alcohol were found on
a premise; and it stiffened the penalties for violating prohibition
law.[31] This law was radical in its approach to temperance but not
in its approach to the conditions of women. Anthony needed more
experience and a deeper political consciousness of the fundamental
issues that caused the subordination of women in society before she
could realize that radical change would elude her as long as she
confined her work to temperance.

Campaigning for the Maine law was Anthony's first experience
in demanding legal change. Strategy came naturally to her. Within
a few short months, Anthony and the co-workers she had mobilized
gathered twenty-eight thousand signatures on a petition demanding
that New York pass the equivalent of the Maine law. Immediately
thereafter, she organized a hearing before the New York legislature—the first time a delegation of women in America had ever
carried their own demands before a legislative body.

In petitioning for the Maine law, Susan B. Anthony made what
she considered "my first declaration for woman suffrage," which in
fact surpassed the principle of suffrage and called upon women to
actually vote if men's theories proved false.[32] "Men tell us they vote
for us by proxy," she declared. Well, if that is true, put it to the
test, she urged women. Since she could not vote, woman should
"duly instruct her husband, son, father or brother how she would
have him vote, and if he longer continues to misrepresent her, take

the right, march to the ballot-box and deposit a vote indicative of her highest ideas of practical temperance." But if men "fail to represent our true sentiments, let us send up, from every nook & corner of the State one united resolve to refuse to trust them as our agents."[33]

Here was the core of Anthony's organizing strategy: Take a concrete issue, such as intemperance; analyze the problem; formulate a specific demand, such as the Maine law; then urge women to take practical, confrontational, and effective actions that logically followed from her analysis of the issue. She was determined not only to act on behalf of women, but to mobilize women to act for themselves. If, in each of their private circumstances, they could test the theory that men "vote for us by proxy" then it was likely that they would be able to confront the reality behind it. The aim of her organizing strategies was to spark political consciousness in women; she was not interested in merely cultivating followers. She knew that women had to personally experience the limits of men's ability to act on their behalf if they were to begin to act for themselves, and that they could experience these limits only by testing men's claims.

This was not the image of a lady reformer nor was it respectable behavior. As an article in the *Utica Evening Herald* pointed out:

> With a degree of impiety which was both startling and disgusting, this shrewish *maiden* counseled the numerous wives and mothers present to separate from their husbands whenever they became intemperate, *and particularly not to allow the said husbands to add another child to the family* (probably no married advocate of woman's rights would have made this remark). Think of such advice given in public by one who claims to be a *maiden* lady.[34]

But if Anthony's strategies in the field came naturally and without compromise, in her first years of public work she was somewhat naive about political maneuvering. At the first anniversary meeting of the Woman's State Temperance Society in June 1853, she acquiesced to the conservative women's demands that men be admitted and granted voting privileges in the society. As soon as the men were given a voice and vote, they deposed Stanton from the presidency because of her strong woman's rights positions. Anthony had known that Stanton's demand for the right of a woman to divorce a drunkard was too radical for most members of their organization. But she had seriously underestimated the counterforce it would produce. She was shocked when Stanton was put out of office. Along with Stanton she severed all connections with the first organization she had founded. Indignant, they returned to the hearth of Mrs. Stanton's old-fashioned fireplace to plot and plan new campaigns.[35]

During these years Susan was a constant thorn in Mrs. Stanton's side, trying to push her into the world. At the same time, it took Mrs. Stanton over six months to get Susan into the Bloomer dress. The bond between Mrs. Stanton and Susan gave Susan the love and care she had lost upon the death of her cousin Margaret. But this was more than intense womanly affection, it was a deeply political bond as well. "So entirely one are we, that in all our associations, ever side by side on the same platform, not one feeling of jealousy or envy has ever shadowed our lives," Stanton noted. What was intimate and personal between them was simultaneously public and political. Mrs. Stanton and Susan did not separate their personal relationship from their political work, which gave Susan a commitment that followed her into the world and stayed with her in her work. Later Mrs. Stanton recalled that it was like a perfect marriage. "Soon fastened heart to heart with hooks of steel in a friendship that thirty years of confidence and affection have steadily strengthened, we have labored faithfully together."[36]

The depression that overcame Susan in Canajoharie was gone. Her expanding consciousness of the conditions of women's lives, provoked by the treatment she and Mrs. Stanton had received from the male temperance leaders, released in her a new energy. As it became apparent in reform circles that she had more drive than most people around her, her unbounded energy took on a new kind of daring.

By mid-1852, the Bloomer dress had become a political statement of the "ultras," as the most advanced, radical, and controversial of the woman's rights advocates came to be known. In December of 1852, Susan B. Anthony reported from Mrs. Stanton's house, "Well at least I am in short skirts and trousers!"[37] Having turned up the hem of her dress until the skirt fell just below her knees, she abandoned her layers of petticoats and instead put on a pair of Bloomer trousers that she had made for her. Wearing this looser and lighter dress in a spirit of new freedom and with an air of defiance, she also uncoiled her long, thick brown hair and had it clipped into a bob. Off she went to woman's rights conventions and lecturing in her own defiant style.

Only a few months ago, Anthony had attended her first convention where she found the convention hall filled with women sporting the new dress and haircut. Except for Mrs. Stanton, most of the luminaries of the young woman's rights movement were there: Lucy Stone, Antoinette Brown, and Ernestine Rose. Their strong speeches more than matched their militant presence, and the air was alive with the spirit of change. Although this was Anthony's first woman's rights convention, she was already well known for her temperance work. But this was the first time many of the "ultras" had seen her in action.

When the meeting opened, Lucretia Mott's husband James nominated for president Elizabeth Oakes Smith, the fashionable literary figure. Anthony took the floor to protest. As Smith was dressed in a white, low-necked, sleeveless gown, a bit seductive and in high fashion, Anthony, her moralistic piety still intermingled with her developing political ethics, argued that Smith could not represent "the earnest, solid hardworking women of this country."[38] James Mott tried to subdue Anthony by tactfully pointing out that not everyone could be expected to dress as plainly as the Quakers. But that was not the point. Their woman's rights movement was demanding equal rights on behalf of housewives, seamstresses, the mill workers, the launderers, and domestics who Anthony reiterated would find it difficult to believe a woman dressed in such a fashion could represent their sex. But even this response could not hide her prudery. Eventually her argument prevailed and the convention elected her own nominee, Lucretia Mott, as president. A few months later, Anthony herself began wearing the Bloomer dress, an "ultra" symbol of woman's rights. Feminism prevailed over femininity. As controversial as the Bloomer dress was, Anthony did not see it as alienating to the hardworking women of America.

In mid-nineteenth-century America conventioneering was a highly popular activity. In his observations of America, de Tocqueville found that it was in their democratic institutions that Americans, who were unknown and unrelated to each other and from different social strata, worked together in meetings, conventions, and other gatherings on common projects. For de Tocqueville, democracy—as it advanced from its early revolutionary stages—made equality work. The social meetings, conventions, and projects that brought Americans together broke through the isolated individualism fostered by equality. De Tocqueville contrasted American democracy with European aristocratic tradition, which had had the "effect of closely binding every man to several of his fellow citizens" in aristocratic social bonds that were rigidly tied to lineage and privilege. These "fixed positions" in aristocratic societies defeated the idea of equality and prevented different classes from mingling with each other. Americans more socially isolated by individualism but able to cross class lines could come together on common projects, where they were in this period particularly concerned with the betterment of the human condition.[39]

In view of our understanding today of the exploitation of workers during industrialization, de Tocqueville's observations appear at best to be naive. Looking at American democracy with the eyes of a European aristocrat, black slavery, the subjugation of women, and the exploitation of the new growing working class did not seem to de Tocqueville to contradict democratic values. Not even in the liberal reform movements were disfranchised groups—women and blacks in particular—given serious voice or vote. In early nineteenth-century America, when it was still considered a flagrant violation of treasured social custom for a woman to speak in public, the participants of conventions and meetings where de Tocqueville observed that different classes mingled were notably white and male. Instead of experiencing equality in the reform world, women had to fight that male-dominated arena also.

The public forum, whether in the United States Congress or a temperance convention, had been held by men for the promotion of their political goals. For too long men had controlled the temperance movement. Temperance was essentially a woman's issue. Men were the offenders as Anthony argued, "I am not aware that we have any inebriate females among us."[40] Seizing control of the male temperance movement became one of the first steps for women toward creating their own arena for action and a forum for their voices.

Now if they were to have their own movement, women were going to be forced to carve out a social space for it. They needed more than a convention hall, for "social and cultural space implies room to experiment with making the future."[41] Domination—whether in slavery, through marriage, or under colonization of another group—is most effective when it has denied the group it oppresses the possibility of formulating their own future. For women social space meant the necessity to locate themselves outside the conditions of domination in marriage, which had defined their total existence. To develop their own convictions, to test their own theories, to act from an independent position which they envisioned to be a necessary condition of their liberation, women needed not only a hall for a convention but social distance from the direct, continuous, and un-interrupted experience of domination. With all of the insecurity of neophytes, they had to find and speak in their own voice, to test their abilities and to form new kinds of bonds with each other that would be based on their own political commitments to their sex. In doing so, they would essentially define their space, out of which they would build their own movements of protest.

For the previous two decades women had been carving out their own social space in schools and in associations they formed through their mill work and other jobs. Now they demanded and took social space essential for their own political and reform movements. One of their first confrontations was with the temperance clergy. Once begun, there was no stopping them. This was evident in the fall of 1853 when the women activists descended upon New York City, the site of that year's World's Fair. Most of the reform movements had called their conventions to coincide with the opening of the fair. Before the fall conventions in New York City, Susan went off to Seneca Falls to confer with her partner. This was one of those times which Mrs. Stanton would later recall, "whenever I saw that stately Quaker girl coming across my lawn, I knew that some happy con-vocation of the sons of Adam were to be set by the ears, by one of our appeals or resolutions."[42] This time Susan thought it would be just the right thing if Mrs. Stanton would come with her to New York City. After the temperance conventions, there would be an-tislavery meetings and finally the woman's rights convention that same week. And, Susan told her, before she left for New York City she intended to say a word at the State Teachers Convention in Rochester. Susan was high with energy and ideas.

"Say not one word to me about another convention, any paper, or any individual," Mrs. Stanton ordered Susan, "for I swear to you that while I am nursing this baby I will not be tormented with suf-fering humanity."

Susan insisted that Mrs. Stanton was only reacting to their recent defeats. "You ask me if I am not plunged in grief at my defeat at the recent convention for the presidency of our society." Came the reply: "Not at all. I am only too happy in the relief I feel from this additional care."[43] This time Mrs. Stanton would not budge, and Susan went off to New York City alone.

First there was the men's World's Temperance Convention. The reformers called a *Whole* World's Temperance Convention to highlight what they considered the arrogance of male temperance clergy who in claiming to represent the "world" actually excluded over one-half of it—the women. The woman's temperance organizations sent Reverend Antoinette Brown as their delegate to the World's Temperance Convention. As the first woman to be ordained a minister of a recognized church in the United States, she went as one of the clergy but was certainly not accepted as such. The hostility of the temperance men was so extreme that afterward William Lloyd Garrison, who had weathered many a stormy convention, declared that "on no occasion have I ever seen anything more disagreeable to our common humanity." The *New York Tribune* summarized the convention thus: "First day—Crowding a woman off the platform; second day—Gagging her; third day—Voting that she shall stay gagged."[44]

The temperance men finally took on the character that women had always been accused of—benevolent do-gooders who tried to impose their own moralistic piety on others. By unmasking the intent of the male temperance reformers to silence them and by exposing the men's sexist hypocrisy, the women gained control of the temperance movement.

This was a significant advance for women in claiming their own public presence—that is, the political space for their own actions. It confirmed their political consciousness of their condition *as women*. The woman's rights movement effectively took control of the temperance issue and subsumed it into their larger agenda by expanding the issue from men's intemperance into the fuller definition of male domination of women. The feminists saw that other conditions that confined women's lives, appropriated their labor, and denied them a political voice and vote superceded the issue of alcohol. After the mid-1850s, there was little evidence of a temperance movement in New York State, and it did not reappear again with any force until Frances Willard took it over from the Woman's Christian Temperance Union in 1879 and converted it from a "praying society" to a woman's reform organization.

Antislavery meetings were scheduled to be held after the temperance conventions. The tension the reformers had created in New York City escalated, and these meetings were disrupted by street mobs of men and boys who had been roaming the city during the World's Fair. But the mobs made up of proslavery, reactionary, and often drunk males were at their most menacing when they reached the National Woman's Rights Convention, where they hurled abusive remarks at the speakers. The mobs used any excuse to taunt women, but this time they seemed to be especially provoked by the "unfeminine" appearance of the women. Anthony reflected later that this was "the first overt exhibition of that public sentiment woman was then combating, the mob represented more than itself; it evidenced that general masculine opinion of woman, which condensed into law forges the chains which enslave her."[45]

It was in their demands for their rights that women elicited the direct expression of the "general masculine opinion of woman." That opinion either remains invisible for women who, when they are isolated from each other, may find it too painful to recognize, or, when it becomes evident in settings like these conventions, it stirs woman's consciousness to new heights. For Anthony and many other women, it signaled an urgent call to arms. But they saw not only sex hatred in these meetings. Anthony had poignant memories of the emotions that were stirred when Sojourner Truth rose to speak. "Sojourner combined in herself the two most hated elements of humanity. She was black and she was a woman, and all the insults that could be cast upon color and sex were together hurled at her."[46]

As a former slave in New York State and now a free woman, Sojourner Truth claimed the right of citizenship in the state and hence the right to speak on woman's rights. "We'll have our rights; see if we don't; and you can't stop us from them, see if you can. You may hiss as much as you like, but its commin'." The hissing rose in the crowd, but Sojourner simply turned on them with mockery, likening them to snakes and geese. "I know that it feels a kind o' hissin" and ticklin' like to see a colored woman get up and tell you about things, and Woman's Rights." She not only affirmed the sentiment of the women present but showed them how to respond to the mob. "We have all been thrown down so low that nobody thought we'd ever get up again; but we have been long enough trodden now; we will come up again, and now I am here."[47]

Later in the meeting Susan B. Anthony was asked to report on her disruption of the New York Teachers Convention, which had been widely covered in the press. Susan had an irrepressible sense of humor, loved to play charades, and one can only imagine how she acted out this scene with a hint of sarcasm. "Well," she began, "throughout the reading of reports of the various committees, I listened in vain for one word of recognition for women, either in the professions or in the deliberations of the convention."[48] Women constituted two-thirds of the five hundred teachers present and not one had yet said a word. When she could hold her tongue no longer, to the astonishment of the entire teacher's convention, she rose to speak, "Mr. President."

"What will the lady have?" old President Davies queried. "I wish to speak to the question under discussion," Anthony replied simply. Davies asked for the response of the convention, and only men's voices were heard. Amidst the commotion one man moved, "She shall be heard." Then, as Anthony humorously explained for half an hour the men debated whether she should be heard or not. But it was not so funny when it actually happened. Anthony could feel her heart pounding in her chest when she summoned her resolve to stand before them while they debated. The self-discipline of her earlier years paid off. When she was finally permitted to speak, she addressed her former colleagues like a stern school mistress giving a rebuke, all the while feeling as if her knees would give in under her. Considering the question under discussion, "why the profession of teacher is not as much respected as that of lawyer, doctor, or minister," Anthony responded with clarity.

> It seems to me you fail to comprehend the cause of the disrespect of which you complain. Do you not see that so long as society says woman has not brains enough to be a doctor, lawyer or minister, but has plenty to be a teacher, every man of you who condescends to teach, tacitly admits before all Israel and the sun that he has no more brains than a woman?[49]

Then she sat down. The audience was stunned.

Before leaving the convention, in another provocative act, Anthony nominated for the office of vice president Emma Willard, the now-retired founder and head mistress of the Troy Female Seminary. But Willard, who would have nothing to do with Anthony's bold schemes, politely declined the nomination.[50]

Shortly after the New York City conventions, Anthony went back into the field again to lecture and organize. She planned to canvass New York State and to meet with the local woman's temperance societies she had organized the previous year. As an unmarried woman she had traveled from one village to another, and she was astounded to find that "in every place, except Elmira, those Societies had never existed after the evening of their beginning." It was as if she had not been there at all the year before.

What, then, went wrong? She knew that the women had organizational and writing abilities, and certainly they were committed
to the cause. The answer lay somewhere else. Only months before,
Mrs. Stanton had warned Susan that "it is in vain to look for the
elevation of woman, so long as she is dependent in marriage . . .
The right idea of marriage is at the foundation of all reforms."[51]
This time Anthony went to visit the women in their homes and spent
afternoons talking with them, but most of all she listened intently.
"The reason given, by nearly all the ladies with whom I conversed,
for the failure of their societies was woman's want of *time* and *money*
to meet their demands."[52] With this new information, she pushed
her political analysis beyond her earlier understanding of the individual abuses that stemmed from men's intemperance to a new realization of the depth and extent of woman's subjugation as a class.

Confronting the male clergy forced them to reveal their contempt
for women; and that had been a significant event in the shaping of
Anthony's political consciousness, for it revealed the nature of male
power. But that was not enough. Male power had to be brought
home to her, so to speak. Her consciousness was expanded into
another dimension of women's reality and that was effectively shaped
when she was confronted with male domination in married wom-
en's daily lives. "Reflections like these, cause me to see and really
feel that there was no true freedom for woman without the possession of all her property rights and that these could be obtained
through legislation only, and . . . the sooner the demand was made
of the Legislature, the sooner would we be likely to obtain them."[53]

She listened and reflected over the full range of conditions faced
by married women. She returned to Rochester immediately. Her reflections were a call to action.

Arriving home on November 8 after being "on the road" since
August, she did not bother to rest or unpack her bags. She went
directly to William Henry Channing, who was minister of the
Unitarian Church that was Rochester's center of radical antislavery,
temperance, and woman's rights activity. She proposed a plan to
launch an enormous petition campaign for married woman's property rights. She insisted that they hold a woman's rights convention
in Rochester before the end of the month.

Immediately, in the same authoritarian tone, she turned to Mrs.
Stanton. "Waive household and baby cares and come to Rochester
at the time of the Convention and open your mouth for the good
of the race."[54] Had Mrs. Stanton not warned her only several months

earlier not to send her one more convention call? Susan promised she would at least not make Mrs. Stanton the president of the convention, if that was what worried her. No, again Mrs. Stanton was adament; she refused to move.

During the convention, Anthony organized sixty women for door-to-door petitioning. Then she reported to Mrs. Stanton that they would take their petitions to the New York State legislature in February. Mrs. Stanton could not resist any longer. Her excitement returned, and she admitted that "with the cares of a large family, I might in time, like too many women, have become wholly absorbed in a narrow family selfishness had not my friend been exploring new fields for missionary labors."[55] Now, she told Susan, she was ready to get back to philosophizing, and she had more than a few words to say to the New York State legislature on the question of married woman's property rights. She urgently asked Susan, "Can you get an acute lawyer . . . to look up eight laws concerning us—the very worst in all the code?"[56] Susan went to work and soon brought back the evidence. Now the underlying facts of woman's condition—the laws from Blackstone's *Commentaries* that rendered married women, as property of their husbands, legally dead—would be put to work.

Susan B. Anthony was not the first woman to campaign for married woman's property rights. Ernestine Rose, Paulina Wright Davis, and many other women in New York had demanded and won some limited rights for women in 1848. But as with so many other issues she took on, Anthony, if not the first, must have been the fastest and most persistent. In a record time of ten weeks during New York's harsh winter, she and her workers from the Rochester convention gathered six thousand signatures for married woman's property rights and four thousand for the more radical demand of suffrage. At the same time, she organized another New York State woman's rights meeting in Albany, and won a hearing before the legislature.

In February 1854, Elizabeth Cady Stanton delivered the address and enumerated women's demands before the New York State legislature. She demonstrated to the lawmakers how the legal codes concerning women (the very worst) produced a legal degradation of "woman as woman" and "wife" as "widow" and "mother." She identified the laws that taxed unmarried women's earnings while not giving them the right to representation, and pointed out that while blacks who were denied representation could not be taxed. She showed how a woman's legal servitude made it impossible for her to be tried by a jury of her peers in criminal cases. She also demonstrated that while married women now had the legal right to their property, they were prevented from exercising it as the law placed them in the same position as a convicted criminal by denying them the right to contract, buy, sell, or bequeath in their own names. Meanwhile, the widow was further disadvantaged as the law gave the husband the absolute right to will away his property as he wished.

Anthony quietly sat listening. She and Mrs. Stanton had worked over this talk together, but the power of Mrs. Stanton's delivery and the way she had woven together the legal facts must have made Susan's heart swell with a personal pride in her best friend. She must have felt especially proud when Mrs. Stanton, looking directly from the podium at the legislators assembled before her, demanded, "How could you ever look thus on woman?" With all the indignation she could muster, she proceeded:

> Would to God you could know the burning indignation that fills woman's soul when she turns over the pages of your statute books and sees there how like feudal barons you freemen hold over your women.[57]

Sometime later Stanton would clarify that these fiery speeches were toned-down versions of the real rage in hers and Anthony's hearts. "For Miss Anthony and myself, the English language had no words strong enough to express the indignation we feel in view of the prolonged injustice to woman." After she and Anthony gave "our feelings an outlet" in the most vehement manner, they issued their documents in milder tones. "If the men of the State could have known the stern rebukes, the denunciations, the wit and irony, the sarcasm that were garnered there, and then judiciously pigeon-holed, and milder even more persuasive appeals substituted, they would have been truly thankful they fared no worse."[58]

At the close of Stanton's speech, Ernestine Rose and William Henry Channing came forward and presented the ten thousand petitions to the state assembly. Anthony's work at this point, as she saw it, was to put things into motion. She pushed others forward to give the speeches and present the petitions and had the satisfaction of seeing what she called "subsoil plowing" bear the fruit of protest. Immediately after the meeting was adjourned, Anthony had fifty thousand copies of Stanton's speech printed which was undoubtedly an act of love as well as good political strategy. She put a copy on the desk of every legislator and packed up a bundle of them for her next petition drive.

Just as quickly, the legislators denied the suffrage petitions, and with a little more deliberation they rejected the demand for a law that would give married women control over their own earnings. Anthony immediately went back into the field, escalated her strategies, and pushed on. What she did not know at that moment was that the legislature would continue to deny her petitions every year for the rest of the decade. What the "feudal barons" did not know was that their refusals only fueled the fires of women's consciousness of their servitude.

At the moment, the campaign for dress reform was becoming a private agony—a "mental crucifixion"—for most of the woman's rights advocates sporting the Bloomer. Elizabeth Cady Stanton stopped wearing it by the time of the 1854 Woman's Rights Convention in Albany. Lucy Stone was wavering. "I have bought a nice new dress, which I have had a month, and it is not made because I can't decide whether to make it long or short," Lucy wrote to Susan.[59] But Susan felt very edgy that Lucy even entertained the thought of giving up this dress. Learning of Lucy's hesitancy, her mind flashed back over the scene they had faced a short time before in New York when they had gone to a post office during the noon hour one day while the streets were filled with people. Lucy remembered the details. "Gradually we noticed that we were being encircled. A wall of men and boys at last shut us in, so that to go on or to go back was impossible. There we stood. The crowd was a good-natured one. They laughed at us. They made faces at us. They said impertinent things, and they would not let us out. Every moment brought added numbers, who peered over to see what attracted the crowd."[60] What a relief when a friend who saw the scene left and returned with a policeman who dispersed the crowd before the confrontation escalated further!

Susan had not been afraid, but she was weary. How many more times, she thought to herself, when she had been in the streets and printing offices all day long would she have to face the "rude vulgar men," who, as she described it, "stared at me out of countenance," and then they would yell, "There comes my Bloomer!" At least at home in Rochester she was spared some of this harassment. The Bloomer dress provoked controversy there as elsewhere,[61] but Susan was protected from direct public ridicule because "everyone knew my father and brother, and treated me accordingly."[62]

Stubbornly, Susan B. Anthony, the "ultra" who was in the public eye more than most of the other women, continued to wear her Bloomer dress and suffered for it. Wasn't this, she contended, what was meant by the principle of conforming one's behavior to one's convictions? Day in and day out, on her way to the printers or to rent a hall, to meet with a temperance society or to make arrangements to post a meeting in the newspapers, she turned away from glaring eyes and diverted harassing comments.

As she was preparing for the Woman's Rights Convention in Albany, the harassment got the better of her. Lucy's suggestion that it might be wise to give up the Bloomer, "not that I think any cause will suffer, but simply to save myself a great deal of annoyance," reached Susan at the Albany convention. She took it to her room, read it, and gave in to a long cry—"a bursting of the floods long pent up." Lucy was worried about Susan. "I am sure you are all worn out or you would not feel so intensely about the dress."[63] Susan respected Lucy's words precisely because she knew that Lucy was strong and uncompromising. But she persisted.

Lucy and Mrs. Stanton were unaccustomed to seeing emotional eruptions in this always-proper woman. Her boundless energy and uncompromising stands sometimes left them awed, and often they took her strength and endurance for granted. It was difficult to imagine one so strong giving in to a kind of emotional edginess. Finally, Susan asked Mrs. Stanton for direction, and Mrs. Stanton, who knew Susan better than anyone else, was firm with her. "Let the hem of your dress out today, before tomorrow night's meeting," she insisted. By the end of the convention Susan had still not followed Mrs. Stanton's advice, believing that it was a sign of compromise. Mrs. Stanton became more emphatic. "I hope, Susan, you have let down a dress and petticoat. The cup of ridicule is greater than you can bear. It is not wise, Susan to use up so much energy in that way."[64]

Some months after the convention, Susan reluctantly let down the hems of her dress and petticoats, having worn the Bloomer for little over a year. It seemed like a personal as well as political defeat, but for her it had become "an intellectual slavery; one never could get rid of thinking of herself, and the important thing is to forget self. The attention of my audiences was fixed upon my clothes instead of my words."[65]

Since her days at Canajoharie, when she had abandoned stylish clothes, dances, and parties, a kind of asceticism had begun to characterize Susan's life. She kept her physical needs simple, which seemed to unburden her and give her more energy for her work. When she abandoned the Bloomer, she continued to dress loosely if more cumbersomely, and she decided that she would never take herself to any platform with more than one issue at any one time. From then on, she consistently subdued her own presence and always appeared in dignified black; nothing on her person would distract her listeners from her message. Actually, her simpler appearance was more consistent with her own asceticism than was the novelty of the Bloomer dress. This gave her additional comfort and freed her from another preoccupation with self, as she would say. On the other hand, Susan loved colorful clothes. But her discipline and asceticism required that she enjoy her few colorful dresses at home and in her garden in Rochester; they were not for public work. It would be many more years before her co-workers could coax her into a garnet velvet, and then she would wear it only for "state occasions."

"The important thing is to forget self" was the philosophy behind Susan's asceticism and the force that propelled her through her campaigns. She cared little about her own comforts nor was she concerned with gaining personal rewards for her work. Success was for the cause—for womankind. She put her own needs and satisfactions aside, and thus she was able to plan strategies and mount campaigns that were finely tuned to the issues and the conditions of women's lives from which the issues were drawn. Not surprisingly, given this kind of selfless dedication, her campaigns were highly effective in bringing the situation of women to public consciousness. The woman's rights movement was too radical and controversial to immediately win concrete change. But Anthony was highly successful in commanding new public attention to their demands. This, in turn, brought her greater responsibilities and more attention. Already the heavy weight of organizing national conventions and state petition drives fell on her shoulders almost exclusively. Other women turned to her for direction for their own work, and her authority as a leader grew in proportion to the force that propelled her forward in behalf of her movement.

During this period, Susan B. Anthony's political consciousness grew into a force that shaped her life. Identifying deeply with the women for whom she campaigned, she worked intensely on each strategy and each campaign. But at times this could be a wearying life, and she began to learn that political confrontation takes a personal toll even when it is for a worthy cause.

About this time, as often happens at the beginning of a new social movement, the activists' voices and ideals began to be reflected in new, popular literature. Just when Susan was beginning to feel weary from the struggle, while she was in Albany she bought and read *Bertha and Lily: or the Parsonage of Beech Glen.* Immediately she wrote a note of thanks to the author, the same Elizabeth Oakes Smith whose nomination for president of the Woman's Rights Convention in Syracuse she had contested two years before. "From the very depth of my heart, do I rejoice that the good Father put it into your heart to pen those noble truths, in manner so lovely, so pure that they cannot fail to meet a universal response, not only from the educated and refined, but from the humblest of God's children." Susan also told her that the book "will do a glorious work for women," and she hoped that it could be published in a cheap edition so that "the poorest sewing women may be able to buy a copy of it."[66] These were indeed high praises from someone who considered herself too utilitarian and practical to read romances!

What Susan found so compelling in this novel was the main character, Bertha, who reflected something important about her own life.

> I am an "old maid." . . . Am I happy?" Am I, an isolated, obscure woman, utter and entire mistress of myself, going and coming at mine own will and pleasure, expending money, buying and selling at the dictates of no one, am I happy? Yes, I am happy in all this. I believe it should be thus to the sex, in all external and pecuniary matters.[67]

So speaks Bertha (meaning "brave"), a noble, pure woman, who is an "old maid" who goes to Beech Glen to live with her loyal friend, John True, and his rather unpleasant wife, Defiance. Bertha is the embodiment of the "new true woman," a new image cultivated by woman's rights leaders. In the book, the earnest young parson of Beech Glen, Ernest Helfenstein, learns from Bertha's example and her teachings that until he can "unman" himself of the vain arrogance and self-assured place he assumes in the world by birthright, he will never be morally pure. When the parson falls in love with Bertha, he realizes that she is too good and pure for his earthly, manly, imperfect love. The "new true woman" is a morally superior force, elevated above and beyond even the masculine clergy, who, like Parson Helfenstein, could learn the path to true virtue under Bertha's moral guidance. The parson has rescued two young orphaned children: little Kate, who he has renamed Lily, and her younger brother, Willy. He has nourished them on good food and Christian teachings; but it is Bertha who gives him moral direction practical assistance with the children. Lily blossoms into a kind of earth angel, while her poor struggling younger brother (who is a metaphor for the parson) tries to be good but never quite achieves his sister's state of virtue.

In *Bertha and Lily,* Elizabeth Oakes Smith sounded a theme particularly strong among feminists at the time. Bertha revealed that men could become capable of full, true, and noble union with women of virtue only when they became wise enough to learn from them and to submit to their higher moral judgments. This was a belief in their superiority that women assumed for themselves in part because it was granted to them as keepers of the private sphere.

"Do I reject marriage?" Bertha asked rhetorically, and answered, "God forbid that I should do so. It is very sacred, very lovely, in my eyes, and therefore, to be sustained from pure motives."[68] For feminists, marriage had to be elevated to a state that they considered becoming to the "new true woman." In effect, this placed marriage beyond the realm of practical possibility at the time, considering the changes required of men and the relations between the sexes.

This was not the old moralistic piety that had characterized traditional femininity. Nor was it the sentimental version of love that put women on a pedestal as the object of some idealized masculine vision of womanhood—the bird in a gilded cage. Instead, the "new true woman" was to be self-made and independent; above all, she was to be the central actor of her own life. She would marry only when and if she and her husband could come together in equality; she would no longer face only the choices of "wife" or "old maid."

It was in their image of the "new true woman" that feminists first shifted their struggle from improving the conditions of marriage, as they had emphasized in their temperance campaigns, to the more radical goal of liberating woman herself—as an end in itself. In an era when it was beyond even the revolutionary imagination to challenge the institution of marriage, the most radical demand and confrontational challenge yet made by woman's rights advocates was their call for full equality in marriage. Instead of abandoning the moral superiority gratuitously granted to women (stemming from their biological ability to mother and thus their responsibility to rear children), woman's rights advocates transformed it into a political weapon and proclaimed their intent to wage, as Stanton put it, a "great moral revolution."

Susan had become a living example of Bertha, and Smith's novel had reaffirmed Anthony's life choices when there was little else in the world around her to reflect them. She had made logical choices, ones that seemed consistent to her. These were choices that in fact any common woman freed from marriage could make. But with each choice she was becoming more exceptional, precisely because few common women did make those choices. As such, Susan B. Anthony was herself becoming a symbol of women's future and a representative of their culture.

4

A Passion for Justice

IT WOULD HAVE BEEN CHARACTERISTIC OF SUSAN B. ANTHONY to think that her work was nothing out of the ordinary for a woman—at least in the world of reform. But it was different. A single, independent political woman leader without a husband and family to return to from her work and without a male-led movement for her organizational base (such as the American Anti-slavery Society) was unheard of at this time. For Anthony, unlike the women she admired the most—Lucretia Mott, Abby Kelley Foster, or even Elizabeth Cady Stanton—there was no separation between public work and private life. And there was no model before her when she had to break paths in organizing women's own movement. Stanton had initiated this work when she had called the Seneca Falls convention in 1848. But for the movement to be sustained, a committed political organizer was required.

Until now, most of Anthony's work had been confined to New York State. Her increased responsibility for the organization of the major actions of the woman's movement made her realize that she had to expand her horizons. In the spring of 1854 she decided to take a trip south with Ernestine Rose and to try out the woman's rights message, first in the nation's capital and then in nearby Baltimore, Maryland, and Alexandria, Virginia.

Among her "ultra" friends, Susan could have chosen no one better for this trip than Ernestine Rose. Rose had made many impressive appearances on woman's rights platforms. Ten years Susan's senior, she was worldly and wise, as well as eloquent and beautiful.

She was a Jew from Russian Poland, who had fled her native country at the age of sixteen to avoid a marriage arranged for her by her father. She then traveled throughout Europe for a few years and championed several human rights causes, including a peace group called the Association of All Classes of All Nations. She was a woman of truly independent mind. When she fled her homeland, she left her religious convictions behind and became an avowed atheist. Rose identified herself with the free-thought movement, and after she emigrated to the United States and married, she and her husband joined a community in Skaneateles, New York, which was modeled after the ideas of utopian socialist Robert Dale Owen. In the 1840s, Rose was one of the first to campaign for married woman's property rights in New York State.

Ernestine was a woman of compelling presence. She was described thus in the *History of Woman Suffrage:* "She had a rich musical voice, with just enough of foreign accent and idiom to add to the charm of her oratory. . . . She not only dealt with abstract principles clearly, but in their application touched the deepest emotions of the human soul."[1] But her forthright atheism and her utopian socialism made her too controversial for some woman's rights advocates, who tried to keep her off of their platforms. To Anthony, Rose was courageous and uncompromising.

Anthony and Rose arrived in Washington within days of passage of the Kansas-Nebraska Act, a bill which, in effect, repealed the Missouri Compromise (the 1820 law in which it was agreed that Missouri would be admitted to the Union as a slave state but then prohibited slavery north of the 36°30' line of the Louisiana Territory). The Kansas-Nebraska Act, which allowed slavery to expand beyond those boundaries, was a consequence of several developments. Senator Stephen A. Douglas promoted the legislation to open the Kansas frontier for an extension of the railroad. Southern congressmen were already watching carefully as increased settlement and industry in Kansas and Nebraska meant that those territories would soon apply for admission to the Union. With Westward expansion, slavery became a national issue that was not confined only to North-South antagonisms. Until the Kansas-Nebraska Act, those states were still governed under the Missouri Compromise; this meant that north of 36°30' territories were prohibited from entering the Union as slave states. If Kansas and Nebraska were to be admitted as free states, the southern proslavery balance of power in Congress would be unsettled. Consequently when Kansas and Nebraska sought admission to the Union, pro- and antislavery tensions escalated. In response to southern pressure, Senator Douglas gained presidential and administrative support to repeal the Missouri Compromise.

In its final form, the Kansas-Nebraska Act affirmed a "states-rights" approach to the extension of slavery, which allowed each territory to be organized either as slave or free. Northern abolitionists immediately reacted. The Massachusetts legislature met and created the controversial Emigrant Aid Society. The society was granted $5 million and authorized to encourage northerners with abolitionist sentiments to settle the new territories of Kansas and Nebraska; thus preventing them from entering the Union as slave states.

At the same time, many liberal politicians in the northern and midwestern states who were angry over the new plan to extend slavery into the territories met to find a political means to express their concerns. The result was the nucleus of a new Republican party. Its members were not explicitly abolitionist and some concessions were still made to slavery, but their platform stood clearly against the extension of slavery into new territories.

Controversy surrounding the Kansas-Nebraska Act and hostile suspicion of the abolitionist sympathizers followed Rose and Anthony throughout their tour. This trip was Anthony's first direct contact with southern slavery. Slavery sympathizers in the North had told her to "just go south once, and see Slavery as it is, and then you will talk differently."[2] Instead, Anthony found Mount Vernon consumed with the effects of slavery: "The air of dilapidation and decay that every where meets the eye, tottering out-buildings, the mark of slavery o'ershadows the whole. Oh, the thought that it was here, that he whose name is the pride of this nation was the *Slave Master*."[3]

> How strangely blind must the person be, who hates slavery less, by coming in closer contact with its degrading influence! How wanting in true nobility of soul he must be, who can hear a human being speak of himself as being the property of another, without evincing the least discontent. How unworthy the bond of freedom is the man who sees himself surrounded, for the first time, with beings wearing the human form, from whose face slavery has blotted out almost every token of that Divine spark within, that aspires to a higher, a nobler life, that scorns to be a thing, and from the very depths of his soul hates not slavery more than it were possible for him to ever have done.[4]

It was the absence of "that Divine spark within" that Susan detected when she and Ernestine Rose questioned their chambermaid in Baltimore, where they had taken rooms from a Mrs. Walters. As the young woman was making up their room while a little boy played alongside of her Anthony and Rose wondered if Sarah might be a slave. Mrs. Rose asked her about the little boy, and Sarah told her that he belonged to the proprietor, Mrs. Walters, and that his mother was the cook in the kitchen. His father was also a slave, but he was on the eastern shore and under a master who prevented him from seeing his wife and children.

Susan stiffened and her "blood chilled," as she described the feeling. To her this was a dramatic moment. She had heard stories of families that were brutally separated by slavery, but now here in her own room this young woman and little boy were slaves who belonged to Mrs. Walters. Susan was earnest and determined to not let one aspect of slavery pass her by. Gently she began to question Sarah about her own situation.

SBA: Are you *free* Sarah?
SARAH: No, Miss!
SBA: Do you belong to Mrs. Walters?
SARAH: No, Miss, she hires me of my Master for $8 per month.
SBA: And don't you get any portion of it?
SARAH: No, Miss, only my Master give me my clothes.
SBA: Does he keep you well clothed?
SARAH: Sometimes, Miss, and sometimes I get short.
SBA: And don't you have any pocket money of your own?
SARAH: Yes, Miss, what the ladies give me.

Sarah left the room, and Susan worried about the passivity that slavery bred in many of its victims. "Sarah is a bright girl, fine expression of face. Oh how I long to probe her soul in search of the Divine spark that scorns to be a slave."[5] At this moment Susan faced a dilemma that all genuine reformers must confront sooner or later: the conflict between their desire to provoke anger and stir up rebellion among the enslaved and oppressed classes in order to heighten their intolerance of their conditions until it bursts out into collective rebellion, and the realization that in the short run such anger for individuals with no evident alternatives before them might only increase their pain and suffering. As she looked at Sarah, Susan decided that it was unfair—in fact, it was cruel—to encourage her to rebel when she had no means to free herself. To do so would only add to the burdens of Sarah's wretched life. It was a sensitive but still personal response; it was one that came from her heart and reflected her deep conviction. But it was a response that had not yet formed into a political analysis.

Susan's voice reflected the tone of Harriet Beecher Stowe's *Uncle Tom's Cabin,* which was published in 1852 (two years before Susan went south to take a firsthand look at slavery). By 1853 Beecher Stowe's novel had sold over three hundred thousand copies. Its popularity made it a major instrument for abolitionists, as it was highly effective in intensifying antislavery sentiment. In her novel, Harriet Beecher Stowe tried to break the image promoted by slaveholders that slaves were merely thoughtless, shiftless beings who were happy in their lot. She tried to convey to people in the North a picture of slavery as she thought it must have been felt by mothers who had their babies taken from them, and as it must have been experienced by those degraded and placed on a trader's wagon to be taken to a public sale. Stowe told her mid-century audiences that "the object of these sketches is to awaken sympathy and feeling for the African race, as they exist among us; to show the wrongs and sorrows under a system so necessarily cruel and unjust as to defeat and do away with the good effects of all that can be attempted for them by their best friends under it."[6]

Consistent with the style of women writers at the time, *Uncle Tom's Cabin* is a highly romanticized and sentimental work, with the character of Tom epitomizing self-effacing and submissive Christian virtue. But in its sentimentality it was not slavery that the author romanticized. Her powerful condemnation of slavery made the work a daring and provocative novel in the 1850s. Harriet Beecher Stowe exposed the double burden of slavery for black mothers who were sexually used and abused, while they labored under the slave master. Stowe had five children of her own, and when she sat down to write she imagined—as a woman and a mother—what that experience must be like. Out of this personal identification she wrote swiftly and brought forth strong imagery that she later attributed to visions that came to her from God. Stowe was effective in her portrayal of the slave woman's experience because she attempted to put herself in the place of the slave mother. From this point of personal identification, she made a powerful (if sentimental) appeal to all women through the bonds of motherhood. As she told the story of Eliza who, upon learning that her small son had been sold by her master, managed a desperate escape, she appealed to women to identify with this violation of humanity.

If it were *your* Harry, mother, or your Willie, that were going to be torn from you by a brutal trader, tomorrow morning—if you had seen the man, and heard that the papers were signed and delivered, and you had only from twelve o'clock till morning to make good your escape, how fast could *you* walk? How many miles could you make in those few brief hours, with the darling at your bosom, the little sleepy head on your shoulder, the small soft arms trustingly holding on to your neck?[7]

Susan easily adopted the vigilant spirit of abolitionism. It was the same spirit but a different intent of true womanhood. She personalized abolitionist vigilance and frequently worried that so pernicious was slavery that she herself could be drawn into some of its subtleties if she were not constantly on the lookout for all of its wicked manifestations. One still hears in her the voice of her younger years of unrelenting self-examination:

This noon, I ate my dinner without once asking myself, are these human beings who minister to my wants *Slaves* to be bought and sold and hired out at the will of a master? And when the thought first entered my mind, I said, even I am getting accustomed to Slavery, so much so that I cease continually to be made to feel its blighting, cursing influence, so much so that I can sit down and eat from the hand of a bondman [*sic*], without being once mindful of the fact that he is such.[8]

Then, in a tone not unlike Harriet Beecher Stowe's in *Uncle Tom's Cabin,* Susan lashed out against the daily ways that injustice becomes part of ordinary routine. "Oh Slavery, hateful thing that thou art, thus to blunt the keen edge of men's conscience, even while they strive to shun thy poisonous touch." This kind of conscientious self-examination heightened Susan's sensitivity to slavery. But it is often the case that personal soul-searching conforms to women's private morality rather than producing political action.

One day while they were traveling together Mrs. Rose told Susan that she had heard Lucy Stone and Wendell Phillips express prejudice against the foreigners and say that they even believed that foreigners should not be granted the rights of U.S. citizens. Susan was shocked by Rose's allegations and defended Lucy Stone, whom she thought of as an uncompromising worker and a generous soul. But Mrs. Rose was adamant; she was sure of what she had overheard. A tense silence fell between them and Susan pondered, "It seems to me that she could not ascribe pure motives to any of our Reformers, while to her it seems I am blindly bound to see no fault, however glaring."

Finally, she broke the silence by challenging Mrs. Rose. "There is not one in the Reform ranks, whom you think true, not one but whom panders to the popular feeling." Susan had touched Mrs. Rose's vulnerability. She turned on Susan with painful honesty. "I take them by the words of their own mouths. I trust all until their words or acts declare them false to truth and right . . . no one can tell the hours of anguish I have suffered, as one after another I have seen those whom I trusted betray falsity of motive as I have been compelled to place one after another on the list of panderers to public favor."

This, Susan learned is what it means to be an "ultra,"—the radical who distrusts and challenges every inequality and injustice, both small and large, one who lets no injustice pass by unnoticed. She found that Mrs. Rose "is too much in advance of the extreme ultraists even to be understood by them." And she did not want to be identified with those who would say, "I am ultra enough, mercy knows. I don't want to seem any more so by identifying myself with one whose every sentiment is so shocking to the public mind."[9]

Yet Mrs. Rose found inconsistencies in almost everything. Her "ultra" politics were pointed against her friends and enemies alike. Mrs. Rose was more experienced and realistic than her younger and more naive companion. But she was also more isolated and cynical. Her clear-sighted, unrelenting political scrutiny turned against her when too many severe judgments began to alienate her friends. And finally this kind of constant criticism and judgment of others had the effect of emptying even her closest relationships of the dialogue that could either challenge or confirm her suspicions.

Susan tried to bring her friend out of her isolation by offering herself to elicit a new trust. "Do you know, Mrs. Rose, that I can but feel that you place me too on that list." But Mrs. Rose had already withdrawn to her own world. She coldly and judgmentally responded, "I will tell you when I see you untrue." Susan was stunned and genuinely worried for her friend. "It filled my soul with anguish to see one so noble, so true (even though I felt I could not comprehend her) so bowed down, so overcome with deep swelling emotions." They sat together in silence; there was nothing left to say. After a few moments Susan took some paper from her handbag and copied out a hymn that they had sung that morning, inscribing it "Susan B. Anthony for her dear friend Ernestine L. Rose." She handed it to Mrs. Rose, and they both sat quietly and wept.

For a moment Susan had broken through her friend's barriers, and after a long silence Mrs. Rose offered, "no one knows how I have suffered from not being understood." Susan tried to comfort her. "I know you must suffer and heaven forbid that I should add a feather's weight to your burdens." But there was now a breach between the two women.

After their Baltimore meetings, Anthony and Rose headed north and stopped in Philadelphia for a visit with Lucretia Mott. Sarah Grimké was visiting the Motts when Anthony and Rose arrived. In the early 1820s as young women, Sarah and her sister Angelina had left their home in Charleston, South Carolina, where their slave-holding family had been prominent in the southern aristocracy. They had moved to Philadelphia and become Quakers, who were among the most articulate and daring abolitionists of that era. But in the mid-1830s many male abolitionists, like the general public, reacted strongly against women speaking on public platforms. This prompted Sarah Grimké to write her famous *Letters on the Equality of the Sexes* in 1838, the same year in which proslavery mobs overcame the Philadelphia antislavery conventions, burned the new abolitionist hall, and hanged Mott in effigy. The Grimké sisters were mobbed during their speeches. Angelina married that year, and both sisters retired from public speaking. Sarah moved to New Jersey and lived as an old maid with her sister Angelina and her husband for the rest of her life.

Philadelphia was one of Susan's favorite cities. One morning the two Quaker spinsters, Angelina and Susan, "sallied forth" in search of the tree where William Penn had signed a treaty with the Indians. Mrs. Rose disapproved of Susan's hero worship of Penn, and that aggravated Susan. "Mrs. Rose does not agree with me as regards the worth of Penn, indeed she does not regard the memory of any whom we are accustomed to think of with reverence." In fact, thought Susan, she "sees no good in none save such as the world has traduced." She reasoned that the value of William Penn was in his work to raise the human condition. "It is well that there are some to bring to light the virtues of the neglected and despised.

In the 1850s spiritualism captivated the imagination of many reformers, and Anthony was one of them. In 1848 in a house just outside of Rochester, two young girls began to hear noises that seemed to come from no discernible source. Margaret Fox and her sister responded to the sounds by rapping on tables or the wall and then often received a communication back. These noises and communications continued for several months. As the word of them spread, they became known as the "Rochester rappings." They were assumed to be the spirits of departed loved ones and others who had "gone over to the other side." Soon others began to hear rappings, and spirit circles began to form. The Fox sisters, and particularly Margaret, were recognized as "mediums" who were chosen by the spirits of the other world to convey their messages.

The citizens of Rochester became wary and began demanding an investigation into the authenticity of the communications. Committees were organized to locate the source of the rappings. However, the failure of each investigation to uncover a cause escalated the atmosphere in Rochester to the fervor of a witch hunt. A ladies' committee formed to examine young Margaret for any evidence of trickery on her body or in her clothing. Amy Post, who was notable in Rochester for her woman's rights and abolitionist work, was present at one such examination during which she heard Margaret's cries and protests. She stormed into the room and standing in the doorway with her authoritative presence brought the examination to a halt. She took Margaret away without interference, and then calmed the frightened young girl and returned her to her family.

News of the Fox sisters and their Rochester rappings spread quickly, and soon many mediums began to appear. Some claimed that they could transmit messages from departed loved ones. The source of the rappings was never determined, and the whole phenomenon provoked considerable discussion of the spiritual world. Of what was it constituted—by whom and how?

While Susan and Mrs. Rose were in Philadelphia, sides were drawn on the question of spiritualism during a dinner party at the Motts', and an evening of lively discussion and debate ensued. On the "unbelieving side" was Mrs. Rose, "believing the spirit was inseparable from the body" and therefore concluding that these spirits could not exist. Sarah Grimké, who was a believer in spiritualism, "was all enthusiasm in the faith." Susan was not sure. "The rest of the company with myself, seemed not to know whether or not there is any truth in these modern manifestations," until the discussion went directly to the question of human morality. As they probed "the probable future existence of the mind or soul or spirit of man," Susan observed that "not an argument could one of us bring other than an intuitive feeling that we were not to cease to exist, when the body dies." Mrs. Rose argued that if a human spirit lived on after death then so "must the essence of the tree, the animal, the bird, and the flower." Susan had no argument against such reasoning. Instead, she settled the questions for herself in terms other than those derived from rational logic. "If it be true that we die like the flower, leaving behind only the fragrance . . . while the elements that compose us go to form new bodies, what a dream is the life of man."[10]

Like the philosophes of the eighteenth-century Enlightenment, Susan lodged her beliefs not in a god in a distant realm, but in an optimistic faith in human immortality. Spiritually she believed that human beings do not cease to exist when the body dies. Her spiritual belief in immortality, which meant for her a rejection of the idea that we leave nothing behind us after death, sustained her particularly because her political work often did not bring her immediate rewards. She already knew that her political hope for the liberated "new true woman" might not be realized in her own lifetime. Further, she knew that she could not measure the success of her struggle by the advantages she would gain for herself. Even at the age of thirty-five, she began to realize that she was working for future generations who would probably realize more of the benefits than would she and her own generation. Through her belief in human immortality she connected herself in a way to those future generations.

In her autobiography, Elizabeth Cady Stanton, described Susan's spirituality as that of an agnostic. Susan never denied the existence of God, but her beliefs were secularized and lodged in the world around her. When she was once asked "Do you pray?" she responded, "I pray every single second of my life; not on my knees but with my work. My prayer is to lift women to equality with men. Work and worship are one with me."[11] She did not attach human immortality to a distant god; rather, she found it to be within each individual. This was a concept she had inherited from the Quaker belief in the Inner Light.

Quakerism had served Anthony well with its emphasis on self-reliance and introspection. But by now Susan B. Anthony's spiritual life had outgrown her Quaker heritage. Her father, who had grown increasingly frustrated with the limited world view of the Quakers since the Hicksite separation years before, turned to the Unitarian church. Susan was also sympathetic to Unitarian beliefs. In fact, she signed the church register in Rochester and even attended services when she was at home. She found good sermons particularly inspiring and personally comforting. But her need was not for a formal religion.

In his comparative historical study of leadership in *Puritan Boston and Quaker Philadelphia,* E. Digby Baltzell illustrated how Quakerism—with its emphasis on withdrawal from the world and the repeated schism that followed from its inward orientation—was unable to produce significant political leadership. The more the religion turned inward on itself, the less effective it could be in the world. At this point, Susan B. Anthony's radical egalitarianism became the moral and spiritual base from which she lived. Her conviction that no human being was superior to any other gave her the reference point from which she decided campaign strategies and confrontations even when her closest friends disagreed. Her spiritual life, which found God in every human being and in nature as well, was the inspiration that sustained her moral convictions and therefore her leadership.

Susan B. Anthony would not derive the authority for her work solely from her moral convictions. Her leadership had to be confirmed by her constituency. It was Elizabeth Cady Stanton who recognized the resistance Anthony faced from women,

> Susan B. Anthony circulated petitions both for the civil and political rights of woman throughout the State, traveling in stage coaches and open wagons and sleighs in all seasons, and on foot from door to door through towns and cities, doing her uttermost to rouse women to some sense of their natural rights as human beings, while expending her time, strength, and money to secure these blessings for the women of the State, they would gruffly tell her they had all the rights they wanted, or rudely shut the door in her face, leaving her to stand outside, petition in hand, with as much contempt as if she were asking for alms for herself.[12]

These reactions did not hold her back. She returned home to Rochester from her long southern trip on October 1 to plan another more extensive petition drive and lecture campaign for married woman's property rights. She was indignant over the legislature's audacity in rejecting women's petitions. She recognized that a small band of woman's rights leaders appearing before the state legislature was not enough to put the power of social protest behind their petitions, even if they carried the signatures of thousands. The legislators must be forced to feel the spirit behind the signatures on her petitions. And she knew that their movement was a live, vital force with growing numbers of discontented and protesting women. The force of their discontent must be brought before the legislature if women were to effectively impress their message on those "feudal barons."

Initiating the 1855 canvass, Anthony set for her goal nothing less than the kindling of that consciousness throughout the entire state by taking her message face-to-face to the people of New York. She was determined and even for a moment never entertained a doubt that she would accomplish her goal. Generally heedless of holidays, Susan left home on December 25, 1854, to begin a canvass of New York State's fifty-four counties. In the next four months, she took her lecture and petition drive into each county seat and into as many other villages and cities in each county as she could manage.

Wendell Phillips advanced her fifty dollars to begin the campaign. She opened her first meeting on December 26, which marked the beginning of a strategic schedule she would continue until she had canvassed every one of the fifty-four counties by May 1. She called meetings in the county seat or at a nearby village every other day, using the day in between to travel. When she arrived in a city or village, she immediately went to see that the notices that she had sent beforehand were posted. Then she checked to be sure that the town hall or a local church was secured for her afternoon and evening meetings. After she found her own accommodations, she often had to set up and light the candles in the hall.

In each village Anthony called an afternoon meeting for the ladies. She read half of her newly prepared speech and spent time talking with them about their concerns and her hopes for achieving their property rights. And then she appealed to them to bring their husbands to the evening meeting pointing out that as long as women were disfranchised and had only the power of petition, their husbands held the political power of the vote to give women their rights.

Knowing that it was the husband who carried the family purse, Anthony charged an admission fee for her evening meeting and sold her literature then. That was when she read the second half of her speech and passed around her petitions. She hoped that if men signed them their wives would be willing to follow. She even called out the schoolgirls to meet with her. In Canandaigua she met them at their female seminary, no doubt calculating the potential for recruits to work for the cause when the girls finished school. "She made a special request that all seminary girls should come to hear her as well as all the women and girls in town. She had a large audience and she talked very plainly about our rights and how we ought to stand up for them and said the world would never go right until the women had just as much right to vote and rule as men."[13]

She had large audiences and small. Her diary for December 29, 1854, shows that five towns were represented at one day's meeting, with sixty in attendance in the afternoon and three hundred in the evening, even though "the day very cold, snowy, sleighing very poor." In contrast, "Saturday went to Olean, could not [get] a church, school house or academy [to] speak in —held meeting in a dining room of landlord."[14] She arrived in Riverhead, Long Island, to find that the courthouse had been prepared for her meeting but only the janitor was present. She refused to be disillusioned and simply sat down in the meeting room and waited. "Finally one man after another dropped in, until there were perhaps a dozen. Not at all discouraged, she began her speech. Presently the door opened and she saw a woman's bonnet peep in but it was quickly withdrawn. This was repeated a number of times but not one ventured in."[15]

In contrast to the timidity that characterized the women in some communities, others were militating for their sex. In one city a group of women wearing the Bloomer dress met her. "It does my soul good to see them," she noted privately. And she was encouraged with the meeting in that town as "everyone we met is ready to tell some fact under the cruel laws to woman."[16]

Upstate New York is known for its severe winters. From living in Rochester and teaching in Canajoharie, Susan knew that if she set out in December for a canvass that she planned to complete by May, she would face blistering snowstorms that frequently dropped several feet of snow in one day and easily continued at that rate into the next. She traveled under these conditions, often buffeting icy winds and freezing temperatures in an open sleigh. Most of Susan's fellow reformers obeyed the dictates of the climate and gave up their convention circuits and lecture tours until the spring thaw. Consequently, there were few antislavery and woman's rights conventions to draw Susan away from her canvassing.

She had several other good, strategic reasons for going off the train routes and into the most remote regions of the state under these conditions. The heavy winters forced people into the seclusion of their homes. When they were thus isolated as the winter endured, an opportunity for some diversion was even more appealing than it might have been in the warmer months when they were usually working outside. In many of these remote New York State towns, Susan B. Anthony was the first woman to speak on a public platform, and that novelty provided an additional incentive that prompted many people to bundle up and wade through the deep snows to her meetings.

In mid-February 1855, Anthony paused from her petition campaign to attend the Woman's Rights Convention in Albany and to take the petitions she had just collected to the New York State legislature once again. A few days later, when she was about to leave Albany for her next meeting, she found a pleasant Quaker gentleman in the stagecoach with her. Before the stage began its cold trip to Lake George, the Quaker gentleman heated a plank of wood over a fire and placed it on the floor of the coach for Miss Anthony to warm her feet and the coach during the trip. Each time the stage stopped for passengers he rewarmed the log, thus insuring that she had a relatively comfortable trip. She was pleased to accept his courtesy, but as soon as the stagecoach stopped in Lake George she went directly to her meetings. Again he was waiting for her. When she was ready to leave, he invited her to his home not far from Lake George, which was "presided over by a sister," and drove her there in "his fine sleigh filled with robes and drawn by two spirited gray horses."[17]

Susan enjoyed her visit there and then left for the wilder regions of New York's Adirondack Mountains. He accompanied her and again made his sleigh available to her. After all the weeks of traveling alone, often without even a comforting remark in some villages, his attention must have been a pleasant turn of events. After a few days on the road again, her Quaker friend explained that as a gentleman of some wealth he was ready to provide for her pleasure and attend to her comforts for years to come, if she would only give up this backbreaking work and marry him. He had been courting her! And further—he had assumed that he was rescuing an unmarried woman of thirty-five from the fate of being an old maid. Undoubtedly he could not conceive of a single woman wanting to remain single and finding the full meaning of womanhood in her work. His presumptuous behavior probably seemed natural to him, but it must have seemed impertinent to her. She did not dally for long over his proposal. In fact, she never even recorded it in her diary and told her friend and biographer, Ida Harper, only that her "heart made no response to this appeal." Either she gave it little thought, finding it to be too insignificant to consider, or she was too offended and angry to even mention it.

Anthony conducted over half of the fifty-four sets of meetings and canvasses by herself. Ernestine Rose joined her for thirteen of them, and occasionally she had the assistance of a few other women who were all paid for their time. Anthony approached her canvassing with sound Quaker business sense and raised the money to cover her travel and pay for her speakers by charging a twenty-five cent entry fee for evening lectures, as well as selling literature there. But without the kind of support available to other social movements, such as endowments and trusts, there would always be trouble making ends meet. When she closed her canvass that May, she sat with her accounting books and found that she had taken in $2,367 and paid out $2,291. From the $76 she had left, she returned to Wendell Phillips the $50 he had advanced her. He promptly sent it back to her.

What was the impression Susan left behind in the villages, cities and remote corners of the state?

In an age when speaking had risen to an art form with gilded words and evangelical flourishes, Susan B. Anthony came to her platforms with neither flourish nor flair. Always wearing a simple black dress with a fitted "basque-waist" jacket, she walked with a determined but not heavy stride to the front of her audiences and stood very straight before them, looked directly at them, and delivered her message. In Roundout, New York, the papers reported that Anthony "unattended and unheralded, quietly glided in and ascended the platform." She did not exhibit nervousness or anxiety but instead was "easy and self-possessed as a lady should always be when performing a plain duty, even under 600 curious eyes." Usually she was alone having no one to help her. But once she even had to contend with a difficult custodian who had simply thrown her papers and pamphlets on the platform. But "Miss Anthony gathered them up composedly, placed them on a table disposedly, put her decorous shawl on one chair and very exemplary bonnet on another, sat a moment, smoothed her hair discreetly, and then deliberately walked to the table and addressed the audience." The newspapers in Roundout summarized well the general sense she conveyed when standing before an audience. She was "of pleasing rather than pretty features, decidedly expressive countenance, rich brown hair very effectively and not at all elaborately arranged, neither too tall nor too short, neither too plump nor thin—in brief one of those *juste milieu* persons, the perfection of common sense physically exhibited."[18]

There she stood, just a little taller than most women of her time. She was 5 feet, 5 inches, and weighed 138 pounds. At the age of thirty-five, she was physically strong and constitutionally healthy. She was full-figured; her bust measured 38 inches and her waist was about 31 inches around. She had blue-gray eyes and a rather angular but full face. She wore her thick brown hair parted neatly in the center, pulled over her ears, and coiled at the nape of her neck—a not unpopular hairdo in the 1850s.

Susan carried the countenance and had the commanding presence of a "strong-minded woman," which was the pejorative term used for woman's rights advocates. Already her determination was etched in her face and conveyed in her brisk, upright carriage. A Maine newspaper found her to be "rather above medium stature, and *minus* her gold spectacles, might generally be deemed *good-looking*."[19]

But she was not good-looking to her enemies, whose image of her was caricatured by the antifeminist press that never relented from describing her as a "strident spinster" with a "lean and cadaverous" look. Even though some of her public viewed her sympathetically, it has been the caricatures promoted by the enemies of woman's rights that have formed our contemporary image of her. Combined with the fact that she generally chose the most serious photo taken during a sitting, we are left with a visual image of her that conforms to the most severe stereotypes. By twentieth-century standards (which have lost the eye of mid-nineteenth-century America), her photographs generally give the impression of a woman with a tough exterior who could buffet any storm. This image, generally taken as unwomanly, had the effect of reducing her strength and her unadorned, unapologetic sense of purpose to ridicule of her personal appearance. This is the same problem faced by the self-determined feminist of any age, whose appearance—if it is not conventionally feminine—is caricatured in her own time and to future generations as a way to try to discredit her ideas and politics.

From the beginning, Anthony held her audiences' attention. "Her enunication is very clear and remarkably distinct, and we should judge could easily make herself heard by an audience of from two to three thousand persons" and "her voice is clear and musical, with an emphasis that is accurate and natural." This report went on to confess that from the previous news reports the audience had been led to expect a masculine character and presence, but they found none of that in her. Even those who opposed her had to commend her. "While we differ widely with Miss Anthony, both as regards the propriety of the calling she has assumed, and the notions of which she is advocate, we cheerfully accord to her credit, as a public speaker, much above mediocrity, expressing herself with clearness and many times with elegance and force!"[20]

But Susan B. Anthony never considered herself a good speaker. She confessed her frustration to one of her close friend, Martha Wright, the sister of Lucretia Mott. "Would the good Spirits give me the right words in the right place and time, no earthly tie should bind my tongue, but I fear they'd never make me a *'speaking medium'* whatever else they may do for me."[21] Mrs. Stanton did not agree. "Miss Anthony's style of speaking is always equal to the emergency." Then she described what frequently happened when they were called upon unexpectedly to speak together. "Filled with consternation, I usually appealed to her to go first; and without a moment's hesitation, she could always fill five minutes with some appropriate word and inspire me with thoughts and courage to follow."[22]

Mrs. Stanton gave due credit to what she knew of Susan's speaking ability, but rarely, if ever, did she actually hear her lecture. When they were together in public, Mrs. Stanton delivered the speeches. Her impressions of Anthony's public speaking were therefore limited to what she saw and heard in convention arguments, business reports, resolutions, and Anthony's introductions of her. She never attended any of Anthony's lectures unless she was also a speaker. "Mrs. Stanton faileth to be present at my lecture in evening—she has never yet heard me give a lecture," Susan noted in her diary as late as 1873, twenty years after they had begun going together before the public with their cause.[23] But Susan B. Anthony's reputation as a poor public speaker seems to be the product of her own insecure self-perception.

Anthony clearly did not have Stanton's rhetorical flair. Instead—and this appealed to many of the people who came to her lectures thinking they would see a spectacle—she gave straightforward, no-nonsense, direct speeches. She did not mince words but conveyed her message through the fiery passion of her convictions. If her audiences did not agree with her, she was too much the kind of character they respected to dismiss her—even though she was a woman.

The simplicity of her dress and the directness of her speech revealed a woman of common origins. She was a woman who had retained the simplicity of earlier life even as she had surpassed its limitations. And this was an inspirational image for these village people. Her drive, her committment, and her passion for her cause came through in her presence as well as her words. Yet she was reachable; she spoke their own language. Her magnetism was precisely in her accessibility to working people; wives in particular identified with her as a common woman, though sometimes she had to win their husbands' respect first. Her appeal was underscored by the fact that she doubtless thought about that aspect of herself not at all—except as she grieved over the absence of rhetorical flair in her speeches, the very thing that drew her audiences to her.

Charismatic leadership must be granted by a constituency. It emerges only when the special qualities of a forceful leader are recognized and acknowledged by a "following," whose recognition grants moral authority to this particular kind of leader. Within the woman's rights movement, it was becoming evident that Anthony had a special dedication to "the Cause," which outdistanced most of the rest of the woman's rights leaders. The work of organizing and strategizing was left to her. But at any time, this special form of leadership is never assumed merely because one does more work or because one is willing do the work others will not or cannot do. Anthony's leadership came to be expected of her by the women she represented. They were not passive followers who were to be merely led. Rather, they were engaged participants in their own cause. They actively conveyed to their charismatic leader the sense that she represented their movement because her values, ideas, and actions seem to crystallize their collective mission. It was from her audiences, from the women she met with and organized throughout the state in small villages and large cities and whose lives she touched and expanded with their struggle, that Anthony derived the moral authority for her new work.

It was typical of Susan that she thought little about what it meant to enter a new village every other day, having to secure the confidence and assistance of the people there, and always being somewhat of a foreigner who appeared very strange to those who were unaccustomed to encountering a woman alone in public. She was painfully reminded of her intrusive presence when one Methodist minister responded with overbearing hostility to her request to use

his church for a meeting "If the Bible teaches anything," he forcefully asserted to her, "it is that women should be quiet keepers at
home and not go gadding about the country." Caught off guard,
Susan was momentarily stunned. She concluded that this minister
did not have "the first spark of reverence for humanity" or for God,
and then turned on her heels and marched out to find a meeting
hall. When another minister offered to adjourn his prayer meeting
so that she could use his church, she admitted that "this kindness
made me so weak, the tears came in spite of me, and I explained
the rowdy treatment of the other minister. . . ." But she could not
dismiss the first minister's rudeness. Sitting in the solitude of her
room that evening, she heard his church bells ringing and had "half
a mind to go, to see if he warns his flock to beware of my heresies."
But she didn't go. Her unexpected tears that afternoon gave her
cause to reflect. She was feeling a weariness that went beyond daily
fatigue, and she began to ponder over the work she had chosen for
herself. "Verily, I am embarked in an unpopular cause and must be
content to row upstream," she concluded before going to bed that
night.[24]

Susan was not one to linger over the weight of her work. But
private agonies have a way of making themselves felt and insisting
their way into a daily routine, particularly when they are compounded by exhaustion. She began to feel it in her feet first. She
had been trudging through deep snow in her new, uncomfortable
boots for weeks. When the pain in her feet became too pronounced
to ignore, she decided to try one of the new, popular "water cures."
She ran very cold water over her feet until they were almost numb,
wrapped them in flannel towels, and went to bed. The next morning
she awoke with a deep, driving pain that settled in her lower back
and was unrelenting for days.

Nevertheless, she had meetings scheduled several days ahead; so
every morning she was up early and, although doubled over with
pain, she prepared for her stagecoach trip to her next destination.
The pain persisted, and one day she had to be carried to a sleigh
where she was wrapped in blankets and driven seventeen miles over
the snow to her next meeting, which was not accessible by road.
Her route through the northernmost regions of New York State
took her to Watertown. When she arrived, she went directly to a
hotel and ordered the chambermaid to bring her buckets of water.
Stubbornly she gave herself another version of what she believed to
be the water cure.

After she finished her canvass, Susan returned to Rochester and

from there continued her pace of conventions and meetings; sometimes she had enough time left to tend to home duties. But her back
continued to give her pain. In the early fall of 1855, she visited the
Worcester Hydropathic Institute in Massachusetts where her cousin, Dr. Seth Rogers, took charge of her water cure. He put her on
a regimen that included

> First thing in the morning, dripping sheet; pack at 10 o'clock for forty-
> five minutes, come out of that and take a shower, followed by a sitz
> bath, with a pail of water at 75° poured over the shoulders, after which
> dry sheet and then brisk exercise. At 4 P.M. the programme repeated,
> and then again at 9 P.M.[25]

What was Susan's reaction to this program? "My day is so cut
up with four baths, four dressings and undressings, four exercising,
one drive and three eatings, that I do not have time to put two
thoughts together."[26] She had brought with her a supply of statio-
nery and postage stamps, planning to send out some convention
calls. Finally she gave in to the regimen and in her leisure moments
went back to reading, her favorite pastime. She took up *Villette*
with special sadness, having learned that only a few months before
that Charlotte Brontë had died in England. Brontë and Elizabeth
Barrett Browning (or Elizabeth Barrett as Susan preferred to call
her) were her favorite authors. She saw in their works special gifts
for describing the noble possibilities of the "new true woman," as
well as carefully revealing all the obstacles that were thrown in her
way by the "aristocracy of sex." Susan put their pictures over her
dresser and kept them there for the rest of her life. In a few years,
Brontë's father would convince the English writer Mrs. Gaskell to
write a biography of his daughter, which Susan would also read
with particular care. For now she was steeped in the other literature
that preoccupied the "strong-minded" women of the time: the works
of such daring and controversial French women as Madame de Staël
and George Sand.

That fall Susan left her rest cure to go to the Massachusetts Woman's Rights Convention held in Boston. When she arrived, Lucy Stone
took her to meet the prominent philanthropist Francis Jackson, and
afterwards they went sightseeing together.[27] This proved to be a
fortuitous and lifelong connection, because Jackson became a supporter of the woman's rights movement. Three years after this meeting, he gave the movement five thousand dollars. In later years his
daughter, Eliza Jackson Eddy, would become a friend and benefac-

tor of Susan and the movement. And it was his granddaughter, Sarah Jackson Eddy, who would paint a portrait of Susan B. Anthony forty years later, which captured the tenderness of the moment when children again laid roses in her lap at a celebration in honor of her eightieth birthday.

The elite—even the reformist elite—is nothing without its literati. In these years, the notables of the antislavery and woman's movements mingled easily together. In Boston they came to the woman's rights convention and met for tea at the Garrisons'. Ralph Waldo Emerson was there and so was the wealthy established literary figure Caroline Dall, who had assisted veteran woman's rights advocate Paulina Wright Davis in organizing the Boston convention. Caroline Severence, who had recently moved to Boston with her husband who was a leading banker, also came to the Garrisons' home that evening. And, of course, there was Wendell Phillips, the wealthy Boston abolitionist who was one of the toughest antislavery leaders of the day as well as a Boston aristocrat who had never lost his class' spirit of *noblesse oblige*.

In contrast, Susan B. Anthony was a struggling reformer without aristocratic lineage, new wealth, or the personal connections to privileges and power that facilitated the work of aristocratic reformers. She now realized that these were necessary for her work. But like the women it was organized to represent, the woman's rights movement was poor. Anthony's financial resources depended on the money she could raise from lectures, and the twenty-five-cent admission that was not enough to support a cause.

Perhaps it was William Lloyd Garrison himself who best understood the importance of the Bostonian connection for the struggling reformer. Twenty-five years earlier he had come to Boston as an editor and reformer who had personally defeated many of the limitations of his own insecure and poor childhood in nearby Newburyport. When he met the prominent New England reformers Samuel May, A. Bronson Alcott, and Samuel Sewall, he received the endorsement and support he needed to initiate his antislavery paper, *The Liberator*. Unlike its effect on woman's rights advocates, marriage enabled Garrison's work. By marrying Helen Benson he connected himself not only to a dedicated wife and a prominent New England family. Helen's father, George Benson, a successful merchant, director of a bank, and a trustee of Brown University, had supported the antislavery cause for over fifty years. It was Garrison's principled and confrontational stance against slavery that established his reputation as leader of the antislavery movement, but it was his Boston supporters and the wealth of his wife's father that provided the resources for his work. And it was his wife Helen, "a noble, self-sacrificing woman, loving and loved, surrounded with healthy, happy children in that model home,"[28] as Susan observed, who provided Garrison with the emotional support for his work. Helen Garrison was still the woman her husband had described thus in a letter to his brother-in-law a year after their marriage.

> By her unwearied attentions to my wants, her sympathetic regards, her perfect equanimity of mind, and her sweet and endearing manners, she is no trifling support to abolitionism, inasmuch as she lightens my labors, and enables me to find exquisite delight in the family circle, as an off-set to public authority.[29]

By contrast, Susan struggled alone.

During her visit to Boston Susan prevailed upon Ralph Waldo Emerson and Wendell Phillips until they agreed to speak in an antislavery lecture series she was organizing in Rochester. Lucy Stone and Antoinette Brown said they would think about it, but Lucy had married Henry Blackwell only a few months before and was still hesitant about public work.

Next Susan went to meet Theodore Parker, a distinguished abolitionist and Unitarian minister in Boston. She felt a bit stunned in this great but gentle man's presence when she entered his third-floor study. "The room is lined with books to the very top—16,000 volumes and there at a large table in the center of the room sat the great man himself." Susan thought, "It really seemed audacious to me to be ushered into such a presence and on such commonplace errand." Whatever her intimidation, she left Parker's study with his commitment to speak. Afterwards she reflected that "he received me with such kindness and simplicity that the awe I felt on entering was soon dissipated."[30] The common woman had overcome one more social barrier.

Susan was moved by the breadth of influence, vision, and spiritual understanding she encountered in Boston, especially when she heard the radical Unitarian minister Thomas Wentworth Higginson preach. He had supported the women when they had disrupted and walked out of the World's Temperance Convention a few years before. That spring he had officiated at the wedding of Lucy Stone and Henry Blackwell, afterwards publishing the couple's marriage protest which they modeled after that of the English statesman, John Stuart Mill when he married the feminist Harriet Taylor and promised to relinquish the "odious powers" given by marriage to men over women.

Boston was alive in those days with the new philosophies of transcendentalism, Emerson and Thoreau, and the beginning of Unitarianism, which William Ellery Channing had introduced to the Hub during his long tenure in Boston's Federal Church. Channing combined aspects of his social philosophy of the idea of progress— which viewed humanity as continually evolving toward a state of perfection—with his respect for the individual's responsibility for his or her own destiny. Unitarianism, in which freedom of will and social responsibility was emphasized finally was beginning to wrench Boston free from two hundred years of entrenched Calvinism.

New reforms, such as antislavery, woman's rights, and free and open Unitarian beliefs, coexisted among the aristocratic elite with the power and privilege of their position producing contradictions which limited their potential to be true reformers. Not surprisingly then one could still find the vestiges of the Puritan fathers' moral authority and superiority in the reformist elite of Boston, who dominated both the abolitionist and woman's movements. They controlled the antislavery movement to such an extent that when the black leader Frederick Douglass stepped out of line with their thinking, by not agreeing with their strategy for the abolition of slavery, they attempted to discredit him. The Boston reformist elite supported the woman's rights movement as long as the women did not offend aristocratic sensibilities (which they had for awhile with the daring Bloomer dress) and as long as the women did not challenge the authority of elite leadership. Tensions were mounting over questions of authority between the Boston aristocrats and the women's rights advocates. Because of the continuing acceleration of their demands, it was becoming more difficult to keep Anthony and Stanton in line. Soon married woman's property rights would not be enough; they would eventually challenge marriage itself.

Not all of these contradictions and underlying power struggles were yet evident in the movement. At this moment Susan was inspired by her trip to Boston. When she returned to Rochester she was more elated than ever. Her voice was no longer restrained and hesitant. Her political consciousness forged during her recent travels, confrontations, and petition drives brought out a fearlessness in her that others called courage. To her she was doing what had to be done, which ironically made her seem to others to be all the more courageous.

Nestled away on her family farm for a few weeks, she wrote to

Samuel May in Syracuse that "I can but acknowledge to myself—
that Anti-Slavery has made me richer and braver in spirit—and that
it is the school of schools for the full and true development of the
nobler elements of life." The effects of her recent exposure to New
England's transcendentalism, with its belief of God in nature, were
apparent. She told May that "indeed all nature is clothed in her
most hopeful dress. It really seems to me that the trees and grass
and the larger fields of waving grain did never look so beautiful as
now—It is more probable however, that my soul has grown to appreciate Nature more fully, than that she had taken herself new
charms!"[31]

She already knew that it was not her personal and political convictions that would hold her back, it was her status as "woman,"
and she pondered the meaning of that.

> Had the accident of birth given me place among the aristocracy of sex,
> I doubt not I should be an active, zealous advocate of Republicanism;
> unless perchance, I had received that higher, holier light which would
> have lifted me to the sublime height where now stand Garrison, Phil-
> lips and all that small but noble band whose motto is "No Union with
> Slaveholders."[32]

At this point she still saw that truly powerful, as well as "higher
and holier" leadership, was possible only for men. But not being of
the "aristocracy of sex" did not hold her back; within months she
was part of that "small but noble band." In 1856 Samuel May
wrote to Anthony on behalf of the American Anti-Slavery Society
that the executive committee had met and desired to engage her as
an agent.[33] The Garrisonians hoped that the drive, organizing talent, and political commitment of Susan B. Anthony could be directed to the abolition of slavery. That stubborn, demanding, and
unrelenting drive, which brought her resentment when she tried to
push her women friends back to work in the field, was exactly what
the Anti-Slavery Society wanted from her.

Anthony accepted the Anti-Slavery Society's offer under the condition that she would be able to continue her woman's rights campaigns. The ten dollars a week she earned for her abolitionist work
did not expand her purchasing power, but it did provide her with
a steady income for awhile. On the other hand, because many of
her friends were retiring to marriage and families, Anthony found
it difficult to organize woman's rights meetings for lack of speakers.
She increased her antislavery work and organized several meetings

for Garrision, Phillips, and others "to awaken the conscience of the North." In light of the increasing proslavery agitation, she wrote to Samuel May that "I shall be very glad if I am able to render even the most humble service to this cause. Heaven knows there is need of earnest, effective radical workers. The heart sickens over the delusion of the recent campaign and turns achingly to the unconsidered *whole question.*"[34]

The American Anti-Slavery Society through its executive committee responded to her that "we put all New York into your control and want your name to all letters and your hand in all arrangements." Samuel May added further:

> The Anti-Slavery Society wants you in the field. I really think the efficiency and success of our operation in New York this winter will depend more on your personal attendance and direction than upon that of any other of our workers. We need your earnestness, your practical talent, your energy and perseverence to make these conventions successful. The public mind will be sore this winter, disappointment awaits vast numbers, dismay will overtake many. We want your cheerfulness, your spirit—in short, yourself.[35]

After having schooled themselves in political organizing first in temperance reform and then in woman's rights, Susan B. Anthony and others of this generation of woman's rights advocates became effective abolitionists. Their political consciousness had been forged in their confrontation against the conditions that confined and dominated women's lives. Raising their own movement from their deeply personal connection to domination and from reflection over and connection to the experiences of women such as their mothers, whose lives were even more confined than their own, they found in themselves a strong, personal point for identification—a new motivation to work against slavery.

Although Elizabeth Cady Stanton attended the World Anti-Slavery Convention in London in 1840, she did not go as an abolitionist. She was on her honeymoon there with her abolitionist husband. Susan B. Anthony was familiar with antislavery arguments from her Quaker youth, but the piety of "true womanhood" robbed her of any ability to understand the institutional aspects of this form of domination. Lucy Stone campaigned for woman's rights and antislavery simultaneously. Undoubtedly, her feminist consciousness sparked her antislavery work as much as, if not more than, her abolitionism influenced her feminism. But most importantly, countless other women, less prominent than Anthony and Stone, came to the movement discontented with the conditions of their own and other women's lives, and out of their identification with their cause could understand and feel more deeply the oppression of others.[36]

In the 1850s, most of the women of Anthony's generation who made the woman's rights movement into an active political force had had no prior political or abolitionist experience. In contrast, some of the older generation of feminists, such as Lucretia Mott, Abby Kelley Foster, and the Grimké sisters, had begun as abolitionists and eventually turned to woman's rights. Of this group, only Lucretia Mott remained uncompromisingly committed to the women's movement when it was threatened by a split from the abolitionists.

Through their own woman's rights movement, woman like Susan B. Anthony transcended their earlier socialization and found themselves for the first time in a position to confront the legal, economic, and institutional dimensions of power. After they had acquired this political acumen, the abolitionist movement solicited their aid for the Anti-Slavery Society.

The year 1857 saw the worsening of the slave masters' control with the Dred Scott decision in the Supreme Court, which held that blacks (even free blacks) were not citizens and therefore had no legal rights. The Missouri Compromise was declared unconstitutional, which made it impossible for Congress to limit the right of an American citizen to take any of his property—including slaves— into any territory. All territories were now open to slavery.

Susan accelerated her work with the American Anti-Slavery Society. She organized lectures, arranged for halls, and advertised meetings for every abolitionist she could keep in the field. Under the pressure of the moment, she found her own voice and began to lecture extemporaneously. Speaking to her audiences only from a few notes, she freed herself from the weight of prepared lectures, which she was never able to memorize anyway. Her written speeches choked her energy and contained her passionate convictions; but when she spoke from notes she surpassed her self-restraints.

> Our mission is to deepen sympathy and convert it into right action, to show that men and women of the North are slave-holders, those of the South slave-owners. The guilt rests on the North equally with the South, therefore our work is to rouse the sleeping conscience of the North.

Drawing on her belief in the full equality of all people, she identified with the slave and called upon her audiences to "recognize the facts which we present. We ask you to feel as if you, yourselves were the slaves." Her political analysis flowed from this personal identification.

> The politician talks of slavery as he does of United States banks, tariff or any other commercial question. We demand the abolition of slavery because the slave is a human being, and because man should not hold property in his fellowman. The politician demands it because its existence produces poverty and discord in the nation and imposes taxes on free labor for its support, since the government is dominated by southern rule.
>
> We preach revolution; the politicians reform. We say disobey every unjust law; the politicians say obey them, and meanwhile labor constitutionally for repeal.[37]

In 1857, Anthony attended another New York State teachers' convention. She did not go without one of her bombshells. She stunned the convention with a series of resolutions that denounced "exclusion of colored children from our public schools," found it mean and cruel to fire a teacher in Albany because Negro blood was found in her family, and claimed that preventing graduates of a colored normal school in New York City from having diploma ceremonies "was a gross insult to their scholarship and their womanhood." But it was her proposal for coeducation that created the greatest controversy and foreshadowed future troubles in introducing women's rights alongside of antislavery issues. She proposed "that it is the duty of all our schools, colleges and universities to open their doors to woman and to give her equal and identical educational advantages side by side with her brother man." The same Professor Davies who tried to prevent her from speaking four years earlier reiterated the majority opinion at this meeting. "These resolutions are the first step in the school which seeks to abolish marriage, and behind this picture I see a monster of social deformity."[38] The resolution was defeated. But as one friend noted after observing Anthony in action at a teachers' convention, "She arraigned those assembled teachers for their misdemeanors as she would a class of schoolboys, in perfect unconsciousness that she was doing anything unusual."[39] When Mrs. Stanton heard of the controversy, she wrote to Susan, "I see by the papers that you have once more stirred that pool of intellectual stagnation, the educational convention."[40]

The newspapers reported on Susan B. Anthony's actions at the convention, and their accounts reveal her compelling presence.

> Whatever may be thought of her notions or sense of propriety in her bold and conspicuous position, personally, intellectually and socially speaking, there can be but one opinion as to her superior energy, ability and moral courage; and she may well be regarded as an evangel and heroine of her own sex.[41]

Susan had not been a "heroine of her sex" to the women at this convention—most of whom had voted with the male minority. If they had not, the women's vote would have carried Anthony's resolutions. Mrs. Stanton, who was still at home with her six children and living vicariously through Susan's battles in the world, wrote, "Well, if in order to please men they wish to live on air, let them. The sooner the present generation of women dies out the better. We have idiots enough in the world now without such women propagating more."[42]

Susan was back in the field again and organizing meetings across the state when she wrote to one of her sisters: "I have just returned from the hardest three weeks tour of anti-slavery meetings I have had yet, so cold and disheartening." The lectures were poorly attended; yet, with other abolitionists like Parker Pillsbury, Aaron Powell, and Abby Foster, she trudged on, organizing and speaking and taking hostile rebuffs. This was her work, and she found that "everyday brings to me new conceptions of life and its duties, and it is my constant desire that I may be strong and fearless, baring my arm to the encounter and pressing cheerfully forward, though the way is rough and thorny."[43]

5

The Woman's Enlightenment

INTELLECTUALLY AND POLITICALLY THE 1850S WERE AN exciting and daring time for feminists. It was a time when their movement was marked by their determination to win freedom for their sex. With an explosion of new ideas, they began to put to rest tired old theories of female inferiority. It was during these years that they issued their most radical positions. Among the most important was their critique of marriage, complete with their vision of the future liberated woman. In their image of the "new true woman," they captured an idea of the future possibility for womankind—in fact, she was the woman that they themselves were trying to be.

Susan B. Anthony summarized her image of the "new true woman" in a speech she delivered.

> The true woman will not be exponent of another, or allow another to be such for her. She will be her own individual self,—do her own individual work,—stand or fall by her own individual wisdom and strength. . . . The old idea that *man* was made for himself, and woman for him, that he is the oak, she the vine, he the head, she the heart,— he the great conservator of wisdom principle, she of love, will be reverently laid aside with other long since exploded philosophies of the ignorant past. She will proclaim the "glad tidings of good news" to all women, that women equally with man was made for her own individual happiness, to develop every power of her three-fold nature, to use, worthily, every talent given her by God, in the great work of life, to the best advantage of herself and the race.[1]

The women's movement had found the social space to begin shaping their political consciousness and future. Now they became acting subjects of their own destiny and their movement. When Anthony spoke of "new true woman," she was not only championing the cause of another class of women, such as victims of intemperate husbands or married women who had no right to their property or children, she too had become the object and the subject of her political struggle. The experience of domination was no longer only what others faced. Anthony was speaking for herself as well as to all women when she called upon woman to "be her own individual self, do her own individual work, stand or fall by her own individual wisdom and strength." For the woman's rights advocates, winning their rights was an urgent matter; in fact, it was a question of survival for many women. But surviving abuse and domination was not enough. They wanted their full liberation and conceived of the possibility of it in their vision of the independent, autonomous woman. With that concept, they initiated a revolutionary critique of marriage.

In reality, the "new true woman" proved for many women, including some feminists, to be a difficult role to sustain. While she was single, Lucy Stone was one who had not been able to overcome the social scourge attached to being an "old maid." Lucy Stone had developed an independent spirit in her early years. She had fought against her family to achieve her own education, as her father had been convinced that schooling was not necessary for girls. As she worked her way through Mary Lyon's seminary at Mount Holyoke and then Oberlin, she began to find her life going in different directions from that of her family. Like Anthony, she first became conscious of the condition of women's subjection through reflection upon her own mother's life. By the time she went to Oberlin, the first college to admit blacks and women along with white men, she began to focus her energies on reform and on antislavery and woman's rights in particular. She had been strongly influenced by Abby Kelley Foster, and with her other "strong-minded" classmate, Antoinette Brown, was outspoken on many issues. Working her way through school with no family support and witnessing the abuse of Abby Kelley for speaking in public at her college were the formative influences that pushed Lucy into becoming one of the most radical advocates of woman's rights.

At the age of thirty-seven, after a long courtship, Lucy married Henry Blackwell, an abolitionist from Cincinnati. She withdrew from public work for many years. Before their marriage Lucy confessed to her betrothed, "Do you suppose, dear Harry, that now when I believe I have a right to the marriage relation, after having spent half my days on the barren desert of an unshared life, that I would voluntarily shut myself up to its utter loneliness still longer, if I knew any true door of escape?"[2] The following year Antoinette Brown, Lucy's friend from their college days at Oberlin and another committed woman's rights worker, married Henry's brother, Samuel Blackwell.

It never occurred to Susan that her good friend Lucy Stone would give in to "matrimonial bliss." When it happened, she was more than disappointed with Lucy's decision; she was furious and perhaps a bit intolerant. She and Lucy had been working together and lecturing and organizing for some time. But this was not the first time a woman had thrown all her energy into the woman's rights movement only to withdraw it for the sake of home and husband. In contrast, Susan found that she had more energy than ever before for the cause. She was restless and increasingly frustrated when each time she was ready to mount another vigorous campaign, her friends—the strongest feminists whom she had relied upon as speakers—were not available. She felt abandoned. Mrs. Stanton, whose able pen was ever ready for the cause, had talked of wanting to get back into action. But she was still having babies and rearing her children. After one campaign, Anthony complained to Antoinette Brown Blackwell.

O, dear, dear, how I do wish you could have kept on with me. I can not tell you how utterly awful is the suspense these other women keep me in; first, they can't, then they can, then they won't unless things are so and so; and when I think everything is settled, it all has to be gone over again. The fact is I am not fit to deal with anybody who is not terribly in earnest.[3]

Susan spoke her mind to Lucy and Nettie, but they simply chided her. Nettie told Susan that she had heard of some bachelor inquiring after her and advised, "Get a good husband, that's all dear."[4] When Susan persisted in asking Lucy to speak at one convention after another, Lucy responded with the same sentiments. "I wish you had a good husband, it's a great blessing."[5]

Susan told Paulina Wright Davis that "I get most discouraged with women. They will work for men, but a woman must ride in triumph over everything before they will give her a word of aid or cheer; they are ready enough to take advantage of every step gained, but not ready to help further steps." Almost as if in defiance of their own political consciousness, women were demanding their rights but refusing to take responsibility for their struggle. "Oh, Paulina, when will they be truer and nobler?" But Susan knew the answer. "Not in our day, but we must work on for future generations."[6]

It was not easy for Lucy Stone to subdue her naturally active spirit and silence her radicalism. She sometimes ached to return to the field. She told Susan that she wished she "lived near enough to catch some of your magnetism. For the first time in my life I feel, day after day, completely discouraged. . . . Susan, don't you lecture this winter on pain of my everlasting displeasure. I am going to retire from the field; and if you go to work too soon and kill yourself, the two wheelhorses will have gone and then the chariot will stop."[7]

When Lucy Stone was drawn from her retirement to give a meeting and speak on both woman's rights and antislavery, she confided in Susan that "I feel half disposed to leave all and go at once to work." Susan told Martha Wright, "It cheered my spirit to see and know that she can hardly *keep still* and the Mercy knows I pray she may 'leave all and go at once to work.' "[8]

Ultimately, motherhood forced Lucy Stone into retirement from public work for several years. Absorbed in domesticity, she told Susan, "Quit common work." Defensively she added, "I know you are tired with 'your four months' work, but it is not half as hard as taking care of a child night and day. I shall not assume any responsibility for another convention until I have had my ten daughters."[9] Although Lucy had only one child, the reality and demands of child rearing, as Mrs. Stanton had learned, almost precluded public work. It was true that Mrs. Stanton, more than the other domestically confined woman's rights advocates, made periodic efforts to attend meetings, and Lucy Stone did leave home to speak a few times. But few of the married women could sustain even for periods of time the full-time work of a political organizer, which involved petition drives, traveling and lecturing, and arranging conventions and hearings.

As a single woman with no intention to marry, Susan found motherhood to be no justification for retirement. She reasoned that her friends and co-workers, unlike many women oppressed in marriage, did not have husband and family forced upon them; as she saw it, they chose marriage over their cause. She was unsympathetic precisely because she saw them choosing private satisfactions over the public and collective movement for their sex. She admitted to

Martha Wright that "I feel discouraged when I think of holding a Convention without Lucy or Antoinette—but they are bound to give themselves over to the ineffable joys of Maternity, so we must either abandon Conventions altogether, or learn to do without them."[10]

Stanton gave birth to her daughter Harriot in 1856 and to Robert, her last child, in 1859. When Antoinette had her first child, Mrs. Stanton asked Susan to convey her blessings for her to Nettie, which Susan did. "Mrs. Stanton sends her love to you and says if you are going to have a large family go right on and finish up as she has done." Being no more sentimental about babies than she was about marriage, Susan added, "Mrs. Stanton has only devoted eighteen years out of the very heart of her existence to this great work. But I say, stop now."[11] Nettie went on to have seven more children, losing the first and another in infancy, and her woman's rights work subsided in proportion to her domestic responsibilities.

Mrs. Stanton recognized the mounting tensions between Lucy and Susan. She cautioned Susan, "Let Antoinette and Lucy rest in peace and quietness thinking great thoughts . . . do not keep stirring them up or mourning over their repose."[12] The rupture between Lucy and Susan must have been serious, because when Mrs. Stanton learned it had been patched up she told Susan, "I am glad to hear of Lucy Stone. I think a vast deal of her and Antoinette Brown. I regret so much that you and Lucy should have had a slight interruption to your friendship."[13]

The subject of marriage not only created personal disagreements between friends; Anthony began to see how it prompted woman's loss of her own identity. She took up the question with one of her remaining spinster friends, Lydia Mott, a niece of Lucretia Mott.

> In the depths of my soul there is a continual denial of the self-anni-hilating spiritual or legal union of two human beings. Such union, in the very nature of things, must bring an end to the free action of one or the other, and it matters not to the individual whose freedom has thus departed whether it be the gentle rule of love or the iron hand of law which blotted out from the immortal being the individual soul—stamp of the Good Father. How I do wish those who know something of the real social needs of our age would rescue this greatest, deepest, highest question from the present unphilosophical, unspiritual discussers.[14]

Lydia, who was unmarried, was still loyal to marriage. She told Susan that it was most natural to "fall into habits and trains of thought of those we love." Besides, she warned Susan, take heed, "for this standing alone is not natural and therefore cannot be right." Susan defended her position. "Institutions, among them marriage, are justly chargeable with many social and individual ills." Then she added hopefully, "I am sure my 'true woman' never will be crushed or dwarfed by them."[15] This was Anthony's critique of marriage—one that exposed its exploitation. But hers was a critique that came from a positive vision of the alternative: Women could choose their liberation and fight for it. She was firmly convinced that ultimately women would be able to live free from the limitations and deformations imposed on them by marriage.

This critique of marriage was not unique to Anthony or to American women in the 1850s. This new vision of woman had also been the subject of the recently published novels and poetry of Charlotte Brontë and Elizabeth Barrett Browning, who were among the English writers who eloquently envisioned another possibility for womankind. As noted earlier, Anthony was drawn to their works and regarded them above all other writers. Their characters Jane Eyre and Aurora Leigh were indeed "new true women." They were fictional nineteenth-century characters who refused the dependency and denial of personal identity that marriage traditionally required of women.

Brontë was a thirty-one-year-old spinster when she finished writing *Jane Eyre,* an early and powerful vision of the "new true woman." Even before Brontë approached the question of independence and autonomy in *Jane Eyre,* she had been determined to redefine the heroic woman and to free her from the masculine standards of feminine beauty lodged in aristocratic privilege. Refusing to make Jane Eyre larger than life, Charlotte Brontë promised her sister Emily, the author of *Wuthering Heights,* "I will show you a heroine as plain and as small as myself, who shall be as interesting as any of yours."[16]

In the novel, Jane Eyre—a common woman—becomes a new heroic woman. She fights her way through her orphaned and loveless childhood with a determination out of which she grows into a self-reliant young woman who, in searching for a position as governess, finds her way to Thornfield, the estate of Mr. Rochester, and the promise of an easier life. When Rochester eventually reveals his love for her, the possibility that he might marry her seems as if it will lift her from her social and economic dispossession. As one critical work points out, the diminutive Jane is "invisible as air, the heir to nothing, secretly choking with ire."[17]

Before Jane ever learns that Bertha (the madwoman Rochester has locked in his attic) is actually his wife, Rochester tests her by making it appear that he is going to marry another woman. Jane, hurt and humiliated but still possessing her own moral integrity and her self-reliant spirit, decides to quit Thornfield and leave Rochester. Finally, when Rochester reveals to Jane that it is she he intends to marry, Jane recognizes his arrogance and realizes that Rochester sees her as less than himself.

> Do you think because I am poor, obscure, plain and little, I am soulless and heartless? You think wrong! . . . I am not talking to you now through the medium of custom, conventionalities, nor even of mortal flesh; it is my spirit that addresses your spirit; just as if both had passed through the grave, and we stood at God's feet, equal as we are![18]

The spirit that Jane called forth from herself was the same spirit that Susan B. Anthony called "the divine spark within." For the "new true woman,"that spirit created both the desire and the necessity to overcome the conditions that had limited and constrained her. In her speech on "true womanhood," Anthony found that "the hope of the world's realisation of my ideal of the *true woman,* must be based on the immutable principle that there is indwelling [*sic*] in every human being irrespective of color, or sex, or condition, the indestructible . . . germ of immortal life . . . this imperishable spark of divinity." For Anthony's "new true woman" to emerge on the human scene, she must throw off the chains of barbarism, which "show us woman degraded to a beast of burden . . . she may be beaten and bought and sold in the public market; she is recognized as fit only to minister to man's animal comforts, pleasures and passions. . . ."[19]

Merely lifting woman from these conditions of "barbarism" was not enough for either Brontë or Anthony. Jane Eyre's heroism did not rest solely on her refusal to marry Rochester. It came from a new positive foundation: Her independence and self-reliance bolstered her determination to go alone into the world, risking the unknown without income, possessions, or a home of her own.

Like Jane Eyre, Elizabeth Barrett Browning's Aurora Leigh chooses to make her way alone in the world, having rejected a marriage to her cousin Romney arranged by her aunt and guardian to insure her inheritance of the Leigh family fortune. She chooses her life and career as a poet and writer over Romney's offers of protection and marriage. She struggles as a writer in her London garret, and when her writing finally brings her success and the assurance of economic independence, she moves to Italy. Romney, like Rochester, being possessed of all the arrogance and pride that manhood and wealth confer on him, recognizes the higher values of Aurora Leigh only after he is blinded in local riots when peasants sack and burn his estate. Now blind, he is humbled physically, and without his estate he is left in poverty. Only then is he able to see that Aurora Leigh has more to offer him than he does her. He realizes that it is her writing and ideas that should inspire their love and that he should follow her.[20]

Anthony read *Aurora Leigh* in 1857, the year in which she was forced to cancel the National Woman's Rights Convention because most of the other woman's rights leaders refused to leave home, husbands, and babies. "Nobody seemed to feel any personal responsibility" to the cause, she lamented.[21] At moments like this, Barrett Browning's verse sustained Anthony's hope "that woman may more and more be like Aurora Leigh"[22] and take responsibility for their own lives and independence. This book meant so much to her that she carried it with her for the rest of the century, avidly rereading her favorite underlined sections such as Aurora's response to Romney's proposal of marriage.

> You misconceive the question like a man,
> Who sees a woman as the complement
> Of his sex merely. You forget as much
> That every creature, female as the male,
> Stands single in responsible act and thought
> As also in birth and death. Whoever says
> To a loyal woman, 'Love and work with me,
> Will get fair answers if the work and love,
> Being good themselves, are good for her—the best
> She was born for.[23]

Like Brontë and Barrett Browning, Anthony called on her "new true woman" to create a definite purpose in her life, just as she herself lamented that "it is only the *heroic few* whose earnest spirits are not daunted . . . who venture beyond the prescribed bounds of woman's sphere, and with most natural union of head and heart, work out for themselves an individual name and fame."[24]

In many ways, Susan B. Anthony was her own, albeit unacknowledged, model of the "new true woman." She was the architect and force of her own life; hence, she alone was responsible for her radical choices and was prepared for their consequences. But Anthony was fully aware of what others said of her. She knew well that those "who have worked out for themselves an individual destiny . . . are all of them looked upon with distrust,—hardly counted as women, whispered of, as wanting in that true womanly modesty."[25]

In fiction, Brontë and Barrett Browning were faced with the problem of how to dispossess men of their unjustly held power in order to make marriage possible for their heroines. In real life, Anthony surmounted these inequalities by remaining single. But mid-nineteenth-century literary sensibility, which reflected the imagination of the times, could not conceive of the kind of social change that could make equality in marriage possible. Instead, both authors had to make their male protagonists victims of severe physical catastrophes in order to bring them to the point of a moral crisis, in which they could recognize the superior moral qualities that would come from a relationship of equality with their heroines. Both Rochester in *Jane Eyre* and Romney in *Aurora Leigh* lost their magnificent estates and fortunes. But economic equality was not sufficient to level their masculine sense of privilege. Both men lost their eyesight and were humbled by being made dependent on others. Only then did these men reach the wisdom that enabled them to recognize in their loved ones the "new true woman." Only when masculine love was transformed could Jane Eyre and Aurora Leigh accept it.

For the woman's rights movement, neither fires and blindness nor civil and private catastrophes could be a solution to the problem of masculine privilege. Anthony and Stanton would have to raise the concrete issues, such as married woman's property rights, and the rights to divorce and to vote, which Brontë and Barrett Browning could evade in fiction. But beneath the critique of marriage emerging from both women's literature and their movement was a deeper analysis of women's condition. And that analysis remained unspoken, except in the oblique language used by women activists as well as writers. That was the question of the role of sexual relations in the scheme of male domination.

Because she was unmarried Anthony had a particular vantage point from which to consider sexuality and its role in the exploitation of women. She first began to comprehend the power of sexual surrender in the subordination of women when her married sisters turned away from her and rejected their sisterly society. Stanton had transcended this domination politically and theoretically but not personally—at least not enough to keep her marrige from standing in the way of her love for Susan. Sexuality and its role in women's lives was an unspoken issue in the mid-nineteenth century. It was an issue that women were aware of but were forced to be silent about. Anthony must have known what happened to women who experienced their sexuality in the context of unequal relationships, for she understood well the potential of sex as a form of human fulfillment—something she considered an epitome of human experience. But when relationships were unequal, in sex women were reduced to objects "recognized as fit only to minister to man's animal instincts."[26]

As Anthony was neither a masochist nor unlovable, she would never have chosen to live without sex if she had believed that she could experience it as fulfillment instead of degradation. What we do not know is to what extent she may have wanted to experience this human fulfillment in sexual relations with Stanton, who being tied to her husband made it a living impossibility for Susan. For Susan, a sexual relationship was one intimately and intricately tied to a lifetime loyalty. This loyalty, Susan believed, was one that endured even after the death of a partner, as she would make clear to her brother-in-law when her married sister died.

If it is true that underlying Anthony's critique of marriage was an analysis and awareness of sex as domination—a critique that was known but silenced and not made explicit in the women's movement—then we must assume that it was a tactical decision on Anthony's part not to address the issue. By now, Anthony's ability to interpret women's lives as we are interpreting hers had reached a point of consciousness where not seeing masculine power in its fullness would have been almost impossible. And typical of those who try not to see and not to know what has been concretely established before them, it would reveal personal foibles and contradictions in her that we have not discovered.

If Anthony's "new true woman," Brontë's Jane Eyre, and Elizabeth Barrett Browning's Aurora Leigh embodied new visions and hope for womankind, it was because before the feminist movement women's lives were hidden in a kind of social darkness. Generally excluded from the public world, barely evident in the professions, legally nonexistent in marriage, mid-nineteenth-century women lived in a virtual state of marital feudalism. In marriage women had not progressed beyond feudalism—husband and wife being much like the lord and vassal of tenth century Europe. While vassalage had disappeared centuries before, feudalism continued in marriage. But women were also living during a period when, as Anthony pointed out, they were "enjoying more of social equality, or rather suffering less of abject menial servitude, but still the slave of man." Anthony called this new era a "twilight of civilization." The woman's rights movement was enlightening the condition of women and casting out old myths in favor of new rational reasoning. Like the eighteenth-century *philosophes* who had appealed to reason and science in order to overcome the darkness that religion and economic feudal relations had imposed on human knowledge and social life, the "ultra" women leaders insisted that womanhood be discussed with a new sense of possibility—in a rational discourse rather than with sentimentality.

Anthony had already insisted that they rescue "this greatest, deepest, highest question, from the present unphilosophical, unspiritual discussers," who thought of marriage or any bond like it only in terms of women's weaker and dependent natures. Further, until they challenged the domination of women in marriage it would remain beyond public scrutiny. It had to be made an issue of public concern if the private exploitation of women in their homes was to be challenged. The demand for Married Woman's Property Rights opened the debate. But only an enlightenment of minds and a change in traditions could dispel the unquestioned assumptions upon which marriage had been maintained through the centuries. As Anthony and Stanton began to discuss the deeper issues surrounding marriage, they expanded the philosophical base of the woman's rights movement and ushered in what should be properly understood as a woman's enlightenment.

The eighteenth-century Enlightenment was more than the philosophical writings of several thinkers. Peter Gay has characterized it as a "recovery of nerve," a time when "educated Europeans awoke to a new sense of life."[27] It created a social climate of self-assurance and a new temper focused around the meaning of freedom. It emphasized reason, rationality, secularization, and science—those qualities that would demystify religious beliefs often going back as far as feudalism. The Enlightenment embraced the idea of freedom in its many forms: "freedom from arbitrary power, freedom of speech, freedom of trade, freedom to realize one's talents, freedom of aesthetic response, freedom, in a word, of moral man to make his own way in the world."[28]

The Woman's Enlightenment was not an imitation of that great age of enlightenment that spanned the eighteenth century in Europe and America. Rather, it was a new historical epoch ushered in by women. Yet, it necessarily displayed similarities to the earlier age. As a philosophy, the Enlightenment cannot be reduced to one set of ideas, doctrines, or dogmas. And as a social program, woman's rights was concerned with a broad range of issues.

Largely confined within their private sphere, women remained relatively untouched by the advances of the eighteenth-century Enlightenment. But by the end of the eighteenth century and the French Revolution, French women acted swiftly to claim a place for themselves in the new social order that would lift them from the darkness of feudalism. From the Revolution in 1789 to the Terror, which began in 1793, women took their demands for their rights to the National Assembly. The Society of Revolutionary Women and Olympia de Gouges insisted that women be recognized as citizens and accorded their natural rights. Following the Enlightenment argument, they reasoned that human beings are naturally equal and therefore that sex superiority was unnatural. Women, they insisted, should be equal partners in marriage. For a few years it appeared that women would win some of those rights. But in the Reign of Terror that followed the French Revolution, women's clubs were surpressed and Olympia de Gouges was guillotined for her radical feminist work.[29] Later, when France adopted the Napoleonic Codes, the backlash against the revolutionary feminists was complete. Any rights women had momentarily won were withdrawn. Marriage and women's sphere remained excluded from the advances of the Enlightenment.

In more subtle ways, eighteenth-century women had transformed certain Enlightenment values into what has been called "rational domesticity." Without challenging their domestic arrangements, they attempted to transform them with Enlightenment values by emphasizing rational friendship and love. Aristocratic and middle-class women created rational friendships with each other and developed a climate in which delayed marriage or refusing marriage altogether became acceptable for some women.[30]

But it was not until the mid-nineteenth century that women could create their own enlightenment on their own terms. Now with a movement of their own, the time for a genuine Woman's Enlightenment had arrived. Now they could take up the claims of the earlier generation of revolutionary women.

In the Woman's Enlightenment, Anthony and Stanton questioned all of the assumptions and ideas that were used to justify the confinement of their sex to the private sphere. One of these was the assumed difference in male and female natures. By January 1856, Mrs. Stanton was ready to take on this question by launching with Susan a campaign for coeducation. But when it was time to write the report they had been discussing, entitled "Educating the Sexes Together," and the release their most formidable challenge yet to the ideas of woman's inferior nature, Susan was nowhere to be found. "Where are you Susan & what are you doing? Your silence is truly appalling. Are you dead or married?"[31]

Actually, Susan was off in the snow-driven regions of New York State with Frances Gage. Having promised to organize a series of antislavery lectures, she decided to "initiate" Gage into a winter campaign for woman's rights, leave her to finish it, and return to her antislavery organizing. When Mrs. Stanton was looking for her, Susan was on a sleigh headed for Nunda, New York, where it was twelve below zero and the "trains all blocked by snow." Within a few weeks Frances Gage was called home to family concerns, forcing Susan to excuse herself from the antislavery lectures so she could finish their campaign.

When she finally arrived home, Susan was delighted to hear from Mrs. Stanton for she too was ready to go work on their new project to restore to woman a human and, therefore, equal nature. They knew of Mary Wollstonecraft's valiant efforts in the late eighteenth century to address the question of women's nature and insist on their fuller education in her work *A Vindication of the Rights of Women*. They knew that experiments in coeducation had been going on in places like Oberlin for several years. However, opposition to coeducation was still strong and the advancement of women's education was being undermined by such theories as those of Catharine Beecher. As the leader in the domestic-science movement, she promoted the idea that woman's education must be aimed at training her for domestic life. By now, Susan had reached the height of her irritability with Beecher who, as the head of the American Women's Education Association, exercised a conservative influence on women's education. After one meeting of the association Anthony remarked to Stanton, "Isn't it strange that women such as these—are so stupid? Yes, so false as to work for anything but their highest convictions."[32]

Anthony went to Stanton with her own outline for their report on "Educating the Sexes Together." They set out their work, with Stanton doing most of the writing and Anthony crossing out and changing ideas as they went along. Their report was organized in three parts. Part I, on "The Identity of the Sexes," opened with the question, "In studying Algebra & Geometry, in reading Virgil or the Greek Testament, who ever found any feminine way of extracting the cube root of Xyz, or any masculine way of going through the moods, tenses of verbs?" Thus, they challenged the theory that held that women's smaller brains required a different and less strenuous education.

They insisted that they would not even respond to "the common theory, that man & woman are two distinct creations,—differing in all their manifestations of mind & body, placed here for a different purpose & to fulfill a different destiny." As to the "natural" differences between males and females, "that portion of this human nature in which there is really a difference, is not only physical, but comes not within the range of scholastic discipline. That which is common is precisely what the world has proposed to educate." In the natural world, men and women

> . . . inhale the same vital atmosphere, drink from the same gushing fountains, bask in the same vivifying sunlight, & draw all the resources of their existence & growth from one common storehouse—If then, in relation to the physical, where the principle of sexual does undeniably obtain, it would be ridiculous to talk of male and female atmospheres, male & female springs of rains, male & female sunshine, or male & female elements in any part of nature, how much more ridiculous is it in relation to mind, to soul, to thought, where there is as undeniably no such thing as sex, to talk of male & female education & of male & female schools.

In Part II, Anthony and Stanton contested the argument that "man was made for *himself,* & woman for *him.*" They proclaimed that "we preach a new doctrine. Women equally with man was made for her own individual happiness. . . . It is not for man to point out the sphere in which she may move." In Part III, they argued that "a similar education [is] required for beings of the same instincts, appetites, impulses, passions & powers." Then logically they concluded, "If the same education is desirable for both, why should the sexes be separated in pursuit of it?"

Through coeducation, colleges would become integrated and finally give women access to the same intellectual resources and educational curriculum that had been available to men for three centuries. Four years before Vassar endowed the first woman's college in America, they lamented that "we have no Yales, Harvards, Girards or Lawrences to found & endow colleges for girls."

What they underestimated was how difficult, if not impossible, it would be for women to immediately surmount and compensate for the social inequality between them and men. Men as a group had had access to higher education for over three hundred years in America. From that advantage and their connections to positions of power and influence in society, they found themselves moving from their schooling into important and influential positions. Such social access and political power was unknown to women as a class. And something other than the long, slow progression of history would be necessary if women were to be truly equal. As long as change evolved slowly, the three-hundred-year time lag between men's and women's educational opportunities would persist. Immediate and radical change became the base of all the women's demands.

To claim their natural and inalienable rights and win the access to social power that men had held, the feminists had to demystify woman's nature. Anthony and Stanton culminated their argument for coeducation in the spirit of the Enlightenment: "We have crucified and tortured nature long enough. Let us now follow her dictates & ponder well her simple teachings."[33] Their paper was first delivered by Anthony in New York and then in Massachusetts at the state teachers' convention.

Then in the fall of 1857, Anthony went to a Progressive Friends meeting where she again had to forcibly impose rational discourse onto the mystified, and indeed almost mystical, notions of men and women's separate spheres discussed there. She told Mrs. Stanton that a Mr. D. read a paper that spoke truthfully about reproduction and "abuses in marriage," but that when "he set forth his idea of the Nature of the sexes & their relation to each other," she challenged him. "He said that woman's inherent nature is love," which Anthony noted left wisdom to the nature of man. According to Mr. D., "Love reached out to wisdom & wisdom to love, and together there was a beautiful blending of the two principles."

"My soul was on fire," Anthony told Stanton. Upon hearing Mr. D.'s words, she was on her feet in an instant and declared that this was "the very same doctrine that consigned woman from the beginning to the sphere of affections, that subjugated her to man's wisdom." But her ire did not silence the speaker who continued to elaborate his theory. Finally, by parlimentary rules the question was called. But Anthony was fuming, "I must out." On her feet again she insisted, "Mr. President, I must say a word more." With all eyes focused on her, she turned to the women in the meeting and forcefully asserted that if they accepted this theory, "you may give up all talk of change for woman." Then she offered her most energetic and reasoned argument. If they agreed with the doctrine that love must prevail in woman while wisdom prevails in men then "woman must look to man for wisdom—must ever feel it impossible for her to attain wisdom equal to him."

Anthony personally felt the sting of this message and told the women that "such a doctrine makes my heart sink within me . . . and did I accept it—I would return to my own Father's house and never again raise my voice for woman's rights to the control of her own person." She argued that rights must be earned; if woman went along with these ideas, "she ought not to possess those rights." After the meeting, Anthony reported to Stanton that she had "stirred the waters" and then forced the speaker into a corner from which "he failed to extricate himself."

For many women at this meeting, her daring new argument, the reasoning that came with it, and the courage of convictions that sounded through it must have come like a breath of fresh air. No longer did feminists such as Anthony and Stanton accept the idea of sentimentalized love, which was separated from wisdom and assigned to woman. For them real love could only exist between two free individuals who came together in equality.

Susan said to her friend, "I tell you, Mrs. Stanton, after all, it is very *precious* to the soul of man, that he shall reign supreme in intellect—and it will take centuries if not ages to dispossess him of the fancy that he is born to do so."[34] "Man's wants makes his rights" was the way Stanton described men's individual power over women. Women would fight that arbitrary power by appealing to reason, logic, scientific proof, and especially natural law to claim their natural rights.

The problem for feminists was to find the legal logic from which they could challenge the private, arbitrary authority and power invested in husbands over wives and by extension in men over women.

Further they had to claim authority for their rejection of marriage laws and social practices that were based on myths and superstitions that posited different natures for males and females. With Jefferson and the Declaration of Independence, they turned to "the laws of Nature and Nature's God." They required for women that which the Constitution had guaranteed citizens—positive law that was derived through duly constituted public, legal mechanisms which they hoped would limit what they saw as the arbitrary power that customary law had invested in husbands, a kind of law they believed was crafted by nature.

They called upon nature to validate their claims. They considered human rights and civil and political equality theirs because those rights were unalienable; they existed in nature and men therefore had no valid power to either give or withhold them. Stanton asserted, "I consider my right to property, to suffrage, etc. as natural and inalienable as my right to life and liberty. Man is above all law. The province of law is simply to protect me in what is mine."[35]

Over a half-century after the United States declared its independence from England, these claims sounded more quaint than revolutionary. Even Elizabeth Cady Stanton's militant language in the 1848 Declaration of Woman's Rights, "the history of mankind is a history of repeated injuries and usurpations on the part of man toward woman, having in direct object the establishment of an absolute tyranny over her,"[36] has the ring of clever modeling after the original Declaration. But it does not carry with it the political significance, the weight of history, the authority of a new people that the Declaration of Independence gave to the American people.

In fact, times had changed and once Enlightenment ideas had cast their influence on the shaping of the laws of the new Republic, they became accepted practice. In 1848 revolution was being discussed in entirely different circles. The same year as the Seneca Falls Convention, Karl Marx and Frederich Engels issued the *Communist Manifesto* with the call "Working Men of All Countries, Unite!" The dominant analysis of revolution had shifted from the unjust and arbitrary authority of nations and kings, to the exploitation of workers by the capitalist class. Having established how the capitalists derived their profit by not paying workers the full value of their labor and by controlling and owning the means of production, Marx and Engels called upon the workers, the proletariat class, to rise up in revolution and seize the control of production for themselves.

It would seem that Anthony and Stanton had skipped a beat, so to speak. They were calling for an eighteenth-century revolution in the midst of nineteenth century industrial capitalism. Anthony and Stanton knew of the stirrings in Europe which were beginning to be felt in the United States but the revolutionary ideology of Marx and Engels did not hold for them a compelling interest.

Certainly Anthony and Stanton recognized the exploitation of labor produced by the factory system. Anthony had grown up with it all around her, and she had not forgotten the problems and hardships of the working women she saw in her youth. While the feminists realized that wages were unjust compared to women's work in the home, they were at least set by established rates. They did not require a lifetime commitment and dependency on their employer. They knew that the laborer owed his labor power to his employer, not his gratitude, and that he received wages and not arbitrary familial beneficence from his employer.[37] Even Marx recognized that to revolt against capitalism it was necessary to be free from feudalism. That was the case for white men in the nineteenth century. But it certainly was not the case for women or for blacks each of whom were living under quite different historical circumstances and relations of power.

Women had been confined to their private sphere by marital feudalism. Blacks were confined to their masters' property by slavery. Each group lived in a set of historical conditions which were different from the other and wholly different from that of white men, whatever their class. Furthermore, marital feudalism and slavery were the material, objective bases upon which the industrial revolution was being forged. Cheap, slave-picked cotton made mass production of cloth possible. Women's unpaid domestic labor made possible male labor in the new industries. Any movement that claimed to revolutionize labor without addressing the very structures of racial and sexual power that underpinned it would be of little interest to American feminists.

The woman's rights movement was focused on its own enlightenment precisely because women were living through a different history than men. Eighteenth century values and principles were more appropriate to addressing the conditions of their lives than were the contemporary ideologies around them. In fact these two movements, woman's rights and socialist revolution, were in fundamental conflict with each other. Calling the worker to his own revolution while his wife was his feudalistic vassal meant only to extend and protect his authority—the source of his domination over her.

By the time women began exposing male power and revealing new possibilities for their own sex in the language of an enlightenment, Marx had already shown that the Enlightenment and liberal doctrine had failed to come to terms with the exploitation of workers. But women were only beginning to struggle for the rights that men took for granted for themselves. The Woman's Enlightenment freed women from their privatized morality, which they transformed into civil responsibility and rights based in natural law. It is characteristic of the ideas of an enlightenment to cast the nets wide and to break the chains of doctrinal limitations imposed by religious beliefs and customs. It came like a breath of fresh air— loosening restraints on thought and action, it freed women to introduce into their movement the widest possible range of human rights issues.

In this spirit Susan B. Anthony took on the antislavery cause, demonstrated against capital punishment, attempted to organize a free church in Rochester for the fullest discussion of opinions, and when John Brown's raid failed on Harper's Ferry and he was captured and sentenced to death, took up his defense along with most of transcendental New England. If she did not identify with the Marxist analysis of labor, she certainly understood the abolitionist analysis of slavery.

John Brown had planned to build a private army to free slaves. In October 1859, he had gathered enough men to raid Harper's Ferry. The proslavery men took the raid as irrefutable proof that abolitionists were conspiring with blacks to mount an insurrection. This was a false assertion that was used to justify more proslavery mob violence. The mobs followed antislavery workers wherever they went, particularly if they paid honor to Brown. In this climate, Susan B. Anthony went door to door in Rochester to sell tickets for a meeting she was organizing to honor John Brown. Brown was hanged on December 2, 1859, and antislavery sympathizers mourned his death in public meetings throughout the North. Although she was met with intense hostility, Susan B. Anthony had coaxed out three hundred people in Rochester to pay tribute to their slain hero. As Brown's heroism rose to legendary proportions, proslavery antagonism intensified. But with a new hero whose legend was intensely emotional, Brown's followers began to believe—at least for a moment—that they had the chance to expunge slavery itself.

Anthony continued her antislavery work alongside her woman's rights campaigns, never mixing the two issues but giving up on neither. But abolitionists began to withdraw from the woman's rights conventions. Or, if they came, it was only to introduce "political" issues, by which they meant antislavery and not woman's rights.[38] The abolitionist movement along with the Republican party had effectively forced slavery onto the political platform. Woman's rights were becoming a back-burner issue.

For Susan, the long months of campaigning and facing hostile crowds with her antislavery message, was wearying. Susan told Mrs. Stanton in "one of my very tired moments" that "there is so much midst all that is hopeful, to discourage and dishearten—and I feel alone, still I know I am not alone, but that all those true and good souls both in & out of the body, keep my company, and that the Good Father more than all is ever a host in every good effort." She was tired and felt vulnerable to being pulled like her friends Stone and Blackwell into the comforts and companionship of the home. In one of her private moods, she confided to Mrs. Stanton that "I have *very weak moments*—and long to lay my weary head somewhere and nestle my full soul close to that of another in full sympathy— I sometimes fear that, *I too* shall faint by the wayside—and drop out of the ranks of the faithful few."

Susan knew that it was from Mrs. Stanton herself that she always derived the strength and support to go on. "How I do long to be with you this very minute, to have one look into your very soul and [hear] one sound from your soul stirring voice." Then Susan prodded her friend. "Oh Mrs. Stanton, how my soul longs to see you in the great Battlefield—when will the time come—you say in two or three years—God & angels keep you safe from all hindrances— and free from all mountain barriers." But her approaching despair came through her optimism. "If you come not to the rescue, who shall?"[39]

In fact, Mrs. Stanton was longing to join Susan in the fray. "I glory in your perseverance. Oh, Susan I will do anything to help you on. . . . Courage Susan, this is my last baby. . . . You & I have the prospect of a good long life. We shall not be in our prime before fifty." Then she added, "We shall be good for twenty years at least & if we do not make old Davies shake in his boots or turn in his grave I am mistaken."[40] In fact, they were "good" for over forty more years together.

Susan did not have to wait much longer, Mrs. Stanton was about at her limits with her own domestic confinement. She described her frustration to Susan.

> How rebellious it makes me feel when I see Henry going about where and how he pleases. He can walk at will through the whole wide world or shut himself up alone, if he pleases, within four walls. As I contrast his freedom with my bondage and feel that, because of the false position of woman, I have been compelled to hold all my noblest aspirations in abeyance in order to be a wife, a mother, a nurse, a cook, a household drudge, I am fired anew and long to pour forth from my own experience the whole long story of woman's wrongs.[41]

Soon Stanton would rejoin Anthony in the world of action. Her agitation against her present life was increasing. "I pace up and down like a caged lioness, longing to bring nursing and housekeeping care to a close."[42] And she meant what she said. From her own experience she would expose woman's wrongs, this time with a new demand—the right to divorce.

Anthony was tired, but it was not a time to rest or to give in to weariness. As 1860 approached, the nation was on the brink of civil war and women were about to face their toughest political battles yet. Now with her partner coming to join her, it is likely that it was Mrs. Stanton who was on Susan's mind when she underlined the following in *Aurora Leigh*:

> The world waits
> For help. Beloved, let us love so well,
> Our work shall still be better for our love,
> And still our love be sweeter for our
>   work
> And both commended, for the sake of
>   each
> By all true workers and true lovers
>   born.[43]

Anthony did not have to wait much longer. She arrived in Albany in February 1860 for the State Woman's Rights Convention to find that the Judiciary Committee was about to recommend a radical bill for married women's property rights. It would be before the full legislature within weeks, if not days. Anthony needed Stanton in Albany. There was no time for hesitation or delay. "You must move heaven and earth now to secure this bill, and you can if you will only try." But she was not sure that this would be enough pressure to move Mrs. Stanton into action, so she asked Martha Wright to go to Seneca Falls and make Mrs. Stanton "feel that the salvation of the Empire State, at least the women in it, depends on her bending all her powers to moving the hearts of our law-makers at this time."[44]

"If Napoleon says cross the Alps, they are crossed," Stanton responded to Anthony's command, admitting that "I can not, my dear friend, 'move heaven and earth,' but I will do what I can with pen and brain." She insisted that Susan Anthony must come to her to "start me on the right train of thought, as your practical knowledge of just what is wanted, is everything in getting up the right document."[45]

Two weeks later Stanton stood before the New York state legislature and delivered another powerful argument for woman's "natural rights," which she described as inalienable to civilization. After five years of petition drives, state canvasses, and legislative hearings, the bill was finally adopted by the legislature. For the first time in the history of the state, married women were granted the right to own separate property, to carry on business in their own names, to enter into contracts, to sue and be sued, and to be the joint guardian of their children. Momentarily at least the women of New York State were revived from the legally dead. It would be another ten years, in 1870, before the women of England would win their first legislative victory for married women's property rights. Militant suffragist Sylvia Pankhurst later described their victory as the "first breach in the iniquitous institution 'coverture.' "[46] And she was right. For American women—triumphant for the moment—were soon to learn that their 1860 victory was a temporary one. Even when property rights were finally won for married women, the courts did not generally interpret them in favor of women well into the twentieth century.

Anthony opened the Tenth National Woman's Rights Convention in New York City in May 1860 with a report of their new legislative victories. Success reinvigorated the meeting with new spirit and energy. The woman's rights advocates boldly resolved, "That inasmuch as man, in the progress of his development, found that at each advancing step new wants demanded new rights . . . it is his duty to stand aside and leave to woman the same rights."[47] It is in the struggle to win their rights that women learn the depth of male resistance to woman's emancipation. That resistance and the struggle itself often make it difficult to see and expose other levels of domination. But for a radical movement a victory such as winning a new right exposes other issues and clarifies the direction for the movement's next struggle. Now the Woman's Enlightenment, delayed as it had been for over a century, had acquired its own momentum. Radical women were ready for their next challenge—divorce.

Until this moment woman's rights advocates had approached divorce only in the context of temperance campaigns. They justified divorce and the proposal that women deny their husbands' right to the marital bed with the argument that wife abuse necessitated it. In 1852 the New York State Woman's Temperance Convention had resolved, "Let no woman remain in the relation of wife with the confirmed drunkard. Let no drunkard be the father of her children."[48] Now, Anthony and Stanton reasoned, the right to divorce must be claimed as a new civil right that did not have to be justified only on those terms. Framing divorce as a right permitted women to conceive of it as a part of what was inalienably due to them. The result would be that woman could act as her own independent person either in marriage or out.

The optimistic and energetic 1860 Woman's Rights Convention was unprepared for Elizabeth Cady Stanton's reformulation of the demand for divorce. When she took the podium, she proceeded to redefine marriage as a civil contract and nothing more. She reasoned that marriage was a civil contract that should be "subject to the restraints and privileges of all other contracts." Futher Stanton wanted the convention to go on record in support of a resolution that stated "That any constitution, compact, or covenant between human beings, that failed to produce or promote human happiness, could not, in the nature of things, be of any force or authority; and it would be not only a right but a duty to abolish it."[49]

In demanding woman's right to divorce, Stanton offered her most radical reformulation of marriage. By calling for the union of husband and wife in marriage to be recognized as a contract, she intended to rescue the family from the power of privatized domination and to challenge the religious, romantic, and mystical beliefs in women's inferior nature, which had kept marriage from being contracted on a rational basis. In one swift gesture, she demoted marriage from a sacred act to a civil function and raised divorce from an offense against God to a civil, contractual right. In doing so, the movement challenged both the sentimentalization of love and the religious sacredness of marriage.

It is ironic that John Stuart Mill's essay *On the Subjection of Women* was heralded as a major statement of their movement by women's rights advocates when it was published in 1869. In fact, Mill's essay intentionally excluded divorce as a woman's right and thereby reduced the most radical feminist theories of marriage to a liberal treatise. Mill, a classical liberal theorist and former member of Parliment, published his famous essay in 1860, which was the year the woman's rights movement faced its most difficult tests and was factionalized into the antagonizing groups that would exist for at least two decades. By then feeling demoralized from the splits and the internal opposition against them, Anthony and Stanton were grateful for Mill's work and hailed his essay as a major advance for their cause.

In his essay, Mill rejected the slavery of marriage and argued that in a voluntary association between people it was not necessary that one party be the master. "The equality of married persons before the law, is not only the sole mode in which that particular relation can be made consistent with justice to both sides, and conducive to the happiness of both, but it is the only means of rendering the daily life of mankind, in any high sense, a school of moral cultivation." He called for "the admissibility of women to all the functions and occupations hitherto retained as the monopoly of the stronger sex." And in advance of his times, he defended suffrage and the election to political office as rights of women. Thus far, in his argument and exposition of women's rights, Mill advanced no new ideas beyond those that Anthony and Stanton in the United States and feminists in Britain had been making for nearly two decades. In fact, we have learned that the ideas for his essay on women came from his feminist wife, Harriet Taylor.[50]

Like Stanton, Taylor went much further on the subject of divorce than Mill ever would. Harriet Taylor had argued that divorce should be granted by the consent of both parties, and Stanton had called for a marriage contract that would be null and void when its terms were not kept by either party. Mill recognized that there were conditions under which the marriage contract might require separation of the parties, but like most liberal men of his time he clearly stipulated, "I do not now speak of divorce."[51] Mill excluded the essentially radical feminist demand for divorce from his essay. He also represented the other feminist issues of the mid-nineteenth century in classic liberal language and theory, and that essentially camouflaged the material reality of marital feudalism.

The power relations of male domination became invisible behind Mill's interpretation. In political circles this is now understood to be how liberals co-opt a radical movement. Once co-opted, the woman's movement became characterized by Mill's essay *On the Subjection of Women,* which was a quintessential statement of nineteenth-century liberal ideology that made it appear as if feminists were merely middle-class women seeking to gain more privileges for themselves.[52]

At the 1860 woman's rights meeting, Anthony and Stanton knew that the radical resolution, which demanded the right to divorce as premised on the idea of marriage as a civil contract, would be controversial. But neither woman was prepared for the wrath it would bring down upon them. Antoinette Brown Blackwell was the first to speak against Stanton's resolution. She argued that marriage was a relation "which from its very nature must be permanent" and that "divorce is naturally and morally impossible."[53]

Wendell Phillips was not satisfied to merely speak against the Stanton resolutions. In language that was considered extremely heavy handed for the time, he tried to have the resolutions expunged from the record. "This convention is no Marriage Convention," he argued—separating marriage from the list of wrongs against women and the inequalities they suffered. "I as a man, have exactly equal interest in the essential question of marriage as woman has."[54] Then he moved that the resolutions not appear in the recordings of the convention. Garrison did not support the resolution to censor Stanton, but he voiced his agreement with Phillips's argument.

Stanton was stunned. His "words, tone, and manner came down on me like a clap of thunder."[55] Quickly, Anthony was on her feet. At least a half dozen times before the meeting she had reassured Mrs. Stanton that Garrison and Phillips would be with them on these resolutions.[56] Now she turned to Phillips and asserted, "As to the point that this question does not belong on this platform,— from that I totally dissent." Then to the assembly she defended the new resolution on divorce.

> Marriage has ever been a one-sided matter, resting most unequally upon the sexes. By it, man gains all—woman loses all; tyrant law and lust reign supreme with him—meek submission and ready obedience alone befit her.[57]

When the vote was taken Phillips's motion lost, and the resolutions were published with the convention proceedings. Stanton later sized up the Bostonian aristocrat. "He over-rated his personal power, and was mortified to find it so little. With all his excellence and nobility, Wendell Phillips is a man," she declared.[58] Phillips held his position and wrote to Anthony later that "of course it is no right & no wish of mine to dictate what shall be in our plat- form . . . [But] whenever it is understood that the platform will include these questions, I shall have nothing to do with the Convention."[59]

What elicited such a strong and severe reaction from Phillips? Clearly, as Stanton asserted, he launched his attack against her de- mand for divorce on the assumption that his powerful position of leadership and respect in the abolitionist movement would support his stance at this meeting. But in woman's rights meetings, Phillips was repeatedly finding himself less than the fiery radical he fash- ioned himself to be. He was uncomfortable with Stanton and An- thony's increasing militancy. It is likely that his firm Calvinistic be- liefs, which relied on following God's will as it is given in the Bible and known through good works, provoked this reaction. For men like Phillips challenging marriage was not only an offense against God. It is even possible that his own marital difficulties rested be- hind his public assertions.

From all biographical accounts, Wendell Phillips deeply loved his wife Ann. But from the beginning of their marriage, she was af- flicted with a "defect of nervous organization," a condition that characterized the lives of many confined and stifled upper-class women in the nineteenth century. Fragility, weakness, and easy sus- ceptibility to aches and pains as well as melancholic depressions dominated such women's days. Every effort was made to protect them from stress. For women of this social class, doctors frequently prescribed long European voyages as rest cures. It was only one month after the debates at the Woman's Rights Convention when Ann Phillips fell into another crisis. As he had so many times over the years, her husband completely withdrew from public activity for several months to be with her.

However devoted Phillips was to his marriage, those who have studied his life suggest that it was without either a sexual or social life. Some biographers believe that he sublimated these needs into his abolitionist work. Whatever his unconscious psychological re- sponse was to Stanton's resolution, it is likely that when she posed marriage as a civil contract, Phillips and other men took it as a personal threat. Phillips summoned the power of the Boston aris- tocracy and he bonded with his sex to fight Stanton's proposals.[60]

Anthony and Stanton hoped that Garrison was still a friend. Stanton wrote him a few weeks after the convention that she was still recovering from the shock of Phillips's attack, "when he came so near [to] sweeping me from the face of the earth." She offered a conciliatory gesture to keep their friendship. "I particularly desire to stand acquitted with my friends on this point. I should regret to disagree with you or Mr. Phillips as we are under great obligations to you for all you have done for us in the past."[61] While she did not back down from her position, Stanton had hoped that Phillips's reaction would not destroy her relationship with either him or Garrison. But only time would tell.

While visiting with Mrs. Stanton after the convention, Susan wrote to Garrison that the two women were turning Mrs. Stanton's divorce speech into an article they undoubtedly wanted Garrison to publish. Susan told Garrison, "You will find my traces in Mrs. Stanton's article enclosed—I called for a minute, on my way home, and as is my wont, lent a helping hand to her thought." What is surprising is to see how far Anthony would go to enlist Garrison's support. In reference to the convention she added, "The thought of the New York meetings is on the whole more than usually satisfactory—they were indeed very excellent meetings."[62]

While both women made gestures to reaffirm their friendship with the abolitionists, what they apparently did not realize was that by his actions Phillips was in effect forging a split in the woman's rights movement, which Garrison and most abolitionists were to join. Soon the Civil War would intervene. And the men would take security in their belief that the war had silenced the woman's rights movement. Later in the decade when Anthony and Stanton refused to abandon their movement, these men factionalized it and gave the young and already very powerful Republican party an expedient excuse to turn against the woman's rights movement when it stood in the party's way. But none of these repercussions were evident in 1860. When they became evident, the Civil War was over, and the issues of marriage and divorce had been suppressed.[63]

Stanton was undeterred by the attacks. She told Anthony that "I feel a growing indifference to the praise and blame of my race, and an increasing interest in their weal and woe."[64] Anthony too was beyond concern over the criticism of others.

Cautious, careful people, always casting about to preserve their reputation and social standing, never can bring about a reform. Those who are really in earnest must be willing to be anything or nothing in the world's estimation, and publicly and privately, in season and out, avow their sympathy with despised and persecuted ideas and their advocates, and bear the consequences.[65]

To show their determination, only one month after the 1860 convention Stanton and Anthony went off to a meeting of the Progressive Friends and raised the same arguments and demands for divorce. The extent to which Phillips's action against the radical women was building in force was most evident when Anthony took the daring action of harboring the wife of Senator Phelps from Massachusetts and helping her and her children escape his abuse.

One cold evening in December 1860, Susan B. Anthony was at a bank depository in Albany with Lydia Mott when she was approached by a woman who was so heavily veiled she could not be recognized. She asked Anthony if she might have a word with her. Anthony found them a comfortable place in a secluded corner, and the woman revealed that she was Mrs. Phelps, the wife of a Massachusetts senator, and that she had been hiding with her thirteen-year-old daughter. When she had discovered a few years before that her husband had been having affairs with other women and confronted him with the evidence, he became furious, threw her down the stairs, and continued to abuse her. When she threatened to expose him, he committed her to an insane asylum. After a year and a half, her brother managed to get her released but her husband refused to allow her to have her children.

Then she told Miss Anthony that only a few weeks before her husband had allowed her daughter to visit her, and she decided to flee with her. A Quaker family had given them refuge until her husband learned of their hiding place. Now she was appealing to Miss Anthony to help her find protection and a place to stay. She could not even ask her brother, a United States senator, to help her as he had already told her, "It is of no use for you to say another word. The child belongs by law to the father and it is your place to submit. If you make any more trouble about it we'll send you back to the asylum."

Anthony told her that of course she would help her but first she must make some discreet inquiries. A time was set for their next meeting; meanwhile Anthony verified the woman's story. Anthony then decided that she herself should take Mrs. Phelps and her daughter to New York City and find a safe place for them with friends there. On Christmas Day, the three boarded a train in Albany and arrived in New York City too late to call on friends. After being denied rooms in several hotels because they were not accompanied by a gentleman, Anthony tried to prevail on a friend who also refused them. Finally at midnight, cold and wet, they tried another hotel on Broadway. Again the proprietor explained that he would like to help, "but our house is full."

"I know that is not so," retorted Anthony in anger. "You can give us a place to sleep or we will sit in this office all night." In response to this the proprietor threatened to call the police. Anthony would not be moved. "Very well, we will sit here till they come and take us to the station." The proprietor finally conceded and gave then a room for the night. The next day Susan B. Anthony, Mrs. Phelps, and her daughter trudged the streets of New York all day, going from one friend's door to another. It was 10 o'clock in the evening before they found someone who was willing to harbor a "runaway wife"—but only temporarily.[66] Anthony later told William Lloyd Garrison that "in all those hours of aid and sympathy for that outraged woman I remembered only that I was a human being."[67]

But as far as the abolitionists were concerned, Anthony was breaking the law and embarrassing the reform movements. It had not taken long for word to spread among the Republican and abolitionist ranks that Susan B. Anthony had "abducted a man's child and must surrender it." Wendell Phillips spoke for Garrison and himself when he said, "Let us urge you at once to advise and insist upon this woman's returning to her relatives." Aware that Mrs. Phelps's brother and husband were both politicians they could not ignore, Garrison was concerned with the movement's reputation. "Our identification with the woman's rights movement and the antislavery cause is such that we ought not unnecessarily involve them in any hasty and ill-judged, no matter how well-meant, efforts of our own." To Anthony, they too had become men of expediency.

She replied, "That I should stop to ask if my act would injure the reputation of any movement never crossed my mind, nor will I now allow such a fear to stifle my sympathies or tempt me to expose her to the cruel, inhuman treatment of her own household. Trust me that as I ignore all law to help the slave, so will I ignore it all to protect the enslaved woman."

Garrison confronted Anthony again at an antislavery meeting. "Don't you know that the law of Massachusetts gives the father the entire guardianship and control of the children?"

"Yes, I know it and does not the law of the United States give the slaveholder the ownership of the slave? And don't you break it every time you help a slave to Canada?"

"Yes, I do," Garrison returned, unable for the moment to understand the connection. Anthony continued, "You would die before you would deliver a slave to his master, and I will die before I will give up that child to its father."[68]

Mrs. Stanton had warned Susan after the 1860 convention that "woman's degradation is in man's idea of his sexual rights."[69] Whether Garrison could not or simply would not comprehend Anthony's analogies and explanations can never be determined. One can assume that a man of his stature and political experience was not intellectually obtuse. He also knew that Anthony always carefully investigated any cause before she championed it. The violations Mrs. Phelps experienced were not vague charges. Besides physical abuse and forced imprisonment in a mental asylum, her husband had taken their children from her as well as all of her personal earnings from her writings. In all of these actions he was fully protected by law. But the issue of marriage and divorce came very close to home for men like Garrison and Phillips, and the idea of challenging them posed such a fundamental threat that it caused them either to resort to intended maliciousness or to employ not so conscious self-defense strategies. Anthony's father was among the few men who were capable of seeing the case clearly, and he told his daughter, "My child, I think you have done absolutely right, but don't put a word on paper or make a statement to any one that you are not prepared to face in court. Legally you are wrong, but morally you are right, and I will stand by you."[70]

Mrs. Phelps's brother threatened to have Anthony arrested. "Mrs. Stanton," wrote Anthony with urgency, "the Hon. Phelps of Boston is determined to execute the law on me—I pray you impart nothing of my action to the sister Mrs. Garnsey." Mrs. Garnsey was Mrs. Phelps's sister. Anthony explained that Garrison was pressuring her to reveal Mrs. Phelps's hiding place and that "he says there is not a spot or blemish on Phelps character." Mrs. Stanton, who knew Mrs. Garnsey, must help. Anthony asked her to "get an account of the whole affair, especially her testimony as to Mrs. Phelps sanity." But particularly she wanted evidence against Phelps. "Get Mrs. Garnsey's opinion on his chastity to his Marriage Vow."[71]

Anthony was gathering her ammunition for a fight. But "the Hon. Phelps of Boston" discovered his wife's hiding place and kidnapped his daughter. Mrs. Phelps had no legal redress. His arbitrary, discretionary power ruled, and she was never able to get her daughter back.

The abolitionists betrayed the feminists on the divorce issue and other liberal men joined them. Anthony began to mount another campaign in Albany for a divorce bill then before the Judiciary Committee. The bill would permit divorce in cases of desertion and cruel and inhuman treatment. This time the opposition to divorce was led by Horace Greeley, the powerful editor of the *New York Herald Tribune*. He used his newspaper to lash out against Stanton and divorce and to present the same position as that of Phillips's on divorce: it was an issue of concern to men as well as women and therefore not a legitimate woman's rights issue.

Anthony reported to Stanton that Greeley had gone so far as to encourage petitions against the divorce bill. Anthony and Stanton's liberal supporters, like Garrison and Phillips, made no protest against Greeley's actions. Liberal and conservative men had closed ranks against the women. Then while Anthony was in Albany early in 1862, she heard rumors that the legislature might move to retract the Married Woman's Property Acts of 1860.[72] Clearly this struggle was going to require new alliances. By the end of the decade, the feminists had learned that they had taken their campaigns as far as they could without launching a revolution. But at that moment, the nation was already at war.

The Woman's Enlightenment, compressed into the decade of the 1850s, found women testing the limits of society and pushing their demands as far as they could. In ever-widening circles of influence they expanded outward into to larger society, speaking and acting on a broad range of issues. Having eschewed the privatized morality and personal piety into which they had been socialized, they had fully launched a movement based on civil morality and political action.

6

Which Slaves' Emancipation?

This union's existence, this very hour, is at no less a cost, than that of the lives and the liberties of four million human beings. Therefore, do we say dissolve this union,— overthrow this government, commit its blood-stained Constitution to the flames,—blot our every vestige of that guilty bargain of the Fathers.—Break every fetter, and let the oppressed go free—And on the ashes of the abomination, build up a new government, based on the immortal Declaration of '76—"All men are created free and equal."

Susan B. Anthony, 1858[1]

THE GARRISONIAN ABOLITIONISTS—ANTHONY AMONG THEM— held that the Constitution of the United States was essentially a proslavery document, which, like the Union itself, must be destroyed to end slavery. However, the black abolitionist Frederick Douglass had rejected this position some years before. It was his fear that if the Garrisonians succeeded with their campaign for "No Union with Slaveholders" and the South seceded then the slaves in the South would be left completely to the mercy of their masters. Douglass maintained that if the Constitution were followed to the letter of the law and if a government that truly promoted the general welfare and liberty of the people could be achieved then the Constitution could be interpreted as an antislavery document. Speaking not only for but as one of a disfranchised class, Douglass tried to find ways to make the Constitution and the Union work for blacks. But when he disagreed with Garrison, he was summarily expelled from the Garrisonian antislavery circle. After the Civil War the American Anti-Slavery Society adopted Douglass's position, never admitting that its own authoritarian, white male leadership had been wrong and insensitive in its opposition to Douglass's attempt to make the letter of the law in the Constitution work for blacks and give them another weapon in their struggle for self-determination.

In 1860, when the nation was on the brink of civil war, it was the Garrisonian platform that Anthony championed. It was her belief that nothing, especially "this blood-stained Constitution," could stand in the way of defeating slavery. Her personal concern for the slave as a human being was now accompanied by her political consciousness of the economic power that enforced slavery. She saw that slavery was no longer only a southern evil. Northerners manufactured products and made profit from slave-picked cotton, and some northerners even aided and abetted slave masters in capturing runaway slaves who had headed north. Along with the strongest abolitionists, Anthony considered that the very existence of the nation should be put at stake in the struggle against slavery.

Tension over slavery rose in every city, and the impending crisis made Anthony relentless in her challenge to northern complicity in southern slavery. She arranged meetings for Garrison, Phillips, Aaron Powell, and others throughout New York State. Their abolitionist platform angered proslavery northerners. And in that tense winter before the war, Anthony and her band found virulent mobs awaiting them as they campaigned throughout New York under the motto "No Compromise with Slaveholders. Immediate and Unconditional Emancipation."

In the spring of 1861, when the first guns were fired upon Fort Sumter opening the Civil War, the newly elected President Lincoln insisted that this was insurrection and not war. It was Lincoln's hope that a brief military action would bring control again. In the early months of the war, Anthony continued to arrange meetings for Samuel May, Aaron Powell, Stephen S. Foster, and Elizabeth Cady Stanton, who was back in the field again with Anthony. Their first meeting together was in January 1861 in Buffalo, where the abolitionists were greeted with such hissing, booing, and yelling that it was impossible for them to deliver their messages. The new Republican mayor of Buffalo issued orders to the police to control the mobs, but the police ignored the orders and instead supported the proslavery rioters. When Anthony finally managed to open one of the meetings there, someone turned off the gas. The lights went off and pandemonium broke out. In the melee Anthony assumed the same stance that would carry her through every disrupted meeting;

she stood her ground, refusing to move from the platform until the lights were turned on again. Only then did she adjourn the meeting. Her message was embodied in her person as well as her words—neither would succumb to proslavery intimidation.

Anthony faced similar episodes in most of the other cities she traveled to. In Utica she was denied access to the hall she had engaged for antislavery lectures. The mayor met her outside the locked doors and asked her not to try to hold a meeting. A mob formed around them, and Anthony demanded that the doors be opened. The mayor refused, telling her he would escort her away from the mob. Anthony retorted sharply, "I am not afraid. It is you who are the coward. If you have the power to protect me in person, you also have the power to protect me in the right of free speech. I scorn your assistance." With that he "escorted" her away involuntarily.

Perhaps the scene in Syracuse was the worst of all. "Rotten eggs were thrown, benches broken, and knives and pistols gleamed in every direction." That evening effigies of Susan B. Anthony and Samuel May were carried through the city and burned by the celebrating, victorious rioters.[2]

Albany was the only city where the band of abolitionists was able to conduct meetings. Anthony's own recollections of the event provide the most graphic account.

> The mayor went on the platform and announced that he had placed policemen in various parts of the hall in citizens' clothes, and that whoever made the least disturbance would be at once arrested. Then he laid a revolver across his knees, and there he sat during the morning, afternoon and evening sessions. Several times the mob broke forth, and each time arrests were promptly made.[3]

At the final session of the first day, the mayor prevailed upon Anthony to make the first day the only day. "If you insist upon holding your meetings tomorrow, I shall still protect you, but it will be a difficult thing to hold this rabble in check much longer. If you will adjourn at the close of this session I shall consider it a personal favor." She agreed to his request.

The Civil War changed everything. In the first several weeks of fighting, when several southern states seceded from the Union, Garrison and the Anti-Slavery Society decided to withdraw from public agitation. Anthony was outraged; she considered it unthinkable to stop. She told Martha Wright a month after the war began, "The Abolitionists, for once, seem to have come to a perfect agreement with all the World, that they are emphatically out of time and place, hence should hold their peace. No longer torment this wicked nation before its time, by their keen rebukes and scorching anathema." She saw this as a retreat in the face of battle. "Our position, to me, seems most humiliating," she confessed to Martha, "simply that of the political world, one of expediency not principle."[4]

For similar compromising reasons Anthony was forced to cancel the National Woman's Rights Convention planned for May of 1861. She was angry and confessed to Lydia Mott, "Oh, Lydia," she grieved, "I am sick at heart but I cannot carry the world against the wish and will of our best friends."[5] "All alike say 'Have no conventions at this crisis!' . . . 'Wait until the war excitement abates.' " She considered this reasoning tantamount to saying "ask our opponents if they think we had better speak, or, rather, if they do not think we had better remain silent." At this point, she had no idea that it would be six years before she would be able to call another national meeting for woman's rights.

Susan and Mrs. Stanton were working closely together in the field now, and Susan was often in Seneca Falls between meetings. When Mrs. Stanton was preparing for her family's move to Tenafly, New York, Susan took the Stanton's four boys home with her to Rochester until the move was finished. But life in the political field was not always so compatible for them. Susan felt let down when Mrs. Stanton stood with the abolitionists on the question of canceling public meetings, and many years after the war, Stanton regretted her decision. "I am now equally sure that it was a blunder, and ever since, I have taken my beloved Susan's judgment against the world."[6]

As the war dragged on with the North and South entrenched in fighting, it became apparent to the abolitionists that this was not the time to withdraw from public agitation. Slowly they began to trickle back onto public platforms and to resume their demands for immediate emancipation of the slaves. However, by that time they had effectively silenced any further public discussion of woman's rights.

During this time, Anthony had worried not only that the work of woman's rights would not go forward but that they might indeed lose some precious, hard-fought-for rights if they were not vigilant. She was right. In 1862, with no active political presence to challenge it, the New York State legislature repealed most of the sections of the Married Woman's Property Acts, which had been passed only two years earlier. Reaffirming marital feudalism once again the state lawmakers denied women the right to equal guardianship over their children, and widows lost control over their property and the care and protection of their minor children.[7] Anthony noted, "Well, well; while the old guard sleep the young 'devils' are wide-awake." Reflecting upon the situation, she was angry and concluded that, having forsaken their own woman's movement, "we deserve to suffer for our confidence in 'man's sense of justice,' and to have all we have gained thus snatched from us."[8]

Not all nineteenth-century campaigns for property rights were waged by woman's rights advocates. Many states voted for limited property rights as a way to paternally protect women without fully granting them legal independence.[9] Campaigns such as those waged in New York under Stanton and Anthony's leadership, which had culminated in a temporary victory in 1860, won a broader and more fundamental range of rights, including a woman's right to the guardianship of her children. Neither Anthony nor Stanton believed that controlling one's own property and the right to guardianship would revolutionize women's lives. Rather, just as Douglass had reasoned that blacks needed constitutional protections, Anthony and Stanton knew that these laws would give women some essential legal tools to use in the struggle for further and deeper changes. At some significant, but not necessarily conscious level, those who are in power—legislators, husbands, liberal movement leaders—know that new rights will create new freedoms and that those freedoms would produce independence for women that were never intended in the original legislation. Therefore, it is not surprising that the legislature repealed the Married Woman's Property Rights, and in so doing remandered women to their place. The burning national question was whether slaves would be freed from their place.

In 1861 Abraham Lincoln had been elected by a narrow majority to the United States presidency. His election was a major victory for the young Republican party, which was aggressive against slavery if not abolitionist. On the issue of slavery, Lincoln took office as a chief executive who held a more conservative and anti-Negro position than did most members of his party. In the famous debates held in 1858, when he unsuccessfully challenged Stephen Douglas's seat in Congress, Lincoln conceded that "I have no purpose to introduce political and social equality between the white and black races . . . I am in favor of the race to which I belong having the superior position."[10] And in his inaugural address, he reaffirmed that he had no intention "to interfere with the institution of slavery."

In March of 1862, however, seeing the ravages the Civil War had brought upon the nation and believing his primary responsibility was to save the Union, Lincoln realized that he had to take action against slavery. Reluctantly, he proposed a plan for the gradual emancipation of slaves, which would begin with the freeing of slaves in those border states that had not seceded from the Union. It would take thirty years to abolish slavery under Lincoln's plan, and, according to his proposals, during that time the federal government would sponsor a colonization program—that is, the government would export the freed slaves to somewhere outside of the country, presumably to Africa.

Throughout early 1862, Susan B. Anthony lectured with all the indignation she could muster against Lincoln's position. She called for immediate and unconditional emancipation, and challenged the question raised by politicians: "But, if you do emancipate the Slaves, what will you do with them?"

> What will the black man do with himself, is a question for him to answer. I am yet to learn that the Saxon man is the great reservoir of human rights to be doled out at his discretion to the nations of the earth. "What will you do with the Negroes?" Do with them precisely what you do with the Irish, the Scotch, and the Germans—Educate them. Welcome them to all the blessings of our free institutions;—to our schools & churches, to every department of industry, trade & art. "Do with the Negroes?" What arrogance in us to put the question, what shall we do with a race of men and women who have fed, clothed and supported both themselves and their oppressors for centuries.[11]

The arrogance of masculine domination made white power crystal clear to her.

The abolitionists who returned to the field continued to press for immediate emancipation. On the other side, the slave-owning border states rejected Lincoln's plan for gradual emancipation. By July 1862 the question of emancipation was coming to a climax, and Anthony was among those who were doing everything in their power to maximize the pressure on the president for immediate emancipation. In a speech she delivered on the Fourth of July in Framingham, Massachusetts, Anthony lashed out against Lincoln and Secretary of State William Seward. "The weak & wicked failures of our fifteen months of war, prove one of two things, either we have no leaders or they are crushed out of place & power by mere slave partisanship." While Lincoln was claiming that the most pressing issue was to save the Union, not to end slavery, Anthony pointed out that he and Seward "have the power to crush utterly, a rotten aristocracy, & draw out the poison of class & caste from our glorious institution. . . . This is not simply a question of national existence, but of the value of man."[12]

The border states refused to accept Lincoln's plan, which forced him into a tougher position against slavery. The Republican-dominated Congress was in advance of his position on slavery. Now some Republicans threatened to form a more radical third party. Finally, prodded by the Republicans and provoked by the abolitionists, unable to accommodate the border states, and at the same time witnessing his country ravaged by the greatest war it had ever faced, Lincoln was forced to radically change his position. Historian Stephen Oates has noted that "by his second inaugural, he had reached an apocalyptic conclusion about the nature of the war—had come to see it as a divine punishment for the 'great offense' of slavery, as a terrible retribution God had visited on a guilty people, in North as well as South."[13]

On July 13, 1862, Lincoln announced to his cabinet his plan to issue the Emancipation Proclamation. The proclamation went into effect on January 1, 1863, and freed all slaves in the rebel states. But he conceded to the border states, allowing them to continue slavery because they had not seceded. For the radicals, the Emancipation Proclamation did not go far enough. They demanded that all slaves be freed and their rights constitutionally guaranteed and protected. Anthony and Stanton decided to put that demand into practical action and for that purpose they organized the Woman's National Loyal League. In early March of 1863 Susan went to stay with Mrs. Stanton, who was by then living in New York City. They spent many weeks together, first writing an appeal to the women of the Republic to demonstrate their loyalty to the nation under war with their own "war of ideas not bullets and bayonets." They called women from across the nation to New York City that May to a convention that would launch this new campaign.

Anthony opened the May convention and nominated Lucy Stone for president. Lucy had decided that since her daughter was now five years old and the war held particular urgency, she would venture back to public work from time to time. Later, when Anthony addressed the assembly, she proposed several resolutions that she had written with Stanton beforehand. The most important resolution urged:

That we heartily approve that part of the President's Proclamation which decrees freedom to the slaves of rebel masters, and we earnestly urge him to devise measures for emancipating all slaves throughout the country.

There never can be a true peace in this Republic until the civil and political rights of all citizens of African descent and all women are practically established.[14]

As a presage of what was to come, the convention hotly debated the last resolution because it included woman's rights. Stone had not lost her old radicalism: "If the right of one single human being is to be disregarded by us, we fail in our loyalty to our country." Anthony insisted that "it is not because women suffer, it is not because slaves suffer, it is not because of any individual rights or wrongs—it is the simple assertion of the great fundamental truth of democracy that was proclaimed by our Revolutionary fathers."[15]

Having launched the Woman's National Loyal League, the convention agreed to commend Lincoln—"By a mere stroke of the pen you have emancipated millions from a condition of wholesale concubinage," and to challenge him—"We now ask you to finish the work by declaring that nowhere under our national flag shall the motherhood of any race plead in vain for justice and protection. So long as one slave breathes in this Republic, we drag the chain with him."[16]

With Anthony as its chief organizer, the Woman's National Loyal League initiated a new petition campaign demanding the complete abolition of slavery. With the goal of one million signatures, Anthony sent out appeals for petitioners and began raising money for the league's operation. She went to every friend, as well as every contact she had previously approached in her woman's rights work, and found that fund raising was an even more difficult task in wartime.

She went off to Brooklyn to make a personal visit to the revered preacher of Plymouth Church, the famous Henry Ward Beecher. Beecher was the brother of Harriet Beecher Stowe and the son of Lyman Beecher, the Congregationalist minister who had dominated New England religion and Calvinist beliefs for the better part of the century. While she was wearily climbing the streets of Columbia Heights, she suddenly felt a hand on her shoulder. She turned and there was Beecher grinning at her. "Well, old girl, what do you want now?" Susan, as always, was direct. "I need money for the work of our League."

"Well," Beecher assured her, "I'll take up a collection in Plymouth church next Sunday." He did, and the contribution advanced the funds of the league by two hundred dollars. When the league closed down in 1865, Susan's meticulous bookkeeping showed a deficit of $4.72, which she supplied to balance the ledger.[17]

In Congress the pressure was building for a Thirteenth Amendment to the Constitution that would abolish all slavery. Under Anthony's direction, within nine months following its first convention the Woman's National Loyal League submitted to Congress petitions with one hundred thousand signatures demanding passage of the amendment that would forbid all slavery. This herculean effort was a major part of abolitionist and Republican pressure on the Senate, which resulted in passage of the amendment; but the House was not persuaded. Lincoln however, having become convinced by this time of the need for such an amendment, "put tremendous pressure on the House to endorse the amendment, using all his powers of persuasion and patronage to get it through."[18]

By August 1864, the Woman's National Loyal League, with five thousand members and two thousand people circulating petitions, had acquired almost four hundred thousand signatures. Finally, on January 31, 1865, the House adopted the amendment forbidding slavery within the borders of the United States.

> Neither slavery nor involuntary servitude, except as a punishment for crime, whereof the party shall have been duly convicted, shall exist in the United States, or any place subject to their jurisdiction.

Having concluded the antislavery work for which it had been created, the Woman's National Loyal League closed its doors.

Throughout 1862 Susan pressed vigorously for emancipation. She was "on the road" during most of the year. Then two months before Lincoln issued the Emancipation Proclamation, she returned home for what she intended to be a short visit. It was early November. The days were becoming chillier, and the air was changing in preparation for another long New York winter. But Susan always found the farm to be a warm, cozy place to return to between long and wearying meetings in front of cold and hostile crowds. This was home to her as much as any place was.

One Sunday morning while she was home, Susan sat with her father reading the *Anti-Slavery Standard* and *The Liberator*. They were speculating on what the probable effects of Lincoln's proclamation would be. Suddenly, Daniel Anthony was stricken with severe stomach pains. He was sixty-nine years old, constitutionally strong, and had not been ill for years. Within a short time his daughters and wife had helped him into bed, where he lay for days in acute pain with an illness described only as "neuralgia of the stomach." He died two weeks later on November 25.

Death was an intimate family affair in the nineteenth century. It was the family and especially the women who prepared the body for burial and arranged the funeral. As shock and grief gripped the Anthony family, Susan took charge of the funeral arrangements. She invited Reverend Samuel May, their long-time abolitionist friend, to conduct the services. Frederick Douglass and other noted abolitionists spoke and paid tribute to Daniel Anthony, who had been a highly respected man in Rochester. But undoubtedly, the tribute to Daniel Anthony was a way to recognize his daughter, who by then was known throughout the abolitionist ranks as one of the most uncompromising and enduring antislavery fighters.

In principle Daniel Anthony had been deeply committed to justice and antislavery, and Susan found his beliefs and views to be a comfort to her and a source of assurance. He supported the antislavery cause but had never worked actively for it. When his family was young, he had compromised his convictions when he did not join the Quaker boycott on slave-picked cotton. Unfortunately, he was not the courageous abolitionist that some recorders of the Anthony family history have identified him as.[19] The success of his early mills relied on slave picked cotton and the unpaid, exhausting labor of his wife. His home had not been a Quaker model of female emancipation.

On the other hand, while Daniel has been historically overrated for his influence on his daughter's reform work, he has not been fully recognized for his contribution to the Anthonys' secure family life. What was truly exceptional about Daniel Anthony was his unswerving commitment to his wife and children. It was a loyalty and devotion that provided his family with an unquestioned and lifelong sense of security.

Daniel Anthony's profound effects on Susan can be found and understood best in the tightly woven and secure family circle that Daniel and Lucy Anthony created for their family. When Susan had settled on her life's course—no matter how strange it was for a woman of her time—her parents supported her. Whether she was viewed as controversial or merely peculiar, or whether she inflamed crowds to anger or was at work campaigning for new laws, her family, and particularly her parents, were behind her in ways that helped to foster in her the deepest personal security. When she went into the world, formed her own convictions, and carried them into action, it was with a self-assurance that was envied by many. Although she had learned to derive her strength from her inner self, her parents' secure and unquestioned devotion was an important springboard to her own personal strengths.

Parker Pillsbury understood this about Susan and knew what her father's death meant to her. He wrote in consolation: "You must be stricken sore indeed in the loss of your constant helper in the great mission to which you are devoted, your counselor, your consoler, your all that man could be, besides the endearing relation of father. What or who can supply the loss?"[20]

Still steeped in grief, within three months of her father's death Susan was at Mrs. Stanton's house in New York for some very intensive months of organizing in preparation for the Woman's National Loyal League. In active work Susan was most fully herself. And so she kept moving while she carried within her deep feelings of loss. Her father's death was often on her mind. She reminisced over talks she had had with her father about her brother Daniel Read, whom the family called D.R. He had been an early settler of Kansas as a member of the antislavery-inspired Emmigrant Aid Company, and later was elected mayor of Leavenworth, Kansas. Now her father's pride in her brother came back to Susan. "Last night when my head was on my pillow, I seemed to be in the old carriage jogging homeward with him, while he happily recounted D.R.'s qualifications for this high post and accepted his election as the triumph of the opposition to rebels and slaveholders."[21]

A frenzy of work with the Woman's National Loyal League did not mitigate Susan's grief. One evening after a long day of work she "strolled west on Forty-fifth street to the Hudson river, a mile or more," and her thoughts lingered over her family, the poignancy of her father's death reviving her childhood memories.

> There was newly sawed lumber there and the smell carried me back, back to the old sawmill and childhood days. I looked at the beautiful river and the schooners with their sails spread to the breeze. I felt alone, but my mind traversed the entire round of the loved ones. I doubt if there be any mortal who clings to loved ones with greater tenacity than do I.[22]

Neither in life nor in death did Susan give up her connection to those she loved. From the time of her father's death, she began to record in her diary the number of days and months, then later the years, since the loss of a particular loved one. She realized once again that she had perhaps taken her mother too much for granted, and told her sister Mary that "I often feel as if we did too little to lighten her heart and cheer her path." Her father's death made her realize that their mother would leave them one day as well.

> And, by and by, when we have to reckon her among the invisible, we shall live in remembrance of her wise counsel, tender watching, self-sacrifice and devotion not second to that we now cherish for memory of our father—nay, it will even transcend that in measure, as a mother's constant and ever-present love and care for her children are beyond those of a father.[23]

"I doubt if there be any mortal who clings to loved ones with greater tenacity than do I" is one of the more revealing statements that Susan B. Anthony has given us. She kept her devotion for her own family circle. Over the years, a few women outside that circle would enter this inner sanctum of committed love for Susan. Certainly Mrs. Stanton had been there for a decade. Susan and Mrs. Stanton created for themselves their own sense of family. Mrs. Stanton's children had become Susan's children also. Mrs. Stanton recalled that when she and Susan were at home together, "we took turns on the domestic watchtowers, directing amusements, settling disputes, protecting the weak against the strong, and trying to secure equal rights to all in the home as well as the nation."[24]

When Susan traveled, she frequently wrote to Mrs. Stanton inquiring about "my children." Once when she was frustrated with Mrs. Stanton's difficulties in getting away from home, Susan wrote her in the midst of an abolitionist campaign: "It is a shame that you can never be released from constant presence at your home— I shall make a contract with the Father of my children to watch & care for them one half the time."[25]

While Susan and Mrs. Stanton were working on the Woman's National Loyal League, Susan met Anna Dickenson, a young woman of twenty who was already a powerful antislavery orator. What distinguished her from many other women abolitionists was that she had taken up the *political* issues of antislavery. As had Anthony in her earlier days, many women still approached slavery from the perspective of a mother or a moral reformer. Anna Dickenson was clearly of that new generation of young women who, because of the groundwork laid by Anthony, Stanton, and the woman's rights movement during the preceding decade, were able to begin their work with the kind of political consciousness it had taken Anthony's generation over a decade to develop. Throughout the Civil War, Dickenson had lectured against slavery and had even addressed the House of Representatives on the question of emancipation. Susan was proud. The first time she heard Anna Dickenson speak, she "felt fully repaid for all the years of odium through which we have passed in order to make it possible for women to speak on the political topics of the day."

Anthony had never reconciled herself to the fact that the women's rights movement had been silenced during the war. Nothing could replace the work of that movement in her life, but certainly the networks of woman's rights advocates and their close relationships with each other were a sustaining force while the movement had been inactive. Anna Dickenson's youthful enthusiasm and personal devotion gave Susan hope. "The sunniest of sunny mornings to you, how are you today?" Anna playfully greeted Susan on one occasion. "Well and happy, I hope. To tell the truth I want to see you very much indeed, to hold your hand in mine, to hear your voice, in a word, I want *you*—I can't have you? Well, I will at least put down a little fragment of my foolish self and send it to look up at you."[26]

Anna's personal enthusiasm held all the more significance for Susan because of her powerful, political oratory. "How many lifelong hopes and prayers I realized as I listened to her eloquence; for whatever any woman does well, I feel that I have done it. Just as any poor negro listening to Douglass loses himself in the pride of race, so do I in womanhood," Susan told Martha Wright.[27] Women had become Susan B. Anthony's *people*. But few could understand the idea of someone's taking womankind as her own *people*. Blacks were a people, but women were married to men. They were not viewed as sharing a common culture, a united condition, or even their own history. How, then, could they be considered a people whose collective rights must be championed and whose freedom must be won? Politically women were united in two ways; first in their informal, personal women's networks, bonds of friendship, love and support, and second as an oppressed class tied to the bonds of marital feudalism. It was in both of these senses that Anthony took woman as her people. In turn, by making the cause of women her life's work, she added to women's own consciousness of their oppression as a class.

In taking women as her people, a dialectical relationship developed between Susan B. Anthony and the woman's movement.

Women's value of themselves as women, a class apart, was signified by Anthony's dedication of her life to them—*a people*. They designated their collective identity in their use of "woman," the singular generic identification of their sex. They created a new collective identity of woman by virtue of their analysis of the concrete conditions of woman's oppression and their vision of her future possibilities. Susan B. Anthony, Elizabeth Cady Stanton and others were the catalysts of this new identity.

Anthony's work was her life and her passion, and it was intensely personal to her. As the years progressed, it is clear that the cause of woman consumed all of her time and energy but rarely drained her. Instead, her worst battles spurred her on to greater confrontations. To some she had become "the evangel of her sex," to others, "the Napoleon of woman's rights." But that she was becoming a legend in her own time was of little concern to her.

It was no longer avoidable: Susan B. Anthony had become a charismatic leader. Max Weber noted that it is in times of political stress and crisis that national leaders with charisma seem to appear. From the clarity of vision they acquire through uncompromised principles, charismatic leaders carve a new way through the turmoil and confusion in times of crisis. Such clarity, or the ability to see through that which confuses everyone else, and fearlessness in standing uncompromised on certain absolute principles are the personal attributes of a charismatic leader. "Charisma knows only inner determination and inner restraint."[28]

Susan B. Anthony may seem like an unlikely candidate for charismatic authority. A woman of common origin without the gifts of grace attendant to the aristocratic class or the cultivated charms of femininity is not the usual description of a charismatic leader. But in her own time, Anthony's commitment to her cause, her firm principles, and her personal strength came to be a source of attraction far beyond admiration from those around her. She compelled people to action and inspired woman after woman to work for the cause. In her energy and drive she seemed almost superhuman, often missing a night's sleep to prepare for a meeting or leaving a city immediately after a six-month campaign to begin a new one the next day in another state.

During the decade of the 1850s, Anthony had been steadfast as she created and followed her own life course. Like most charismatic leaders, she eschewed institutional affiliation and political party ties; she lives "outside the ties of this world, outside of routine of occupation, as well as outside the routine obligations of family life."[29] Her only organizational commitment was to the associations she founded to promote her cause. Susan B. Anthony held no regard for any institution, any law, or any document (including the Constitution) that stood in the way of human liberty. She refused to become involved with any political party, as she eventually learned that they all gave in to "expediency," which always led to a political compromise of means to ends.

It is said that "charisma lives in, but not off, this world." Anthony lived frugally. All the money she raised went to the cause, which included covering her minimal expenses. But when she borrowed or was advanced money from friends for a particular campaign, she returned it as soon as she had covered the campaign expenses. Some wealthy reformers occasionally gave her money for her personal use, but she usually spent it to have tracts printed or to rent a hall.

As a child, Susan had learned to deny "the gratification of every imaginary want." Now she became a kind of ascetic—one who was deeply involved in the world but was not of the world. She dressed simply, sensibly, and loosely. Her attire was usually black, which she had preferred since the days when woman's message was turned to ridicule over the Bloomer. It is characteristic of charismatic leaders whose work is identified with their people to subdue their desire for the personal pleasures of life as their cause, its successes and its failures hold the supreme importance in their lives. The life of Ghandi is an example of this. And it has been noted that leaders who do not indulge in sensual pleasures in their own lives, as Anthony and Ghandi did not, can never be conquered or subdued by them. Indeed, there is little to tempt them away from their commitments.

While Susan was organizing for the Woman's National Loyal League and boarding with Mrs. Stanton "at a reduced price," she stopped at a nearby restaurant for lunch each day. "I take always strawberries with two tea-rusks." From day to day her meals were the same, but once when the waitress had placed a dish of strawberries in front of her, she sighed, "All this lacks is a glass of milk from my mother's cellar." And the waitress suggested, "We have very nice Westchester county milk." Susan smiled and thought, "Tomorrow I shall add that to my bill of fare. My lunch costs, berries, five cents, rusks five, and tomorrow the milk will be three."[30] Personal pleasures took these simple forms, but they never assumed an imperative over her.

Many had waited for Susan to marry and to retire from the field. When she did not, they wondered if she could have a personal, private life. That her work was both her personal and public life and that it involved deep and sustaining relationships was not evident to those who assumed that only in marriage and the privacy of the home could women express the intensity of their feelings and passions.

Continuous traveling put Susan in the company of strangers more frequently than that of her own family and friends. Until she returned home or to Mrs. Stanton, she learned to live without the familiarity of being in the midst of those who knew her well. With her family "so widely separated," she comforted herself with what the spiritualists called "soul communing"—the idea of making mental or emotional contact with deceased loved ones. But Susan tried soul communing with the living. "I almost believe in the power of affection to draw unto itself the yearning heart of the absent one," she told one of her sisters, "I often pass blessed moments in these sweet, silent communings."[31]

In 1865 when a forty-five-year-old Susan B. Anthony visited her brothers and sisters, she found that their children had grown into a new generation of young adults. When her sister Guelma's oldest daughter died suddenly at the age of twenty-three, Susan was deeply grieved. Ann Eliza "had ceased to be a child and had become the fullgrown woman, my companion and friend. I loved her merry laugh, her bright, joyous presence."[32] Susan helped her sister bury Ann Eliza and then wrote to her brother Daniel in Kansas:

This new and sorrowful reminder of the brittleness of life's threads should soften all our expressions to each other in our home circles and open our lips to speak only words of tenderness and approbation. We are so wont to utter criticisms and to keep silence about the things we approve. I wish we might be as faithful in expressing our likes as our dislikes, *and not leave our loved ones to take it for granted that their good acts are noted and appreciated and vastly outnumber those we criticize.* (emphasis added).[33]

But Susan's family still took her for granted. They had not yet discovered that there was another passion in their spinster sister.

With the end of the Civil War Susan went to Kansas to visit her brother D.R., who had become editor of his own newspaper. The trip west, which she began in January 1865, proved to be a rugged adventure for her. She stopped in Chicago to visit her Uncle Dickenson—the uncle she had reprimanded many years before for drinking cider at a Quaker Meeting. Heavy winter storms delayed her departure from Chicago. When she finally found a train, there were no sleeping cars as ice on the tracks had caused several cars to derail. Then in Missouri, the train in front of hers derailed, and the passengers had to wait for hours for the track to be cleared. The cars, which were overcrowded with travelers who had been in them for days, became stuffy. As soon as the train stopped, many of the men got up and went outside to stretch their legs and find a place near the road to wash up and get some coffee. Not a woman in the cars budged. Susan hesitated and finally, refusing to be governed and confined by this unspoken division of the sexes, got up, walked out of the car, and went directly to a woman who lived in a "hovel" near the tracks and was pouring coffee for the men. The rest of the women watched from inside the train while Susan asked, "Would you please be so kind as to sell me a cup of coffee?" After turning on her with a look of disapproval, the woman finally agreed and left to make more coffee. While she waited for fresh coffee to be brewed, Susan washed her face and hands in a trough of clear water. Even to take advantage of these ordinary comforts on the road, Susan was defying womanly tradition an act which probably made her relish her coffee all the more. "Oh, did I enjoy it," she marveled, "brass spoon, thick dingy, cracked cup and all."

She reached Leavenworth a little less for wear. But with rest and long visits with her brother, her energy quickly revived and she began to explore the Kansas frontier. "Had a pleasant stage ride— grand old prairie are perfectly splendid and the timber-skirted creeks are delightful," she noted in her diary.[34] She lectured frequently "on politics, negro equality and temperance."[35] She supported new programs to assist the many freed slaves who had flocked to Kansas after the Emancipation Proclamation. And she was deeply disturbed by the Indian wars. "It is cruel as death to retain that old 7th Kansas Regiment to go out to the Plains to fight Indians & the boys feel very much wronged," she noted in another diary entry.[36]

After a few months, her friends in the East began to write entreating her to return, and she missed them. She particularly missed Mrs. Stanton, with whom she had lived during most of the preceding year. "Dear-a-me," she wrote, "how over-full I am, and how I should like to be nestled into some corner away from every chick and child, with you once more. My soul longs to go out to do battle for the Lord once more. Do write me often."[37]

And Mrs. Stanton did write!

I hope in a short time to be comfortably in a new house where we will have a room ready for you when you come East. I long to put my arms around you once more and hear you scold me for my sins and short-comings. Your abuse is sweeter to me than anybody else's praise for, in spite of your severity, your faith and confidence shine through all. O, Susan, you are very dear to me. I should miss you more than any other living being from this earth. You are intertwined with much of my happy and eventful past, and all my future plans are based on you as a coadjutor. Yes, our work is one, we are one in aim and sympathy and we should be together.[38]

Susan received several such missives and entreaties from her friend. Their love for each other was not new, and after ten years their expression of it was as alive and vital as ever. Nevertheless, Susan did not return east for several more months, and when she did it was because a political crisis and not the longing for a loved one, called her back. To return and live with Mrs. Stanton without a definite plan of work would have been to live in and with Mrs. Stanton's marriage. It would not be like sharing the undivided attention of one's beloved, for Mrs. Stanton was still married and living with Mr. Stanton. At least with a project there was a concrete reason to be there; they would have something that focused them on each other. And by this time, Mrs. Stanton had found that her commitments to her husband and children were what she could use to keep Susan's pressing demands on her in check; yet at the same time, Mrs. Stanton could not live without her Susan. Years before Susan seems to have reconciled herself to the divisions that marital loyalty had created between them, as she also had come to terms with her sisters' shifts in loyalty. Mrs. Stanton's marriage limited what their emotional relationship could have been, and Susan knew this and acted from it. Being single Susan never had to anchor her identity in another or shift her identity from herself and away from women in her life. The single woman, unlike the dependent old maid, could keep an unbroken woman's identity. Perhaps this was one of the reasons why she decided to remain in Kansas, despite Mrs. Stanton's loving appeals for her to return.

Susan had been in Kansas almost eight months with no definite plans to return east when one morning, in early August of 1865, she picked up a newspaper in her brother's office and read that a new amendment to the Constitution had been proposed to the House of Representatives. The amendment defined citizens as "all persons born or naturalized in the United States and subject to the jurisdiction thereof" and extended due process and equality of protection to them.

> No State shall make or enforce any law which shall abridge the privileges or immunities of citizens of the United States; nor shall any State deprive any person of life, liberty, or property, without due process of law, nor deny to any person within its jursidiction the equal protection of the laws.

Section 2 of the proposed Fourteenth Amendment also reduced the representation of any state in the United States Congress if any males over the age of twenty-one were denied the right to vote. Stunned and angered, Anthony saw that this amendment would grant due process, extend equal protection, define citizenship, and grant the right to vote only to *male* citizens. In addition, the amendment did not explicitly grant suffrage, which outraged abolitionists like Wendell Phillips. To deliberately exclude women from both the protection of citizenship and the right to vote, the Republicans wrote the word "male" three times into the amendment. The designation of sex had never before appeared in the Constitution. Over thirty years earlier, in 1832, the English government had effectively disfranchised women by writing the world "male" into a reform bill that expanded suffrage. By the mid-1860s, the United States Congress was willing to expand the meaning of "persons" to include corporations and to narrow its meaning to "male" in order to exclude women. In 1882, Roscoe Conkling, a member of the congressional committee that authored the Fourteenth Amendment, argued the amendment before the Supreme Court. Using documents from the 1866 congressional committee, he argued that the committee had intentionally used the word "persons" in other phrases of the amendment in order to include corporations among those granted due process and equal protection. He explained to the Court that when the representatives were framing the amendment, corporations were appealing to Congress for protection from discriminating state taxes.[39] "Person" was intended to mean males of every class and race and even to mean Corporations. In the Fourteenth Amendment it was not meant to mean woman.

Susan put down the newspaper, returned to her brother's house, and began to pack for her trip east. Her mind raced with plans to address this catastrophe. Mrs. Stanton wrote with urgency:

> I have argued constantly with Phillips and the whole fraternity, but I fear one and all will favor enfranchising the negro without us. Wom-

an's cause is in deep water. With the League disbanded, there is pressing need of our Woman's Rights Convention. Come back and help.
There will be a room for you. I seem to stand alone.[40]

Anthony returned to the East immediately and after a brief stop
in Rochester headed straight to New York for a strategy meeting
with Mrs. Stanton. On the way, she visited Martha Wright, who
was pessimistic about being able to revive their woman's movement
at that moment, for she believed that the weight of opinion seemed
so much against them. But Anthony trudged on to the homes of
every possible woman's rights leader in New York, New Jersey, and
New England to raise their interest for new campaigns.

By Christmas, she was back in New York with Mrs. Stanton and
reported that it was not going to be easy to resurrect the woman's
rights movement. As they talked, with Susan sometimes pacing the
floor, their indignation rose. All their strenuous campaigns of the
1850s seemed to evaporate before them: They had lost most of the
married woman's property rights they had won in 1860; the abolitionists had successfully diverted them from promoting their most
radical analysis of marriage and from their demand for divorce; and
their movement had been silenced during the Civil War years. Now
the abolitionists acting in concert with the radical Republicans (whose
representatives in Congress were pushing for passage of the most
advanced legislation to protect blacks and enforce reconstruction as
a punishment to the South), were trying to deny women the fundamental protection of citizenship.

Mrs. Stanton described the new and escalating dissension in the
ranks of the American Anti-Slavery Society to Susan. At the end of
the Civil War, Garrison believed that because the Anti-Slavery Society had met its goal of unconditional and immediate emancipation
there was no need for the society to continue. In opposition, Phillips
argued that emancipation was not enough protection for the freed
slaves, and that there would be no real freedom "unless the negro
has the ballot and the States are prohibited from enacting laws making any distinction among their citizens on account of race or color."[41]
This was the "Negro's hour," proclaimed Phillips along with other
abolitionists and the Republicans.

At the May 1865 meeting of the Anti-Slavery Society, Garrison
declined reelection as president, and Phillips was elected. Garrison
made it known then, even before the Republican Congress had
brought forward the proposed Fourteenth Admendment, that, as he

told Elizabeth Cady Stanton, "I am now engaged in abolishing slavery in a land where abolition of slavery means conferring or recognizing citizenship, and where citizenship supposes the ballot for all men."

Stanton indignantly fired back, "Do you believe the African race is composed entirely of males?"[42] She challenged Phillips "on the apparent opposition in which you place the negro and woman." Garrison and Phillips's influence in Boston made it very difficult for woman's rights advocates there to go against the men, but they could not stifle Anthony and Stanton's determination to force the Republicans to strike the word "male" from the Fourteenth Amendment.

The Republican party proved to be a formidable opponent of woman's rights. After Lincoln's assassination, the Republicans gained control of Congress. The bungling President Andrew Johnson, Lincoln's pro-southern successor, was, as historian Kenneth Stampp pointed out, a man of "tactless, uncompromising, and violent behavior, and the southern politicians' indifference to northern public opinion, eventually forced moderates into an alliance with the radicals."[43] The Republican alliance against Johnson enabled Congress to vigorously pursue a suffrage amendment for black men after the Fourteenth Amendment was approved. The radical Republicans had bitterly opposed the plan introduced by Lincoln before his assassination in April 1865, in which he proposed limited suffrage for some blacks only—"the very intelligent, and especially those who have fought gallantly in our ranks."[44] With his assassination, the Republicans seized the moment and pushed for full suffrage for all black men. At the same time, they aggresssively instituted a punitive reconstruction program to finally break the economic hold of the southern plantation aristocracy.

In fact, the Republicans were as self-serving as they were noble in championing of blacks' rights and protections. Many of them represented northern industrial capitalists, and they were determined to use reconstruction to break the economic power of the South. It is evident that granting suffrage to black men meant more than political protection to the Republicans. They believed that suffrage would enable blacks to leave the plantations, where many were still very dependent, and that with new reconstruction programs the former black slaves could become free workers, "able to respond to the rational demands of the marketplace."[45]

In fact, the Republicans were courting a new potential class of voters.[46] With another constitutional amendment explicitly granting black men the right to vote, they knew that their antislavery sympathies and their new reconstruction policies would bring that bloc of votes into their camp. Women, however, might not be such a political asset if they had the vote. Politicians worried that because women had been excluded from political affairs for so long, they might tend to vote as their husbands did. The home was woman's sphere; if she became a voter, it might be as a conservative to protect her interests there.

It was only over many months that the power and intent of the radical Republicans became clear to Anthony and Stanton. Moreover, the abolitionist alliance with the Republican agenda for the Fourteenth Amendment began to shift the position of the Anti-slavery Society away from universal rights, which included universal suffrage, to a restricted commitment to male citizens.

In the study of women's history, the question that has persisted is: Why was suffrage so important to these women? One can feel their indignation and the betrayal they experienced, but for many that has not been sufficient to explain the extent of their reaction to the Fourteenth Amendment and subsequent amendments that extended the full rights and protections of citizenship to blacks. Late-twentieth-century thinkers, who presume suffrage as a granted right, do not tend to empathize with the urgency it held for Stanton and Anthony—even though historians have generally accepted suffrage to have been a necessity for black men during this period.

But in the second half of the nineteenth century, suffrage was one of the most salient political rights of the times. It was considered an ultimate *protection* of citizens. As Senator Charles Sumner told Congress:

> The ballot is like charity, which never faileth, and without which man is only as sounding brass or a tinkling cymbal. The ballot is the one thing needful, without which rights of testimony and all other rights will be no better than cobwebs, which the master will break through with impunity. To him who has the ballot all other things shall be given-protection, opportunity, education, a homestead.[47]

If by the end of the Civil War being admitted to suffrage was tantamount to being granted the full protection of citizenship, it is not surprising that women insisted on its purported protections and privileges for themselves. As Anthony argued "Disfranchisement *in a republic* is as great an anomaly, if not cruelty, as slavery itself."[48]

There was another reason why Anthony and Stanton felt so keenly the sting that came when the word "male" was introduced into the Constitution. Until the Civil War, the Declaration of Independence was the governing document of social movements. Its emphasis on liberty and personal rights provided the antislavery and woman's rights causes with validation of their claims. But the Civil War brought the United States Constitution to the center of public attention. The secession of the southern states created major questions of constitutionality. With national unity more seriously threatened than ever before, Lincoln raised the meaning of the Constitution to the importance of a religious creed. In his campaigns for national identity, he called for a "political religion of the nation."

As the war progressed, the need for change in this less-than-perfect document became part of the pledge to sustain it. Only a constitutional amendment to eliminate slavery could save the Union. Along with his compelling campaigns for national unity, which centered around the Constitution, Lincoln envisioned his country as a national family into which he was willing—through suffrage—to admit some loyal blacks after the war. But Republicans and abolitionists wanted more; they wanted to open up the national family to all blacks.

The struggle for suffrage for the black man was recognized as necessary to win an essential constitutional protection. Black women, still the most oppressed and therefore vulnerable group in the society, were excluded. Further, black women's identification with the struggle of blacks now effectively separated them from the woman's rights movement by virtue of the white male campaign for the "Negro's Hour." Black women, still without the social space to militate on their own behalf, would not find the opportunity to raise their own demands for woman's rights for many years. It was in this context that white women's continued demand for their rights was perceived by abolitionists as a contemptible act—an interpretation that has been reaffirmed in the writing of the history of that era. In defiant response, Anthony and Stanton insisted that the protection women could derive from suffrage would enable them politically to win other long overdue rights. Suffrage would put them on equal ground with men of their class. They correctly believed that if they had the vote, it would enable them to radically change the condition of women.

"The real fact is that we have so long held woman's claims in abeyance to the Negro's that to name them now is received as impertinence," Anthony told the well-known writer Caroline Dall.

Anthony felt an infantilizing of women embedded in the instructions they received from the radical white men, who counseled them to sit back and not stand in the way of full male enfranchisement. She sent off a package of petitions to Dall, who always kept her distance from Anthony so as not to be associated with radical ideas. "I hope the petitions will not shock your good taste. . . . You will see the petition assumes that Congress will move to amend the constitution to prohibit Negro disfranchisement and then to admit woman is to give universal suffrage. To me the broad ground of republicanism is the one true place for all advanced minds to occupy."[49]

In an attempt to accommodate both the women and Phillips, in December 1865 Theodore Tilton proposed the formation of a National Equal Rights Society with Phillips as president. Still hoping to keep their platform of universal rights and suffrage, Anthony agreed with the plan and decided to propose consolidation of the Anti-Slavery Society and the woman's rights societies organized in different states. Unaware of its dangers, she and Stanton entered into the political minefield of coalition politics.

Forming coalitions and bringing different movements together can be effective political strategy, if each of those movements has the same status and access to political power relative to the others in the world of reform. But those groups that hold the lowest status in society are also the most vulnerable among political and reform movements. They are the ones most likely to be co-opted to the purposes and goals of the others. The woman's rights movement, while tolerated and sometimes even supported by other political movements, actually had the same status in the reform movement— as did women in the society as a whole. They were viewed as the easiest to sacrifice for expediency, and their demands, while granted a grain of seriousness, were not considered very important, and certainly not paramount. To have agreed to enter into coalition politics under these conditions was to court political suicide. But neither Anthony nor Stanton could see at this point the actual stature they held in the men's eyes; nor were they politically experienced enough to recognize the risks. Further, by now what was obscured was the fact that the campaign against suffrage for women stemmed from a reaction against the radical women's demand for divorce and reformulation of the marriage contract. Yet, the questions remain: To what extent did the white male politicians merely use the convenient issue of black suffrage as a foil for their deep concern to prevent a challenge to the rights and power of men in marriage? Did they strategically force an opposition between blacks and women in order to discredit the woman's movement for their own purposes?

To promote her plan to campaign for universal suffrage and Tilton's proposal to form a National Equal Rights Society, Anthony scheduled the Eleventh National Woman's Rights Convention (the first since 1860), which was to be held a week after the anti-slavery convention in New York City in May 1866. She and Stanton appealed to women to militate against the Fourteenth Amendment, which they described as "the proposed class legislation in Congress" that would "deny that 'necessity of citizenship' to woman." To be sure there was no uncertainty about their aims, they declared their radical intention: "To build a true republic, the church and the home must undergo the same upheaving we now see in the State."[50]

At the anti-slavery convention, with the weight of the presidency of the Anti-Slavery Society now behind him, Phillips defeated Anthony's proposal for consolidation of the two societies into a National Equal Rights Society. Phillips's having killed the plan for the new organization could not deter Anthony from introducing at the Woman's Rights Convention the following week another resolution to unite the antislavery and woman's rights movements into another association. She argued that "all associations based on special claims for special classes are too narrow and partial for the hour" and urged that in the spirit of coalition, "All we, assembled in our Eleventh National Woman's Rights Convention, bury the woman in the citizen, and our organization in that of the American Equal Rights Association."[51] The convention passed the new resolution to consolidate then adopted several more resolutions that identified the work of the new association. It was concluded with the launching of new petition drives.

The women's relationship with the American Anti-Slavery Society, now headed by Phillips, was further strained as he pursued his "Negro's-Hour" agenda. "The gate is shut, wholly," Anthony declared a few months later when Gerrit Smith and Phillips refused to print a letter from Stanton in the *Anti-Slavery Standard*. Mockingly she chided, "It ain't as it used to was." She had believed that they were all part of the same movement, but she was disappointed by the narrowness of the men's agenda. "Time was when we professed to have a free platform but surely those proud days are not now. I am sorry that the good old ship has thus anchored in the harbor of non-intervention."[52] Resentment was growing rapidly to any challenge made by women to the Fourteenth-Amendment strategy.

While Anthony and Stanton worked on the formation of the American Equal Rights Association, they were making plans to address their concerns to the constitutional convention called to amend the New York Constitution. At a time when the forces were mounting against them, Lucretia Mott sent a fifty-dollar donation and wrote to Susan:

> We cordially hail the movement at this time for your state, in view of the approaching revision of your Constitution. The negro's hour came with his emancipation by law, from cruel bondage. He now has Advocates not a few for his right to the ballot. Intelligent as these advocates are, they must see that this right cannot be consistently withheld from woman.[53]

One day when a small group of the major reformers was gathered in the office of the American Equal Rights Society preparing for the New York Constitutional Convention, Wendell Phillips proposed that "now the time is ripe to demand that the word white be struck from the New York State Constitution." Tilton agreed and the men began to discuss Phillips's plan. They decided that Anthony and Stanton should be the ones to canvass and petition the entire state to remove the word "white"—but not the word "male"—from the Constitution, in order to win full male suffrage. Of course, Tilton and Phillips assumed that Anthony would take charge of this plan.

The women stood there silently listening while the men presented their plan. The puzzle for both women was Tilton, who had solidly backed Stanton and Anthony until now when he proposed that they continue to support woman's suffrage as an "intellectual theory." Stanton seemed to be dazzled by Phillips and Tilton's rhetoric, and appeared to be going along with them. Anthony was indignant and declared, "I would sooner cut off my right hand than ask the ballot for the black man and not for woman," spelling out the full, and until then unstated, implication of the men's proposal. Then she turned on her heel and marched out of the office. As she went out the door she overheard Tilton say "What does ail Susan? She acts like one possessed," and Mrs. Stanton responded, "I cannot imagine; I never before saw her so unreasonable and absolutely rude."

Susan knew that Mrs. Stanton would not intentionally betray her; in fact, Mrs. Stanton was genuinely confused. By the time she reached home she knew that the problem was not with Susan. But in the moment, when male eloquence camouflaged the underlying motivations in proposals such as the one made by Phillips, even a powerful mind such as Mrs. Stanton's was caught in an unanticipated confusion.

As soon as her afternoon meeting concluded, Susan went directly to Mrs. Stanton's and found her friend in deep anxiety. She was pacing back and forth in her parlor, wringing her hands. They embraced. "I never was so glad to see you," Mrs. Stanton exclaimed, still very confused with Susan's behavior that afternoon. "Do tell me what is the matter with me? I feel as if I had been scourged from the crown of my head to the soles of me feet!"[54] Throughout most of that evening, they sat in the parlor and talked over the afternoon's events. As they examined all the surprises, all the unanticipated letdowns, all the strange turns of events against them, they realized that they had few allies any longer. And they talked with each other about how, if necessary, they must stand alone and fight together for their beliefs and their sex.

Letters began to pour in from all over the country condemning them for their position; but they could not be intimidated. Indignation sprang from their belief that not only they, but womankind—their people—had been grievously wronged. Stanton responded in this spirit to one hostile letter they received.

> With three bills before Congress to exclude us from all hope of representation in the future, I thank God that *two* women of the nation felt the insult and decided to rouse the rest to use the only right we have in the government—the right of petition. If the petition goes with our names alone, ours be the glory, and the disgrace to all the rest! . . . When your granddaughters hear that against such insults you made no protest, they will blush for their ancestry.[55]

7

The Male Betrayal

There is a great stir about colored men getting their rights, but not a word about the colored women; and if colored men get their rights, and not colored women theirs, you see the colored men will be masters over the women, and it will be just as bad as it was before. . . . I suppose I am about the only colored woman that goes about to speak for the rights of the colored women. I want to keep the thing stirring, now that the ice is cracked. . . . I don't want to take up time, but I calculate to live. Now if you want me to get out of the world, you had better get the women votin' soon.[1]

Sojourner Truth

SUSAN B. ANTHONY INTRODUCED SOJOURNER TRUTH TO THE American Equal Rights Association at its first anniversary meeting in May of 1867 by reminding the audience that this eighty-year-old veteran had been a slave in New York State for forty years. "She is not a product of the barbarism of South Carolina," Anthony told the audience, "but of the barbarism of New York, and one of her fingers was chopped off by her cruel master in a moment of anger."[2]

While the American Equal Rights Association was meeting in New York, Lucy Stone and her husband, Henry Blackwell, were in Kansas beginning one of the toughest and ugliest campaigns yet waged for woman's suffrage. In early March Anthony had received an urgent appeal from Samuel N. Wood, the Republican senator from Kansas, to send her strongest speakers to stomp the state for woman's suffrage. The Kansas legislature had just submitted amendments for woman's and Negro suffrage to the people. Anthony and Stanton, busy preparing for the forthcoming New York State Constitutional Convention where they would vigorously campaign to have the word "male" struck from the state constitution, could not leave New York before July. They lost the battle to strike the word "male" from the Fourteenth Amendment when it was adopted in 1868. Undaunted, they left immediately for Kansas in July, 1868.

In March when Senator Wood first contacted her, Anthony turned to Lucy Stone and appealed to her to come out of retirement. Although their relations had been tense in the past and although Stone had been away from movement work for several years, Anthony and Stanton coaxed her back to work. She had returned to the public platform for a brief time during the war to support the Woman's National Loyal League. But she was still hesitant and somewhat reluctant to re-enter public work. Finally she agreed to go to Kansas and her husband, Henry Blackwell, decided to join her.

When they began to organize for Kansas, Stone and Anthony decided that Stone should use the money left in the fund Francis Jackson had created for the woman's rights movement several years earlier. Immediately, Wendell Phillips, as third party to the fund and vigilant in his determination to thwart the woman's rights movement, moved to block their use of it. Lucy Stone and Susan B. Anthony outvoted him and appropriated fifteen hundred dollars for Stone's work in Kansas. Unfortunately, Stone's campaign depleted the fund, as Anthony discovered when she began to figure the expenses for her trip with Mrs. Stanton to Kansas that summer. As a result, she had to turn to the American Equal Rights Association for support and went to Kansas as its general agent. Phillips would not forget that these strong-minded women had prevailed over him on the question of money. In a matter of months, he would contrive reasons to accuse Anthony of mismanagement of funds in the Kansas campaign in order to discredit her woman's suffrage work.

In Kansas, Stone rediscovered her old anger at "woman's wrongs" and liberal men's benevolent control of women. She wrote Anthony questioning whether Phillips had supported them through the convention of the American Equal Rights Association. When she found he had not, she told Anthony that as for men who supported woman's suffrage, "If they volunteer, very well, but I have been for the last time on my knees to Phillips, Higginson or any of them." With determined assurance she added, "If they help now, they should ask us and not we them."[3]

Lucy reported that all of Republican Kansas seemed to be turning against woman's suffrage, and that even Susan's brother, Daniel R.

Anthony, had personally defected from woman's suffrage although his paper *The Leaveworth Bulletin* did support it. For some months the Republicans remained undecided about woman's suffrage. When faced with an actual decision, the Kansas Republican party followed the position of the national Republican party on woman's suffrage and called a meeting for the purpose of eliminating from the Kansas Republican platform the amendment to enfranchise women.[4] Before she left Kansas, Lucy warned Susan that "the negroes are all against us," presumably having been convinced by Republicans that to support woman's suffrage would weaken the case for black male suffrage in the state.

A few Republicans continued to support woman's suffrage. In May Henry Blackwell wrote assuring their friends in the East that Senator Samuel Wood was on their side and more. "We owe everything to Wood, and he is really a thoroughly noble, good fellow, and a hero." He described Wood as "a short, rather thick set, somewhat awkward, and slouchy man, extremely careless in his dress, blunt and abrupt in his manner, with a queer inexpressive face, little blue eyes which can look dull or flash fire or twinkle with the wickedest fun. He is so witty, sarcastic, and cutting, that he is a terrible foe, and will put the laugh even on his best friends."[5] Blackwell's introduction of his friend Wood to their friends in the East established Wood as the person through whom the campaign for woman's suffrage would be coordinated.

Blackwell was actually working behind the scenes with Wood, contriving a plan to bring a flamboyant and anti-Negro Democrat, George Francis Train, to Kansas to champion the woman's cause with Susan B. Anthony. Wood and Blackwell had decided that Train would attract attention and Democratic votes to their cause, which they desperately needed to boost their losing battle. And they decided that tough and uncompromising Anthony would be just the person to campaign with Train and to keep him in line and control his anti-Republican, anti-black rhetoric.

Anthony knew nothing of this strategy. While it was being planned in Kansas, she and Stanton were strategizing against another self-proclaimed Republican opponent of woman's suffrage, the powerful editor of the *New York Tribune,* Horace Greeley, who was a key figure at the New York State Constitutional Convention. Politically, Greeley was the quintessential liberal. Even if he did champion such controversial issues as antislavery, he managed not to have the onerous burden of raising reformist demands before their time, when they were unpopular, nor was he seen backsliding on essential liberties. He helped elect Lincoln to the presidency and then persisted in pressuring him to emancipate the slaves, while he consistently attacked the Garrisonian abolitionists for being too radical. Although he was highly opinionated and he was idiosyncratic in his behavior, he usually was on the right side of an issue.

Greeley was chief of the nation's most influential paper and was also one of the best writers and editors, taking positions and writing in a tone that ranged from "quiet, conversational to loud, militant, oratorical." He had the reputation of being personally disagreeable and difficult. He had few friends, was reputed to alienate his editors and printers, and was particularly known for misjudging people and engaging in petty animosities.[6] During the first years of the reconstruction era, by which time Greeley had made peace with the abolitionists, he championed the demand for "universal suffrage and universal amnesty," which included women. But as Anthony and Stanton recalled later, he would not break ranks from the Republicans and abolitionists for long, because "a few cracks of the party whip brought him into line."[7] Soon he became an ardent opponent of woman's rights. And once he decided to strike out against the militant women, he did so with a vengeance. Anthony and Stanton, who soon tired of Greeley's hackneyed expression "the best women I know do not want to vote," had their plans too.

Anthony initiated another massive petition campaign to remove the word "male" from the New York Constitution and traveled the state, as she put it, "like the flying of the shuttle in the loom of the weaver."[8] One of her visits was to Mrs. Horace Greeley, a supporter of woman's suffrage. She agreed to help.

On June 27, 1867, the galleries of the constitutional convention were full in anticipation of Greeley's expected negative report on woman's suffrage. But first Stanton spoke. Neither she nor Anthony could take an official part in the proceedings, not even to present their petitions. So they chose the prominent man-of-letters George William Curtis to speak for them. Just before Greeley was introduced, Curtis rose and asked for the attention of the assembly. "Mr. President, I hold in my hand a petition from Mrs. Horace Greeley and three hundred other women citizens of Westchester, asking that the word 'male' be stricken from the Constitution."[9] Greeley was shaken. The women had taken the moment, and everyone present knew it!

Greeley later confronted Anthony and Stanton. "You two ladies are the most maneuvering politicians in the State of New York. You set out to annoy me in the Constitutional Convention and you did it effectually. I saw in the manner my wife's petition was presented, that Mr. Curtis was acting under instructions. I saw the reporters prick up their ears and knew that my report and Mrs. Greeley's petition would come out together, with large headings in the city papers, and probably be called out by the newsboys in the street."[10] Greeley's relationship with his wife had not been a good one since the beginning of their marriage. He was an ill-tempered man, who was an undoubtedly a difficult husband. One can only imagine the state of their marital affairs after his wife's petitions reached the constitutional convention.

Greeley went before the constitutional convention with no little anger. As rumored, his report came out for *manhood* suffrage. In addition to rejecting the women's platform for universal suffrage, Greeley's report also included one clause that stung the women in particular: "That idiots, lunatics, persons under guardianship, felons, and persons convicted of bribery, unless pardoned or otherwise restored to civil rights, shall not be entitled to vote."[11] If his report were adopted, all women would be classified *de facto* with lunatics and criminals as a class that should be excluded from suffrage. They were indignant. How much more insult, indignation, and humiliation would their former male allies heap upon the female sex? They knew that the men were closing ranks, and that they were being forced to either submit or fully proclaim their determination to fight it out for their sex. Then came the next blow. On July 25, 1867, the amendment to strike the word "male" from the Constitution went down to defeat, with 125 men opposing it to only 19 in support.

There was no time to dwell over this defeat. Urgent reports from Kansas indicated that Lucy Stone was besieged with mounting Republican opposition to woman's suffrage. Immediately after the constitutional convention, Anthony and Stanton prepared to leave for Kansas, as there was still the possibility of winning suffrage there when it came up for popular vote in November.

Meanwhile, Lucy Stone and her husband had returned east at the end of May, 1867 in time for Stone to testify before the constitutional convention. While she was in New York, she had long meetings with Anthony and Stanton briefing them on the problems and strategies in Kansas. Senator Wood was waiting for their arrival,

Blackwell told them, and Wood had laid out plans for their campaign that would take them through to the November election. At the moment the odds were against woman's suffrage, but Stone was enthusiastic. Although the response to the campaign from Republican party politicians had not been favorable, she had had large audiences and the response from the people in villages and cities had been positive.

Anthony and Stanton arrived in Kansas and began their work in early September. The state Republican party had met, agreed to find the "best method for defeating the proposition to strike the word 'male' from the Constitution of Kansas," and formed an Anti-Female Suffrage Committee.[12] Republican opposition was solidified, the women had to look elsewhere for support.

Then, as the *History of Woman Suffrage* recalls, "at this auspicious moment," when Anthony and Stanton were deciding they would have to appeal to the Democratic vote if there were to be any hope for woman's suffrage, a telegram came from George Francis Train. He was nearby in Omaha and ready to come to Kansas if they wanted him. He said he had been invited by the secretary and other members of the St. Louis Suffrage Association to go to Kansas and help in the woman's campaign.[13] As Anthony did not know Train, she polled the woman's suffrage committee. They all agreed that they should accept his offer and telegramed him to "come to Kansas."

George Francis Train was an eccentric, wealthy Democrat who was an entertaining and powerfully convincing speaker. Although he was a Democrat, he was associated with so many diverse causes that it was difficult to identify him with any one political orientation. As a Fenian he was steeped in the Irish rebellions against England, for which he was imprisoned more than once in England. Attractive, controversial, and capable of dramatic flair, he commanded large audiences, particularly of Irish immigrants and other members of the working classes whose rights he often championed. He was uncompromising in his support for woman's suffrage and was a self-proclaimed candidate for the presidency of the United States. The Republicans hated him for his "copperhead" position on the money question and even more for his anti-Negro attitudes.

According to the plan devised by Senator Wood, Stanton left for her tour of the state with ex-Governor Robinson, another one of the few male supporters of woman's suffrage in Kansas. When Anthony learned that Train was soon to arrive and accompany her, she organized an itinerary for them that followed her usual canvassing strategy: to saturate the state by speaking in all possible towns, villages, and watering holes not covered by Stanton, regardless of whether they were Democratic or Republican strongholds. By traveling through the state separately, Anthony and Stanton would cover all of Kansas with their suffrage demand before the elections on November 6. They knew that woman's rights issues, such as married woman's property rights and suffrage, were not essentially partisan issues, although one party or the other might try to use them to their own advantage. From their standpoint, it was men who had to vote to grant women their rights, as it was men as a class—not as members of one particular party—that had withheld those rights from women.

Anthony arranged meetings for Train and herself. Because woman's suffrage was not a partisan issue she paid no attention to the fact that she had scheduled Train (one of the most controversial Democrats) to speak in Republican strongholds. Train spoke only on woman's suffrage, but his reputation as a Democrat preceded him. The results were catastrophic. They met hostile rebuffs from Republicans at every turn. Had Anthony scheduled the meetings for Train along the railroad, where the working-class Irish and pro-Fenians were to be found, Train's presence in the women's campaign, while problematic because of his known proslavery attitudes, would have had less of an impact. He undoubtedly would have been more effective in drawing in the votes. Despite those problems, when Henry Blackwell returned to Kansas in late October, he told his wife that "had not Mrs. S and Susan come out & Olympia Brown made the most heroic and persevering fight ever known, it would have been a complete fizzle." And then he admitted, "As it is we are beat."

At first glance it may seem strange that Anthony, who was recognized by both woman's rights and antislavery workers as the most effective and strategic organizer in the field, should make such costly blunders and demonstrate such ineptness by taking Train into the most hostile, anti-Democratic parts of the state. What she did not know then was that by doing so she ran counter to the admittedly risky Blackwell-Wood plan to use a controversial Democrat to campaign for woman's suffrage.

Yet, there are other questions lurking unanswered behind the by now infamous Anthony-Train association. The questions are provoked not so much by Train as by the severity with which the Republicans and abolitionists repudiated Anthony when she returned

£ast after the Kansas campaign. Something else must have been at play in this political minefield. In closely examining the details preceding Train's appearance in Kansas, the underlying question that until now has never been asked is: Why and how did Train appear at this "auspicious moment." Anthony had neither invited nor expected him; his appearance was a complete surprise to her.

For the first time, it is possible to answer this question. Because of the discovery of some old correspondence that has remained hidden away for over a century in an attic of an old Beecher family home in Hartford, Connecticut, I was able to unravel the full story. Among the papers now held by the Stowe-Day Foundation, I found letters from Isabella Beecher Hooker revealing that Henry Blackwell had made a secret plan with Senator Wood to use Train in Kansas that spring. Hooker, a newcomer to the woman's rights movement in 1867 and someone determined to find the answers to these same questions, learned from Blackwell that his plan had backfired. The discovery of the Beecher letters made it possible for me to interpret and explain the contradictory accounts of this important controversy in the history of woman's suffrage. Blackwell's account of what happened contradicted the version in Anthony's biography, which itself does not agree with the account in *The History of Woman Suffrage* edited by Stanton and Anthony. We are now able to unravel what happened when Blackwell returned to the East. As he faced possible exposure for his complicity in bringing Train to Kansas when the plan backfired, he and Stone blamed the entire association of Train with the woman's movement on Anthony. Then he joined with the abolitionists and Republicans when they resoundingly condemned her. In this context, it also has become evident that at least part of Blackwell's motivation was personal. He wanted to set his wife, Lucy Stone, against Anthony and Stanton. In fact, Stone did sever her friendship with them. But Blackwell and the Republicans' motivations were not merely personal. With this plan, they forged the most damaging split of the century in the women's movement. But this split had really begun in 1860 when Stanton introduced woman's right to divorce as part of the woman's movement platform.

The actual split did not occur until two years after the Kansas campaign. By that time the Anthony-Train association became a national controversy. Isabella Beecher Hooker decided to find out for herself the real story behind the antagonism between Lucy Stone and Susan B. Anthony. Because she was of the prominent Beecher family, various parties to the story were willing to tell her their side as the Beechers' favor was constantly being courted in reform circles.

The most revealing information came from Isabella Beecher Hooker's interview with Henry Blackwell in December of 1870. Hooker subsequently reported her account in complete confidence to her friend Susan Howard, who kept Hooker's confidence. Hooker also wrote a note to Henry Blackwell, telling him that "our talk was not only confidential, but useful," and that she felt "fully possessed now of both sides & certainly shall make no ill use of any confidence bestowed by either." And she kept her word. It is now more than a century later that her confidential knowledge of the controversy can become known through the discovery of these letters.

Here is Isabella Beecher Hooker's report of her conversation with Henry Blackwell.

> [Lucy Stone's] husband told me in the course of a long conversation on the "differences"—that Mr. Train went to Kansas on the invitation of one Wood, a republican, to lecture to whomever would hear on Woman Suffrage among other things . . . Mr. Blackwell & Gov. Robinson & two or three others who were conducting the W.S. campaign thought it might be well for Susan to accompany Train & so get democratic votes—while at the same time she could perhaps keep him straight on the negro question—Train being there against negro suffrage. *They accordingly advised & promoted her Kansas trips with Train* and she went as General Agent of the Equal Rights Association & with their full approval on that whole Kansas campaign.

By the time she interviewed Blackwell, Hooker knew of the story spread by the abolitionists that blamed the entire association of Train with the woman's rights movement on Anthony. Therefore, Mrs. Hooker was stunned when she heard Blackwell's account. "I could hardly believe my ears when Mr. Blackwell quietly told me this, the beginning of the story—& so I waited a while & then asked him if I understood him rightly in saying thus & so—he said I did & then went on to show me that the thing didn't work out well, that they thought they lost more republican votes for W. Suffrage by Train's advocacy than they gained democratic & were disgusted with the experiment."[14]

The "auspicious moment" of Train's telegram announcing his willingness to campaign in Kansas was the result of this plan or, as Blackwell put it, his and Robinson's "experiments." In piecing together the details of this strategy, it appears that Blackwell or Wood must have arranged for the St. Louis Suffrage Association to invite Train to speak in Kansas. It is highly unlikely that Missouri women in the St. Louis Suffrage Association would have taken the initiative to bring Train into a campaign outside of their own territory unless it had been proposed to them in advance by Kansas organizers. But as identified Republicans, Blackwell and Wood could not directly invite Train themselves. One can only imagine how much fun Train would have had in his lectures poking ridicule at Republicans who had to reach for Democratic help to support woman's suffrage.

The extent to which the Blackwell-Wood plan was a conspiracy first to use Anthony without her knowledge and later to use her association with Train to discredit and repudiate her as a leader of woman's rights becomes evident when one compares Blackwell's story—given in confidence to Isabella Hooker—with the "official" version he published many years later in *The Woman's Journal*.

> After my wife and I had returned from our campaign work in Kansas, *George Francis Train was invited into the State by Miss Anthony*, at the insistence of friends in Missouri, to speak in behalf of the woman suffrage amendment. While undoubtedly done with the best intentions, this was most unwise. Mr. Train, as everyone knows, was a semi-lunatic . . . He was also a virulent copperhead, and the last person who should have been asked to speak for woman suffrage in a strongly Republican state, like radical Kansas. . . .
>
> When the officers of the American Equal Rights Association at the East read in the papers that this fantastic personage was speaking for the suffrage amendment in Kansas, they could not believe it, and thought it must be some monstrous hoax invented by the enemy. When they found his meetings were actually being advertised in Kansas as held under the auspices of the American Equal Rights Association, Lucy Stone, as chairman of its executive committee, published a card stating the fact that the Association was in no wise responsible (emphasis added).[15]

Stanton claimed that she and Anthony did not "see through the game of the politicians until nearly the end of the canvass" in Kansas.[16] But considering the disparity in Blackwell's various accounts of the events in Kansas, it is likely they never fully understood the game at all. Nor could Blackwell, Wood, and Robinson, in devising their strategy, have anticipated the unexpected consequences of setting up Anthony to campaign with Train. Not only did the Republicans err in assuming that Anthony would organize the Kansas campaign along the lines of partisan politics, but they assumed they could manipulate Democratic support for her cause and then expected her to reject it when they, the Republicans, no longer saw it as useful. All along, they never doubted Anthony's and Stanton's allegiance to them. Further, these Republican men assumed that they would remain loyal to their party, even when that party set itself against woman's suffrage. Republicans and abolitionists could attack and condemn the women, but it was unthinkable to them that the women would break ranks with the Republicans. But that was, in effect, what Anthony did while campaigning in Kansas with Train. As a charismatic leader Anthony's direction was determined independent of Republican or abolitionist politics. What infuriated the abolitionists and Republicans is that they could not penetrate or buy off her radical egalitarianism. She refused to accept any group as a priority over any other in the demand for rights. Thus, there were no conditions under which she would abandon the woman's cause.

Train arrived in Kansas in October and submitted himself to Anthony's rigorous canvassing schedule. He soon found that her practice of canvassing a city a day was too strenuous. He protested to her, and she told him in her matter-of-fact way, "I will go alone if you cannot handle it." He replied, "Miss Anthony, you know how to make a man feel ashamed,"[17] and this odd couple trudged on from city to city.

On one trip they had to take a lumber wagon and ride through steady rain to get to Ottawa, Kansas. In the midst of darkness and torrential storms their driver lost his way, and Train had to get out and lead the wagon by foot. It was late by the time they reached their destination, where Anthony had scheduled Train to speak that evening. Anthony recounted what happened next. Because Mr. Train was fastidious about his appearance, he insisted on going to his hotel to change before speaking. She, on the other hand, was used to going to work as soon as she arrived in a town no matter what her private comfort required.

Leaving Mr. Train to attend to himself, Anthony with muddied skirt hems and a still wet dress, went on to the meeting where a General Blunt was now holding forth with a strong Republican condemnation of woman's suffrage. She had already challenged Blunt in another town, so this time, quietly entering from the rear, she took a seat in the back and listened. In the middle of his long speech,

Blunt shifted his attack from woman's suffrage to George Francis Train. By that time, Train had dressed and come down to the meeting. He had also been listening to Blunt from behind the scenes. With one of his usual well-timed dramatic gestures, he entered from the top of a stairway to the rostrum. Impeccable in a full dress suit complete with white vest and lavender kid gloves, he interrupted Blunt in midsentence.

> Are politicians so pure, politics so exalted, the polls so immaculate, men so moral that women would pollute the ballot and contaminate the voters? Would revolvers, bowie-knives, whisky bottles, profane oaths, brutal towdyism be the feature of elections if women were present? Woman's presence purifies the atmosphere. Enter any Western hotel and what do you see, General? Sitting around the stove you will see dirty, unwashed-looking men, with hats on, and feet on the chairs; huge cuds of tobacco on the floor, spittle in pools all about; filth and dirt, condensed tobacco smoke and a stench of whisky from the bar and the breath on every side. This General is the manhood picture. Now turn to the womanhood picture. She, you think, now will debase and lower the morals of the elections.[18]

By reducing Blunt to ridicule, Train swayed the audience and won the day.

Train was one of the few male allies to break through the Kansas Republican's barriers against woman's rights. Shortly before the amendments came to a vote in Kansas, he offered another important and unexpected support to the women's movement. During their travels, Anthony had mentioned to him her desire to start a woman's rights newspaper. Deciding that Anthony and Stanton were worthy of an investment beyond this work in Kansas, Train made a surprising announcement at the end of their campaign. "Ladies and gentlemen," he began, "when Miss Anthony gets back to New York she is going to start a woman suffrage paper. Its name is to be The Revolution; its motto, 'Men, their rights, and nothing more; women their rights, and nothing less.' This paper is to be a weekly, price $2 per year; its editors, Elizabeth Cady Stanton and Parker Pillsbury; its proprietor, Susan B. Anthony. Let everybody subscribe for it!"[19] His announcement was complete with his commitment to finance the paper.

Both woman's and Negro suffrage lost in Kansas. But Anthony left the state satisfied that over nine thousand of a total of thirty thousand votes were cast for women—the first ever. She blamed their defeat on the East Coast Republicans, who she believed set the pace for the western reaction against woman's suffrage. With Train's support for the new paper that she and Mrs. Stanton were about to launch, she decided to return east immediately.

Had Anthony and Stanton severed their association with Train after the Kansas campaign they would have simply been following unknowingly the Blackwell-Wood plan to use Train. As a result, the slanderous campaign initiated by eastern Republicans against them would never have occurred and become the accepted historical record of this campaign until now. Blackwell had not foreseen how far Train would go to support woman's suffrage or that Anthony and Stanton would accept his support. When they returned East with Train and strengthened their women's movement with his support, eastern Republicans moved in concert against them.

Newspaper reports warned the eastern Republican and abolitionists that Anthony was lecturing across the country with Train on her way back from Kansas. By December, Anthony and Train were lecturing in New York State. The abolitionists were furious, and Garrison, in particular, was "mortified and astonished beyond measure in seeing Elizabeth Cady Stanton and Susan B. Anthony travelling about the country with that harlequin and semi-lunatic, George Francis Train, in advocacy of Woman's Rights, denouncing Republicanism and lauding Copperheadism, and assailing Henry Ward Beecher and Wendell Phillips as no longer true to that cause. They seem to have taken leave of common sense."[20] In truth, Garrison, Phillips, and the Republicans had already abandoned the woman's suffrage campaign. Train then used their defection from woman's rights to denounce the Republican party as being weak on woman's suffrage.

Abolitionists and Republicans were shocked and outraged that Anthony had agreed to campaign with Train in Kansas, but they might have been willing to look beyond that if she had not had the unmitigated gall (in their perception of her actions) to accept Train's support. They declared her a traitor to them, while in Kansas some of these men had seen her as just the right person to contain Train's proslavery positions.

Few have understood Anthony and Stanton's desperation and the isolation that resulted from the Republican and abolitionist opposition to them during the Train episode. Because they were committed to not prioritizing the rights of one group over another and because theirs was a special commitment to women, they refused to abandon the woman's cause or to subordinate it or themselves to the men who tried to dominate them. In doing so, they appeared to be taking a proslavery or antiblack position, thus prioritizing rights after all. But what they knew was that there was a powerful movement and political party against proslavery forces, while they were the only radical representatives left fighting the antiwoman forces. At this moment, because they refused to give up their cause in the face of all opposition, Anthony and Stanton faced a reality of the struggle for woman's rights that few, if any, women had ever experienced—that is, that women have no natural allies for their own liberation outside of their own sex. In those painful moments of isolation, Anthony and Stanton learned that no political party or reform movement led by men could be their sustained natural ally, such as Republicans and abolitionists had been for black male slaves. Men—as a group—in whatever party or movement they organize, cannot form a material alliance with women's rights—however supportive some individual men might be. In reflecting on the Kansas campaign and how women had been deceived by the Republicans and abolitionists during the Civil War, Stanton noted that "if the leaders in the Republican and abolition camps could deceive us, whom could we trust?"[21] They knew that there would have been no hope for their cause if they had not accepted whatever token support was proffered to them.

This time the women had gone too far, and their former colleagues made every effort to block them. Greeley refused to print any notice of their paper in the *Tribune*. Likewise, Phillips censored them from the *The Liberator*. Some members of the Equal Rights Association tried to prevent them from renting a room in a building on Park Row in New York City for their paper. But Anthony and Stanton prevailed. Against considerable odds they rented a room for their headquarters and defiantly brought out the first issue of *The Revolution* on January 8, 1868.

Outraged, the officers of the American Equal Rights Association in retaliation called a special closed meeting and charged Anthony, who had gone to Kansas as their general agent, with misuse of funds in the Kansas campaign. Anthony had raised most of the money for her trip to Kansas but was additionally supported by the Equal Rights Association, since she and Stone had used up the Francis Jackson fund for Stone's trip to Kansas. Now the abolitionists and Republicans, finding that they could not stop Anthony's paper, decided to try to discredit her. In Anthony's absence, the meeting "passed a vote after [she was] gone not to have Susan [as] General Agent," according to Isabella Beecher Hooker's notes from her confidential meeting with Henry Blackwell, and a special committee was appointed "to examine Susan's accts." Dutifully, Anthony presented her account books and explained every expenditure in detail. Accountants were assigned to examine her books and finally declared "no vouchers irregular." Anthony noted that "accounts all thoroughly examined and the committee voted to pay them."

If the investigation was a humiliating experience for Susan, she did not say so; rather, she endured the inquiry and provided the committee with any documents and information it required. However, she was thankful that the investigation had been conducted in private, as she knew how easily a prejudiced public opinion could affect her work and her newspaper if even suspicion of her accounting became public knowledge.

Suspicions and allegations continued, but Anthony and Stanton refused to capitulate. In reality, Anthony and Stanton's association with and support from Train lasted for only three months. He abandoned the women and *The Revolution* on the day its first issue was published. His Irish Fenian causes beckoned him to Europe, which resulted in a friendly but unexpected departure from *The Revolution*. On January 8, 1868, he left for England. It was only a short time before he was in a Dublin jail, where he remained for the rest of the year. Train wrote to Susan from jail encouraging her to hold to her course. "Measure your power by the force of abuse showered upon you. They were fair-weather friends. They left you in Kansas to die." Unlike Anthony, Train probably knew of the Republican plan to use him in Kansas. "I know the load I had to carry in the woman's question, but you did not know the load you had to carry in Train!"[22] *The Revolution* continued to carry Train's articles until May of 1869, when it announced that it was dissolving its relationship with him because of his departure and withdrawal of support.

At this point, the Republicans escalated their "Negro's Hour" campaigns to ratify the Fourteenth Amendment. They argued that because their power was precarious, they could not support woman's suffrage at the same time that they were championing it for Negro men. The evidence suggests something different. Historian Kenneth Stampp has pointed out that "by 1865, the Republican party was no longer the spontaneous grass-roots movement it had been at the time of its birth in the 1850s. It had become institutionalized, it was dominated by professional politicians; and it had developed powerful political machines in the various northern states. Playing the political game according to a familiar set of rules, Republicans made the winning of elections and control of the patronage ends in themselves."[23]

In fact, the radical Republicans constituted the largest bloc in Congress by 1865. Even though the party was defeated in four state elections in 1867, the radical Republicans in the U.S. House of Representatives in that same year were voted in by large majorities in many states.

In 1868 when President Johnson defied Congress by challenging the Tenure of Office Act, which had been passed by the Congress to limit his presidential powers, the Republicans attempted to impeach him and lost. They viewed this as a major defeat. But in the same year, they won the presidential election with a landslide victory for the popular hero and Civil War victor, Ulysses Grant, who had taken the surrender of the South from General Lee. Nevertheless, the Republicans insisted that they had to focus their political strength on the "Negro's Hour" as their power was too precarious to risk if they included woman's suffrage. But in reality, they were at the height of their political power. They held enough power to nationally ratify the Fourteenth Amendment by July 1868 and then to require the southern states to ratify it as a condition of regaining their state representation in Congress. They had come to believe in themselves as the saviors of the nation and were sure of the black vote because of their history of antislavery positions. Ultimately, their commitment to black suffrage was an expedient way to keep themselves in office.[24]

At the 1868 American Equal Rights meeting, Olympia Brown charged that the Republican party was no better than the Democrats and asserted that "we want a party who will adopt a platform of Universal Suffrage for every color and every sex." Frederick Douglass challenged her by pointing out that "the present claim for the negro is one of the most *urgent* necessity" and argued that the women were wrong in going against Greeley, Phillips, and Theodore Tilton who were opposing them. Olympia Brown angrily responded to him, trying to force him to admit to the anti-Negro attitudes of the Republicans, "why did Republican Kansas vote down negro suffrage?" But Douglass was ready with the Republican party line, "Because of your ally, George Francis Train!" Because of their association with Train the women were now made responsible for Republican anti-Negro sentiment in Kansas.

Lucy Stone took the floor and challenged Douglass and the Republican party. Her position was consistent with that of Anthony and Stanton. But after she spoke the argument turned back again to Train, whom Republicans and abolitionists had made into a symbol of the women's disloyalty to them. In fact, it was Anthony and Stanton's leadership in the movement they intended to subvert.

Stanton later reacted thus to the Equal Rights Association: "For anyone to question our devotion to this cause is to us amazing. The treatment of us by Abolitionists also is enough to try the soul of better saints than we. The secret of all this furor is Republican spite. They want to stave off our question until after the presidential campaign."[25] The feminists were not politically naive to the Republican manipulation of the black male vote and their assumption that women, being less politically coalesced, would confound the voting in the presidential campaign.

Lucy Stone claimed that the Train-Anthony association in Kansas must have been "a monstrous hoax invented by the enemy."[26] But the question of movement leadership was an even more sensitive issue for Stone, who had returned to the movement feeling a much lesser luminary than she had been in her younger years. She simply did not now command the following that Anthony and Stanton had acquired. In addition, although Stone had stood with her old friends against the Republicans so far in this meeting, she was fighting competing loyalties—her husband was a Republican.

It is not surprising, therefore, that as the argument in the meeting centered on movement leadership, Stone broke her alliance with Anthony and reintroduced the charges that Anthony had misused funds in the Kansas campaign—even though Anthony had already been cleared of those charges. Anthony refused to fight Stone on those grounds; after the meeting, she pointed only to the brilliance of her former friend's feminist oratory. She told Thomas Higginson:

> I was sorry you were not present Thursday evening—to see & hear Lucy Stone out do her old self even—It was most delightful I can assure you—to all of us—I felt as if I ought & would overlook her every word and insinuation against me *personally*—Indeed I had done that before—but that speech at the close of that last meeting at 10 o'clock—melted all hearts into a recognition of woman's urgent need of the power of self-protection in her own hands.[27]

In February 1869, the Republican Congress proposed the Fifteenth Amendment to the Constitution. It stated that "the right of citizens of the United States to vote shall not be denied or abridged by the United States or any State on account of race, color or condition of previous servitude." The radical woman's rights advocates responded with anger. "Or sex" was the wording they had expected the Republicans to add to this amendment. The fact that the Republicans refused to do so was further evidence to Stanton of "Republican spite." They had had enough.

The women activists had opposed the Fourteenth Amendment on the basis that it explicitly defined citizenship and implicitly extended suffrage and equal protection to men only. Now, the Fifteenth Amendment explicitly extended suffrage to all men. In their *History of Woman Suffrage*, Stanton and Anthony stated that their opposition to the Fourteenth Amendment "did not grow out of any hostility to 'negro suffrage,'" for they themselves were abolitionists. After the Civil War, they sought the broad platform of universal human rights. As Anthony told Caroline Dall, "I think the time has come to bury the Negro & (Mrs. Stanton would have added) the woman, in the human being, the citizen."[28] But they could not forget Greeley's amendment introduced at the New York Constitutional Convention for "manhood" suffrage, which had assigned women to disfranchisement along with lunatics and criminals. The justification they offered for their position was that they "were opposed to another class of ignorant men to be lifted above their heads, to be their law-makers and Governors; to prescribe the moral code and political status of their daughters."[29]

Anthony and Stanton looked with disdain on their accusers. "In criticising such good and noble men as Gerrit Smith and Wendell Phillips for their apathy on woman's enfranchisement at this hour, it is not because we think their course at all remarkable, not that we have the least hope of influencing them, but simply to rouse the women of the country to the fact that they must not look to these men as their champions at this hour."[30] They saw their struggle as akin to Frederick Douglass's, and they argued that in their movement, as well as his, "White men could only be taught the lesson of a common humanity by just such resistance as these oppressed classes made."[31]

With all the moral authority of their privileged Bostonian heritage, which dated back to the tyranny of the Puritan fathers, the Massachusetts abolitionists demanded first from the former slave—Frederick Douglass—and later from the rebellious women—Stanton and Anthony—a kind of gratitude and reciprocity for their generosity, a stance which historian Eugene Genovese in his study of slavery found to be the essential characteristic of the slave master. Genovese sees slavery sustained by a "delicate fabric of implicit reciprocal duties, the acceptance of which by both masters and slaves alone could keep the regime intact."[32] In return for small rewards and for not being too severe in their punishment of the slaves, the masters expected gratitude. Reciprocity was established between master and slave through the slaves' recognition that acts of kindness (or absence of whipping, for example) must be repaid through hard work and in gratitude. What astounded the master was the ingratitude of the runaway slave. As Genovese pointed out, "The masters desperately needed the gratitude of their slaves in order to define themselves as moral beings."[33]

Genovese's model reveals the dynamics of domination by exploring the idea that gratitude enters into a relationship when equality is out of the question. Thus, the oppressed are expected to be grateful not so much for what they receive as for the generosity of the giver himself. That is what the abolitionists expected of Anthony and Stanton.

First they tried to discredit Anthony by challenging her financial records, but that did not stop her. Then they used Anthony's association with Democrat Train as the most visible evidence that Anthony and Stanton had stepped out of their place in Republican politics. But the women persisted and published their newspaper. Finally, at the American Equal Rights Association meetings in May 1869, Stephen S. Foster launched another attack on behalf of the Bostonians. Foster moved that Anthony and Stanton be asked to withdraw from the Association because of *The Revolution*'s association with George Francis Train. He noted that the Massachusetts Society (which included Phillips, Blackwell, Higginson, Stone, and others) refused to work with Anthony and Stanton any longer because they had repudiated the principles of the Association. The point was somewhat overdone, as Train had already severed his connection with the paper by the time of its first publication. Mary Livermore, editor of the woman's rights paper *The Agitator*, quipped with not a little sarcasm that Foster's reference to Train was "generous," considering that Train had already retired from *The Revolution*. This brought Foster to his point: He wanted the women to repudiate Train and apologize for their association with him. "The Revolution," Foster contended, "does not repudiate him. He goes out; it does not cast him out."

"Of course it does not," Anthony firmly and unflinchingly responded.

"My friend says yes to what I have said," Foster went on, even more concerned with the slate of officers that had been reported for the following year, which included Stanton as vice-president and Anthony as a member of the executive committee. "I thought it was so. I only wanted to tell you why the Massachusetts Society cannot coalesce with the party here and why we want these women to retire and leave us to nominate officers who can receive the respect of both parties." He concluded by stating that he refused "to put officers here that ridicule the negro." At that point, even Henry Blackwell recognized that Foster in his pompous authoritarian manner had seriously overstated the case. Blackwell benevolently offered, "You who know the real opinions of Miss Anthony and Mrs. Stanton on the question of negro suffrage do not believe that they mean to create antagonism between the negro and the women question."[34]

Then Frederick Douglass asked that the convention support the proposed Fifteenth Amendment, which guaranteed that "the right of citizens of the United States to vote shall not be denied or abridged by the United States or any state, on account of race, color or previous condition of servitude." Anthony argued that this new amendment "put 2,000,000 colored men in the position of tyrants over 2,000,000 colored women," and then she finally restated the principles from which she had not deviated for twenty years.

> The question of precedence has no place on an equal rights platform. The only reason it ever forced itself here was because certain persons insisted that woman must stand back and wait until another class should be enfranchised. In answer we say: If you will not give the whole loaf of justice to the entire people, if you are determined to extend the suffrage piece by piece, then give it first to women, to the most intelligent and capable of them at least.

Her logic was lodged in her radical egalitarianism, which exposed their prioritizing rights. Then she turned on Phillips and Tilton for their assertion that woman's rights was ony a theoretical idea and not a political movement.

> I repudiated this downright insolence, when for fifteen years I had canvassed the entire State, county by county, with petition in hand asking for woman suffrage! To think that those two men, among the most progressive in the nation, should *dare to look me in the face and*

speak of this great principle for which I had toiled, as a mere intellectual theory! (emphasis added).[35]

Meanwhile, when Douglass stated that he could not see how anyone could pretend that there was the same urgency in giving the ballot to the woman as to the Negro there was great applause. Anthony responded.

If Mr. Douglass had noticed who applauded when he said "black men first and white women afterwards," he would have seen that it was only the men. When he tells us that the case of black men is so perilous, I tell him that even outraged as they are by the hateful prejudice against color, he himself would not today exchange his sex and color with Elizabeth Cady Stanton.[36]

Some years after these events, when Anthony and Stanton began writing the *History of Woman Suffrage,* Stanton insisted that they not include this response of Anthony's to Douglass and that they should be careful not to mention some of their antagonists by name. Stanton also wanted to gloss over the events that led to their repudiation in antislavery circles at that time. Anthony accepted her friend's position until later in her life. When Ida Harper was writing her biography, Anthony insisted that she be vindicated on the charges that had been leveled against her during the "Negro's Hour." She particularly wanted it noted that her description of the convention discussion, after Phillips had made his speech, did not agree with what was actually published. She later said that his speech "filled the leaders with sadness, for they recognized his skillful evasion of the one point at issue—that of making common cause of negro and woman suffrage!" She also wanted it to be clear that her argument was that "precedence has no place on an equal rights platform." That statement, her recollection of Theodore Tilton and Wendell Phillips's proposal that woman's suffrage be dealt with as an "intellectual theory," and her challenge to the abolitionists' "insolence" were deleted from the *History of Women Suffrage* by Stanton.[37] In the void created by those deletions, Anthony was renounced as a racist and her radical egalitarian commitment to universal rights was reduced to personal opportunism.

Why would her best friend rewrite history in this way? There are some obvious answers. First until Anthony had talked her out of it, Stanton had accepted Phillips and Tilton's proposal that they take woman's suffrage as an intellectual theory and that she and Anthony campaign New York State to have the word "white" struck from its Constitution. But also Stanton was never subjected to the full extent of public humiliation and slander that the abolitionists heaped on Anthony. Stanton was able to keep favor with these men because in the refuge of her home and family she was protected from their constant attacks. And finally, Stanton had come to expect that Anthony would take these blows and keep on fighting— an expectation women typically make of men.

In the struggle of every oppressed group for its liberation and self-determination, it is understood that its leaders will always place their cause above all others. That is how Frederick Douglass behaved when he turned his back on woman's rights in favor of black men after the Civil War. That Douglass should have been loyal to the men of his race, holding their claims above all others, has gone unquestioned. But as society refuses to accept women as a group unto themselves and further refuses to recognize their oppression, that understanding which is basic to all liberation movements has rarely been accorded to feminism. But that did not stop Anthony from acting as a leader of an oppressed group and expecting that her commitment to her sex—her own group—be recognized as something she valued above all else.

When the American Equal Rights Association voted to endorse the proposed Fifteenth Amendment, Anthony and Stanton "repudiated" the men. "There had been so much trouble with men in the Equal Rights Society" that Stanton and Anthony decided to call a reception at the newly opened Women's Bureau in New York City and invited women only. With representatives from nineteen states present, the women organized their own independent society and named it the National Woman Suffrage Association. "Sad experience had taught them that in trying emergencies they would be left to fight their own battles, and therefore it was best to fit themselves for their responsibilities by filling the positions of trust exclusively with women." But "they had to concede the right of membership to men, in order to carry the main point, as several ladies would not join unless men also could be admitted."[38] The purpose of the association would be to secure a Sixteenth Amendment to the Constitution giving women equal suffrage with men. Woman's rights and the cause of blacks had been effectively split. Now the entire terrain of the movement shifted, and the radical women were forced to go their own way.

8

Reformers versus Radicals

THE IDEA OF FORMING A NATIONAL WOMAN SUFFRAGE ASSO-
ciation had been on Anthony's mind for three or four years. In 1866,
she had told Caroline Dall that it was still too early for a national
organization "because our immediate work must be for our own
State," but in a year or two "we may fix upon a national organization."[1]

Undoubtedly, if a national society had been formed earlier, as
Anthony had hoped, it would have included Lucy Stone. However,
by 1869 a united national society was no longer possible. In the fall
of that year, Lucy Stone and Henry Blackwell with the Massachusetts reformers called a convention in Cleveland to form the American Woman Suffrage Association, which they claimed was not meant
to be a rival to the National. In fact, they organized their society
specifically to avoid collision with the Republicans over the Fifteenth Amendment by calling for woman's suffrage on a state-by-
state basis.

In the summer of that very tense year, Isabella Beecher Hooker
made her appearance in the woman's rights movement. She had
broken away from her older sisters, Catharine Beecher and Harriet
Beecher Stowe, and fully embraced the cause of woman's rights,
although she was torn between its factions. Isabella, who was a
daughter of Lyman Beecher's second marriage, had lived for years
in the shadow of her highly prominent and successful older sisters
and her brother Henry Ward Beecher.

She had married John Hooker, who became a prominent lawyer,

and raised their three children. As was typical of wealthy women in the nineteenth century, she eventually began to show signs of deteriorating health. From Isabella's correspondence, the Beecher family biographer described her condition as an "excessive menstrual flow, the leaden feeling of a displaced uterus, headaches, back pains, dyspepsia, constipation, nasal polyps that deadened her sense of taste and, most disturbing, a 'diseased nervous system.' "[2] But Isabella refused to give in to the fashionable role of a delicate invalid.[3] Instead, she forayed directly into the woman's movement at a time when its crises and controversies were at their peak.

Isabella avoided taking sides in controversies—a Beecher characteristic. But once convinced of an issue, she embraced it wholeheartedly. Initially her woman's rights allegiances were Boston based, which would have been a natural inclination for the powerful New England Beecher family. Consequently, her first impressions of Anthony and Stanton came from the Bostonian reformers and turned her against them. And even though Garrison, Phillips, and Blackwell were courting her attention because she was a Beecher, she proved that she had a mind of her own.

Paulina Wright Davis, who confessed that "I once had a prejudice against Susan B. Anthony but am ashamed of it," believed that if Isabella Hooker had the opportunity to meet the supposedly villainous woman, she would change her mind. She invited Hooker, Stanton, and Anthony to her home in Providence, Rhode Island, for several days. After the meeting, Isabella told Caroline Severance (a principal of the Boston faction) that, in contrast to how Mrs. Stanton and Miss Anthony were treated, they spoke of Lucy Stone with love and tenderness "and regard her present statements which are so injurious to them as misconception on her part, rather brought on by the state of her health."[4] Stanton had attributed Lucy Stone's behavior to menopausal crisis. Privately and optimistically, she told Paulina Wright Davis that "Mrs. Stone is at that period of a woman's life when they are often morbid. Hers has a jealous turn and in a few years she will see sunshine where shadows dwell today."[5]

Isabella Hooker soon came to love Mrs. Stanton. But before she relinquished her prejudices against Anthony, she studied Susan "day and night for nearly a week in all." She watched for the flaws she had heard about; instead, she saw "a woman of *uncorruptible dignity* & thought of guile is not in her heart. In unselfishness and benevolence she has scarcely an equal, and her energy and executive ability are bounded only by her physical power which for a human being is immense. Sometimes she fails in judgment according to their [her friends'] standard, which they own may be an imperfect one, but in right intentions never for her faithfulness to her friends & her cause whatever it may be, death alone can interrupt that."[6] Drawn like a magnet to Susan, Isabella gave her "allegiance to both as the leaders and representatives of the great movement," while remaining in open sympathetic communication with the Boston faction.

She invited both factions to Hartford, Connecticut, for a woman's rights convention she had organized. Although they disliked sharing a platform with Susan B. Anthony, many Bostonians came because it was a "Beecher" convention. Tempers flared during the meeting when Paulina Wright Davis warmly eulogized Mrs. Stanton and Susan B. Anthony. Garrison was incensed when Davis recommended *The Revolution* and the National Woman Suffrage Association to the audience. "That brought me to my feet and I went in for Mrs. Livermore's *Agitator* as against *The Revolution*—denied there was any national organization properly speaking—and advertised the Cleveland Convention to come next month."[7]

Garrison was losing favor in the women's movement. In the next issue of *The Revolution* that came out after the Hartford convention, Stanton issued a blistering editorial attack against him. Finding Stanton's attack "bold to audacity, and often coarse," Garrison wrote a fourteen-page letter to Isabella Hooker attempting to exonerate himself from Mrs. Stanton's charges. "With the highest respect for you personally, let me caution you against committing yourself to an endorsement of their course, without further and very careful investigation."[8]

He told a friend that he was convinced that Mrs. Hooker "has been so thoroughly manipulated by ECS and SA . . . that it will be difficult to open her eyes."[9] Garrison's letter was a specimen of masculine condescension, written in infantilizing language, and explicating Stanton's errors line by line. He began with one of Stanton's statements at the Hartford convention: "Mr. Garrison fired one terrific broadside into the National Association, The Revolution and The Bible, which knocked the platform into spiritual splinters a few moments, and quickened the circulation of all who heard." He charged Stanton with manipulation, writing "the impression here intended to be conveyed is, that I censured the Bible as I did 'the Revolution,' whereas I did no such thing."

What angered him most was that "she talks of my arrogance in the Hartford Convention in denouncing The Revolution, as if I had no right to give my honest opinion of it." He was furious when Stanton said that she and Anthony had reconciled themselves much earlier to his lack of magnanimity, and he could not believe their audacity in quoting from a private letter he had written to Anthony chastising her for her association with Train. "That private note was forthrightly paraded in print as though it was actually written for publication in 'The Revolution.'" He simply could not comprehend their defiance of him.

Garrison's point was, of course, that he thought Anthony and Stanton were fighting dirty, especially for ladies. Having used the same strategy of exposing his own enemies in print many times in *The Liberator,* he could not now conceive of himself as the enemy that the women would expose. Mrs. Stanton's ungratefulness could not be imagined! He pointed out to Mrs. Hooker how Mrs. Stanton went on to say, "Mr. Garrison always was, and probably always will be, as imperious as Caesar toward those who do not see all things through his spectacles." The man who had become accustomed to reverence, at least within the world of reform, found himself accused by one of the most prominent women in the country of being "despotic in spirit and purpose." In conclusion, Stanton drove home her attack. "Abolitionists, even, cannot brook self assertion, either in women or negroes."

What Garrison did not mention in his letter to Hooker was that in her editorial Stanton recalled Garrison's treatment of Frederick Douglass years before, when Douglass had started his own anti-slavery paper. "Mr. Garrison denounced him and his journal, through which he uttered his gospel of black man's rights."[10]

Then Stanton took on the New England reformers, who had called the Cleveland convention for the purpose of organizing an American Woman Suffrage Association.

> As to the fifty grave and reverend gentlemen who have signed the call for a new Woman's Suffrage Association, if they are about to meet for the very amiable and humane purpose of conferring the right of suffrage on their wives and daughters, all well; but if they go there to make a Republican or Abolition platform on which the Woman's Suffrage movement in the country is to be judged, I advise them to finish up their work in their respective parties, and leave Woman's Suffrage to stand on its own merits.

Rather than behaving like abject slaves, Stanton and Anthony proudly proclaimed in *The Revolution* woman's superiority over the male politicians. "If there are people who cannot come over to our broad, catholic ground and demand suffrage for all—even negro suffrage, without distinction of sex—why, let them have another association until they are educated for the higher platform the present Association proposes."[11] The point was not lost on Garrison. He found the statement conceited, invidious, and insolent. And he certainly hoped that Mrs. Hooker would not be taken in by such women.

One of the questions smoldering not too far under the surface of these tensions was the challenge to Anthony and Stanton's leadership in the woman's rights movement. When Stanton was confronted, she was clear.

> When the Boston malcontents first consulted me on this point, I said, if your hostility to the National Woman's Suffrage Association is one of leadership alone, as it seems to be, and any other woman desires to be the President of the Association, I will gladly resign at any moment. As I do not hold this post by inheritance, or divine right, at the end of the year when all new officers are voted in, if I did not resign of my own free will, I could be easily supplanted by the voice of the majority.[12]

But the question of leadership was not only one of holding an office in an association, for although Anthony rarely held important offices her leadership had already taken on the character of charismatic authority. Even when she was under the fiercest attack, she told Higginson, "You know, today, no human prejudice or power can rob me of the joy, the compensation I have stored up therefrom—That it is wholly spiritual." After twenty years, "I need but tell you that this day, I have not two hundred dollars more than I had the day I entered upon the public work of woman's rights and Anti-Slavery."[13]

To Isabella Hooker, Susan B. Anthony was "a powerful instrument in God's hand, one not to be despised nor set aside." It was a surprise to her "after our Convention, to find that the one woman I had brought forward with fear & trembling as the monster who might drag us all into the depths of disgrace, was the one most commended by gentlemen and ladies as *gentle, wise, logical & reasoning*." Isabella, who still accepted uncritically the masculinist idea that there was an inherent, natural weakness in the female sex, concluded that "I am resolved to work by her side, come what may & to endure what I cannot prevent in her of woman infirmity & of injudicious management flowing therefrom."[14]

Isabella Hooker became a veritable disciple of Susan B. Anthony.

Although she was close to Susan in age, she epitomized the new generation of women who came to the movement two decades after its founding and apprenticed themselves to Anthony. Despite the diversity of their ages, these women constituted a second generation of feminism. They brought new commitment and energy to the work, but they could not fully appreciate the years of struggle behind the debates and schisms. They were attracted to Anthony particularly because of her uncompromised commitment to their sex. Her political anger reflected their feelings and helped to shape their understanding of oppression. But they had no memory of the enormous odds against women in the earlier days, when it was considered a contemptible act for a woman to speak on a public platform. And their anger did not come from their own struggle against domination as much as it was inspired by women like Anthony and Stanton.

Their feminism was formed in a world different from the one in which Anthony and Stanton had become conscious of their condition as women. The new generation could take for granted many of the opportunities for which Anthony and Stanton had had to struggle. In particular, the most important difference distinguishing Anthony and Stanton's political consciousness from the approach of Hooker's generation was that "woman's rights" were defined as individual rights for the second generation, who had no coherent analysis of women as a group subjected to domination. Instead, they only saw individual women who had unjustly been denied rights. Thus, they did not share the vision of Anthony and Stanton's generation of how political power in the hands of women would change the conditions of their class. The second generation feminists had a strong commitment to fight for their rights, but without a consciousness of power relations their movement was no longer characterized by political consciousness.

Rather, the second generation's individual-rights approach followed the direction of reform movements of the day. These movements had been influenced by the break in the collective campaign for universal rights forced by white, liberal men when they decided to prioritize rights. Once the old abolitionists and liberal Republicans had effectively severed the rights of black men from those of black women and white women, there was no more binding ideology of collective struggle and a people's movement. The men had reduced rights to individuals and not classes. Stanton and Anthony continued to demand rights for their sex—their class of women. In this way, the approach of the liberal reformers began to characterize the woman's movement in general. Their approach was to treat individual injustices in much the same way that the early temperance workers had proposed to solve the problem of alcoholism—by reforming each individual drunkard. By reducing social problems to individual ills, liberal reform masked the base of power that creates those problems in the first place. For example, in the presence of industrial poverty liberal reformers did not expose the economic structures that produced poverty. Instead, they focused on feeding and clothing the poor. Liberal reform became a new kind of charity.

Isabella Hooker typified the second generation of the women's movement. Women of Hooker's generation had opportunities that were the result of the earlier generation's struggle. This allowed them to assume that the odds against woman's rights were not as extreme as Anthony and Stanton saw them. They were able to isolate specific issues and become dedicated workers; but without a radical analysis of male power, many of them were unable to comprehend the uncompromising politics of their predecessors. As a result, the former analysis of woman's feudal condition was no longer sharply focused. The feminist analysis of Stanton, Anthony, and the first generation was inspiring; however, when it conflicted with this narrow individualistic approach, its political significance was lost on the second generation. There was a void produced by the absence of political consciousness and the struggle for it. Instead, the woman's rights reformers saw only that there were different sides or points of view. What were to Anthony on one side and Stone on the other deep political differences were merely two different positions on the same issue to the new reformers, who had no underlying theory and analysis of woman's condition. This opened the doors for more conservative and traditional politics in the women's rights movement, at a time when the radical women were under the most severe attack.

Isabella's commitment to woman's rights was representative of this generation. Although Isabella's participation was a radical departure for a Beecher woman, many of her private sentiments remained traditionally feminine. For example, she thought it indecent that Lucy Stone traveled around the country with her husband while signing the hotel registers in her maiden name, and she felt sorry for Anthony's spinsterhood. She was conventional in her defense of marriage and did not find that in conflict with her feminism. She once told Henry Blackwell, "I am deeply sensible that I owe largely to my husband any spirit of caution, any careful considerations of feelings of others, which I may now possess—& as Susan has never had the benefit of such close companionship, such friendly and unselfish advice, my heart warms to her—& until she throws me off, I shall undoubtedly cleave to her with a strong and patient heart." Without a feminist analysis, she was unable to see the contradiction between her feminism and her belief that Susan was deprived of— rather than freed from—marriage.

With considerable naiveté and blinded by her unquestioned loyalty to marriage, Hooker accounted for Susan's errors by the fact that she did not have a husband. She told Blackwell, "I fear that even you have hardly considered how much the fellowship that you & Lucy have enjoyed in this work, has prevented you from misjudgments & mistakes—while your constant sympathy with each other must have made weary work often seem light."[15]

On the other hand, Isabella was drawn by Anthony's charisma and offered her friendship. Anthony was pleased when Isabella decided to abandon the role of peacemaker between the National and American associations. "For the same amount of time, money and vitality put to the work of arousing the sleeping, the unconverted will do vastly more toward hastening the good day," Susan assured her.[16]

Although uninvited and unexpected, Anthony decided to attend the American convention in Cleveland. Before she left, she admitted to Isabella that "exactly what is in store for me I don't know." Pausing, she pondered over the situation and felt that her course had been set. "I know only this—'thus far have I been led.'"

Once Elizabeth Cady Stanton said of her friend that in their half-century of friendship she never heard Susan utter a word against another. In the midst of the Train controversy Susan told Higginson, "I want you to know that it is impossible for me to lay a straw in the way of any one who personally wrongs me—if only that one will work nobly for the cause—They may try to hinder my success but I never theirs."[17] Because she was secure with herself, her charisma was uncompromised.

Anthony called for unity at every turn—but not at any cost. She was determined to steer "the helm of the ship" back onto course. The newspapers followed her to Cleveland. "Miss Anthony is certainly a woman of indomitable resolution. When she says she'll do something, she'll do it. The particular thing she has laid out to do, in connection with the woman's rights cause, is to attend all the meetings Lucy Stone gets up," one newpaper reporter noted. "Lucy is the leader of the reform branch of the movement and don't [*sic*] want Susan around. But so far Susan has been there every time; just as sure as the bills were out, the show advertised, and the speakers ushered upon the platform, there was Susan in the midst of them calmly beaming on the cause through her specs."[18]

At that time, it was traditional to invite all prominent persons in the audience at a convention to come and sit on the platform. At the opening of the American convention, it would have been too public a humiliation for the organizers not to include Susan B. Anthony, and so she was invited up. Sitting there she may have winced internally, but she never betrayed her pain when she heard the Boston reformers castigate her own organization, the National, as an "irregular and irresponsible affair" begun by persons without delegated authority and "conducted in slipshod and reprehensible manner."[19] Nor did she respond to the threatening statement that the American would replace the National and likewise that the new *Woman's Journal,* to be edited by Henry Blackwell and Lucy Stone, would replace *The Revolution.*

Anthony was not there to argue but to work, and when Lucy Stone spoke of the work of the movement, Anthony found the common ground between them. She had been watching Stone in action and knew that when she applied herself to the work of the cause she was among the most dedicated. As one reporter observed, "She can make a telling speech at any time without a moment's notice, for there is nothing about women's rights that she don't [*sic*] know and hasn't said many and many a time. Her hands are full of tracts, and petitions and documents all the time, and she works unceasingly." Stone was vigorous and pleasant faced (as the *New York World* described her), and her appearance was as subdued as Anthony's.

> Lucy appeared with uncovered head, her hair combed in the old-fashioned, smooth, simple style. She wore a plain black dress, with a black basque, open in front, much like a gentleman's vest, and edged with white ruffling passing around the neck. No jewelry was displayed except a delicate breast-pin.[20]

To the surprise of everyone, when Lucy Stone finished her speech Susan B. Anthony stood up and, with more than her usual sobriety, walked to the podium. A young man in the audience was heard to comment, "Oh! Ain't she got the nerve." He was drowned out by thunderous applause.[21]

Anthony began by saying, "I cannot resist speaking because Lucy Stone has struck the key-note of success." She then pleaded for national action.

> Our fathers undertook to elevate all men in the shape of manhood to an equality; and the women must not cease to demand a Sixteenth amendment of the Constitution, giving suffrage to all conditions of men and women. I ask of the convention, at this early stage, not only to demand the favorable action of state legislatures, but of Congress. I care not if this association shall crush out the organization of which I am a member, and the *Revolution* to which I have given two years' labor, for if this association will come up to its great work and accomplish it so help me High Heaven, I will be content.[22]

The applause was warm and effusive, and the American organizers were not pleased. Despite Anthony's dogged determination, the split in the movement could not be bridged.

The woman's rights movement was split for almost three decades into two suffrage associations, each with its own publication. *The Revolution* was a movement newspaper, and its editorial policy was militant. It spoke out on women's most radical demands, taking up the cause of workers, the poor, and women unjustly condemned. The editors wrote and solicited articles on any issue that affected women's lives. They also took as their province such questions as currency, land reform, and particularly the increasingly pressing question of labor reform; they applied their "analytical tweezers" and feminist thinking to any political question they considered important. Controversial and daring, the paper was always deeply in debt after Train abandoned it.

On the first anniversary of *The Revolution* on January 8, 1870, *The Woman's Journal,* the official organ of the American Woman Suffrage Association, appeared. Limiting its scope to woman's suffrage, the paper appealed to a specific audience, composed of women who were beginning to enter professions, women writers, and club women. Supported by the reformist elite, the publication's constituency was drawn from the middle class and the professionals. Thus, *The Woman's Journal* was "proper" and well financed.

Susan B. Anthony's parents, Daniel and Lucy

Daniel Anthony set the austere tone of Quaker plain-living for the Anthony household, which had neither toys nor music when Susan was a child. Both parents provided a deeply loving and secure home for their children. (Courtesy of the University of Rochester Library.)

BIRTH PLACE OF MISS SUSAN B. ANTHONY

The Anthony homestead in Adams, Massachusetts

Born in this house built by her father at the base of Mount Greylock, Susan, who loved nature, had the great outdoors as her playground. (Courtesy of the University of Rochester Library.)

Susan's sampler

And she had many brothers and sisters as shown in this sampler she started at the age of eleven. But her childhood days were also filled with quilting, stitching, baking bread, and helping with the family laundry. (Courtesy of the University of Rochester Library.)

Susan B. Anthony, age twenty-eight, in a plaid dress

By the age of twenty-eight, Susan had broken away from Quaker plain living. By then an independent school-teacher, she appeared at socials in Canajoharie in this white, blue, purple, and brown plaid, complete with a fancy bonnet, and she reported home that rumors went through the village that the schoolmarm was so attractive that "someone might be smitten" and carry her away. But her interests lay elsewhere. (Courtesy of the University of Rochester Library.)

Susan B. Anthony and Elizabeth Cady Stanton, 1850s

By 1852 Anthony had met Elizabeth Cady Stanton, who had called the first American woman's rights convention in Seneca Falls in 1848. A near-perfect match, they became one of the greatest couples of the nineteenth century, often launching their campaigns from Mrs. Stanton's living room where they wrote petitions and demands for property rights for married women. The legislators were stunned by their audacity. "If the men of the State could have known the stern rebukes, the denunciations, the wit and irony, the sarcasm that were garnered there . . . they would have been truly thankful they fared no worse." (Courtesy of The Ella Strong Denison Library of the Claremont Colleges, Claremont, California.)

**Note written by Isabella Hooker
after a confidential meeting with Henry Blackwell in 1869.**

By the end of the Civil War, Anthony and Stanton's radical demands for women's rights had gone too far for the liberals and abolitionists, who tried to silence their movement by insisting that all reform energies be turned to "the Negro's hour." When Anthony and Stanton persisted in women's rights, Henry Blackwell was among the liberal men who tried to discredit them by bringing a racist Democrat, George Francis Train, into the Kansas campaign for suffrage. This note, recently discovered in Connecticut, reveals that it was not Anthony but a Kansas Republican, "Wood [who] invited Train for woman suff—was Republican himself—a shystering politician—mother Quaker—not so strong on negro suffrage. Train in favor women but up to this time opposed to negro—2 or 3 weeks—Susan and Train 30 lectures—not over 1000 democrats—drove off 3000." (Courtesy of the Stowe-Day Foundation, Hartford, Connecticut.)

Isabella Beecher Hooker

Here at eighty-one, Isabella Hooker, the younger sister of Catharine Beecher and Harriet Beecher Stowe, who had entered the movement thirty-five years earlier at the height of controversy when charges against Anthony and Stanton initiated by liberal men were meant to force them to give up their work for woman's rights. Before taking sides, Hooker decided to interview all the main characters, which is what prompted her to meet Henry Blackwell and record the note (opposite) during their meeting. (Courtesy of the University of Rochester Library.)

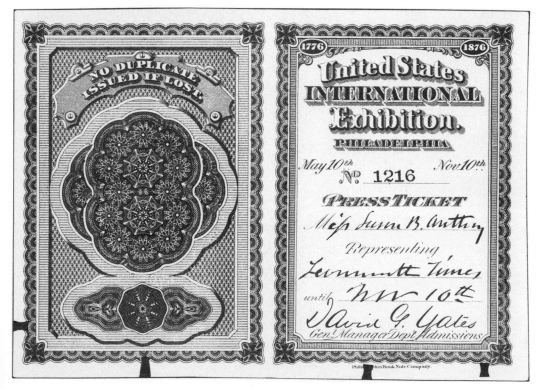

Susan B. Anthony's press pass
for the 1876 Centennial Celebration of the nation's birth

Nothing could hold Anthony back from demonstrating that women were as excluded from the rights of the Declaration of Independence as the feminists were from its national Centennial Celebration in Philadelphia. With this press pass issued by her brother from his Kansas newspaper, Anthony gained entry and then she took over the stage, from which she read a Declaration of Women's Rights and walked out. (Courtesy of the Rochester Public Library, Local History Division.)

International Council of Women, Washington, D.C., 1888

Even international boundaries could not contain Anthony's determination to form a great united sisterhood for woman's rights. After traveling throughout Europe and turning her first real vacation into meetings with feminists in several countries, with Stanton she called the International Council of Women to meet in Washington in 1888, to "impress the important lesson that the position of women anywhere affects their position everywhere. (Reprinted by permission of the Seneca Falls Historical Society.)

Top row, left to right: Bessie Starr Keefer (Canada), Rachel Foster (USA: Philadelphia), Sophia Groth (Norway), Margaret Dilke (England), May Wright Sewall (USA: Indianapolis), Alice Scatcherd (England), Margaret Moore (Ireland). *Bottom row, left to right:* Laura O Chant (Scotland), Susan B. Anthony (USA: Rochester, New York), Isabelle Bogelot (France), Elizabeth Cady Stanton (USA: New York), Matilda Joselyn Gage (USA: Fayetteville, NY), Alexandra Gripenberg (Finland).

Lucy Stone

Noticeably missing from the International Council of Women photograph was Lucy Stone, who had just begun negotiations with Anthony to unite their suffrage organizations that had been separated for over twenty years. Shortly after this meeting, the new organization became known as The National-American Woman Suffrage Association. (Courtesy of the University of Rochester Library.)

Susan B. Anthony with riding party, Yosemite, 1895

At the age of seventy-five, Susan rode through Yosemite Valley on her steed "Moses" with her faithful suffrage "lieutenants," just before launching an enormous campaign in California for woman's suffrage. (Courtesy of The Schlesinger Library, Radcliffe College.)

The 1896 California suffrage campaign

Anthony (center) posed with her "lieutenants" Emma Sweet and Carrie Catt to her right and Anna Shaw and Lucy Anthony to her left, with other organizers in the California woman's suffrage campaign. One of the most intensive ever launched, woman's suffrage was defeated that time by the liquor dealers. (Courtesy of The Susan B. Anthony Home, Rochester, New York.)

The Anthony home in Rochester from 1866 to 1907,
now a National historical monument
(Courtesy of the University of Rochester Library.)

The parlor of Susan and sister Mary's Rochester home.
(Courtesy of the University of Rochester Library.)

The attic workroom of Susan B. Anthony's Rochester home, circa 1900.

During the 1890s, sister Mary and woman's suffrage societies spruced up the Anthony home in expectation of Susan's semiretirement. Susan, before leaving for more campaigns, filled it with assistants and secretaries to work with Ida Harper on her biography and gave them the attic for their workroom. (Courtesy of the Library of Congress.)

Susan B. Anthony with Rochester neighbor Mrs. Greenleaf

"The girls are in," Anthony reported to Mrs. Greenleaf after having won the victory of forcing the University of Rochester to accept women students. This strenuous and bitter campaign took its toll on Anthony. University officials had resisted to the very end when Anthony put up her own life insurance to guarantee the funds she raised to cover the cost the university placed on admitting women. The day of their victory, she suffered a stroke, but a few months later, against doctor's orders, she was in Madison Square Garden to promote the woman's suffrage cause. (Reprinted by permission of the Seneca Falls Historical Society.)

Anna Howard Shaw. (Courtesy of the University of Rochester Library.)

Carrie Chapman Catt. (Courtesy of the University of Rochester Library.)

Susan B. Anthony

By 1900 it was time to turn the woman's suffrage movement over to a younger generation. When Anthony resigned the presidency of the National-American, her closest companion, Reverend Anna Howard Shaw, was in contention with the dynamic organizer Carrie Chapman Catt to replace her. When votes were taken, the eighty-year-old Anthony raised the arm of Carrie Chapman Catt and announced to an emotional audience, "I give you my successor." (Courtesy of The Schlesinger Library, Radcliffe College.)

The casket of Elizabeth Cady Stanton, 1902

No loss could have been greater for Susan than the death of her beloved Mrs. Stanton. "The voice is hushed that I have longed to hear for fifty years." The mutuality of their love was evident, for even when Mrs. Stanton died it was Susan's photo that rested on top of her casket and their photo together was placed on the table next to it near where Susan sat through the funeral. (Courtesy of the Douglass Library, Rutgers University.)

Banquet, International Council of Women, Berlin, 1904

From a small meeting in Seneca Falls in 1848 to the International Council of Women in 1904, the woman suffrage movement now stretched across the globe. Eighty-four-year-old Susan B. Anthony celebrating with her sister Mary and suffragists from numerous countries contentedly declared "This is the climax of my career." (Courtesy of the University of Rochester Library.)

Susan and sister Mary, 1905

"Let it be sister Mary, first and always," Susan wrote home when she was unable to be there for her youngest sister's seventy-fifth birthday. Mary, a former school-teacher and principal, had virtually kept their home together all the years Susan was on the road. Home more frequently by the age of eighty-five, Susan agreed to pose with her sister because the aspiring photographer, Grace Woodworth, was from Seneca Falls. Grace Woodworth found that "a few minutes with her gave me the feeling of wanting to do something worthwhile and also the feeling that I had the ability to do it." (Reprinted by permission of the Seneca Falls Historical Society.)

Now for the first time since the inception of the movement, opposition to the radical militancy of Anthony and Stanton was voiced through formal organizations and in a publication from *within* the woman's rights movement. Having traditionally united against their external enemies, the radicals and reformers were now split, and the radical edge—the militant presence in the movement—was in serious jeopardy. In *The Revolution,* Anthony and Stanton warned their readers of coming dangers.

> In the present stage of the Woman's Suffrage movement in this country a division in our ranks is rather to be deplored, for when friends disagree new-comers hesitate as to which side to join; and from fear of being involved in personal bickerings they withhold their names and influence altogether; still more deplorable is the result to the old friends themselves, when instead of fighting the common enemy, prejudice, custom, unjust laws and a false public sentiment, they turn, as the old Abolitionists in their divisions did, and rend each other.[23]

There were other fundamental political differences between the National and the American. The National was open to all. Anyone who paid a dollar to join and then attended meetings held a voice and vote. Although Stanton and Anthony had hoped initially to organize the National exclusively for women, they found that women were not yet ready for their own separate organization. But they drew the line on permitting men to hold office. The American was organized on a delegate basis. Members had to be elected from local suffrage organizations, which were to be made auxiliaries of the American. Men were not only welcome but could hold office. In fact, Henry Ward Beecher was elected the American's first president.

With a minimal organizational structure, the National retained the character of a social movement that was oriented toward grassroots organizing. Any woman was welcome, and all were encouraged to organize local societies. The more traditional structure of the American required that local societies formally become auxiliary to the American and send official delegates to its conventions.

It was clear in the first weeks and months of the split that Henry Blackwell intended to use the American's hierarchical structure to try to bring all existing woman's suffrage societies under the American. For weeks he wrote letter after letter to suffrage organizations (many of which Anthony had helped to organize) and to prominent woman's rights advocates telling them they must affiliate with the

American. He invited Isabella Hooker to be an officer in the American and proposed to make her Connecticut Woman's Suffrage Society an auxiliary of the American. Hooker, who had been disturbed for some time by Blackwell's scheming, refused.[24] That same week, Martha Wright, a long-time friend of Anthony and Stanton, received a letter from Blackwell. After listing "all the sins of ECS & SBA and *The Revolution*," Blackwell advised her that "the time was very near when our State [New York] assn. must decide whether it would become auxiliary to the American Ass."[25]

Anthony was insulted; but instead of reacting to Blackwell, she proceeded with her plans for a National Woman Suffrage convention to be held in January 1870 in Washington, D.C. She reasoned that they would be better located to make their demand for a Sixteenth Amendment in the nation's capital. Anthony instructed Isabella Hooker, who was responsible for organizing the convention, to invite Lucy Stone and Blackwell. "It is our National that has called the Convention and our National must not exclude any of the old or new representative speakers—we cannot afford to be narrow or spiteful or retaliative." She even insisted that Thomas Higginson and William Lloyd Garrison be invited. "Am I not right?" she asked Isabella. "You see to do otherwise, would be to do no better than they & we can't afford that." But the split taught her another lesson—the need to keep control of her organization. "We must marshall our forces and hold the reigns to the end."[26]

, The Bostonians did not attend, and the National convention was a success without them. But the tension between the National and American escalated when both organizations had meetings scheduled at the same time in New York City a few months later. Charging that the National had usurped leadership of the movement, Blackwell offered the rival organization an opportunity to become auxiliary to the American. Anthony would not budge. To her the American was just like the South during the Civil War—they were the seceders. Her position was firm, as she revealed to Isabella Hooker in another one of the long letters recently discovered in the collection in Hartford, Connecticut.

> Then you see—theirs is a Mass Convention called on the same days in the same city when and where they knew the National Society always held its anniversary. . . . and that too after the regular call for regular anniversary had been a month or six weeks published. You see, we the Nationals have nothing to explain & concede. . . . nothing in the world to do but go right strait [sic] ahead about

our work of organizing the Nation to secure the 16th Amendment. If they, the Boston Cleveland seceders, individually or collectively come to our National Anniversary, make themselves members—pay their dollars—speak, vote, & generally act in good order—they shall be received and the same as we ourselves, clothed with rights & privileges—and with us—abide the majority decision, by fair open vote & discussion—of officers of the National & every question of plan & work. If they won't allow the majority to rule, why then "secession" & "new organization" is all there is left for them.

Anthony's confidence rested in her constituency, the thousands of people she and Stanton had been lecturing to across the country. She continued:

Mrs. Hooker, let us just go strait ahead gladly welcoming to our Society every worker & believer who comes. You have seen enough of the animus to know that if the people should vote Stanton or Anthony to prominent office, certain prime movers of that Society would not feel happy to say the least—& after all this—to vote them out of office would be to sanction the Lucy Stone allegations against them. And that the friends will never do, for the people out here believe in Stanton & Anthony and will ask the reason why—if their names are not recognized. The friends in every town are taking sides & of course, mainly with us because our Revolution is out among them.[27]

Undeterred, Anthony conceded neither her movement nor her militancy to these latest threats. *The Revolution* continued to represent the movement's most radical, wide-ranging, and controversial positions. When the United States Internal Revenue Service notified Anthony that she owed the government taxes on her newspaper, she responded:

THE REVOLUTION, you are aware, is a journal, the main object of which is to apply to these degenerate times the great principles on which our ancestors fought the battles of the Revolution, and whereon they intended to base our Republican government, viz, that "Taxation and representation should go together;" and that to inflict taxation upon any class of the people, without at the same time conferring upon them the right of representation, is tyranny.

I am not represented in the United States government, and yet that government taxes me; and it taxes me, too, for publishing a paper the chief purpose of which is to point out and rebuke the glaring and oppressive inconsistency between its professions and its practices.

Under the circumstances, the Federal government ought to be ashamed to exact this tax of me. However, as there is such pressing need of money to supply a treasury which is so sadly depleted by extravagant expenditures and clandestine abstractions by its own officials, I consent to contribute to its necessities this large sum ($14.10), assuring you that when the women get the ballot and become their own representatives, as they surely will and that very soon, they will conduct themselves more generously and equitably toward the men than men now do toward them; for we shall then not only *permit* you to pay taxes, but *compel* you to vote also. I had thought of resisting the payment of this tax on high moral grounds, as an unjustifiable exaction, but learning that the courts do not take cognizance of moral questions, I have decided to send you the sum ($14.10) enclosed.[28]

The most essential disagreement between the radicals and the reformists lay in their political strategies. The then-recent woman's suffrage campaigns in Kansas and New York had taught Anthony that a *national* constitutional amendment was woman's only hope to establish this right throughout the land. In opposition, the American campaigned for suffrage state by state to avoid conflict with the Republicans, who had launched a national campaign for the Fifteenth Amendment. Lucy Stone's position on the Fifteenth Amendment was that "every effort should be made to include women, but that if this proved impossible, the Amendment ought nevertheless to pass."[29] By agreeing with the liberal Republican party, the American situated itself as a reform association within the larger Republican-dominated political world.

Anthony and Stanton were appalled that in constructing the Fifteenth Amendment, the Republicans refused to extend protection against disfranchisement to women. The political scene in Washington had shifted since the campaign for the Fourteenth Amendment, and the Republicans influence in Congress was beginning to wane. Blacks were in increased jeopardy in the South, as state legislatures began to erode the effects of the new constitutional amendments. Especially menacing was the growth of the Ku Klux Klan, which had originated at the end of the Civil War as an organization pledged to retaining white supremacy in the South. Anthony and Stanton were aware of these developments and were not insensitive to them, but they refused to organize their movement as a secondary cause. They considered the abolitionist idea that they campaign state by state an attempt to reduce their cause to a single issue with a limited strategy. After all, that had been the position adopted by abolitionists previously when they had been faced in the past with the stubborn refusal of feminists to submerge their cause into silence or into the background. The radical women knew that the men intended to locate the woman's rights movement outside of their own sphere of action, where they waged national campaigns for constitutional amendments. Further, the radical women had no intention of limiting their movement to suffrage campaigns, particularly in the face of such pressing questions as divorce and labor.

By the time the Fourteenth Amendment was adopted, enfranchisement had become acceptable in reform movements. Now many well-known figures, who had stayed away from public commitment when suffrage was too controversial, began to appear on the American platform. The more moderate tone of the American program, which explicitly excluded the controversial divorce issue, appealed to many prominent women, such as Julia Ward Howe, author of the "Battle Hymn of the Republic," and Mary Livermore, a reform worker. Drawing from the more conservative classes and rejecting the militant politics of the National, the American actually helped to expand the numerical base of the woman's movement and to give it social credibility.

In strategy, organizational style, and goals, the reformers charted a different path from the militant, radical women. They dissociated themselves from any militant woman's rights actions, and the reformers won social legitimization and financial support. They were coopted by liberalism. One of the most damaging consequences of liberal reform is its ability to isolate radicalism. A movement devolves to reform when it disavows and isolates its radical edge. It loses sight of its goal—that is, radical social change and the self-determination of its people. As a result, reform becomes a compromise to change some things but not the whole system. The first response of radicals to isolation is to strengthen their militancy, as Stanton and Anthony did after the Civil War. But eventually isolation forces them to narrow their focus to only their most radical demand. A single issue movement was a contradiction to their original political consciousness which refused to prioritize or isolate women's issues. The question was: How long, in the face of powerful organizing against them within their movement, would Anthony and Stanton retain their radical analysis and militant spirit? The answer would determine the life of their movement.

A call for unity between the National and American was issued throughout the reform ranks. While Anthony and Stanton were campaigning in the West in the spring of 1870, several reformers met in New York City with Blackwell, Stone, and other American leaders to try to bring about a unification of the two organizations. Seventy-seven-year-old Lucretia Mott, who rarely left home anymore, traveled to New York hoping to resolve the problems. Anthony and Stanton wired from the West that they would not stand in the way of unity, although Anthony carefully added, "united national organization for the Sixteenth Amendment,"[30] reiterating that she refused to reduce their movement to state campaigns. Stanton again offered to resign her office and said that she would accept an organization under Beecher or Lucretia Mott. In her words, "I am willing to work with any and all or to get out of the way entirely."[31]

Anthony took a position that was fair but not conciliatory. This was an approach that would characterize her organizing—for better or for worse—for the rest of the century. She contended that

> The American was organized by persons who ignored the two persons, Stanton & Anthony, who had stood in the front ranks of the suffrage army (if not its acting generals), ignored the National Society of which they were officers, ignored the Revolution of which they were Editor & Proprietor, ignored every instrumentality which they found in existence, when they took up their public work. They are persons who are either new converts and new workers, or old ones who had been comparatively silent, out of the public field for the last ten or fifteen years. These two classes combined called the Cleveland Convention & then formed the American ass. & started the Woman's Journal all on the basis that there was no organization, no woman's suffrage paper, no Stanton & Anthony.

> Now surely, it is not for Stanton & Anthony & National Association to make proposals of peace to them & theirs. It would prove just as futile as did the Congressional attempt of the North in its overtures to Jeff Davis and his compeers.[32]

Liberals have interpreted this split in the movement as one that expanded the woman's rights movement by enlarging its constituency and opening its membership to middle class and elite women.[33] But with second generation feminism having bypassed the struggles of political consciousness, the split could only have had the effect of narrowing the movement and reducing its radicalism to reformism.

One of the controversial positions espoused by *The Revolution* that embarrassed the reformist elite was the feminists' position on labor.

In an early edition of their paper, Anthony and Stanton supported women who were hired to fill the places of the striking men, when Local No. 6 of the National Typographical Union went out on strike against the *New York World* in 1867. Excluded from labor unions (including Local No. 6) and barred from gainful employment by management except when they were used as scab labor, the women workers reasoned that the short time they would hold their jobs would give them not only income but also valuable training and on-the-job experience. Women strikebreakers put it to the male unions this way, "Just as often as possible we shall step into new places, and then get us out if you can. If you won't let us in any other way, we must enter in this."[34] Anthony and Stanton heartily agreed and urged them to fight to keep their jobs. In the eyes of labor and the world of reform, Anthony and Stanton were simply supporting strikebreakers and scab labor. In Anthony and Stanton's terms, both male unions and male management needed to be taught the lesson of woman's bargaining power.

Anthony had not forgotten the plight of working women. In her youth, when industrialization was in its early stages, she had witnessed the hardships of mill girls. By the second half of the nineteenth century, the exploitation of labor had intensified. A heavy influx of immigrants provided a new pool of exploitable labor to feed the rapid pace of industrialization. Working conditions deteriorated, and tenements appeared and created overcrowded slum conditions. The time was ripe for a new labor movement.

In the fall of 1868, Anthony began organizing women workers into groups where women from different jobs could come together, build mutual support, and teach themselves how to fight for their rights. The women were not content to confine their grievances to a specific labor issue against one employer. As Anthony reasoned, it was the wide range of wrongs against women in different occupations and the fuller scope of women's rights—from labor grievances to political power—that provided the necessary movement context for their organizing.

But Anthony had another goal—to gain a foothold in the upcoming September convention of the National Labor Union. In early September of 1868, she formed Working Women's Association No. 1, which met at the office of *The Revolution* and consisted of typesetters and clerks employed by her paper. A few weeks later she organized Working Women's Association No. 2 at a boardinghouse in an old tenement, where many factory girls lived. A hundred women attended the first meeting. Anthony began by explaining the importance of the ballot for working women and then asked for the "facts." She wanted to know the women's working conditions. "I get two dollars a piece for making ladies' cloth cloaks," one young woman offered. "How long does it take you to make them?" Anthony queried. "Less than a day, its partly machine and partly handwork."

Embarrassed silence filled the room, which Anthony broke with "Well, go on girls." One very pale girl spoke up. "I make lace collars for twenty-two cents a dozen. I can make three dozen in a day, twelve hours' work, that's sixty-six cents." The young women's reticence to speak gave way, and their anger began to rise. One after another reported her working conditions until one of them began to stretch the "facts" a bit too far and others laughed, charging that what she claimed just wasn't true. Anthony chimed in, "I am here to find out your wants, and to help you to make more money. Pray do not make it any worse than it is. Heaven knows, it is bad enough."

Then a young woman who was obviously ill began to speak in a low, weak voice. "I am a carpet-sewer. I work for one of the largest carpet-houses in the Bowery. The Brussels carpets are very stiff sometimes, and I blister my hands very badly." She raised her hands to show the sores, scratches, and blisters. Everyone in the room listened attentively. She continued, "I work nearly three days, and I sew fifty yards of carpet, and when I asked him to pay me for sewing the borders which is additional work, he laughed and said it was 'chucked in.'" The tension in the room broke into cries for the man's name. Anthony interjected that this was "the crime of the system, not of an individual."

As a good organizer, Anthony wanted to focus their anger. "Have a spirit of independence among you, a wholesome discontent. And you will get better wages for yourselves." She told them to "get together and discuss, and meet again to discuss this question, and all the time have a wholesome discontent, or you will never achieve your rights. You must not work for these starving prices any longer. Talk to one another, and I will come and talk to you, and the press will support you, and by and by we will have an immense mass meeting of women, where all can talk if they choose, and all the good men and women of America, listening to your appeal will come forward and stand by you."[35] Anthony closed the meeting and announced that she would be back the next Thursday, after "I have organized my type-setting girls."

Anthony had a special interest in the "type-setting girls," the women compositors and clerks in printing firms. Mrs. Stanton explained, "One of Miss Anthony's most cherished plans is to have a magnificent printing establishment, and a daily paper, owned and controlled and all the work done by women, thus giving employment to hundreds and making the world ring with the new evangel for women." The plan was part of a feminist vision: "Let women of wealth and brains step out of the circles of fashion and folly, and fit themselves for the trades, arts, and professions, and become employers, instead of subordinates; thus making labor honorable for all, and elevating their sex, by opening new avenues for aspiration and ambition."[36]

Anthony was never satisfied with organizing aimed only at delineating the wrongs against women; nor did she stop with her dreams of creating exclusive women's organizations and projects. Since the early 1850s, her organizing strategy had been twofold: to create separate women's groups, as she did in organizing women's temperance associations, and to challenge male control of the women's movement, as she did when she militantly confronted one male temperance convention after another. Now with a growing labor movement that excluded women, Anthony's strategies were not essentially different nor were the reactions of the men.

Immediately after the Civil War, many individual labor unions were consolidated into the National Labor Union, which was organized by William Sylvis. By 1868, the leadership of the National Labor Union and that of *The Revolution* had found common ground. Both advocated the eight-hour day and unionization of working women. Under Sylvis's leadership, the NLU supported suffrage as an essential political tool that was necessary for women to gain entrance to and command equal wages in the trades. However, the NLU excluded women from its ranks.

Anthony had intentionally organized the Working Women's Association only a few weeks before the 1868 convention of the National Labor Union and then applied for NLU membership. Anthony went to the NLU convention as a delegate from the Working Women's Association. Stanton accompanied her as a delegate of the Woman Suffrage Association of America, an organization they hastily put together for the purpose of getting another woman and the issue of suffrage into the convention. The women had not been invited, but that did not stop Anthony from writing to other working women's associations she had formed asking them to also send delegates to this "working men's national congress."

Spontaneous, grass-roots organizing is usually viewed as a menace by properly structured organizations that function according to adopted rules and guidelines. When necessary, those who do this type of organizing disregard all protocol that may stand in the way of their own agenda. The union men knew what Stanton and Anthony were up to, and they had not forgotten the women's support for strikebreakers in the 1867 strike against the *New York World*. It was not without considerable objection and controversy that the women were seated as delegates and thus broke the sex barrier of the NLU. So major was this breakthrough that even Karl Marx noted the complete equality with which the NLU accepted women.[37]

Within a month, Anthony and Stanton had succeeded in opening the National Labor Union Congress to women. Their breakthrough enabled Augusta Lewis, a journalist and trained typesetter who had helped form the Working Women's Association with Anthony's assistance, to form the Women's Typographical Union. Anthony addressed their first meeting.

> Girls, you must take this matter to heart seriously now, for you have established a union, and for the first time in woman's history in the United States you are placed, and by your own efforts, on a level with men, as far as possible, to obtain wages for your labor. I need not say that you have taken a great momentous step forward in the path of success.[38]

Not including the women used for strikebreaking, women constituted fifteen to twenty percent of the typographers working in the printing trades in New York City at this time.[39]

There were significant differences between Augusta Lewis's agenda for the Women's Typographical Union and Anthony's goals for the Working Women's Association. Specifically, Lewis disagreed with Anthony and Stanton on including suffrage with labor issues. Her Women's Typographical Union took women's labor reform as its only goal, because it could not support women strikebreakers and at the same time maintain its legitimacy as a union. This led Anthony and Lewis down different and conflicting paths when Local No. 6 of the National Typographical Union went out on strike against bookbinders and printers in January of 1869. Lewis and the Women's Typographical Union supported Local No. 6. On the other hand, Anthony struck while the iron was hot as she later explained:

> Last spring some one came into my office and said: "Miss Anthony, now is your time. You have been talking to your workingwomen's association about establishing a training school for learning girls to set

type. Now is your time, while these employing printers are in distress to make them for over some cash to establish a school." Well, of course, I am not in the Working Women's Association especially to advance men's wages; I am there specially to help women out of the kitchen and sewing-room, so I put my bonnet on in a twinkling and went over to Astor House. Those gentlemen with a broad grin on their faces, looked and sneered as I walked in the room, but I told them why I came there . . . I appealed to their self-interest to establish a school for the education of girls in typesetting. They appointed a committee to take the matter into consideration, . . . and I said to girls who applied to me by the fifties, go in and learn your trade. I knew full well that when Union No. 6 came in line with the employers, or the employers with them, the girls would be turned adrift; but I said to myself, they will have acquired a little education, a little help, and I will have helped them this much. The result was that some forty or fifty young girls served with Gray and Green and others, during a few months while the strike was in progress.[40]

Anthony was the organizer of working *women,* not a *labor-union* organizer. The printing firm for *The Revolution* responded by setting up a program to train fifty-three women during the strike. Unions saw this as scab labor. Of course, this made Local No. 6's negotiations to end its strike more difficult. Those involved in labor reform considered this a fundamental violation of labor-union principles. On the other hand, the radical women insisted that their position was strengthened because by having women trained as typesetters neither unions nor management could argue that there were no qualified women for these jobs. Now the unions would be forced to see that trained women got the jobs they deserved.

Anthony was satisfied that several women had been trained during the strike and could now be hired by the printing firm of *The Revolution*. She further argued that as a representative of the Working Women's Association, she was not bound by the unions' rules. "I admit that this Working Woman's Association is not a *trade* organization; and while I join heart and hand with the working people in their trade unions, and in everything else by which they can protect themselves against the oppression of capitalists and employers, I say that this association of ours is more upon the broad platform of philosophizing on the general questions of labor, and to discuss what can be done to ameliorate the condition of working people generally."[41]

At the 1869 National Labor Union convention, Augusta Lewis

and the Women's Typographical Union were seated as delegates. Anthony noted with satisfaction that since she had broken the sex barrier the year before, there were now several black delegates seated as a result of a NLU resolution to invite representatives "regardless of race or sex."

But if Anthony had paved the way for others, she had virtually closed the door for herself. At the convention a delegate from Local No. 6 challenged her credentials and charged that the working women's associations she represented were not trade unions, that the printers of her *Revolution* opposed organized labor, that the women typesetters were not paid equal wages, and, most importantly, that she had solicited aid to procure positions for women from the employers that Local No. 6 had been striking against. Anthony responded to the charges by arguing that the Working Women's Association was not a labor union and asserting that the printers of *The Revolution* had trained women typesetters who were paid at a higher rate than other typesetters in the City. Then she charged the unions with opposing her because they were against her campaigns for woman's suffrage and political independence. Votes were taken, and her credentials were revoked.

In defense of the labor movement, Anthony has been viewed either as monomaniacal or naive or opportunistic or bourgeois for her strikebreaking.[42] But she firmly believed that no other issue, cause, or grievance could be placed above the representation of her sex. Further, as she considered political power essential to gaining all other women's rights, mixing suffrage with labor reform was a necessary strategy to her. Ironically, as Anthony's position on labor brought down the wrath of the labor reform movement, it also boosted her charismatic authority among her followers.

The Working Women's Association would not limit its grievances to those of women in the trades. There were also the marginal women, who were poor and untrained and were the least recognized and represented. These women were forced to accept menial, degrading labor and, particularly, domestic work. Domestic labor was the only form of work available to black women recently freed from southern slavery, and it was the major occupation of immigrant women. It was with this commitment to the broader base of "wrongs against women" that the Working Women's Association and *The Revolution* took up the case of Hester Vaughan, a young immigrant girl from Gloucestershire in England who upon arrival in the United States discovered that her husband was already married. Deserted and alone, Hester had to fend for herself. Elizabeth Cady Stanton's report of Hester's story in *The Revolution* best conveys the tone of the cause.

Then came the tug of war for Hester Vaughan, as every other woman who, from what cause soever, finds herself compelled to fight the battle of life alone. This of this young girl, a stranger in a strange land, with neither friend nor relative to advise or comfort. For several weeks she lived out as servant in a family at Jenkintown; was then recommended as dairy maid to another family, and here misfortune befell her. Overcome, not in a moment of weakness and passion, but by superior strength—*brute force*—Hester Vaughan fell a victim to lust and the gallows. The man also went his way. Three months after this terrible occurrence, Hester moved to Philadelphia and hired a room there. She supported herself by little odd jobs of work from different families always giving the most perfect satisfaction. During one of the fiercest storms of last winter she was without food or fire or comfortable apparel. She had been ill and partially unconscious for three days before her confinement and a child was born to Hester Vaughan. Hours passed before she could drag herself to the door and cry out for assistance, and when she did it was to be dragged to a prison.[43]

Hester's baby died before she could get help, and she was charged with murder—infanticide. Anthony and Stanton brought the best women doctors to visit and examine Hester in prison out of concern for her health and to assure the veracity of her story. Anthony and Stanton went into action to raise legal and financial support for Hester Vaughan. They took a demand for unconditional pardon to the governor after she was convicted of murder and sentenced to death. The governor told Mrs. Stanton that he did not think Hester was a bad woman by nature, but his hands were tied because the jury had found her guilty. Then he added, "You have no idea how rapidly the crime of 'infanticide' is increasing. Some woman must be made an example of it. It is for the establishment of a principle, ma'am." Stanton retorted with all her anger, " 'Establishment of a principle,' indeed!! I suggest you inaugurate the good work by hanging a few women."[44] Nevertheless, by using the influence of their paper and their organizations, Anthony and Stanton, were able to bring enough pressure on the governor to secure the release of Hester Vaughan. With the money they raised, she returned to England.

Although she was the figure most hated by abolitionists, Republicans, and labor leaders, Susan B. Anthony was becoming one of the most beloved figures to her own constituency—women. Older women remembered the early years of resistance to women's rights, and younger women were invigorated by her spirit. Anthony was out among them most of the time, lecturing and organizing. On the occasion of her fiftieth birthday on February 15, 1870, friends and followers chose to demonstrate their loyalty and love with a major celebration. Susan resisted the idea of a birthday party, especially if it were to be a testimonial to her; but eventually she conceded. The celebration was held on the day of her birthday at the newly opened Women's Bureau in New York. Susan stood at the entrance to greet her friends and well-wishers, wearing "a dress of rich shot silk, dark red and black, cut square in front, with a stomacher of white lace and a pretty little cameo brooch." Her hair, which had still not grayed, was held in the same, but by now old-fashioned, style she had worn twenty years earlier, as she still continued to disregard female vanities. The *New York World* reported that she wore "no hoop, train, panier, chignon, powder, paint, rouge, patches, no nonsense of any sort."

Susan had wanted her family to be with her for this special event. But her mother was too ill to travel, and, as always, her sisters Hannah and Guelma were preoccupied with their family cares. Even Mrs. Stanton was at home and ill and could not be at Susan's side this evening. As the guests settled into the parlor, Susan was ushered to the seat of honor. She listened attentively, if impatiently, while testimonials and telegrams were read, honors bestowed, and poems written especially for this occasion were presented to her.

Finally, she rose to speak but was overwhelmed and could barely collect herself. She betrayed her awkwardness by telling the gathering that "if this were an assembled mob opposing the rights of women I should know what to say. I never made a speech except to rouse people to action. My work is that of subsoil plowing." She wanted to respond to the testimonials with the kind of eloquence and flourish with which they were presented. But finally she did what was most familiar and comfortable for her; she turned her birthday party into an organizing event and issued a call for action.

> I ask you tonight, as your best testimony of my services, on this, the twentieth anniversary of my public work, to join me in making a demand on Congress for a Sixteenth Amendment giving women the right to vote, and then to go with me before the several legislatures to secure its ratification; and when the Secretary of State proclaims that that

amendment has been ratified by the twenty-eight states, then Susan B. Anthony will stop work—but not before.[45]

Susan B. Anthony found that she had become a legend in her own time. By her fiftieth birthday, she was one of the most loved and hated women in the country. To her enemies she was a witch. "Ask nine men out of every ten to give you their idea of Miss Anthony, and they will describe you a woman unsexed—a witch personified. They dry, tan and shrivel her, and drain her heart of everything but the hate of men." The same reporter who wrote these words met this "hobgoblin of the public mind" on one of her campaigns and was surprised to discover that Susan B. Anthony was an ordinary mortal. "She chats on ordinary topics of the day, as other women do, except that she shows a wider scope of reflection and observation."[46]

Revealing nicknames began to be attached to her: Napoleon, — Bismarck—and even St. Anthony. The *Cincinnati Gazette* compared her to Christ's apostles. "The paramount reason why Susan B. Anthony should be the Apostle of the Woman's Rights cause is that she has never surrendered to man her independence, nor annihilated her personality by marriage, nor promised to honor and obey a male master, nor parted with that state of virgin purity— which in all ages of the world and among all people has been regarded as proof of the mortal weaknesses." She was equated with Elizabeth the First and the biblical Deborah. And when Matilda Joslyn Gage was speaking on woman's rights through New York State, she heard everywhere "the praises of our Susan. Her vigor, her persistency, her untiring devotion were everywhere spoken of." One woman told Gage that Anthony "is more to be revered than General Washington." Larger than life, nearer to the gods, Anthony's charismatic force among women had taken on a life of its own.

It was Anthony's "single blessedness" which confirmed to her followers the purity of her commitment to womankind. One woman reporter noted that while Mrs. Stanton had surrendered her independence and sovereignty to marriage, "the vestal Anthony is above this base spirit, because she has never submitted to this state of servitude." These kinds of statements are usually read as inflammatory rhetoric, a way to discredit them, but more to deny the reality for which they stand, that of a single woman committed to her own sex. By virtue of her life, Anthony had revealed a possibility for womankind, which could only be realized if women refused to be dominated. This made other women's acceptance of domination all too obvious. Some women began to observe that in woman's rights meetings when allusions were made to Susan's unmarried state "by the sister advocates who are or have been married, it is done in a manner which is simply a boasting of their marriage, which is in fact the degraded pride of a slave in his own servile condition." In contrast, these same women saw Susan B. Anthony as uncompromised before *man*kind. "She can hold all men enemies in war, in peace friends—enemies if they assert their usurpation over her inherent political rights; friends if they recognize her equal sovereignty."[47]

This laudatory recognition, with the valid critique of how women (even the woman's rights advocates) relied on their marriages to define them, had negative consequences for Anthony. Followers often invest their charismatic leaders with symbolic meaning that is beyond the leaders' intentions. This was certainly true for many of the woman's rights advocates. They found a source of pride in Susan's refusal to subjugate herself to a man, but then they actually made her into a surrogate husband—the one whom they had to and usually wanted to please and the one on whom they would confer all the responsibilities for their movement. Not only to reporters and admirers had "the Cause" become synonymous with the name Susan B. Anthony, but to her everlasting frustration this was the attitude of Mrs. Stanton, Isabella Hooker, and a number of other women with whom she worked. It was no longer uncommon for her to receive letters from women who wanted to help *her* with *her* movement and *her* campaigns. Instead of embracing the movement as their own, many of her co-workers followed her directives to please her personally.

For example, there was a circular that Isabella Hooker had just written. Susan picked it up from the table and as she read it she knew that Mrs. Hooker had revised it to meet the "General's" specifications, even though she did not agree with it herself. Susan knew that this personal devotion would ultimately undermine these women's commitment to the cause and that it increased her own responsibilities. "Mrs. Hooker, it pains me to have you do anything against your feelings for my sake personally." She went on to explain to Isabella that "even Mrs. Stanton writes she comes back to the Washington Convention—wholly out of regard for me personally—I can't understand it—I do it for the pushing of the work—that is I think I do—I may be mistaken."

Realizing that Mrs. Hooker did not see the distinction between doing the work for her personally and doing it for the cause, Susan pushed her point further. "Look," she emphasized, "Mrs. Stanton is President, you Vice President of Advisory Council of the National—I nothing—really hold no honorary or responsible position in the society—still not one other person seems to feel the thing theirs—all talk to me as if it were mine—Isn't it a little funny."[48] Susan refused to take the male role with her women friends. And they were generally unconscious of putting her in it.

By the spring of 1870, it became apparent that there was no way to keep *The Revolution* solvent. Anthony, who seemed to her friends to have an unrelenting capacity to go on in the face of any hardships was heartbroken. But very few friends noticed how difficult it was for her when she had to give up her paper. For years it had been her dream to become an effective vehicle to promote their issues, to introduce their ideas, and to convey their positions on a wide range of women's concerns.

Susan had sustained *The Revolution* for twenty-nine months, mostly on subscriptions. Train's initial three-thousand-dollar investment and the seven-thousand-dollar investment of his friend Melliss, the Democratic editor of the *New York World,* had been consumed in the early months of publication. Susan had attempted to form a stock company to keep the paper alive. But *The Revolution* and its editors were so steeped in controversy and so constantly the subject of vociferous attack that the supporters of woman's rights would not invest in it or contribute the sorely need funds.

Expenses soared—the highest quality paper; the best typesetters; light, airy offices—and Susan refused to cut back on costs when the going got tough. It was a matter of womanly pride, a reflection of her esteem for her sex. When the editors were forced to cut back, it was felt personally. Mrs. Stanton took no salary, Susan was paid only her expenses, and Parker Pillsbury drew a very small salary. These were the kinds of sacrifices movement leaders learned to accept when it was necessary for the cause, but that kind of principled position did not lighten Susan's need for self-support or Mrs. Stanton's financial responsibility for her children.

In the final months of her proprietorship of *The Revolution,* Susan clung to her dying dream. "My paper must not, shall not go down," she insisted to her cousin, Anson Lapham, who loaned her four thousand dollars to keep the paper afloat. But it was a drop in the sea of mounting debts she faced. Her despair mounted. "I would say 'amen,' but to live and fail—it would be too terrible to bear."[49]

For the first time in a long time Susan's family began to worry about her. Her brothers and sisters saw the emotional and spiritual toll her work was taking on her. Daniel offered to help with the stock company. Mary, who was a schoolteacher in Rochester, spent her summer vacation in New York "holding down the fort" of *The Revolution* offices, while Susan threw herself into a feverish lecture tour to raise money and sell subscriptions. Her energy had an edge of desperation to it. "She is working like a whole plantation of slaves," Martha Wright noticed.[50]

When Susan returned to New York and walked into their offices a flood of anguish swept over her. Standing in the center of the room at the round table with its pretty cloth, she looked at the portraits of Lucretia Mott and Mary Wollstonecraft and remembered how she and Mrs. Stanton had chosen and hung them when they had first settled into their work there. Here they had all their documents and shelves of speeches and pamphlets over by the windows that looked out to city hall park. There was Mill's new essay *On the Subjection of Women* and old speeches of Higginson and Phillips. These offices had become a kind of second home for her and Mrs. Stanton. "There is an atmosphere of womanly purity and delicacy about the place," one reporter noted, "everything is refreshingly neat and clean, and suggestive of reform."[51] It was not only a newspaper office but also a center of woman's rights activity, where women could drop by for a visit or to organize for their Working Women's Associations.

Mary Anthony had been with her sister Susan for days in *The Revolution* offices. "Susan, you cannot begin to know how you have changed." She could see that this work was taking a toll on her sister; something was different in her countenance and her carriage. It was not exactly a hardness; she was tough. It was more than fatigue. Susan seemed depleted. It worried Mary to the extent that she could barely hold back her tears. "Please Susan, I beg of you for your own sake and for ours, do not persevere in the work unless people will aid you enough to do credit to yourself as you always have done." Even D.R. wrote and advised that she must make a change.

Susan could not let go. *The Revolution*'s debt must be paid, and woman's right to vote must be won. This was not the moment to measure personal cost. But Mary was insistent. "Make a plain statement to your friends, and if they will not come to your rescue, go down as gracefully as possible and with far less indebtedness than you will have three months from now."[52]

Susan was weary but detached in a certain way. "I feel a great, calm sadness like that of a mother binding out a dear child that she could not support."[53]

It was Mary who finally told her, "Susan it is very hard for all of us to feel that you are working so hard and being so misunderstood." She worried that the charges of financial recklessness launched against her sister after the Kansas campaigns would be revived and refueled. With the pressing debts Susan could hold on no longer. She and Mrs. Stanton asked Anna Dickenson to take over the paper, but Anna refused. Finally on May 22, 1870, the proprietorship of *The Revolution* passed from Susan's hands to Laura Curtis Bullard and Theodore Tilton. Susan was left with the paper's ten-thousand-dollar debt, which she was determined to work off lecture by lecture—"hundred by hundred."

Now all was lost. Susan conceded that "I suppose it is for the best that I give up *The Revolution*." But she knew that "it will seem pretty tough to see it fall so below its old standards."[54] When the new editors turned it into a literary and society journal she grieved, "It's like signing my own death warrant." Even their revolutionary motto, "Men their rights and nothing more; women their rights and nothing less," was turned into "What God has joined together, let no man put asunder."

The new editors refused to have anything to do with the old radicals. As Susan reported, "According to the new regime, publishers and editors must be thrown overboard, so overboard we went, P.P., E.C.S., and S.B.A." But Susan's despair gave way to a more philosophical view of the situation. "I am not complaining for mine is the fate of almost every originator, pioneer, who has ever opened up the way. I have the joy of knowing that I showed the thing possible—to publish a live out-and-out woman's paper; taught other women to invest, to enter in and reap when I had sown—sown in faith too, such as no canting priest or echoing follower ever dreamed of."[55]

With that she left New York for more lecturing. "I sanguinely hope to cancel this debt in two years of hard work, and I must cheerfully look forward to turning every possible dollar into that channel."[56]

Looking back over the preceding few years, would she have done it differently?

> If you should to-day hold $25,000 in your hand and ask me to choose between the possession of it this hour in place of the agitation, the immense work done by my revolution, during those twenty-nine months by which I sank that amount, I should chose the work done—not the cash in hand. So, you see, I don't groan or murmur—not a bit of it.[57]

9

The Vagaries of Love

IN MAY 1870, THE SAME MONTH THAT SUSAN B. ANTHONY WAS forced to give up *The Revolution,* she and Mrs. Stanton called a mass public meeting "for women only" to protest the MacFarland-Richardson trial. MacFarland was the alcoholic, tyrannical, and abusive husband of actress Abby Sage, who, until she won a legal divorce from him, had been the sole support of their family. Shortly after the divorce, knowing his ex-wife had been having an affair, MacFarland walked into the New York offices of the *Tribune* and shot reporter Albert Richardson, Abby's lover and the man she planned to marry. Abby was immediately befriended by many liberal New Yorkers, including Henry Ward Beecher who, when he heard of the shooting, had immediately rushed to the *Tribune* offices to join Abby to the dying Richardson in marriage. Some weeks later, MacFarland went on trial for murder. He won an acquittal with an insanity defense and was given custody of his and Abby Sage's young son.

This case signaled a new danger to feminists. They saw that neither women's economic independence nor their right to divorce could protect them from arbitrary male power exercised either in the courts or in the family. Before a gathering of two thousand protesting women in Apollo Hall in New York, Anthony and Stanton condemned the judge and jury in the MacFarland-Richardson trial for letting MacFarland go free and giving him custody of the child. They demanded that the governor commit MacFarland to an insane asylum. But for conservative women like Catharine Beecher (Henry's sister), the problem was not MacFarland's freedom; it was Abby Sage's adultery. Beecher told Mrs. Stanton that even "if Mrs. MacFarland was sure she could prove adultery, she was morally free to marry again—but could she be justified on any other grounds without denying the authority of the Lord Jesus Christ."[1]

It was neither a commitment to woman's right to divorce nor his sister's view of marriage as a sacred institution that had inspired Henry Ward Beecher to administer the deathbed wedding vows to Richardson and Sage. Rather, he was caught up in "soul communing," as he called his spiritually purified version of romantic love. For Beecher, Abby Sage's affair with Richardson represented that kind of love. He fancied himself as the vanguard of a new revolution of love, one which brought partners together through their spiritual affinity and elevated the feelings they shared to paramount importance. Spiritual love came from the soul and therefore could not be tied to rules and laws. Beecher saw this as a morally elevated release from legal restrictions. He did not mean to promote a general kind of promiscuity or the pedestrian version, which turned romantic love into passionate and impulsive behaviors. Soul communing was a refined, spiritual love that was deeply romantic.

Although it seemed to place equal emphasis on men's and women's feelings, romantic love actually gave men a new psychological and emotional control over their homes. As they spent increasingly more time away from home to work in the factories and new industries, they had to rely on the binding forces of romantic love to keep their place and power intact in the home. As a social ideal and widespread practice, romantic love was still relatively new to American society. But it was quickly replacing sentimental love as the basis for marriage. Women were no longer going to be birds in gilded cages, objects for adornment and admiration. They were to become emotionally involved and active in the love relation. However, romantic relations did not alter the basis of marital feudalistic power with its arbitrary exercise of beneficence or abuse. Instead women were now expected to emotionally internalize those power relations and then to understand them as love.

Henry Ward Beecher had become one of the chief spokesmen for the higher ideals of romantic love. Beecher, whose beliefs were typical of Protestant ministers at the time, had revised his father's Calvinist theology to reject the belief that fear of hell and atonement should guide individual lives. In its place he proclaimed a new theology of love in which spiritual, holy love, not external law, should determine the bonds of marriage. In theology he elevated vulgarized romantic love to a spiritual, pure union of two loving souls drawn together, not by the traditional obligatory bonds of marriage but through soul communing.

At first glance, Beecher's "Gospel of Love" appeared to be consistent with (if a slightly altered version of) the feminist idea of what love should be—a relation based on equality.[2] He too appeared to reject the idea that the man was made for wisdom and woman for love. Now they were both made for a kind of love that placed emotion over the intellect and made the binding force of marriage spiritual affinity rather than duty. Equality was not what Beecher had in mind at all. He undoubtedly considered himself and his philosophy above an issue such as that.

Anthony would have none of romantic love! As she saw it "true marriage" was "the real marriage of souls when two people take each other on terms of perfect equality, without the desire to control the other, [or] to make the other subservient[,] is a beautiful thing. It is the truest and highest state of all." Anthony anchored her view of love in the objective conditions of equality that must precede marriage. "For a woman to marry a man for support is a demoralizing condition. And for a man to marry a woman merely because she has a beautiful figure is a degradation."[3]

Stanton had proposed that the marriage contract be given the force of a legal contract that is broken when either party fails to comply with it. But Beecher believed that love and not contract should be the binding force of marriage.[4] In contrast to Stanton's idea, Beecher's doctrine drifted into moral vagueness; he neither rejected the passionate, blind intensity of romantic love nor promoted it.

For awhile, Beecher would have it both ways—a higher, purer, love he preached in church and a passionate, yielding, and intense romantic love for some of his female parishioners. For some time, there had been rumors that Beecher had been involved in affairs with women in his congregation. Then, in May 1870, Theodore Tilton's wife Elizabeth, the former poetry editor of *The Revolution* and a friend of Anthony and Stanton, privately admitted to her husband that she had been having an affair since 1868 with his friend and spiritual mentor Henry Ward Beecher. The Beecher-Tilton affair did not reach the proportions of a notorious scandal until late in 1872, when Victoria Woodhull, a proponent of free love, exposed it in her newspaper, *Woodhull and Claflin's Weekly*. As Theodore Tilton and Henry Ward Beecher had maneuvered themselves into the presidencies of the opposing woman's suffrage associations, the scandal of Beecher's affair with Tilton's wife had ramifications throughout the woman's movement. (In April of 1870, Anthony and Stanton agreed that Tilton could organize a Union Suffrage Association for the purpose of bringing the National and American Suffrage associations together under Henry Ward Beecher. Tilton was unsuccessful in his reconciliation efforts. He then launched his own suffrage association anyway and was elected its president.)

Elizabeth Tilton's affair with Beecher began only several months after her husband had concluded an adulterous relationship with another woman. Before Elizabeth accepted the intimate overtures Beecher had been making to her for some time, she had tried with her husband to put their marriage back together. In seeking his wife's forgiveness, Tilton proposed to reinvigorate their long and difficult marital relationship with new ideas of romantic love. The Tiltons' marriage had been a traditional one—they were bound by duty instead of united in love. Now Elizabeth found a new excitement in trying Theodore's "soul loving" to which he had "awakened" her. In this new wedding of two souls (this "higher love" of Beecher's "Gospel of Love"), Elizabeth took responsibility for her husband's infidelity. "Oh, Theodore, darling, I am haunted night and day by the remorse of knowing that because of my harshness and indifference to you, you were driven to despair—perhaps sin, and these last years of unhappiness . . . I am the chief of sinners!"[5]

But this new romantic love did not last for the Tiltons. It was only a matter of months before they returned to the same difficulties they had before. But this time Elizabeth turned in another direction. For over a year she had resisted the sexual advances of Henry Ward Beecher, who was her husband's friend and a frequent visitor to their home. When Theodore turned away from her after their own experiment with romantic love, Beecher's advances took on a different meaning for Elizabeth and their affair began.

Actually, Beecher's "soul communing" was a veiled version of Victoria Woodhull's open platform of free love, which condemned sexual hypocrisy in marriage and promoted open sexual liaisons. But Beecher condemned Woodhull for her ideas and for her impulsive passions, which he believed did not stem from the refined "affinity" of the "higher love" that he preached. At the same time that Tilton found his way to the presidency of his new Union Suffrage Association, Victoria Woodhull, the self-proclaimed proponent of "free love," catapulted herself to the center of the woman's rights movement by announcing her candidacy for President of the United States in her "first Pronunciamento," which was published in the *New York Herald* in April 1870. "Love" was bound to be at the center of the next major woman's rights controversy.

Ironically, Victoria grew up in Ohio under the influence of Lyman Beecher's revival meetings. The patriarch of the prodigious Beecher clan had left a family of famous reformers and a legacy of tamed Calvinism. Victoria Woodhull had other influences as well. She heard voices as a young child and believed she had the ability to predict the future. These experiences led to an interest in spiritualism. But by that time spiritualism had lost considerable credibility from its early days, when the rappings heard by Margaret Fox had led to spiritual gatherings and attempts to make contact with departed loved ones. Woodhull's family moved frequently, and her insecure, spiritually intense youth led her into an impulsive marriage, which lasted only weeks when she discovered that her husband was a drunkard who frequented prostitutes. Victoria, still only a young girl, had a child and then left her painful marriage. Within a short time she had became attracted to an officer, a Colonel Blood, who taught her about free love. Shortly after their meeting and their open and spontaneous sexual liaison, Blood abandoned his family and he and Victoria traveled together for months practicing free love. In 1866, he divorced his wife and married Victoria. They divorced two years later to insure their sexual freedom, while openly living together. By this time, they were living in New York City with other members of Victoria's family. Her sister had recently made the acquaintance of Commodore Vanderbuilt, and he helped the two women open their own brokerage firm in New York in 1870. Despite their business success, Victoria's "tainted" character opened her to attack from respectable society and particularly from the Beechers—Catharine, Harriet, and Henry. To them she was a symbol of degenerate morality. To her they represented sexual hypocrisy.

In promoting free love Woodhull went a step further than Anthony and Stanton had gone and called for the repeal of all marriage laws. "I have an inalienable constitutional, and natural right to love whom I may, to love as long or as short a period as I can, to change that love every day if I please."[6] To Anthony free love was not a "natural right" but merely a "variety system," and women like Woodhull seemed to have a "more numerous record of husbands that are not husbands" than the woman in the Bible who Christ noted had five husbands.[7] But that was not the point. What aggravated Anthony was that Woodhull preached her ideas about free love as part of her woman's rights platform. At first Anthony took the free-love issue lightly with a "let-them-do-what-they-may" attitude, concluding that if this was how Woodhull wanted to conduct her private life, so be it. Likewise, as rumors of the Beecher-Tilton affair began to spread, she ignored them. Concerned as she was for her friend Elizabeth Tilton, she considered these questions to be private matters that had no place in public, particularly not in any discussion of the women's movement.

During the 1850s, the feminist critique of sexual domination was expressed primarily in terms of women's refusal to be the objects of men's lust. Now the emotional role of women was meant to involve them more deeply in their marriages at a time when they were becoming more active in the public world. Anthony argued that "women's subsistence is in the hands of men, and most arbitrarily and unjustly does he exercise his consequent power."[8] Her analysis was essentially correct. She also saw the ideological manipulations behind the debate. "The present howl is an old trick of the arch-fiend to divert public thought from the main question, viz: woman's equal freedom and equal power to make and control her own conditions in the state, in the church and, most of all, in the home."[9] Whatever the changes in the economy, the home was still a feudalistic enclave. Wives still owed their husbands sex, children, child-rearing, and housekeeping, and they were now expected to add to that free love or "soul communing." This was actually how women were to become the means of by which factories could continue to exploit male workers. Although their working conditions might be poor, the men knew that they were sent home each day to their own "castles" and emotional comforts.[10]

Anthony told Martha Wright in the midst of the free-love controversy that "we are fallen upon strange times, but there is no way but to live through them." For her the issue of free love was an economic one. It was not free love that women needed but rather the protection from "fallen men," who "feel it no crime to despoil any woman's virtue they meet."[11] Anthony once told a friend that poverty-stricken homeless girls were the ones who must be put above men's seductive reach. She believed that the movement's work was not to reform fallen women but to "open all doors to all profitable & honorable work to women" and perhaps to reform the fallen men who preyed on the most vulnerable of them.[12]

For Anthony both sentimental and romantic love were impossible, and she probably came the closest to expressing her personal feelings about it to Nellie Bly in an interview. "In fact, I never felt I could give up my life of freedom to become a man's housekeeper. When I was young, if a girl married poor, she became a housekeeper and a drudge. If she married wealth she became a pet and a doll. Just think, had I married at twenty, I would have been a drudge or a doll for fifty-five years. Think of it!"[13]

She had very definite ideas about the marriage commitment, beliefs that remained constant throughout her life. "I am not even a believer in second marriages after one of the parties is dead, so sacred and binding do I consider the marriage relation." There was a time after her sister Guelma died when Susan suspected that her brother-in-law was interested in another woman. She was furious; she believed that the spirit lived on after death; therefore, his marriage to her sister was an eternal bond. On the other hand, she still believed that this inviolable union was dangerous to freedom. "It is almost impossible for a man and a woman to have a close sympathetic friendship without the tendrils of one soul becoming fastened around the other, with the result of infinite pain and anguish."[14] Had Anthony had the possibility and seen the importance of raising this point in public she would have moved into the core of the question of emotional and sexual domination—an issue that remains an unresolved question even for late-twentieth-century feminists. Why she chose not to raise the issue is hard to say. It may have been because she was embattled on so many other fronts and was narrowing her focus to suffrage, or because she had learned that as a single woman she was not considered a legitimate speaker on the subject. She may have truly believed this to be a private matter. It is likely that all of these factors played into her position that there was no place on the woman's rights platform for free love.

In January of 1871, Victoria Woodhull won a hearing before the Judiciary Committee of the House of Representatives to argue that women already had the right to vote under the Fourteenth and Fifteenth amendments to the Constitution. She asked for a declaratory act from Congress to enable their rights under these amendments. Her proposal was not new but had never reached the higher halls of Congress before. Only a year before, *the Revolution* had carried the legal arguments of Francis Minor, a Missouri lawyer. He had argued in behalf of his wife Virginia's case that women already had the right to vote according to his legal interpretation of the Constitution. Until Woodhull's hearing was announced in the newspapers, neither Anthony nor any of the women of the National knew anything about it. They had scheduled their National Woman's Suffrage Association convention to open in Washington the same day.

Susan B. Anthony called her organizers together to decide what to do. Isabella Hooker would not consider associating with a women of such ill repute. Others suggested they ignore the proceedings. Anthony finally convinced them that they must reschedule their convention to open in the afternoon and attend Woodhull's hearing that morning.

In the antechamber to the committee room before the hearing, Victoria overheard some lady say that Isabella Hooker had intended to snub Mrs. Woodhull. Victoria remembered later that a gentleman stepped forward and said, "It would ill become these women, and especially a Beecher, to talk of antecedents or to cast any smirch on Mrs. Woodhull, for I am reliably assured that Henry Ward Beecher preaches to at least twenty of his mistresses every Sunday."[15] At this point it was only rumor, as word had not yet spread of Beecher's affair with Elizabeth Tilton.

Anthony glanced at Victoria Woodhull before she began her presentation to the committee. The young woman was pale, and when she began to speak she was almost inaudible. Anthony noticed that "her voice trembled slightly with emotion which only made the reading more effective."[16] But as Victoria Woodhull worked her way into her message, "her voice strengthened. She became caught up with a sense of her own message and as always in such a case, her cheeks flushed, her eyes began to shine."[17] Her appeal was strong, clear, and forthright.

In her memorial to Congress in 1871, Woodhull claimed that women already had the right to vote under the Fourteenth and Fifteenth amendments and that it was necessary only that Congress enact appropriate legislation to guarantee to exercise of that right. Her argument was built on clear feminist logic that turned meanings of terms intended to discriminate against women into a radical analysis in women's favor.

The Constitution defines a woman born or naturalized in the United States, and subject to the jurisdiction thereof, to be a citizen. It recognizes the right of a citizen to vote. It declares that the right of a citizen to vote shall not be denied or abridged by the United States or any state on the account of "race, color, or previous condition of servitude."

Having defined woman as a citizen, she analyzed the constitutional definition of race.

Women, black and white, belong to races, although different races. A race of people comprises all the people, male and female. The right to vote cannot be denied on account of race. All people included in the term race have a right to vote, unless otherwise prohibited.

And then she defined the meaning of "color" in the Fifteenth Amendment.

Women of all races are white, black, or some intermediate color. Color comprises all people, of all races and both sexes. The right to vote cannot be denied on account of color. All people included in the term color have the right to vote unless otherwise prohibited.[18]

When Victoria Woodhull finished her presentation, Anthony quickly turned to Congressman Benjamin Butler, from Massachusetts. She reminded him of the Civil War days when he—General Butler—had declared that all black people who escaped from southern plantation masters to his lines in the border state of Virginia were to be treated as "contraband of war." By this act, he gave official military sanction to not returning slaves to their owners. Long before the Emancipation Proclamation, Congress had upheld his actions by passing the First Confiscation Act. There in Congress, exactly a decade later, Anthony told Butler, "Now I wish, General Butler, that you would say 'contraband' for us."[19]

Susan B. Anthony was at Victoria Woodhull's side to congratulate her as soon as the meeting adjourned. Other delegates to the convention waited in the antechamber of the committee room to welcome her to their cause. That afternoon Anthony escorted Woodhull to the convention, where she marched to the platform between Anthony and Isabella Hooker to take her seat among the notables of the woman's rights movement and again deliver the memorial she had presented to Congress.

Exactly a month after Victoria Woodhull's hearing before the Judiciary Committee, its chairman, Representative John A. Bingham of Ohio, issued a committee report that denied her demand for a declaratory act. The congressional committee refused to interpret the Fourteenth and Fifteenth amendments as already granting woman's suffrage. In effect, Bingham's report remanded the women back to the states, by claiming that Congress could not take this action "without the consent of the people of the States and against their constitutions' laws."[20] Anthony proclaimed that this was woman's "Dred Scott decision." She reasoned that Bingham's report was similar to the Supreme Court decision, which had returned Dred Scott to his master, asserting that a slave could not be a citizen and therefore did not have the right to sue in federal court.

Woodhull was condemned by women in and out of the movement for her advocacy of free love and her own promiscuity. Reaction set in both within the National and from the more conservative American against Woodhull's presence on the platform for woman's suffrage. Isabella Hooker, typifying second generation women who learned woman's rights without changing consciousness, had altered her opinion of Woodhull after hearing her presentation before the congressional committee. Now Hooker considered her "a remarkable woman & of a sweetness I have seldom seen." But Hooker was pressured by her sisters, especially Catharine Beecher and Harriet Beecher Stowe, to dissociate herself from this woman. And, it seems, her husband John could not sleep, as "he has been so harassed by my three sisters in keeping quiet." Catharine and Harriet, who obviously had not yet heard the gossip throughout the reform movement of their brother's affair of at least two years with Elizabeth Tilton, unrelentingly wrote "imploring me to have nothing to do with her."[21]

Isabella's position was one of studied ambivalence. She could see the value Mrs. Woodhull brought to the movement and felt akin to her spiritualism, but she was vulnerable to pressures from her family and worried about the stress the situation caused her ill husband. Anthony cautioned Mrs. Hooker, "When we women *begin* to search individual records and antecedents of those who bring influence, brains and cash to our work of enfranchising women—we shall *begin* with the men." She told Martha Wright that she had heard rumors of "undue familiarity with persons of the opposite sex" about Beecher, Higginson, Butler, and others.

> Before I shall consent to an arraignment of Woodhull or any other earnest woman worker who shall come to our Platform in Washington or elsewhere—I shall insist upon the closest investigation into all the scandals afloat about those men—not one of whom have I heard Mrs.

Hooker or any other woman express any fears of accepting whatever they may say or do for us.

When we shall require of the men, who shall speak—vote, work for us—to prove that they have never been unduly familiar with any woman, never guilty of trifling with or desecrating womanhood—it will be time enough for us to demand of women to prove that no man has ever trifled with or desecrated them.[22]

Anthony was forceful in her defense of Woodhull. But afterwards she worried that she had been too harsh on her friends. She told Mrs. Wright, "I know that so soon as Mrs. Hooker shall stop to think a minute—she, too, will say the same—It isn't for you nor me nor Mrs. Hooker to say who may & who may not be worthy to stand on our platform & plead & argue the Constitutional law for woman."[23] As long as Woodhull kept the issue of free love separated from her women's rights work, Anthony welcomed her to the cause.

Anthony was reinvigorated by the spunk, the energy, and the clear political strategizing of this young woman. "I feel a new inspiration—spoke as if the very gods were whistling through me," she told Mrs. Hooker. She was, however, concerned with Woodhull's reliance on men in her political work, and also told Mrs. Hooker to tell Victoria not to trust men to write her editorials. "They can't express thoughts for us women."[24]

Still optimistic, Anthony invited Woodhull to the National's May anniversary meeting and then told Isabella Hooker, "We must make our May meeting bristle all over, every session, with work plans and purposes. Don't let us be bored with mere theorizing in the propriety of voting. I am sick to death of the old time pleadings, prayings: if you please master would let us!!! Ours is possession—verification of the ground—and that is with us, as with every other class—nine tenths of the law, & we must hold on to it."[25]

The May meeting was a smashing success and became known as the "Woodhull convention." The feminists were still stinging from the Bingham report, which they took as their "Dred Scott." Some women were concerned about a woman of Woodhull's repute mixing with decent ladies in the convention. But Anthony noted that "the American is sick unto death with propriety"[26] and saw to it that Victoria Woodhull was seated on their platform between Elizabeth Cady Stanton and Lucretia Mott, giving her full legitimization. Woodhull delivered the major convention address and fired another bolt at women's enemies.

If the very next Congress refuses women all the legitimate results of citizenship . . . we shall proceed to call another convention expressly to frame a new constitution and to erect a new government . . . We mean treason; we mean secession, and on a thousand times grander scale than was that of the South. We are plotting a revolution; we will overthrow this bogus Republic and plant a government of righteousness in its stead.[27]

Behind Woodhull's rhetoric was her plan to dissolve the National into a People's Convention, which would then nominate her for president of the United States. Woman's rights and free love would be her platform; however, this was a plan not yet fully unveiled.

Meanwhile, the other Beecher sisters kept up their attack of Woodhull. Harriet published a weekly story in a newspaper column and in it she ridiculed Woodhull, although not by name. Hoping to reconcile her family to her woman's right work, Isabella asked her sister Catharine to call upon Mrs. Woodhull. She did, and in a long conversation attacked her sexual attitudes which questioned the sanctity of marriage and undermined the foundations of Christianity. Catharine equated free love with animal instincts, and went on and on until Victoria quietly pointed out to her that her brother, Henry Ward Beecher, was also a practitioner of free love. Catharine was stunned but not subdued. In reaction, she unwisely threatened Victoria with retribution if she continued to make such outlandish charges.

By now, the Henry Ward Beecher-Elizabeth Tilton affair had been whispered about throughout the reform world. Anthony and Stanton decided not to discuss it with anyone, but Stanton confided the story of the Beecher-Tilton affair to Woodhull to assure her of her belief that "we have had enough women sacrificed to this sentimental, hypocritical prating about purity."[28] Stanton had felt an instant attraction and connection to the young, fiery Woodhull. It is likely that when Woodhull preached that marriage should not be governed by a legal contract, Stanton thought she had found sympathy with her own position that marriage should be *only* a legal contract. Initially, Stanton believed that there was a closer similarity to their positions on marriage than actually existed.

No one anticipated Victoria Woodhull's next move. In a letter published in the *New York World*, she charged that sexual purity did not reign in the world of reform. She made no direct accusation against any persons, but everyone knew she was referring to the Beecher-Tilton affair. Her exposé was as much an attack on the self-righteous morality of the Beecher sisters as it was a good way to keep her name at the center of controversy. It was her strategy to keep attention of the press focused on her as she soon would announce her candidacy for president of the United States.

Anthony again defended Woodhull, this time explaining that she considered Woodhull's free-love platform to be a badge of her oppression as a woman.

> Not until we catechise and refuse men—will I consent to question women—And it is only that Mrs. Woodhull is a woman, & that we are women—all of an enslaved class—that we ever dream of such a thing—I know the pressure upon you & I know more—that so soon as you get breath you will rebound in spirit & say with me—come one, come all—the deeper the gall of bitterness the poor woman's soul has drank—the more does she need the saving grace of absolute freedom from dependence on men for the control of her circumstances.[29]

Woodhull's letter to the *World* put Henry Ward Beecher on guard. He had formerly preached against Mrs. Woodhull's loose morals. Now he wanted to silence her. He met with Theodore Tilton and they decided that the best way to control Mrs. Woodhull was for Tilton to gain her confidence and become her friend. He would then be able to suppress any future exposure of Beecher's affair with Elizabeth Tilton. Tilton visited Mrs. Woodhull in her office, they discussed her letter to the *New York World* and then he invited her home to dinner. Over the next few weeks his friendly overtures led to a sexual affair with her. Rumors flew! Anthony's only comment was that there was something humiliating about all of the "kissing & hugging & putting away old men & getting new ones to hug & kiss emblazoned in print constantly. Your leading W. S. women, its simply sickening!"[30]

Thinking they would leave the free-love controversy and gossip behind, Susan B. Anthony and Elizabeth Cady Stanton departed for their first trip across the continent and a rigorous lecture tour on the West Coast. They spoke in one city after another en route to California. When they reached the Rockies, there were finally some relaxing moments, and they began to enjoy the magnificent mountain vista together. After a short stop in Laramie, Wyoming, where a hundred women accompanied them to the train station and Mrs. Stanton gave a short rallying speech from the train, she and Susan settled into a "drawing room" they had all to themselves. The familiarity and affection of their long years together had created intimate bonds. There was a warm feeling between them, and sometimes they sat close to each other in the car watching the Rocky Mountains unfold before them. Susan was happy. "Here we are just as cozy and happy as lovers." They described their own relationship when they talked of the meaning of love, and Mrs. Stanton noted, "In all that there is real bliss, if only the two are perfect equals, two loving people, neither assuming to control the other." They discussed how "love for and faith in each other alone can make . . . a heaven, and without these any home is a hell." Their love, expressed in embraces and warm closeness, held meaning for Susan that was more spiritual than physical. "It is not the outside things which make life, but the inner spirit of love which casteth out all devils and bringeth in all angels."[31]

The train rambled on over rugged mountain passes and through verdant mountain meadows. It was early July when they entered California. One morning when the porter came to their drawing room and called them out to see Donner Lake and the Sierra Nevada range from the Donner Pass, Susan gazed upon a view that was "sublime—beyond anything I've ever seen."[32] A flood of memories swept over her as she felt once again the delight in nature that had moved her so deeply as a young woman.

Both press and friends of woman's suffrage were waiting for them when they arrived in San Francisco on July 9. They found their suite of rooms in the newly opened Grand Hotel filled and constantly replenished with fresh flowers and fruit. Amidst all the attention, they were even able to slip away from the crowds to some of northern California's most stunning sights. "We had many delightful sails in the harbor and drives to the seashore and for miles along the beach," Mrs. Stanton remembered. They reveled in the lushness of the country and the majesty of the ocean. Along the coastal road they stopped at the Ocean House and spent several hours "watching the gambols of the celebrated seals."[33]

In San Francisco they visited Laura Fair at the county jail. She was a prostitute who had been condemned for killing her lover, a prominent San Franciscan. Since her trial she had become the city's pariah. The press doggedly followed the famous couple to the jail and just as determinedly castigated them for dignifying a prostitute with a visit.

That night Anthony confronted the sexual hypocrisy of a society that claimed to protect women, while leaving women like Laura

Fair abandoned and defenseless. She told her audience of twelve hundred that every day the newspapers carried stories proving that men did not protect women as they claimed they did. She talked about the thirteen hundred infants who had been left in baskets at a foundling hospital in New York City the year before. "These figures prove that thirteen hundred women in that city, forced to give up their children, were not being protected by men." The crowd was not pleased with her linking ordinary poverty and hardship to men's power over women. A storm of hisses and boos followed when she dared to suggest that "if all men had protected all women as they would have their own wives and daughters protected, you would have no Laura Fair in your jail tonight."[34] The audience nearly became riotous and refused to let her speak. Anthony stood silent before them, but she refused to move from the platform. Soon the audience quieted down, and Anthony, with even more force, repeated her original statement. Again the hisses and boos reverberated throughout the auditorium, and again, after she silenced them, she repeated the same statement another time. Her determination and perseverance even under such heated attack drew her audiences to her; they had to admire her. After the speech she went back to the Grand Hotel, and noted with pride that she had turned twelve hundred hisses to cheers.[35] That night she had a contented sleep knowing she had driven her message home against all odds.

The next morning she opened the newspapers to find that "every paper came out against me and my speech last night—never before got such a raking."[36] Within a few days, the story was carried in newspapers across the nation. The adverse publicity caused her audience turnout to diminish markedly—"The shadow of the newspapers hangs over me every minute."[37] No one wanted to be associated with her, even those who agreed and admired her stand. Susan's sister Mary read of the controversy in the Rochester papers and wrote, "If your words for Mrs. Fair have made your trip a failure, so let it be—it is no disgrace to you. It is scandalous the way the papers talk of you, but stick to what you feel to be right and let the world wag."[38] Mary knew that the personal attacks not only caused her sister pain, but that the smaller audiences would cut into Susan's earning power. She was still paying off the enormous debt from *The Revolution.*

Susan's West Coast visit lasted until the end of the year. In the fall, when she went on a lecture tour to Portland, Oregon, and later traveled through the Northwest to British Columbia and Vancouver, she was hounded by the Laura Fair controversy. The nearly

universal castigation of her in the press affected her more than it
ever had before. And through it all Mrs. Stanton left Susan to fend
for herself. Susan was hurt. In the summer while they were still
together, she and Mrs. Stanton would sometimes sit at a table and
write letters. But to her dismay, she had not yet read or seen one
word in refutation of the press's outrageous treatment of my lecture."[39] Despondent, Susan sat in her room one evening wondering,
"Could she—would she if she could do so much to put Editors right
as to what I say & do?" In San Francisco, Susan had taken Mrs.
Stanton's speech to every newspaper to insure that they would not
misquote her. That was what Mrs. Stanton expected of her; but she
did not reciprocate. This was yet another of those times when Mrs.
Stanton took Susan as a kind of surrogate husband—someone who
would protect her but one who needed no protection herself.

Some weeks later, traveling alone in Oregon Susan enjoyed the
attention she received. People came to visit because they wanted to
see *her,* "instead of merely sitting a lay figure and listening to the
brilliant scintillations as they emanated from her [Mrs. Stanton's]
never exhausted magazine." Susan rarely gave in to her personal
need for recognition. She confided to her sister, "There is no alternative—whoever goes into a parlor or before an audience with that
woman does it at the cost of a fearful overshadowing."[40]

Usually Susan claimed that she did not mind being overshadowed, "because I felt that our cause was most profited by her being
seen and heard." But there was something besides Stanton's magnetic and charming presence and radical arguments that attracted
all the attention to her. She was soft and matronly and she chatted
about her family, told stories of motherhood, and related her experiences as a wife. Being a wife and mother mediated being a woman
unto herself.

But despite Anthony's personal difficulties with Stanton, before
she left for Oregon, they set out on an expedition in mid-July to
Yosemite Valley. The trip temporarily lifted Susan's spirits and diverted her from the depression that had set in with the Laura Fair
controversy a few weeks before. She and Stanton had had bloomers
made for their horseback ride into the Yosemite Valley. The rugged
descent down the slopes was the only way to the hotel in the valley
after the stage left visitors at the highest mountain village, accessible
only by coach. They wrote ahead to order a sturdy horse for Mrs.
Stanton. Susan joked about whether "Mrs. Stanton's 180 over de-
pois will break the back of the Yosemite mustang?"[41]

Susan was taller and leaner than Mrs. Stanton, but she still mounted her horse with difficulty, finally adjusting herself into the man's saddle. Mrs. Stanton's horse was strong enough to sustain her weight, but mounting it proved to be a major task. "My steed was so broad that I could not reach the stirrups, and the moment we began to descend, I felt as if I were going over his head." She finally slid down from the horse and insisted on walking down into the valley.

Susan rode on ahead with most of the party. She became confident as she watched her horse "fastening one foot after another in the rocks and earth and thus carefully easing me down the steeps, while my guide baited me on by saying, 'you are doing nicely, that is the worst place on the trail,' when the fact was it hardly began to match what was coming." When she finally arrived at the hotel, "a more used-up mortal than I could not well exist," she worried about "poor Mrs. Stanton, four hours behind in the broiling sun, fairly sliding down the mountain." She had a lunch prepared and sent it back with her guide to Mrs. Stanton.

It was about six o'clock in the evening when someone spotted Mrs. Stanton's party in the distance. Mrs. Stanton, who had a marvelous capacity to laugh at herself and to find the comic in some of her near tragic moments, later recounted the rest of the story. She told how she had made it down the mountain but refused to hike across the valley floor to the hotel. "I can neither ride nor walk further, tell Mr. Hutchins to send a wheelbarrow or four men with a blanket to transport me to the hotel," she instructed her guide. And with that she laid down in the grass and fell asleep. They found a carriage to send to her, and Susan was waiting on the steps of the hotel to welcome her. Mrs. Stanton later complained that when Susan saw her coming, she "laughed immoderately at my helpless plight."[42]

Mrs. Stanton slept in until noon the next day, but Susan was up and on her horse by eight o'clock in the morning to ride out to the Vernal and Nevada falls, which cascaded from the tops of the mountains into the rivers that wended their way through the valley. The next day Susan explored parts of the valley on horse from early morning until seven in the evening, when she reached the hotel "tired-tired. Not a muscle, not one inch of flesh from my heels to my hands that was not sore and lame." She and Mrs. Stanton sat talking in the evening as she rubbed her aching muscles with powerful camphor that her mother had packed for her.

When she awoke on Sunday morning it was still dark. She planned to ride with a party to Mirror Lake, the still surface that perfectly reflected Half Dome, which rose massively above the lake to an elevation of eighty-two hundred feet. The party had planned a sunrise service, where Susan would be able to watch "the coming of the sun over the rocky spires, reflected in the placid water."

> Such a glory mortal never beheld elsewhere. The lake was smooth as finest glass; the lofty granite peaks with their trees and shrubs were reflected more perfectly than costliest mirror ever sent back the face of most beautiful woman, and as the sun slowly emerged from behind a point of rock, the thinnest, flakiest white clouds approached or hung round it, and the reflection shaded them with the most delicate, yet most perfect and riches hues of the rainbow.

Like the transcendentalists who found God immanent in nature, Susan found the richness of her spiritual life in the glories of the natural world. "While we watched and worshipped we trembled lest some rude fish or bubble should break our mirror and forever shatter the picture seemingly wrought for our special eyes that Sunday morning." She later told her mother that as she stood on the edge of Mirror Lake, "Then and there, in that holy hour, I thought of you dear Mother, in the body, and of dear father, in the beyond." She had looked around her and was in wonder. "O, how nothing seemed manmade—temples, creeds and codes!"[43]

After the July Yosemite trip, Mrs. Stanton returned east while Susan prepared for a long lecture trip through the Northwest which would last until the end of the year. It was not until December, when Susan returned to San Francisco to begin her trip east, that the "flurry of prejudice" against her died out.

In January of 1872, while crossing the Rockies, the train in which Susan was a passenger was "stuck in a snow drift five miles west of Sherman, on a steep grade, with one hundred men shovelling in front of us."[44] Sitting out this "fearful ordeal," Susan recorded her work for 1871: "six months on East, six months on West." She had given sixty-three lectures to June 1: twenty-six on the way to California; and eighty-two in Oregon and Washington. She guessed that she had traveled thirteen thousand miles. Her gross receipts were $4318, which after her own expenses made only a small dent in the large *Revolution* debt.

If the women's movement was steeped in controversy in its leadership, it was open, alive, and responsive at the grass-roots level. Anthony and Stanton had been encouraged by the general response to their lecture trip during which they saw the life of their movement in women's organizing and actions in small towns and remote western cities. But Anthony remained concerned about the movement leadership and was rightly worried that this second generation feminism was losing its unifying force and political direction. The movement had been racked by internal splits and fighting between the National and the American; she had seen the demise of their own woman's paper; and now the free-love controversy was edging its way into the center of their attention. She had gone along with Victoria Woodhull when she had acted independently to get a hearing before Congress. But she undoubtedly had Woodhull in mind as a potential threat to the movement when she wrote to Mrs. Stanton, "Remember that *you*—E.C.S.—are *President* of the National W.S. Committee—and that is *your immediate duty as such*—to *issue the call forthwith, at once*—*without delay*—for the 7th Annual Convention at Washington the 3rd week of January 1872." Susan also wrote, "You must go before the Judiciary Committee this winter—and speak too in Representative Hall. We must conquer that room—by opening its doors."

Mrs. Stanton was as used to receiving these kinds of orders as she was to ignoring them. Susan, fully aware of this, admitted that she was trying to "fire your soul to the importance of seizing the helm of our ship again." She saw that the issues were becoming clouded and insisted to Mrs. Stanton that "your nature abhors a vacuum." Stanton must take control of the governing committee of the National. "If you as head of our National Committee step boldly to the front at Washington. . . . You owe it to yourself & the cause to be there first—I was almost going to say *to me too*—for our obligations to the movement are one & that is to hold the helm & keep the ship from running on to shoals & quicksands. So I beg you write the Call—good, strong, singing bugle blast—inviting every earnest worker & speaker to come—every society to send representatives—every State surely one good strong woman—to get a Declaratory Act."[45]

Rather than engage in disputes over leadership, Anthony's strategy was to map out new campaigns, to march forward, and to let political action speak for her. She arrived in Washington, D.C., in time for the January convention at which the leadership of the National declared that women should assume their right to vote under the Fourteenth and Fifteenth amendments. Then she pressed Congress again for a declaratory act which would interpret the Fourteenth Amendment as giving women the right to vote. She had previously told Hooker that she wanted to "drive both Congress & the courts to declare against 14th Amendment if they will & then if they dare against 16th—that would drive us all back to our States— and compel us to work to get suffrage through one plan that would greatly multiply our power."

Strategically, Anthony saw that their besieged movement would mobilize in response to attacks and unify at the grass-roots level. But first they must force Congress and the courts to act and declare themselves in favor of woman's suffrage or be the explicit enemies of woman. Then she would call for mass meetings in every city in the country to mobilize women to seize their right to go to the polls and vote. "Everywhere I make women pledge themselves to do so & to carry their case into Court." She hoped that the "new Dred Scott decision of Bingham's" would fire women to the anger they should have over their servile status. "The more Fugitive Slave Laws & Dred Scott against us—the faster will our idea find its way— nothing helps the right like outrageous violations of it inflicted upon intelligent people."[46]

This was Anthony's organizing strategy for 1872, which she proposed in her lectures and would present to the National convention. But while she was lecturing in Kansas, after a brief visit home to Rochester during the spring of 1872, a man handed her a copy of Woodhull's newly published paper. In it was a call for the National's May meeting. "This convention will declare the platform of the People's Party, and consider the nominations of candidates for President and Vice-President of the United States." Anthony was furious, especially when she saw that the call had been signed with her own name as well as with the names of Stanton, Hooker, and Matilda Joslyn Gage (who was not fully involved with the National). Anthony knew, and she expected Stanton to know that Woodhull's candidacy would divert the National from suffrage.

"Never did Mrs. Stanton do so foolish a thing,"[47] Anthony proclaimed. But when she returned east, she rented the hall for their meeting and then went directly to Tenafly to confer with Mrs. Stanton. She found that her friend had complete confidence in Woodhull's plan and was just as sure that it presented no threat to their movement. Susan argued that it was not Mrs. Woodhull who was the threat but the men behind her, particularly those from the spiritualist movement.

If she were influenced by *women* spirits, either in the body or out of it, in the direction she steers, I might consent to be a mere sail-hoister for her; but as it is, she is wholly owned and dominated by *men* spirits and I spurn the control of the whole lot of them, just precisely the same when reflected through her woman's tongue and pen as if they spoke directly for themselves.[48]

But Mrs. Stanton disagreed. She sided with what she considered to be Woodhull's courageous confrontation against moral hypocrisy.

Whatever the consequence of their arguments before the convention, Susan and Mrs. Stanton left Tenafly together for New York City. When they arrived at Steinway Hall for the opening of the convention, their public demeanor was "like husband and wife, each has the feeling that we must have no differences in public." They marched down the aisle together, went up to the platform, and opened the meeting. This was not the first, nor would it be the only, time in their years together that in the midst of disagreement they presented this image. "To the world we always seem to agree and uniformly reflect each other."[49] But as Stanton pointed out, their loyalty was not blind, their criticism was free and open, and each was in her own way a strong-minded woman.

So was Victoria Woodhull, who, after Anthony opened the meeting, marched down the aisle and took the platform. She announced that this was not only the National Woman's Suffrage Association convention but a meetings of the People's party. Anthony was furious. She countered Woodhull by stating that she had rented the hall in her own name for the National meeting only. Anthony asked all those who were there for the meeting of the People's party to leave the hall. In the jargon of the women's movement, this would have been considered "a most unsisterly act." Many women in attendance that day thought that Victoria Woodhull was, after all, a woman who championed the rights of women. Anthony's friends had seen her take strong and uncompromising positions in the face of the worst attack, but some, including Hooker and Stanton, were aghast at how far she would go to control the helm of the ship. Hooker and Stanton charged Anthony with being "narrow" and "bigoted." Was not their platform open to all who would work for woman's rights? Was that not the very position Anthony herself had defended for so many years?

Woodhull and her supporters left the hall, Stanton resigned from the presidency of the National, and Anthony was elected in her place. But the events were not yet concluded. At the evening session of the National meeting, Woodhull entered again, took the platform where Anthony was presiding, and announced that the People's convention would meet the next day at Apollo Hall. Contentiously, Woodhull moved that the National meeting be adjourned. Anthony refused to put her motion to a vote, so Woodhull called for it herself and received responsive "ayes" from the audience. Rapping her gavel, Anthony declared the meeting out-of-order, at which point Woodhull began to speak. As she talked on about the People's party, Susan B. Anthony walked off the platform and out of the building. In a few minutes, the gas lights went out in the hall. Having found the janitor, Anthony had instructed him to extinguish the lights. With that, the evening session was concluded. Susan B. Anthony had severed Woodhull's candidacy for president from the National's campaign for woman's suffrage.

Apparently, Mrs. Hooker and Mrs. Stanton abandoned Anthony and the National convention to go to the People's convention the next day. The meeting was attended by six hundred enthusiastic supporters of Woodhull, who was nominated as their presidential candidate. Then, without his consent or knowledge, Mrs. Hooker encouraged the convention to nominate Frederick Douglass as Woodhull's vice-presidential running mate. Anthony was at her limit with Isabella Hooker's naive and irresponsible behavior in this matter and told her that such an act was humiliating to Mr. Douglass, particularly since "neither you [Mrs. Hooker] nor Mrs. Stanton would ever think of" running as second to Woodhull.[50]

Woodhull had won the moment. Hooker was carried away with the "sublimity of this hour," but Anthony was "too much in the condition of total collapse of body & soul and all the outer habitments as well—to be able to see or say the word or work of the hour." She told Isabella Hooker that she was no more impressed with the sublimity of this hour than "I have been at the sublimity of every hour and day for the past twenty years."[51]

Although she remained self-assured and adamant in public, Anthony's confidence crumbled in private for the first time in her career. It is a measure of her loyalty to Mrs. Stanton that Susan never confided to anyone the added burden she must have felt from what she saw as Stanton's defection to Woodhull. It was true that in the past they had argued and disagreed as much as they had agreed and supported each other. Now more than ever they began to go their own ways, although on only some political questions. Nevertheless, when she was weary from her lecture tours, weighed down by the *Revolution* debt, and worn down by years of attack, Susan still turned to Mrs. Stanton for support. "I tell you I feel utterly disheartened, not that our cause is going to die or be defeated but as to my place and work."[52] Then she admitted to Martha Wright, "I tell you Mrs. Wright, I am feeling today that *life doesn't pay*— the way seems so blocked up to me on all sides." Anthony wanted more than anything to talk over the whole episode with her trusted friends Mrs. Wright and Matilda Joslyn Gage, "the two sane women, I do hope," for "I tell you I am thrown half off my own feet— really not knowing whether it is I who am gone stark mad or some other people."

If she was near spiritual and emotional collapse, her material condition was no better. After telling Gage and Wright she needed to meet with them, she tried to postpone their meeting for a few weeks "as that is the earliest I can get a whole and decent dress to wear in anybody's house."[53] She had been on the road so continuously for over a year that she had not found the time until then to attend to her clothes, which were in every state of disrepair. But if Gage and Wright insisted that they meet immediately, "I will say amen to that and go in my rags."

Until this moment, Susan B. Anthony had always had "sure knowledge that I was in the right place & way." She told Mrs. Hooker that there is "nothing but such sure faith in one's self can give strength to stand alone without sympathy or aid from those who once stood with us."[54] During the confrontation with Victoria Woodhull she seemed to be standing alone, for even her best friends did not support her. Later, they gave her the support in private they had withheld from her in public. Then it was Mrs. Stanton's advice she valued above all others—"my oldest and longest tried woman friend, ECS" who "sees & knows all my faults quicker & surer than anyone else & I always thought she was free to tell them to me."[55] Even in this controversy, the foundation of their friendship had not been shaken.

Stanton had not retreated from her position on Woodhull; but neither did she continue to support her. In the weeks and months following the convention blow-up, Woodhull's opportunism must have become clear to Stanton, especially when she and Anthony became the subject of an exposé and attack in Woodhull's paper. Woodhull printed a letter from a Dr. D. Orvis implicating Anthony in some scandalous behavior, "which is a perfect fabrication, of course," Anthony told Mrs. Hooker. The contents of Dr. Orvis's assertions about Anthony have not survived in the historical record; thus, we have no document that reveals his charges. But we do know that when Anthony went to the leading woman's suffrage women—including Mrs. Stanton—"each & all of them say the charge is wholly false—none but an evil doer could report me thus." Anthony's response was a bit stronger. "He's a Jack _____," she wrote to Mrs. Hooker, adding that "you may supply the blank or not as you please!"[56]

Mrs. Hooker urged Susan to respond to the new charges. However, Susan knew that Woodhull was then writing a book, and she asserted, "I have not & shall not reply—because it is merely a trap to get a letter from me to publish in their book and they don't get it." But worse than manipulation was that "if she does gather up every supposed and suspected weakness & wickedness of everybody & give them all in detail it will be a sickening heap—for poor human nature is awfully weak & wanting," as Susan told Mrs. Hooker one afternoon.[57] She was certainly thinking of Henry Ward Beecher and Theodore Tilton and of their various love affairs.

While Woodhull had launched an attack against sexual hypocrisy, Susan B. Anthony and others as well began to believe that Woodhull's campaigns and exposés came largely out of her need to draw attention to herself. "Next to Horace Greeley she is the most taken off her feet by the honors conferred upon her," insisted Susan to Mrs. Wright.[58] Anthony also knew that Victoria Woodhull was behind the most recent efforts to discredit her. She firmly believed that Woodhull was set on a course against woman's freedom, so she held firmly to her position and did not give any further attention to it. "I shall welcome her work, every bit of it, for women's freedom—though I do not choose to follow her into a party with those men!!"[59]

Through it all Woodhull never received the attention she personally needed and had tried to get from Tilton and Beecher. The presidential campaigns were moving into full gear for the November elections, and Henry Ward Beecher campaigned with the Republican party for the reelection of Ulysses Grant. Tilton, with whom Woodhull had been having an affair, left her to go off to stump for Horace Greeley, who was the nominee of the new Liberal Republican party. Woodhull would not be ignored, and she published her Beecher-Tilton exposé at election time. But even without Woodhull's opportunistic strategies, the November 1872 election appeared to be heading for some dramatic and unanticipated moments. Susan B. Anthony had moved into action again, which was always her most effective response to despair or depression.

10

Convicted of Being a Woman

"WELL, I HAVE BEEN & GONE & DONE IT!! POSITIVELY VOTED the Republican ticket—strait—this A.M. at 7 o'clock & swore my vote in at that," Anthony triumphantly announced to Stanton on election day.[1]

It was not exactly a spontaneous decision on the part of Susan B. Anthony to respond to the editorial call in the Rochester newspapers on November 1, 1872. The article notified citizens that they had only one more day to register to vote and not to forsake this near-sacred right. "If you were not permitted to vote, you would fight for the right, undergo all privations for it, face death for it."[2] When she was arrested for the crime of being a woman and voting, Anthony told the court that "I have been resolved for three years to vote at the first election when I had been home for thirty days before."[3]

On registration day, Susan called together her sisters Guelma, Hannah, and Mary, and the four Anthony women went off to register to vote at the office set up in the nearby barber shop. In all, nearly fifty women in Rochester registered to vote that week, fourteen in the Anthonys' ward alone. The "prim spinster with no thoughts of girlish or coquettish wiles" led her sisters into the barber-shop-turned-registry-office, remembered young E. T. Marsh, a neighbor of the Anthonys' and an election inspector. Anthony surveyed the scene. Each of these young men serving as registrars was young enough to be her son, as Mrs. Stanton would say. Susan mustered her determination, walked directly to the registrars, and "DE-

MANDED that we register them as voters," as Marsh testified later.

As soon as he and his partners responded that they could not register them, Anthony, armed with legal documents, proceeded politely but firmly to read to them the Fourteenth Amendment to the United States Constitution and an article from the New York Constitution, which contained no sex qualification for voting. Still the men refused to allow her to register. Anthony summoned her dignity and spoke to them with the kind of argument she was sure they would understand. "If you still refuse us our rights as citizens, I will bring charges against you in Criminal Court and I will sue each of you personally for large, exemplary damages!"

The inspectors were a bit stunned. She continued, "I know I can win. I have Judge Selden as a lawyer." This reference to Henry Selden, who was highly respected in the Rochester community, seemed to evoke something from the men. Then, she issued her biggest and, unknown to the inspectors, her most hollow threat. The woman with a ten-thousand-dollar debt hanging over her told the men that "there is any amount of money to back me, and if I have to, I will push to the 'last ditch' in both courts." At least that is how Inspector Marsh remembered it. The inspectors talked over the situation and decided that they should have legal counsel before taking another step. John Van Voorhis, another prominent lawyer and strong supporter of women's right to vote, counseled them to have the women take all the oaths of registry, because "that would put the entire onus of the affair on them." Anthony and her sisters were then registered to vote.[4]

The afternoon papers called for the arrest of the inspectors. Anthony immediately returned to the registry office to encourage the young men to not back down. She also assured them that she would be personally responsible for any costs resulting from legal action against them. On November 5, early in the morning so as to avoid the scene that would inevitably result from the spectacle of women voting, Susan B. Anthony and the fourteen other women voted. The press loudly called for the arrest of anyone who allowed women to vote. The inspectors in other wards were so intimidated that in Rochester no other women's votes were accepted from among the nearly fifty women who had registered some days before.

Since 1868, women had been defying the law, registering to vote and voting throughout the country. In 1871 and 1872, over one hundred fifty women in ten states had tried to vote with some of them succeeding. Most, however, were prevented from voting by the registrars. When Susan B. Anthony voted, it became a national controversy.

Over three weeks later, on November 28, Susan's sister summoned her to the parlor. There was a gentleman who wished to see her. Susan entered and took stock of the "tall gentleman in most irreproachable attire, nervously dangling in his gloved hands a well-brushed high hat."[5] The slightly embarrassed and bumbling deputy United States marshall tried through his stammering to tell her that "the commissioner wishes to arrest you." Susan was caught off-guard. "I never dreamed of the U.S. officers prosecuting me for voting—thought only that if I was refused—I should bring action against the inspectors," she later told Martha Wright. She stood there watching this representative of justice and refused to help him with his discomfort or his "in-the-presence-of-ladies" type of awkwardness. If " 'Uncle Sam' waxes wrath with holy indignation at such violation of his laws,"[6] then she insisted that they be executed without regard for her sex and to the letter. "Is this your usual method of serving a warrant?" she demanded of the marshal, glaring at him.

Reminded of his official duty, he promptly and politely produced the warrant for her arrest. She told him "I am not dressed properly to go to court." And he responded, "Oh, just come on down to the courthouse when you are ready," trying to be careful not to offend this venerable lady. She could only wonder how he could possibly think that she would be willing to go to court on her own, when she had committed no crime. She emphatically told him that she would not take herself to court and he waited in the parlor until she changed her dress. She came back downstairs some minutes later, stood before him and held out her wrists to be handcuffed like any other ordinary criminal. She did not want to miss one ironic moment of this episode. The marshal mumbled that he did not think that was necessary, and escorted her out of the house and to court.

The office of U.S. Commissioner William C. Storrs where she was questioned and examined on her crime was "the same dingy little room where, in the olden days, fugitive slaves were examined and returned to their master." When she arrived, Anthony was surprised to find that the inspectors had been arrested, along with the fourteen other women from her ward who had voted.

At their examination, when U.S. Commissioner Storrs set a date for the preliminary hearing, Miss Anthony told him that she had several lectures and other engagements scheduled until December

10 and could not make it. "But you are supposed to be in custody all this time," the district attorney retorted to her seemingly indifferent attitude toward their authority. Anthony turned and looked at him. "Oh, is that so? I had forgotten all about that."[7] In the second hearing on December 23, all parties were bound over for trial and then released on five-hundred-dollars bail. Anthony was the only defendant to refuse bail.

With all these unanticipated turns of events Anthony was caught up with new excitement. She was charged with voting for a representative of the Congress of the United States without having a lawful right to vote. Properly prosecuted this charge would take her to the Supreme Court if she lost in the lower courts. Finally, women would get the national action they had demanded for their suffrage. Through her lawyer she applied for a writ of *habeas corpus,* which challenged the right of the government to imprison her, arguing that she had exercised a right and not committed a crime. She was released pending court action on the writ.

On January 21, 1873, Anthony and her lawyer went before a U.S. district judge, who, after listening to arguments, denied her writ and increased her bail to one thousand dollars. Again she refused to give bail, making it known that she would rather go to jail than cooperate with the courts. But her attorney, Henry Selden, who otherwise had provided a solid legal defense for her case, conceded to chivalry and insisted that he must put up her bail. Anthony objected, but Selden paid it.

Anthony did not know the full legal implication of his action until she and Selden were leaving the courtroom and she met John Van Voorhis and told him what Selden had done. Astonished, Van Voorhis responded, "You have lost your chance to get your case before the Supreme Court by writ of *habeas corpus!*" Anthony turned to Selden. "Did you not know that you stopped me from carrying my case to the Supreme Court?" she demanded. "Yes," Selden admitted, "but I could not see a lady I respected put in jail." Anthony said not another word. Judge Selden was a kind man and a good lawyer, she thought, but how many times had she been controlled and undone in her own strategies by men's "protection." Yet despite her anger, when her case was concluded and Selden refused to send her a bill, she raised the money from her Rochester friends and supporters to pay him.

The next day, Susan B. Anthony was indicted by a grand jury. While awaiting her trial, she voted again in a local election on March

4. "But the rest of the women all frightened lest fine and imprisonment," she wrote in her diary while sitting alone that evening.[8] This time she was the only woman voter.

Meanwhile Anthony found herself doggedly pursued by the press, not only because of her own case but for comment on Woodhull's most recent action. Only a few days before Anthony had voted that preceding November, Victoria Woodhull (whose campaign for the presidency never went beyond her attempt to organize a People's party) published a special edition of *Woodhull and Chaflin's Weekly*. In it she exposed the Beecher-Tilton affair in full detail, naming all parties. The self-proclaimed purity crusader Anthony Comstock found enough in the articles to indict Woodhull and her sister with sending obscene literature through the mails. They were arrested and jailed, although they were eventually acquitted of the charges.

In January 1873, Woodhull, by then discredited and alienated from the world of reform, tried to rewin favor with Susan B. Anthony. Believing that Anthony's was only an individual case, Woodhull told her that she did not think that her indictment for voting represented all women. "But since you are noticed by the courts, everybody should join in your defense."[9] Anthony did not believe that Woodhull was sincere and refused to answer her letter.

In another court action—this time prompted by Woodhull's exposé—the Beecher-Tilton affair had gone to court when Tilton filed for divorce in the summer of 1874. The press hounded Anthony for comment. Both Tilton and Beecher tried to pressure her into testifying in their behalf. But as the *Chicago Tribune* reported: "Miss Anthony keeps her own counsel on this matter with a resolution which would do credit to General Grant." She refused to speak a word that could incriminate a woman. Her only comment was that "in this case, men proved themselves the champion gossips of the world"; she would have none of it.[10] Before Tilton's divorce trial, Beecher's Plymouth Church congregation held their own investigation into the case and ultimately exonerated their preacher. In divorce court no verdict was reached on the Tilton case, but Stanton and Anthony noted that Elizabeth Tilton was not allowed to testify in her own behalf. Shortly after the trial, she admitted publicly to having had an affair with Beecher. Later, Woodhull left the movement, the country and even her free love theories. She underwent a religious conversion and settled into a marriage in England with a titled English gentleman.

Susan B. Anthony went to trial for voting. Her lawyers assured her that if they could get "a strictly judicial opinion" in the case, there was no doubt that she would be acquitted. But Anthony did not trust leaving her case in the hands of the courts, as she knew from long political experience that "men partisan opinions are the rule."[11] Certain that her case would not be free from political manipulation, she went back to the field. She visited every village in her county—twenty-nine post-office districts in all—"to educate any possible jurymen" before her trial opened on May 13, 1873.[12] "Friends and *Fellow-Citizens*," she began each speech, "I stand before you under indictment for the alleged crime of having voted at the last presidential election, without having a lawful right to vote." Since the years when she had campaigned to abolish slavery, she had been committed to civil disobedience in order to "disobey every unjust law." She emphatically reaffirmed her position now. "We no longer petition legislature or Congress to give us the right to vote, but appeal to women everywhere to exercise their too long neglected 'citizen's right.'" And she reminded her audience that "we throw to the winds the old dogma that governments can give rights. The Declaration of Independence, the United States Constitution, the constitutions of the several States and the organic laws of the Territories, all alike propose to *protect* the people in the exercise of their God-given rights. Not one of them pretends to bestow rights."[13]

The judge declared that Anthony had prejudiced any possible jury, and on May 23 he moved her case out of Monroe County to Canandaigua in Ontario County. Her trial was postponed for a month and was rescheduled for June 17. Undaunted, Anthony immediately launched a thorough canvass of twenty districts in Ontario County before her trial. Matilda Joslyn Gage came to the rescue and spoke with Anthony in sixteen of the townships on "the United States on trial, not Susan B. Anthony." Visiting a village a day, the two women carried their message to the entire county and concluded the night before the trial in Canandaigua, the court seat.

The trial opened, and United States Associate Justice Ward Hunt heard the arguments of both sides. In response to the charges, the defense conceded that Anthony was a woman and that she had voted. Anthony was declared incompetent as a witness in her own defense because she was a woman. Judge Selden who was her attorney, offered himself as a witness in her behalf and testified that he had advised Anthony to vote. Selden argued for three hours in her defense, and the district attorney responded for two hours. At the conclusion, Justice Hunt drew from his pocket a paper and read the court his opinion, which he had evidently prepared even before the case had begun. According to his interpretation, the Fourteenth Amendment was a protection of the rights of citizens, and as a general protection of rights it did not cover Anthony's right to vote. On the basis of this opinion, he *directed* the jury to bring in a verdict of guilty, even though this was a criminal case that was constitutionally protected by the right to trial by jury. Selden protested. Hunt instructed the clerk to take the verdict from the jury. Selden then demanded that the jury be polled individually. Instead, Hunt discharged the jury without having heard the verdict from them. Then he ordered the defendant to stand. Susan B. Anthony rose to her feet, and Hunt asked, "Has the prisoner anything to say why sentence shall not be pronounced?"

What Anthony later described as "sublime silence" filled the courtroom.[14] Then she replied, "Yes, your honor, I have many things to say; for in your ordered verdict of guilty you have trampled under foot every vital principle of our government. My natural rights, my civil rights, my political rights, my judicial rights, are all alike ignored. Robbed of the fundamental privilege of citizenship, I am degraded from the status of a citizen to that of a subject; and not only myself individually but all of my sex are, by your honor's verdict, doomed to political subjection under this so-called republican form of government."

"The Court cannot listen to a rehearsal of argument which the prisoner's counsel has already consumed three hours in presenting," Justice Hunt insisted. But it would listen, for Anthony went right on talking. She reviewed the rights of representation, of consent of the governed, of taxpayers, and the right of trial by jury. Again Hunt interrupted Anthony, "The Court cannot allow the prisoner to go on." Again Anthony continued, protesting "this high-handed outrage upon my citizen's rights."

Hunt was exasperated and ordered the prisoner to sit down. Ignoring his command, Anthony proceeded to tell him what she meant by "peers."

> . . . from the corner grocery politician who entered the complaint, to the United States marshal, commissioner, district-attorney, district-judge, your honor on the bench—not one is my peer, but each and all are my political sovereigns; and had your honor submitted my case to the jury, as was clearly your duty, even then I should have had just cause to protest, for not one of those men was my peer; but, native or foreign born, white or black, rich or poor, educated or ignorant, sober or drunk,

each and every man of them was my political superior; hence, in no sense, my peer. Under such circumstances a commoner of England, tried before of jury of lords, would have far less cause to complain than have I, a woman, tried before a jury of men. Even my counsel, Hon. Henry R. Selden, who has argued my cause so ably, so earnestly, so unanswerably before your honor, is my political sovereign.

The judge became defensive. "The Court must insist—the prisoner has been tried according to the established forms of law."

"But by forms of law all made by men, interpreted by men, administered by men, in favor of men and against women," Anthony retorted, and then explained that it once was an established form of law to punish anyone giving "a cup of cold water, a crust of bread or a night's shelter to a panting fugitive tracking his way to Canada." Just as slaves had to take their freedom, so must women, she preached, and defiantly proclaimed, "I have taken mine, and mean to take it at every opportunity."

"The Court orders the prisoner to sit down." Anthony went right on until she finished and then told the judge that, failing to get justice, "I ask not leniency at your hands but rather the full rigor of the law." This was an abomination to Hunt, who again interrupted her with "the Court must insist." Anthony sat down. "The prisoner will stand up," Hunt boomed, not seeming to be able to control his courtroom. Anthony rose. "The sentence of the Court is that you pay a fine of $100 and the costs of prosecution."

"May it please your honor, I will never pay a dollar of your unjust penalty. All the stock in trade I possess is a debt of ten thousand dollars incurred by publishing my paper *The Revolution*—the sole object of which was to educate all women to do precisely as I have done, rebel against your man-made, unjust, unconstitutional forms of law, which tax, fine, imprison and hang women, while denying them the right of representation in the government; and I will work on with might and main to pay every dollar of that honest debt, but not a penny shall go to this unjust claim. And I shall earnestly and persistently continue to urge all women to the practical recognition of the old Revolutionary maxim, 'Resistance to tyranny is obedience to God.'"

"Madam," the judge intoned in the silent, almost disbelieving courtroom, "the Court will not order you to stand committed until the fine is paid."[15] Hunt's statement was illogical and contradictory: Anthony refused to pay the fine and he refused to imprison her until it was paid. But Hunt knew what he was doing. His was a well-maneuvered act to prevent Anthony from appealing to the Supreme Court, which she could have if he had ordered her imprisoned until the fine was paid.

Anthony remained in Canandaigua for the trial of the inspectors, who were convicted some days later of illegally registering a woman to vote. They were fined twenty-five dollars; refusing to pay the fine, they were later imprisoned. Anthony began the work of writing pleas to have them exonerated.

For many years now the press had been following Anthony from city to city and through every controversy. Their coverage, prejudiced or sympathetic, kept the woman's rights issues before the public. Their coverage of her trial and conviction and of her constant public denunciations of the system that had trampled over her rights elevated her for many to the stature of a martyr. For others, it lowered her to the status of a criminal. For better and for worse, she was a force that had to be reckoned with.

Throughout the trial and the months of preparation preceding it, Susan B. Anthony was still trying to work off *The Revolution*'s debts. But as desperately as she needed money, for the rest of the year she was unable to leave home to lecture. Her older sister was dying of tuberculosis. Day in and day out she sat by Guelma's bed, tending to her while she watched her die. In September she told Isabella Hooker that "I can only urge the rest to work while I watch the slow but sure approach of the disease most deluding—consumption—my dear, dear sister is very weak, barely skin and bones left."[16]

One day Guelma's married daughter Maggie came and had her mother's piano removed to her own house, apparently with her father's approval. "It just broke me down," Susan confessed, "the lack of feeling for Mary and self." Susan recalled their youthful days in Battenville, their sisterly society, their ties with their mother, then her struggle to keep their sisterly society from being broken when Guelma married Aaron McLean many years before. But here at the end the sisters' devotion to each other remained intact, and Susan consoled herself that the "husband & child possessors of all things *material,* but the spiritual still belongs to the sisters and mother."[17]

Comforting Guelma while feeling "powerless to save," Susan sat watching her "dear, elder sister, only seventeen months my senior," so close that "we were cradled together."[18] Guelma's suffering continued through October, and there were times when Susan felt as if her heart would break. It was Mary who was sitting with Guelma when she died before daybreak on November 6. She summoned Susan and Hannah, and the three sisters with Guelma's daughter solemnly "performed the last sad offices ourselves," preparing their sister's body for burial. Lucy Anthony saw her first born child buried. A month later in the midst of their sadness, Mary and Hannah and Susan quietly celebrated their mother's eightieth birthday with her.

Occupied with her voting trial and her sister's illness, Anthony had been able to do little to work off *The Revolution* debt during the entire year of 1873. One of her debtors, a Mr. Stillman, was threatening legal action, and she had to return to the lecture circuit immediately to raise money.

Susan had to carry her grief over her sister's death with her as she traveled from lecture to lecture filled with deep sadness. She wrote to her mother that "except for the hour that I am on the platform, how continually is the thought of you and your loss and my own with me!" Sitting in the train or in a hotel room she wondered frequently, "Our Guelma, does she look down upon us, does she still live, and shall we all live again and know each other, and work together and love and enjoy one another. In spite of instinct, in spite of faith, these questions will come up again and again."[19]

Seeing no end in sight for working off her enormous debt, shortly before Thanksgiving Susan wrote in her diary: "How like a millstone that *Revolution* debt hangs about my spirit."[20] On Thanksgiving evening after a family dinner, Cousin Anson Lapham, whom Susan loved almost as much as her own dear deceased father, handed her some papers. They were canceled notes for her four-thousand-dollar debt to him. She tried to speak, to thank him, to tell him of her gratitude, but he held up his hand to silence her, saying, "I feel the money was well spent." In her diary later that evening Susan wrote that "his manner made me feel his respect for & confidence in me—& that is more to me than the wealth of the Indies."[21]

Stillman continued to press for his money and gave Susan until February 1, 1874, or he would sue. Considering that at this point Susan was earning twenty-five dollars per lecture or "3/4 of gross receipts with admission not exceeding 25 cts" or "entire gross receipts with admission 10 cts—they defraying all local expenses,"[22] she was not likely to earn that money in a few months or even a year. She tried to be philosophical about it. "It is always out of pocket—but the good that is done is much greater than a mere lecture of Mrs. Livermore to 3,000 people and $100 in her pocket—

The Mischief is those women who can make money out of talking on women's rights, don't give themselves not any of their money to help carry the movement."[23]

Stillman proceeded with his suit, which named Elizabeth Cady Stanton as one of the responsible parties. Mrs. Stanton told Mary that the Anthony family should pay the debt. Mary and her mother were offended, and Susan was hurt, for her own family "got none of the good from *The Revolution* & Mrs. Stanton got a great deal." No, Susan resolved, this time she would not go to her own family for help. *The Revolution* was a responsibility of the woman's movement. But "none of them, not Mrs. Davis, not Mrs. Stanton—not one of them felt the slightest responsibility to aid me."[24]

Susan knew that Mrs. Stanton had used much of the fifty thousand dollars her father had left her over a decade before for her children's education; and that she was proud that just as she had attended the first important female seminary at Troy decades earlier, so were her daughters now attending Vassar, the first endowed college for women in the United States. But Anthony also knew that Mrs. Stanton was fully engaged in the lecture circuit, earning her own money. Inevitably, Susan was forced to turn to her family for help. Mary gave her five hundred dollars from her savings earned as a principal in Rochester schools, and Susan settled the suit with Stillman a few weeks later.

This was not the first time Anthony found herself left with the responsibility for their movement, and Stanton was not the only one of the woman's rights leaders to leave the financial responsibilities to Susan. Paulina Wright Davis had invested several hundred dollars in the newspaper; when it folded, she waited for Susan to pay the money back to her as if it were a personal debt. As the *feme sole,* Anthony was legally responsible for all business transacted first for *The Revolution* and then for the National. On this matter, her friends had no choice; being married, they were unable to enter into contracts and conduct business under their own signatures.

The legal structure of marriage had effectively shaped women's relationships with each other, to their movement, and to the public world. Denied the right to enter into contracts in their own names, in its place married women were relieved from responsibility for financial matters—a kind of gratuitous reward or beneficence for accepting their role in marriage that came without rights. They im-

plicitly traded independence for "protection," an unspoken consequence, not an explicit stipulation of the marriage contract.

Protection from responsibility for the decisions over their lives
reduced women's decisions and choices to the minute details of daily
life. It blocked their ability to think about their future in terms of
making choices and decisions for which they would be responsible.
By denying married women this possibility, marriage diminished their
sense of the future. They conceded both their identity and their future to another. In this case, the responsibility was given to Anthony; in this way, Stanton, Davis, and others again made her into
a kind of surrogate husband. They believed that without a family,
she could shoulder these responsibilities. Marriage had taught them
that they had no reason to think they should or could assume it
themselves.

In effect, married women differentiated themselves from each other
and from other women. When they married they changed their social and legal status, lost their single woman's identity and relinquished their basic legal rights. They shifted their identities from
themselves and their sex to the identities of their individual husbands. This structured their relationship to women and to their
movement later on.

Anthony was well aware of this difference between her and her
married woman friends. It was one of the things that convinced her
that there must be a new age, a new historical period. She called it
an "epoch of single women," which would correct this condition
and shift women from always living at least two centuries behind
men, where "the man of the nineteenth century insists upon having
a wife of the seventeenth century." But she had no illusion that it
was as simple as that. "It is perhaps nearer the truth to say that he
demands the spirit of the *two* centuries combined in one woman:
The activity and liberality of thought which characterize the present
era, with the submission to authority which belonged to the past."
She outlined her solution in a speech entitled "The Homes of Single
Women,"[25] which she wrote in the home of a single woman she
was visiting in Denver. In the speech she pointed out that "in woman's transition from the position of subject to sovereign, there must
needs be an era of self-sustained self-supported homes, where her
freedom and equality shall be unquestioned." She was convinced
that "the logic of events, points, inevitably, to an *epoch of single
women*. If women will not accept marriage *with subjection,* nor men
proffer it *without,* there is, there can be, no *alternative.*" Single women

were not old maids. Rather, they were single, professionally autonomous, economically independent women. Yet because they refused
to be defined as wife and mother and created their own social identity, they were, like old maids, considered with suspicion and viewed
as different and abnormal.

Susan B. Anthony embraced these women as her own. They were
the realization of her earliest vision of the "new true woman." She
saw an example in the lives of single women that "as young women
become educated in the industries of the world, thereby learning
the sweetness of independent bread, it will be more and more impossible for them to accept the Blackstone marriage limitation that
'husband and wife are one, and that the one the husband.'" Now
as Anthony traveled she met more and more single women, an expanding circle of women whose lives were more like her own than
were the lives of her married women friends.

But most feminists were married, and the social condemnation of
single women was not one of the issues they decided to champion
in their woman's rights movement. Anthony herself had abetted this
neglect of single women by emphasizing political issues that included them, but not the ones special to them. Now with her new
speech she intended to represent and defend her single sisters' rights
also.

If a woman did not marry, it was thought that she should live
with her married relatives. Only married couples with a family were
entitled to a home of their own. Anthony rejected this rationale. "A
Home of one's own is the want, the necessity of every human being,
the one thing above all others longed for, worked for. Whether the
humblest cottage or the proudest palace, a home of our own is the
soul's dream of rest, the one hope that will not die until we have
reached the very portals of the everlasting home." She asked her
audiences to look at the examples of the homes of single women
she laid out before them. "All this done from pure love of home,
no spurious second-hand domesticity affected for the praise of some
man, or conscientiously maintained for the comfort of the one who
furnishes the money." She challenged them to rethink the idea that
single women were not entitled to their own homes. "Do any of
you Gentlemen and Ladies doubt the truth of my picturings of the
homes of unmarried women? Do any of you still cling to the old
theory, that single women, women's rights women, professional
women, have no home instincts?"

It was probably Susan's own quiet longing for a home of her own led her to write "The Homes of Single Women." At the age of fifty-four, she may well have thought of herself as approaching old age. Although she retained the vitality and energy that she had brought to her work twenty years earlier, age was making itself apparent. Her friends were becoming grandparents, and some were thinking of how to bring about their retirement from public work. With her older sister's recent death, she began to lose many close and deep friends. For the first time since she had begun her public work, she wanted a home of her own. She admitted that she felt as much a stranger in Rochester as in Chicago or New York.[26] For years she had been a boarder in Guelma's home and was still one since her death. During her trial for voting in 1873, many friends and co-workers came to Rochester for the trial, but she could not even invite them to stay with her. "Oh, if I only had the spacious home & help to say to all come & break bread with me—but nature is not thus lavish with me—so I'll be content with my lot," she confided sadly to Isabella Hooker. But of course, there was the positive side. "I am free from all such responsibility & pleasure & so can give all my time & strength to the work in our vineyard."[27]

Economically, there was no way Susan could shoulder the financial burden of the woman's movement and support a home of her own, however much she yearned for it, especially as she was getting older. So she placed the caring sentiments she would have put into a home, if she had had one, into her work for women. When she rented a hall for their National meeting in 1875, she notified the proprietor:

Now as to the *Hall*—please be sure & have it thoroughly *heated*—to go into a cold hall just *chills* & *kills* a meeting—So don't fail to give us a *well warmed room to begin with*.

Then, without fail—please—give us a *carpet on the platform*—With a dozen *easy* chairs & a sofa—if possible—and three or four small tables along the front—*Not* that great long one—put that please, on the floor in front of the platform for the Reporters.

Then can you not give us a flag or two over the platform—& make the hall *wear a lady-like* appearance generally—for though we are *strong-minded* we do not wish to have things about us look *Manish*.

Especially—Do have the hall floor cleaned thoroughly—also the *ante rooms*—They were *simply filthy* last year—we had them just after some sort of *tobacco spitting* performance—So please give us every-

thing clean as silver, and all in real *woman housekeeping* order—&
we will not only pay our rent promptly—but say a thousand thanks
besides.[28]

Not having a home of her own was only part of her grief. What
was worse was the social ostracism of single women. For example,
there was the way that Susan was excluded from forums that included her married women friends and co-workers, as when the
Boston suffrage movement organized a Woman's Congress and did
not invite her to their meeting, even though Isabella Hooker and
Elizabeth Cady Stanton were invited. When Henry Blackwell, the
congress's organizer, was confronted by her, he claimed that Susan
B. Anthony "was specially invited to participate & declined to do
so."[29] Anthony publicly clarified Blackwell's insinuation that she
had refused to participate, stating, "That if my name was left out
because it was not wanted, all right so far as I was concerned, but
if from any lack of mine, I made haste to say that I surely desired
to be reckoned among those who wished to do all in their power
for the uplifting of all womankind in all departments of life." If the
reform-minded Bostonians and particularly Henry Blackwell did not
want to be associated with the National, why had Hooker and Stanton been invited?

Did the Boston women fear that she would command all the attention? Surely not, for it was always Mrs. Stanton who was the
center of attention when they appeared in programs together. And
if they wanted to avoid being associated with controversy, how did
they explain their association with Mrs. Hooker and Mrs. Stanton,
who, as Susan pointed out, the Bostonians considered "the two
greatest Woodhull sinners." Perhaps, Susan thought, it was that the
Boston friends "try to persuade themselves that my prosecution verdict & sentence are a disgrace and that they shrink from affiliation
with an adjudged criminal."[30]

Actually, Anthony learned that she was excluded by the organizers for deeper reasons. "If they let me in, I could not be managed."[31] Antoinette Brown Blackwell told one of her friends a short
time later that she was afraid to be associated publicly with Susan
B. Anthony because her theories on marriage were "dangerous."[32]

Single women personified independence and autonomy. There was
no husband, lover, or partner to mediate their presence or justify
their existence. Responsible for their own lives they did not internalize the passivity that married women had; and Anthony knew

it. "The woman who *will not be ruled* must live without marriage."
She personally represented the refusal of that subjugation in the public
eye and increasingly found herself socially excluded from many
events—even in the woman's rights movement—although always
expected to be organizationally responsible. These snubs had to be
bitter pills to swallow, and by now the only psychological and personally strategic way Anthony had learned to live with this reality
was to keep herself immersed in her work and to keep her vision
on the future of womankind.

It was at this time, when she was being left more often with responsibility for the movement, that Anthony decided that the movement must focus its energy on attaining political power for women
through the ballot. As second generation feminists diversified and
diluted the concentrated political force of the movement, Anthony
thought it could be reasserted by focusing on the ballot. She reasoned that with access to political power, the ballot, women would
be in a position to grant themselves their remaining rights.

In planning a campaign in 1875, she told Matilda Joslyn Gage that
she wanted their platform to represent only their demand for woman's suffrage.

> I want it to be on the one & *sole point of women disfranchised*—
> separate & alone—and not mixed up with—or one of 19 *other points
> of protest*—each all of the 19 good & proper perchance . . . however
> good and needed, we must keep our claim first and most important
> overshadowing every other. Mrs. Stanton answered me that she agrees
> with me—just women & her disfranchised—leaving the other 19 de-
> mands of the *Old Liberty* to wait our emancipation.[33]

As the other nineteen points no longer originated from political
consciousness, they lacked coherence. In response to a friend's query
of what to do about fallen women, Anthony wrote: "Alas, alas—
the first thing needed is to reform the fallen men & their name is
legion—while even the very elect of men feel it no crime to despoil
any woman's virtue they meet. It will be very, very hard work to
lift poverty stricken homeless girls above their seductive reach—
nothing but to make woman's work easy, profitable, honorable can
do it—And that can't be done while no woman even washes her
own dishes who can find a man either in or out of marriage to pay
for the doing it for them. If the ballot in the hands of women shall

fail to do the desired work of elevating women, then I shall not despair—but look in some other direction for help."[34]

This was Anthony's first major departure from her twenty-five-year-long radical organizing strategy. This was the first time she insisted on narrowing the original woman's rights platform to one issue. Anthony was not alone in this analysis of political power. By 1895, Engels had recognized that radical change was the result of long and patient work with the masses, who must gain essential rights, such as the right to vote and exercise power, as an important step toward deeper change.[35]

Clearly, some rights, such as suffrage, enabled other rights and could be part of a revolutionary program that recognized that fully disfranchised classes had no basis for revolt. But the danger lay in prioritizing issues at a time when the movement was beginning to lose its political focus. Anthony would not be able to prevent her single focus from devolving into an essentially reformist strategy. This was a major step in silencing radical feminism which had begun with the first split in the movement.

During the early 1870s, Anthony's new political orientation was marked by her political desperation. In 1872 she had decided to work with Henry Blackwell and stump for the Republican party because it offered women, if not a platform, at least a "splinter" on woman's suffrage. While not fully endorsing woman's suffrage, the Republicans' splinter recognized women as making demands like "any class of citizens for equal rights." Likening herself and the movement to "the drowning man," Anthony admitted that she would clutch this splinter "and cling to it until something stronger and surer shall present itself." More optimistically, she saw that this was the first opportunity to "have the question of women's claims introduced into politics. It is the hour I have worked for with might and main because I have seen that so soon as we could get this, editors and orators of both parties must of necessity discuss the subject."[36]

Anthony was reinvigorated by action. With a new sense of hope, she turned to Stanton. "I tell you the Fort Sumter gun of our war is fired, and we'll go on to victory almost without a repulse from this date."[37] She maintained her position of working for the Republicans if they supported woman's suffrage. It did not matter to her that "Blackwell wants us to work for them because they are this and that on other questions."[38] She had no commitment to the Republican party; rather, "All I know or care of parties now and until women are free, is 'woman and her disfranchised-crucified.' "[39] Similarly, it was her commitment to women and not the Republican "splinter" that made her decide to vote in the 1872 election—something she had been planning and urging women to do for some years.

Stanton had a different reaction. "I do not feel jubilant over the situation; in fact I never was so blue in my life." As for the splinter Susan was clinging to for dear life, "Between nothing and that, there is no choice, and we must accept it." Stanton was indignant. "It makes me feel intensely bitter to have my rights discussed by popinjay priests and politicians . . . striplings of twenty-one." She finally admitted that as to the work of the hour, "I am under a cloud and see nothing."[40] When Stanton found her next issue, which would be against religious domination, she and Anthony would be heading in different directions with their work, although they still had many joint struggles before them.

Meanwhile, Anthony still had a criminal judgment against her. Hunt had closed all the doors of appeal to the Supreme Court by not ordering Anthony imprisoned when she refused to pay the fine. She suspected that this maneuver as well as the judge's decision that had been obviously written before her trial were the results of a meeting between Hunt and Senator Roscoe Conkling, a known opponent of woman's rights whose patronage had won Hunt's appointment as a U.S. district judge. The Republican party was becoming increasingly corrupt, and Conkling's plan to protect the railroad corporations in their right to set fees as a way to increase profits by giving corporations the rights of persons under the Fourteenth Amendment was an example of this. It was not only Anthony who suspected that Conkling had conferred with Hunt before her case went to trial in order to prevent her from getting justice in the higher courts.

Anthony had another plan. In January 1874, she appealed to Congress to remit her fine, asking, "inasmuch as the law had provided no means of reviewing the decision of the judge, or of correcting his errors, that the fine imposed upon your petitioner be remitted, as an expression of the sense of this high tribunal that her conviction was unjust." Not surprisingly, even to Anthony, Congress denied her appeal. The House Judiciary Committee found that she had had a "fair and constitutional trial by an impartial jury."

At the time of their trial, Anthony had urged the inspectors to stand by her and to refuse to pay their fine so they could appeal their case to the president for executive clemency. They agreed. On

February 26, 1874, the inspectors were jailed for refusing to pay the fine of twenty-five dollars each. Anthony visited them in jail. "They are plucky," she told a friend. She was encouraged by their stamina and their commitment to her case and immediately began to arrange their appeal to President Grant, who, on March 2, pardoned the inspectors and remitted their fine. The entire case of the *United States of America* v. *Susan B. Anthony* was closed.

Susan B. Anthony's fine was never pardoned nor was it remitted. Why did she herself not appeal to the president of the United States for clemency, as she had encouraged the inspectors to? There is some evidence that her lawyer, Henry Selden, may have paid her fine for her, just as he had bailed her out when she initially refused bail. Before he died in the early 1980s, George Selden, Jr., a descendant of Henry Selden, confided to J. Sheldon Fisher, an early director of the Rochester Historical Society, that Henry Selden had in fact paid the fine.[41]

It was the case of Virginia Minor that was finally heard before the Supreme Court. The suit was filed by her husband Francis Minor as she could not bring suit in her own name, when the inspectors refused to register her to vote. In affirming the judgments of lower courts, the Supreme Court found in the *Minor* case that suffrage was not coextensive with citizenship and that the Constitution "does not confer the right of suffrage upon anyone." The Court concluded that "no argument as to woman's need of suffrage can be considered. We can only act upon her rights as they exist. It is not for us to look at the hardship of withholding."[42] The argument for woman's right to vote under the Fourteenth Amendment was closed. The only alternative was a constitutional amendment granting women the right to vote.

Anthony responded to their defeat in the Supreme Court by accelerating the campaign for a Sixteenth Amendment to enfranchise woman. Was she discouraged? Consider what happened in Michigan for an example. At the same time that the *Minor* case was lost, women lost another opportunity for suffrage when it came to a vote in Michigan and lost by fifteen thousand votes. With her irrepressible ability to turn failure into success, Anthony declared that the forty thousand votes cast for woman's suffrage were really a wonderful success—a triumph. "Whenever before, on first trial—did 40,000 of a sovereign class freely vote to share their power with a subject class? Never—Never—So I count Michigan a *grand triumph; not a failure.*" Concluding that there were now only fifteen thousand of the sovereign class left to be educated in Michigan in order for woman's suffrage to triumph, Anthony pointed to Iowa, where there was another opportunity to get the legislature to address the question before it came up in Michigan again.[43] The essential optimism that had always framed her campaign strategizing would now carry her through the rest of the century.

In January 1875, only a little over a year after Guelma's death, Susan received word one day when she was on her way to visit Lydia Mott in Albany that Martha Wright had died suddenly of pneumonia while visiting her daughter Ellen in Boston. "No, it can't be." Susan was shocked. "I was struck dumb!" Martha was only sixty-nine years old. Susan's reveries went back to Guelma. "How strange it is that we are never ready to let go of our loved ones." When Guelma died, "It seemed as if part of myself had been wrenched away." Now Susan worried about how Martha's death would affect Lucretia Mott, Martha's older sister, who had just passed her eighty-second birthday. "How little any of us dreamed she would be left to mourn her sister Martha."[44]

Only a year later Susan received word that "our dear Sister Hannah [is] going the way our dear sister Mrs. McLean went." Susan was torn between her attention to Hannah, who was leaving for Denver where it was thought the climate would help her recover, "I feel that I must drop all to go with her—It is too cruel to see her going down,"[45]—and her concern for the emergency facing the movement—the nation's Centennial Celebration of 1876. For four years the Centennial Commission had been planning the six-month celebration, complete with a grand exposition of the industrial and cultural accomplishments of the last hundred years.

The women's rights advocates, having all doors closed by both Congress and the courts to their enfranchisment, were indignant. From the New Year's Eve that ushered in the centennial year of 1876 to the Fourth of July ceremonies, there were celebrations and patriotic rallies in one city after another. The women's rights advocates were not elated; instead, they were determined to highlight the hypocrisy of celebrating political freedom and championing democracy, while denying its rights to over one-half of the population. "Some suggested that the women in their various towns and cities, draped in black, should march in solemn procession bells slowly tolling, bearing banners with the inscriptions: 'Taxation without

representation is tyranny.' " Others proposed that the national leaders should be forced to sit through the celebrations in sackcloth and
ashes "in humiliation of spirit, as those who repented in olden times
were wont to do."[46]

The National convention issued a protest against "the Political
Sovereigns of the United States in Independence Hall" and agreed
to set up a women's headquarters in Philadelphia. There they would
pronounce a Declaration of Rights for Women and draw up articles
of impeachment against the "Political Sovereigns," which "we now
submit to the impartial judgment of the people." As the celebrants
hailed the founding fathers—George Washington, John Adams, and
the others—the women resurrected the spirit of Abigail Adams, "the
wife of one president and mother of another." They frequently quoted
her warning: "We will not hold ourselves bound to obey laws
in which we have no voice or representation."[47] The National
resolved: "That with Abigail Adams, in 1776, we believe that
'the passion for liberty cannot be strong in the breasts of those
who are accustomed to deprive their fellow-creatures of liberty';
that, as Abigail Adams predicted, 'We are determined to foment a
rebellion.' "[48]

The women went to work to plan their confrontation of the Centennial Celebration. Where was Mrs. Stanton now, Susan wondered. Mrs. Stanton had been traveling more or less continuously
on a Lyceum lecture tour since the previous October. On June 15,
she arrived at their Philadelphia offices. "I found them pleasantly
situated . . . with the work for the coming month clearly mapped
out."[49] Susan was surely "glad enough to see her & feel her strength
come in."[50] The first order of business was to get into the Centennial Celebration on the Fourth of July. Anthony asked the president
of the Centennial Commission for seats for fifty officers of the
National Woman's Suffrage Association; when her request was
rejected, Stanton asked for seats on the platform and "permission
to read our Declaration of Rights immediately after the reading of
the Declaration of Independence."[51] Stanton's requests were also
denied.

They had other plans. Susan acquired from her brother Daniel a
reporter's pass for his newspaper, the *Leavenworth Times*. Now
that she had access the next step was strategy. Then a few days
before the celebration, the women received a half-dozen official in-
vitations.

Stanton, Anthony, and Gage worked sixteen hours a day writing their declaration, and then "after many twists from our analytical tweezers, with a critical consideration of every word and sentence, it was at last, by a consensus of the competent, pronounced very good." Then they proceeded to the laborious work required of all political organizers. "Thousands were ordered to be printed, and were folded, put in envelopes, stamped, directed, and scattered."[52] The question now was what else to do with the declaration. Anthony insisted that it be read at the celebration. Mrs. Stanton and Lucretia Mott were so indignant over the way they had been treated that they refused to attend. Instead, they opened the alternative convention called by the women at the same time as the Centennial Celebration. But "others more brave and determined . . . decided to take the risk of public insult in order to present the woman's declaration and thus make it an historic document," Stanton acknowledged.[53]

Anthony, like Mott and Stanton, was also indignant but she had no choice. By now her reputation preceded her everywhere she went; she had become synonymous with the woman's rights movement. As its symbolic and charismatic leader—on a platform giving a lecture or in confrontation with the "masculine government" at her trial and now at the Centennial Celebration—Susan B. Anthony personified woman's rights. She had to embody and personify the women's movement with her visible, physical, and confrontational presence before their opponents. More than any other woman's rights leader, by her presence she represented uncompromised womanhood.

On July 4, Anthony, Gage, and three other women marched off to the Centennial Celebration with their Declaration of Rights for Women. "Their tickets of admission proved open sesame through the military and all other barriers, and a few moments before the opening of the ceremonies, these women found themselves within the precincts from which most of their sex were excluded," the *History of Woman Suffrage* recalled. While the Declaration of Independence was read to open the ceremonies, the women sat listening and keenly eyeing the platform. They were trying to see how they could gain access to it, for they firmly intended to read their own declaration immediately after the one of 1776.

Not quite sure how their approach might be met—not quite certain if at this final moment they would be permitted to reach the presiding officer—those ladies arose and made their way down the aisle. The bustle of preparation for the Brazilian hymn covered their advance.

The foreign guests, the military and civil officers who filled the space directly in front of the speakers stand, courteously made way, while Miss Anthony in fitting words presented the declaration. Mr. Ferry's face paled, as bowing low, with no word, he received the declaration, which thus became part of the day's proceedings; the ladies turned, scattering printed copies, as they deliberately walked down the platform.[54]

On their way out of the hall, they marched through the aisles distributing their declaration, while the master of ceremonies tried to regain control of the program. The women left Independence Hall and proceeded to a platform that had been erected outside for the band; it was now surrounded by a large and eager crowd. Matilda Joslyn Gage followed Susan B. Anthony to the center of the platform and opened an umbrella to protect her from the scorching July sun while Anthony read to the large crowd the declaration she had presented inside. It enumerated the violations of the "fundamental principles of our government" from which women suffered, and presented The Women's Articles of Impeachment, which claimed that a bill of attainder had been passed by the introduction of the word "male" into the Constitution and that the writ of *habeas corpus* "is held inoperative in every State of the Union, in case of a married woman against her husband—the marital rights of the husband being in all cases primary, and the rights of the wife secondary." The declaration protested denial of woman's right of trial by a jury of one's peers, taxation without representation, and the unequal legal codes for men and women.

A month after the centennial protest, Susan and Mrs. Stanton were at Tenafly rummaging through old papers and reading letters, convention calls, and newspaper clippings they had collected over the past twenty-five years. Susan reported that in this "delightfully quiet & pleasant home—[we] are working for dear life—trying to gather up the threads of our Woman's Rights History in this country—we propose to have a general history—and interwoven with it a brief sketch of one & another of the leaders—with their pictures—all to be condensed of course—as we propose 1 vol—octavion of 6 or 8 hundred pages."[55] They were accurate in estimating the length of the first volume, but the *History* grew to four volumes during Anthony's lifetime and two more volumes were published after she died.

In preparation for the work before them, Susan had trunks and boxes of old papers shipped from Rochester to Mrs. Stanton's home. Ever since she had called the Seneca Falls convention in 1848, Elizabeth Cady Stanton had wanted to write a history of women. Now she, Anthony, and Gage would write their own history, the *History of Woman Suffrage*. As there would be publisher's contracts, sales to arrange, and receipts to collect, Anthony had to be the proprietor of this project. The three women began the work of arranging their book, calling for contributions and recollections from other women in their movement. Lucy Stone remains noticibly absent from the volume. During its preparation she wrote that she would not furnish a biographical sketch for it and that she trusted Mrs. Stanton would not try to write one for her. "Yours with ceaseless regret that any 'wing' of suffragists should attempt to write the history of the other."[56]

Nestled away with Mrs. Stanton at Tenafly, Susan found that the task of reading old papers was almost more than she could bear. "It makes me sad and tired to read them over, to see the terrible strain I was under every minute then, have been since, am now and shall be for the rest of my life."[57] By early September she had a bad cold and was feeling very blue. "This attempt to write our history is simply appalling, it weighs me down," she confided to her diary.[58] She could not work, so she and Mrs. Stanton sat darning the children's stockings, and Susan worried that her cold could turn into a fatal illness. Sister Hannah now showed symptoms of consumption, and "it just seems that all of us were to follow dear Gula."[59]

While she and Mrs. Stanton were tackling the "appalling" work on their history, they received word that another close friend, Paulina Wright Davis, had died at her home in Providence, Rhode Island. Paulina had been one of the few New England women who continued to support the National and *The Revolution* through the split in their movement. She had introduced Isabella Hooker to Elizabeth Cady Stanton and Susan B. Anthony during the days when they were characterized throughout the world of reform as pure demons. Susan, always the subject of attack, was reluctant to go to the funeral, but knowing that "not one of the old Boston W.S. Women will pay the last tribute of respect & I will—be my reception what it may."

Mrs. Stanton spoke at the funeral in what Susan described as "the most touching manner & matter of the dead & her sacrifices for women & made an earnest appeal to the women present to try to so live & work as to leave an easier path for the women who shall follow them." Then in the hush of the funeral ceremonies, Susan stepped forward and opened a copy of an old diary of Theodore Parker's and read about the time when "he was deserted by all his old friends because of his heretical beliefs—how alone—how ostracized—and closed with hate—words on the illusion of life—seeking ever to find a full & true communion with some other soul—but that as we come into the world alone & go out alone—so in our deepest & holiest lives—each one of us—must live alone—each one who was true to himself & herself must 'tread the winepress alone' and the work of the true teacher should be to dispel this illusion from the mind of the young."[60]

During the funeral Susan learned that "Paulina has left word for the $500 to be cancelled." She was moved. "I cannot tell you what a relief it is to me that Mr. Davis spoke so cheerfully and whole souled when he handed me the note," she confided to Isabella Hooker.[61]

Within a month Susan was on her way to Kansas, where her sister Hannah was alone and near death. Susan deeply regretted the family decision to send Hannah to the West. "It was dreadfully cruel for us all to let her be out here so all alone—for well as I am—I can't help but feel how very alone & sad it would be if I were sick and struggling to get health and strength." Hannah died a month after Susan arrived, and Susan clung to her sister's memory. "Her precious spirit does brood upon me so constantly and so lovingly—wherever I turn she is more & more near. 'Oh, that I could clutch her back to life & health & her old sprightliness again' will rush through my almost every thought."[62]

Again, Mrs. Stanton worried about Susan. They were getting older and did not have the stamina of their youth, and they were losing dear ones to death. Although more to be expected with advancing age, these losses were never easy to reconcile. "Do be careful, dear Susan, you cannot stand what you once did. I should feel desolate indeed with you gone."

Age was making itself felt. Susan's carefree spirit, which had kept her on the trains more than settled in one place for over thirty years, needed a home of its own. And Mrs. Stanton, more frequently on the lecture circuit, began to feel what that meant for her friend. "As I go dragging around these despicable hotels, I think of you and often wish we had at least the little comfort of enduring it together. When is your agony over?" She forwarded some of her children's letters to Susan to cheer her and remind her of her other family. "I send you letters from *our* children. As the environments of the mother influence the child in prenatal life, and you were with me so much, there is no doubt you have had a part in making them what they are. There are a depth and earnestness in these younger ones and a love for you that delights my heart."[63] Their friendship had endured over a quarter of a century, and their love could not be broken even through their severest disagreements with each other. As Mrs. Stanton explained to one woman:

> Our friendship is of too long standing and has too deep roots to be easily shattered. I think we have said worse things to each other, face to face, then we have ever said about each other. Nothing that Susan could say or do could break my friendship with her; and I know nothing could uproot her affection for me.[64]

11

The Unity of Women— At What Cost?

BETWEEN 1877 AND 1883 ANTHONY CAMPAIGNED FROM STATE to state, returning to Washington every year for the annual National convention at which time she usually arranged to testify on behalf of woman's suffrage before a House or Senate committee. These were years filled with the repetitiveness of one campaign after another. It was work that had to be done whether or not it held the excitement and challenge of the earlier days. And these years were also filled with great sadness. Susan lost her sister Hannah in 1877 and her mother in 1880. And they were filled with another great labor as Anthony and Stanton produced the first volume of the *History of Woman Suffrage,* "a royal octavo of 900 pages," in 1881.

By 1883 it was time for a change. Susan had crossed the continent several times, often with the press at her heels, but never had she crossed the ocean. It was a momentous event when she sailed for Europe in 1883, with her friends, admirers, followers, state officials, and the famous and common alike giving her the kind of sendoff filled with pomp and circumstance that was usually accorded to heads of state. Newspapers throughout the nation announced her trip and reported on the banquets, receptions, honors, and recognition accorded her.

Farewell wishes even came from people such as Harriet Beecher Stowe, who had found the name of Susan B. Anthony too bold and controversial to be associated with only a few years earlier, and Frederick Douglass, who had fought against Anthony with the same toughness he had displayed when he had worked with her. And even such an enemy of woman's rights as Senator Ingalls, the Kansas Republican who Anthony thought "made an *ass* of himself in speaking against us,"[1] proclaimed that though he did not "sympathize with the opinions whose advocacy has made you famous," he joined with the others to wish her a warm farewell, safe voyage, and speedy return.

Her brother Daniel R. in Kansas wired: "Sixty-three years have crowned you with the honor and respect of the people of America, and with the love of your brothers and sisters." Susan B. Anthony's charismatic authority had spread far beyond her influence and leadership of the woman's rights movement. She had captured the imagination of the American public. And she would soon find that her reputation had preceded her to Europe.

Susan B. Anthony embarked on the *British Prince* early on the cold and dreary morning of February 23, 1883, with Rachel Avery, a young woman of twenty-five and a new apprentice to woman's rights who would be her traveling companion and guide through the languages of the countries they planned to visit—including Italy, France, and Germany. A crowd stood on the wharf hoping to catch a glimpse of Susan B. Anthony while she said her farewells to her sister Mary and close friends as they were ushered down the gangplank. She stood on the deck, pulled her beaver-lined black cape more tightly around her shoulders, and fought back that wrenching feeling that had gripped her every time since childhood when she had to part from loved ones. Why had sister Mary so stubbornly refused to join her on this trip, she wondered. Mary had made so much of Susan's work possible by taking care of family responsibilities at home in Rochester. Even after their mother died three years before at the age of eighty-seven, Mary still had the care of Guelma's children. But now they were young women attending the Free Academy in Rochester, and Susan had tried to persuade Mary to join her on this trip and to bring their nieces along. "What a jolly lot of tramps we would make!" she told Mary.

Susan settled into her comfortable stateroom filled with flowers and farewell gifts. As she untied the ribbons of her black velvet bonnet and set it on the table next to her and rested in an easy chair, she knew that while she still had brothers and sister Mary, she also had another kind of family—a privilege few women shared. By now there was a core group of young women who had apprenticed themselves to her and had become her adopted nieces, a true family to her. Rachel Foster was one of them. "What may I call you?" she had asked. "It is too familiar to say 'Susan' and too cold and distant to say 'Miss Anthony.' Mayn't I call you 'Aunt Susan.'"[2]

Rachel was the daughter of a wealthy newspaper owner and had been working with Anthony for over a year on woman's suffrage campaigns. She had managed the Nebraska campaign the year before, keeping eleven speakers in the field until suffrage came up for a vote in that state. During that time, Anthony had spoken in forty towns in a few months and had debated the leading politicians. As the suffrage amendment went down in defeat, the women had been confronted with the same virulent antiwoman attitudes that had followed Anthony during her campaigns thirty years before. Few people of the time realized how little the male attitude toward women had changed from the 1850s. Before Rachel and Aunt Susan had left Nebraska, Susan B. Anthony had been raised in effigy and carried in a coffin through the streets. She was used to confronting this hatred of her sex, but, she wondered, would Rachel be able to endure it over the long years? Would she succumb to the temptations and comforts of marriage and family? So many had come and gone from their movement over the years. Aunt Susan affectionately told her adopted niece, "How I wish you were made of iron—so you couldn't tire out—I fear all the time you will put on that added ounce that breaks the camel's back. You understand just how to make agitation & that is the secret of successful work."[3]

There were moments when the ocean voyage was stormy, and more than once while reclining in a deck chair or walking along the promenade, Susan was pitched into a heap on the deck. As she described it, "A sudden lurch of the ship took both my feet from me and I was flat on my back." There were dinners at the captain's table, to which she was usually invited even if the service had to be fastened to the tables. She prided herself on the strength of her constitution. "I haven't lost a meal during the whole trip."

After several days at sea, they were called to see the first view of land. Susan hastened to the bridge, excited to see the Emerald Isle. Soon they would arrive in England, and there would be an even more beautiful sight to Susan's eyes. Mrs. Stanton was "on tiptoe of expectation" to greet her "beloved Susan" and announced in her characteristic way, "I came up to London the moment I heard of your arrival on the *British Prince*. To think of your choosing a 'Prince' when a 'Queen' was coming!"[4] Mrs. Stanton had sailed to Europe with her daughter Harriot shortly after she and Susan had published the second volume of the *History of Woman Suffrage* in 1882. By the time Susan arrived, Mrs. Stanton had already been there for a year.

Susan and her adopted niece Rachel went sightseeing in London with Mrs. Stanton and her daughter Harriot. They were aghast at the place assigned to ladies to observe the workings of the House of Commons. "It is really a disgrace to a country ruled by an Empress," Mrs. Stanton asserted.[5] Stanton had been in Europe long enough to realize that the conditions faced by women in England and on the Continent and their growing anger were not unlike what she had seen at home. She talked with Susan about forming an international movement for woman's rights, and they met with woman's suffrage clubs. There they heard reports of the great demonstrations on behalf of woman's rights that had begun in Manchester three years before to overflowing crowds in halls that held more than five thousand people. The demonstration had spread quickly throughout England: to Bristol, Nottingham, Birmingham, Sheffield, and Glasgow. They celebrated the success of the Married Women's Property Act, which had finally made its way through both houses of Parliament the year before. In 1870, English women had won the right to retain their own earnings. With this new law, they had the same power as a single woman to enter into a contract and to sue and be sued. The old common law was finally beginning to crack.[6]

The English feminist Josephine Butler founded a movement to abolish the Contagious Disease Acts, which had legalized prostitution for the military in garrison towns. When Anthony arrived in England, Butler was only two years away from success in eliminating the acts. Under these acts any woman or girl on the streets could be arrested, forced to submit to a physical examination, and be officially registered as a prostitute. Once registered they were known as prostitutes and were refused any other employment. As a result, many poor and working women were forced into prostitution.

In 1869, the first National Society for Women's Suffrage was organized in England. That same year Mill's essay, *On The Subjection of Women,* was published and, although it compromised the issue of divorce, it gave a great boost to the suffrage movement. By the 1870s advances had been made in many fields for women, but the demand for suffrage was still relatively new. Because they were facing the first intensive phases of resistance to their demands at home, many English feminists were not ready to escalate the struggle to form an international movement. Consequently, when in her first weeks in England Anthony proposed a plan for a great international council of women, the idea was not well received.

A visit to the Brontë parsonage in Haworth in the moor country in northern England was a kind of pilgrimage for Susan. "A most sad day it was to me," Susan noted, "as I looked into the little parlor where the sisters walked up and down with their arms around each other and planned their novels, or sat before the fireplace and built air-castles." How difficult the climate on those frail young women! she thought. "Think of those delicate women sitting in that fireless, mouldy church, listening to their old father's dry, hard theology, with their feet on the cold, carpetless stones which covered their loved dead. It was too horrible!" Susan walked through the gate and went out through the fields toward the moor wondering, "How much the world of literature has lost because of their short and ill-environed lives, we can guess only from its increased wealth in spite of all their adverse conditions."[7]

There had been teas and visits and excursions and meetings. After a busy month in England, Aunt Susan and Rachel left for the Continent; their first stop was Italy. Italian women had been agitating for suffrage and working to promote educational opportunities for women. In 1876, a bill had been reported favoring the right of women to vote in municipal elections.

The Old World was a wonder of sights to Susan, who eventually relaxed into the role of a tourist. After a three-day trip from London to Milan, she and Rachel rested and toured the city for a few days, and then they were off to Genoa and Naples. They journeyed to Pompeii and finally Rome and the Vatican, where "one is simply dazed with the wealth of marble." But the Baroque churches and their art were too much for Susan. "One becomes fairly sickened with the ghastly spectacle of the dead Christ."[8] And she noted that she had never seen the extent of poverty in America that she found on the streets of Europe.

Later in her trip she visited Ireland. One day she was walking through a market in Killarney, when she noticed some boys on a bridge gawking at "a ragged, bareheaded, barefooted woman tossing a wee baby over her shoulders and trying to get her apron switched around to hold it fast on her back." Then she bent over to pick up another baby in a bundle on the ground. Susan scurried quickly down the hillside to help the woman and learned that she had just left the poorhouse for a ten-mile walk to see her dying mother. That would not do. Hurrying back up the hillside again, Susan found a boy with a "jaunting cart," brought food for the woman, her babies, the boy, and the horse, then "off we went!"

Over the years Susan had become an international figure but had never lost a sense of her ordinary origins. She was as much at ease with common folks in simple settings as she had become in congressional hearings or at meetings with dignitaries. She chatted comfortably with the Irish woman on their way to the village. When they arrived, the young mother led Susan into her mother's home, which consisted of one windowless room. The room was smoky from the peat burning for warmth, and there was some straw in the corner, with a blanket covering it, for a bed. There Susan found more children that "God had given them." She heard the same story in home after home. By the time she left Killarney, Susan was heartsick and angry. "What a dreadful creature their 'God' must be to keep sending hungry mouths while he withholds the bread to fill them!"[9]

In Paris, Anthony met with women leaders and found that "the majority of liberals say it is not the time to demand the ballot for France. That her civil rights should come first—and then their deepest fear is that if the women had the right of suffrage—the vast majority of them being Catholic—they would vote that church back into absolute power!!" The monarchy of the Second Empire under Louis Napoleon had fallen with the Siege of Paris and the Commune of 1871. But monarchists continued to hold control in the new Third Republic through the rest of the decade. Only two years before Anthony's visit had the Republicans won enough governmental power to remove the prohibition against public meetings and the guarantee of freedom of the press. Now French feminists had begun again to vigorously, but cautiously, pursue their legal rights.[10]

The Napoleonic Code, which was promulgated at the beginning of the nineteenth century, gave the husband full legal powers over his wife, her property, and her children. It was the French equivalent of the English Common Law, which rendered married woman legally dead. But in some ways it went further by stipulating that a woman could be imprisoned for two years if she committed adultery and that if her husband killed her for it, he could not be charged with murder, while there were no sanctions for adultery on his part. The Napoleonic Code found powerful church support in this Catholic country. And the liberals, who opposed the religious power of the state, tried to discourage the feminists from pressing their demands for suffrage, as it was widely believed that women were traditionally more religious than men, and that if they were granted the vote, they would vote for conservative, church-supported measures.[11]

French feminists had much to protest. However, they were limited by the power of the Church on the one hand and by the suspicion of the government on the other. Women who had been active revolutionaries and fighters in the Paris Commune, such as Louise Michel, were known as *petroleuses* (incendiaries) and were thought to have set Paris on fire during the uprising of the Commune. Since then women's organizing had been viewed with suspicion. Nevertheless, Louise Michel and others had succeeded in founding the Société pour la revendication des droits de la femme (Society for the Demand of Woman's Rights), and Hubertine Auclert, among the most radical of the French feminists, edited the feminist paper *La Citoyenne*.

By the time Anthony visited France, the French movement for woman's rights had adopted a gradualist approach, trying to influence legislators and important public figures to get them to take up their own "republican" demands. But Auclert remained outspoken, one of the few who asserted the more radical demand for *universal* suffrage. In fact, she attempted to vote in 1880. In their politics, strategies, and commitment to women, she and Anthony had much in common when they met in Paris. Given their convergence of ideas, Anthony was even more frustrated with the language barrier. "I cannot tell you how I constantly long to be able to speak and understand French." She particularly wanted to confront Leon Richer, a male movement leader who favored the gradualist approach of the French woman's movement, for his failure to understand suffrage as political power. "He thinks it inopportune to demand suffrage for women in France now, when they are yet without their civil rights. I wanted so much to tell him that political power was the greater right which included the less."[12]

Despite the political restrictions surrounding French feminism, the Congrès international du droit des femmes was held in Paris in 1878. Mrs. Stanton's son Theodore, who was then living in Paris, attended as a representative from the United States. Ten other countries and sixteen organizations were represented. There were 219 delegates and 400 others attending. But the political rights of women were not discussed. The women took up issues of equal pay, educational equality, and, under the influence of Josephine Butler's work in England, the issue of regulated and forced prostitution. Like women in many other countries, French women had campaigned for the right to divorce. When divorce was granted, it was not on their terms of mutual consent but rather only in cases of adultery, grievous injury, or criminal conviction.[13] Anthony found that despite the differences in their cultures, languages, and governments, French and American women had much in common in their cause. And she was pleased to report to the English women later that the idea of an international women's movement had already begun on the Continent.

For Susan, springtime in Paris was not just a time for politics and meetings. Theodore was like a son to Susan and she was able to relax with him. He took her on tours in Paris and to the countryside as well as to the grand opera. Her tour of the Continent, which was supposed to be a vacation, had been scheduled at her usual busy pace. In Paris, she finally began to relax in ways she never had experienced before. When Madame de Barron invited her to be a guest for a few days in her home, Susan was surprised to awake and to find "my continental breakfast—rolls, butter and coffee—was sent to my room and, for the first time in my life, I ate it in bed. What would my mother have said?"[14]

The new sights and some relaxation gave Susan pause for thought. "All life should not be given to one's work at home, whether that be woman suffrage, journalism or government affairs."[15] Time was passing, her age was advancing, and as the Old World opened up before her, she began to realize how much she had not seen and experienced. "I am getting a good relish for a more deliberate tour later someday." And leaving Paris she knew she had changed. "I have enjoyed the last three months exceedingly, but I am very, very tired; and yet it is a new set of faculties which are weary, and the old ones so long harped upon, are really restive."[16]

Susan's spirits rebounded, and her energy soared again. Instead of giving up her life of work, when she returned to England from the Continent she sought out Mrs. Stanton. "I met Susan face to face in the streets of London with a new light in her eyes. Behold there were more worlds to conquer. She had decided on an international council in Washington, so I had to return with her to the scenes of our conflict." Then Mrs. Stanton conceded, "Well, I prefer a tyrant of my own sex, so I shall not deny the patent fact of my subjection; for I do believe that I have developed into much more of a woman under her jurisdictions, fed on statute laws and constitutional amendments, than if left to myself reading novels in an easy chair, lost in sweet reveries of the golden age to come without any effort of my own."[17]

They met several more times with the English women, who were increasingly receptive to the idea of an international congress. And by the time Susan left, after friendships had been struck up, confidences opened, and lessons from women in other countries discussed, it was agreed that the women would call an International Council of Women. Anthony had been in Europe for nine months, and on November 16, 1883, she sailed for America, feeling quite satisfied with her trip.

When Anthony returned to "the scenes of conflict," her tone had changed; she no longer believed that victory was around the corner. In 1884, she testified before the House and Senate committees in Congress to demand a sixteenth constitutional amendment to enfranchise women. She pointed out to the legislators that this was the fifteenth consecutive year that they, as women, had come in person before the Congress with their demands and the nineteenth year that they had come to petition for woman's right to vote. She assured Congress that if they submitted a new constitutional amendment to the public for a vote, "You need not fear that our enfranchisement will come too suddenly or too soon by this method. After the proposition shall have passed Congress by the requisite two-thirds vote, it may require five, ten or twenty years to secure its ratification by the necessary three-fourths of the State legislatures."[18]

Militancy had yielded to the slow, patient work of change. In 1887, Anthony saw their proposed Sixteenth Amendment—"The rights of citizens of the United States to vote shall not be denied or abridged by the United States or any State on account of sex"— come to its first congressional vote and go down to defeat.

By 1887, Anthony began to organize the International Council of Women, which would meet for the first time in Washington, D.C., in 1888, and it would celebrate the fortieth anniversary of the Seneca Falls convention. It was time, Anthony felt, to turn some of the organizational responsibilities over to the younger women. Rachel Foster and another suffrage worker, May Wright Sewall, took charge.

However, everything passed through the hands of the "General," who in turn sent drafts of everything to Stanton who was back in England with her daughter Harriot. Stanton was overwhelmed. When she received the sixteen-page program for the eight-day event, which was revised with each new printing and was sent out to forty thousand people, she realized that her colleagues had turned the meeting into an enormous project. Make it manageable, Stanton cautioned.

She also complained to Susan that the younger women were too verbose; in her opinion, they left nothing in their writing to the imagination.[19] She insisted that Susan oversee everything. "Do not, I pray you, let one go out until you and & Mrs. Mann put every sentence through your metaphysical, rhetorical & common sense tweezers." Accordingly, Susan instructed Rachel to study and become a nonrepetitious writer. But it was more than a question of style, for the radical spirit that had captured Susan and Mrs. Stanton's political consciousness back in the 1850s and had sharpened their tongues and pens as well was gone. The calls for meetings now began to sound more like hollow rhetoric than confrontational challenges. Anthony and Stanton did not relinquish control of the congress to the second generation feminists. The call reflected their spirit. "Much is said of universal brotherhood, but for weal or woe, more subtle and more binding is universal sisterhood." But in contrast to the grass-roots approach used to organize the National almost two decades earlier (when anyone who paid their dollar was seated and could vote), "universal sisterhood" now meant official delegates. "Literary Clubs, Art Unions, Temperance Unions, Labor Leagues, Missionary, Peace and Moral Purity Societies, Charitable, Professional, Educational and Industrial Associations will thus be offered equal opportunity with Suffrage Societies to be represented in what should be the ablest and most imposing body of women ever assembled."[20] Anthony invited the social-reform women to the council hoping they would see the need for women's political rights.

Although suffrage was a major issue for American feminists, it was absent from the congress. The more broadly based their woman's movement, the more they had to tailor their issues to the varying conditions of women's lives. But the International Council did reflect women's unity in their diversity, as the call continued: "However the governments, religions, laws and customs of nations may differ, all are agreed on one point, namely: man's sovereignty in the State, in the Church and in the Home . . . Such a Council will impress the important lesson that the position of the women anywhere affects their position everywhere."

For months this organizing went on without Mrs. Stanton's help. Susan eagerly awaited her return. "Oh dear—how I wish I had Mrs. Stanton here—and I could galvanize her to make beautiful my crude glimmering of ideas."[21] Stanton had written at one point that "we have jogged along pretty well for forty years or more. Perhaps mid the wreck of thrones and the undoing of so many friendships, sects, parties and families, you and I deserve some credit for sticking together through all adverse winds, with so few ripples on the surface. When I get back to America, I intend to cling to you closer than ever. I am thoroughly rested now and full of fight and fire, ready to travel and speak from Maine to Florida. Tell our suffrage daughters to brace up and get ready for a long pull, a strong pull, and a pull all together when I come back."[22]

Then, less than two months before the International Council, Susan received a letter from Mrs. Stanton saying it was doubtful that she would be home in time for the meeting. She was afraid of the ocean voyage, and she decided to stay in England. Susan sank into her chair. Imagine! "A fortieth anniversary of the Seneca Falls convention without the woman who called it!" What could she do? "I am ablaze," she uttered in an anger almost unbecoming of her. And for the rest of the day, she "was too incensed to write." Then Rachel came in with another letter from Mrs. Stanton, "bidding her to get Susan ready to make the opening speech & get along without her." This was too much. "I was more on fire than ever." Susan went to her desk, and "I wrote the most terrific letter to Mrs. Stanton; it will start every white hair on her head." She told her that "she will never be forgiven by me or any of our association, if she fails to come!" Then she asked Elizabeth Smith Miller to write Mrs. Stanton that "the very evil fates will persecute her if she dares to be absent!!"[23]

Almost as soon as she had mailed the letter, Susan had second thoughts. That night she lay awake, tossing in her bed with her heart aching so much because of "my terrible arraignment, whether it touches her feelings or not." Often during the next ten days she paced the floor, wringing her hands, and finally one day a cablegram arrived from Mrs. Stanton. Susan hurriedly opened it with no small amount of anxiety. "Coming" was the only written message, but it conveyed more than a point won or a crisis passed. Susan intuitively knew that somehow Mrs. Stanton understood, and even if Susan had been too harsh with her, she forgave her. For the first time since this ordeal had begun, Susan relaxed a bit. "My mind is so relieved, I feel as if I were treading on air."[24]

But her problems were not over. Mrs. Stanton did arrive in Washington a few days before the Council began, as she had promised, but without her opening address. They both knew in that instant that they had been through this scene many times before. Stanton recalled that "Miss Anthony ordered me to remain conscientiously in my own apartment and to prepare a speech for delivery before the committees of the Senate and House, and another as President for the opening of the council." But just to be sure she stayed there, Susan had one of the younger women placed outside of Mrs. Stanton's door as a guard. Mrs. Stanton yielded to Susan's protective custody in moments like this. Susan arranged with Mrs. Spofford, the proprietor of the Riggs House where they stayed and a friend of woman's suffrage, to place "her carriage at our service," and Mrs. Stanton "was permitted to drive an hour or two every day about that magnificent city."[25]

Two years later, Mrs. Stanton paid tribute to Susan's demanding and insistent character, which she saw as the core of their friendship.

> If there is one part of my life which gives me more intense satisfaction than another, it is my friendship of more than forty years' standing with Susan B. Anthony . . . Emerson says, "It is better to be a thorn in the side of your friend than his echo." If this adds weight and stability to friendship, then ours will endure forever, for we have indeed been thorns in the side of each other. Sub rosa, dear friends, I have had no peace for forty years, since the day we started together on the suffrage expedition in search of woman's place in the National Constitution. She has kept me on the war-path at the point of the bayonet so long that I have often wished my untiring coadjutor might, like Elijah, be translated a few years before I was summoned, that I might spend the sunset of my life in some quiet chimney-corner and lag superfluous on the stage no longer.[26]

Susan confessed that "what she said is true; I have been a thorn in her side and in that of her family too, I fear. I never expect to know any joy in this world equal to that of going up and down the land, getting good editorials written, engaging halls and circulating Mrs. Stanton's speeches. If I ever have had any inspiration she has given it to me, for I never could have done my work if I had not had this woman at my right hand."[27]

The International Council of Women opened on March 25 and continued for one week, to April 1, 1888. Fifty-three organizations and forty-nine other delegates from England, France, Ireland, Norway, Denmark, Finland, India, Canada, and the United States met in seven days of meetings in which over eighty speakers were heard. President and Mrs. Grover Cleveland welcomed the International Council with a reception, and Reverend Anna Howard Shaw, a young woman who worked with Frances Willard in the Woman's Christian Temperance Union, preached the Sunday sermon at the grand-opera house. Susan B. Anthony opened the Council's first session in the vast auditorium and presided over most of the events. Soft music played while she walked across the platform filled with fragrant evergreens and flowers. Above hung a portrait of Lucretia Mott, which was surrounded by smilax and lilies of the valley. Anthony welcomed the gathering, telling them, "I have the pleasure of introducing to you this morning the woman who not only joined with Lucretia Mott in calling the first convention, but who for the greater part of twenty years has been president of the National Woman's Suffrage Association—Mrs. Elizabeth Cady Stanton."

Mrs. Stanton, now seventy-three years old, plump and matronly, and adorned with her famous locks of white curls, stepped forward. The audience rose in profound applause, with hands clapping and handkerchiefs waving. This morning her theme was unity. "Whether our feet are compressed in iron shoes, our faces hidden with veils and masks; whether yoked with cows to draw the plow through its furrows, or classed with idiots, lunatics and criminals in the laws and constitutions of the State, the principle is the same; for the humiliations of spirit are as real as the visible badges of servitude."[28]

After Stanton's speech, Anthony introduced the foreign delegates and read messages from abroad. But there was another unity of women represented on this platform—one that had particular importance to the American movement. For the first time in twenty years, officers and leaders of the National and American Woman Suffrage associations sat together. Susan B. Anthony introduced Lucy Stone and the suffrage leaders of both associations. Then she invited to the stage Frederick Douglass and Robert Purvis. Purvis was one of the few black men who had stood by the woman's rights movement during the "Negro's hour," claiming he could not fight for his rights unless they included his daughters'. These men had signed the first Declaration of Sentiments in 1848—the fortieth anniversary of which they were now celebrating. Few besides Anthony, Stanton, and Stone could realize what the unity on this platform meant to the woman's movement, which until that moment had been factionalized for twenty years.

Actually, negotiations between the National and American had been underway for some time. While they had been preparing for the International Council, Susan B. Anthony and Lucy Stone had met for the first time since the split and had begun to talk about unity at home. Overtures had begun a few years before. Anthony had noticed a change in Lucy Stone's attitude. Stone had been printing letters to and from women in the National in her own paper, *The Woman's Journal,* and initially that had made Anthony suspicious. "What does it mean, save that she feels that we are on the winning side!!!"[29] Of course Anthony wanted unity, but initially she feared that if she made overtures to Lucy Stone they would again be rebuffed.

Even though suffrage was now the major emphasis of both organizations, Anthony saw that "our only difference from the American Society is that they place men in official positions—and we do not—it is that little point of difference that makes our society a live one and theirs a dead one in comparison. For men cannot make women's disfranchisement hurt them—as it hurts us, hence cannot be our guides and ultimate appeals—as to principles & policies of action."[30]

At the time of the split, Mrs. Stanton's proposals for "easy divorce," as Lucy Stone described this position, was another major difference between the two factions. It was one that had been forged before the Civil War when the liberal men turned against the women's movement over this issue. But since Anthony had placed political rights and suffrage above all other issues, Stone and the American now reasoned that "the methods of the National, as time passed on, had gradually lost the characteristics that had aroused so much objection in its early years. The question of easy divorce was no longer pressed at its meetings."[31]

Nevertheless, Lucy Stone's husband, Henry Blackwell, regularly put obstacles in the path of peace and unity for the women's movement. For instance, he made periodic comments that Anthony seemed to be coming more into line with the American, which insulted her. She did not consider that by raising suffrage to the primary concern of the National she was reducing its platform to the conservative goals of reform. But the fact remains that even though Anthony's commitment to suffrage was for the radical reasons Engels articulated for the working classes, her shift in the woman's rights platform to suffrage opened the doors to the American's making the first overtures toward unity and to its highly conservative influence on the movement.

In its fall 1887 convention, the American Woman Suffrage Association had resolved "that Mrs. Lucy Stone be appointed a committee of one from the American Woman Suffrage Association to confer with Miss Susan B. Anthony of the National . . . to consider a satisfactory basis of union."[32] On December 21, 1887, three months before the opening of the International Council of Women, Susan B. Anthony and Lucy Stone met in Boston with Lucy's daughter Alice Stone Blackwell and Susan's "niece" Rachel to discuss the unity of their two societies. Anthony was skeptical. "It looks *cheeky* to me," she told Rachel Foster, "but let's wait for the development."[33] It was the younger women who were enthusiastic. "The elders were not keen for it on either side," Alice recalled after the meeting. In fact, Lucy's daughter can be credited with bringing about unification of the two societies.

Stone and the American wanted negotiations to take place through committees appointed by each society. The committees would propose whatever modifications were needed, and when they were agreed upon the two societies would unite. Concessions were not the point, Anthony said. "I do not wish to exact any pledges from Lucy Stone and her adherents, nor can I give any for Mrs. Stanton and her followers." Trust was the only basis for unity, she insisted.[34] The best way to unite was to go ahead and unite the two societies and then discuss any remaining issues afterwards. In fact, negotiations continued for two years.

Susan had been looking for some time for someone to succeed her. "I shall leave the helm of the good National ship to Rachel," she told Rachel one day, because "we older ones must learn to surrender our wills to those who *do the work*."[35] But in 1889, just when Anthony thought her twenty-nine-year-old "niece" could carry more of the leadership responsibilities, Rachel secretly adopted a baby; a year later she married and became Rachel Foster Avery. Anticipating Aunt Susan's reaction to the adoption, Rachel carefully concealed her plan until it was completed. Finally, May Wright Sewall "leaked the news," and Susan was "appalled." She confronted Rachel with "the cat is out of the bag!" Nearing seventy, she desperately wanted new leadership and now she could no longer count on Rachel; but she was happy for her too. She convinced herself that this one child would not hurt Rachel, "provided she doesn't lose her head in love with it altogether."[36] Then in her own characteristic humor, she wrote a letter to Rachel's adopted infant.

Dear Miriam Alice, It is doubtful whether Aunt Susan welcomes your little ladyship to the home of 748 North 14th St. Phila.! She is thinking whether you will not divert all the love of the *foster* mamas from the great work for emancipation of *woman*—to the little business of caring for the material & moral wants of the one well one—your little self. So my dear, if you would win Aunt Susan's best will—so deport yourself as to help the junior Aunties to be more—to do more—for the *woman general* than ever before you came to them.[37]

Susan's sights were still set on finding a dynamic, gifted, and above all tireless woman from this younger generation who would not give in to marriage and motherhood and could follow in her steps. One evening during the International Council, while she was on her way back to her hotel room, she was thinking about the powerful preaching and strong dedication to women she had heard in young Reverend Anna Shaw's voice at the opening of their sessions. Before getting to her own room, she gently rapped on Anna's door. "I had gone to bed—indeed, I was almost asleep when she came, for the day had been as exhausting as it was interesting." Still fresh and full of energy, Anthony told her, "I have a great deal to say." She then settled herself into the easy chair near the bed and tucked a lap rug around her knees. Anna sat up, propped some pillows behind her, and was all attention.

"Hours passed and the dawn peered wanly through the windows, but Miss Anthony talked of the Cause—always the Cause—and what we must do for it," Anna remembered later. For years ahead there were many more campaigns before them, Susan told Anna, "Forgetting nothing, forseeing everything, and sweeping me with her in her flight toward our common goal, until I who am not easily carried off my feet, experienced an almost dizzy sense of exhilaration."

When morning light poured into the room, Anthony was surprised. "My we seemed to have talked all night." She stood up and walked to the door. "I must dress now, I've called a meeting before the morning session." Then remembering that Anna Shaw had not slept a wink that night, as she went out the door she suggested that "perhaps you ought to have a cup of coffee."[38]

International and national unity opened old wounds and provoked new factions in the American women's movement. Almost as if it were the realization of the "divide-and-conquer" theory of oppression, new lines of disagreement immediately appeared. Over the years the movement had expanded and diversified, but with the oppressed set up against each other by the dominating class, diversification meant clashes as much as it also meant a broader base for the movement. At one end, there were reform women like Frances Willard, president of the Woman's Christian Temperance Union (WCTU), who still saw women's place as being in the home—even while she campaigned for reforms to improve their situation in the world. On the other hand, women like Elizabeth Cady Stanton were attacking the ideological roots of patriarchal power in religious authority, something that was a particularly timely issue as liberals in the country were worried about the conservative influence of the growing Catholic minority population. Anthony still stood apart. She could not be pulled toward the conservative women although she respected much of their work, and she could not be dislodged from her radical egalitarianism into what she saw as basically a war of words against religious authority.

She supported Frances Willard insofar as Willard supported suffrage. Further, Anthony saw the WCTU address many issues she herself had long championed, such as dress reform and labor reform. Willard campaigned adamantly to discourage women from corseting themselves. She had been inducted into the radical leftist Knights of Labor for her campaigns for the eight-hour day and was recognized by them for her understanding that it was the exploitation of labor that caused men to turn to alcohol. Willard worked for prison reform and campaigned for free kindergartens. She advocated the right of a woman to a sober husband and for a woman's right to a portion of her husband's earnings in recompense for her household labor.[39]

Willard's program encompassed the broadest range of social reform, including many of the demands of the woman's rights movement. But Willard contradicted the possibilities these vast social reforms could produce by compromising on women's domesticity. Her religious beliefs caused her to defend the home as woman's appropriate sphere. Anthony would have none of it; she cautioned Willard against making an alliance with the Prohibition party.[40] Willard ignored her warnings and during the presidential campaign of 1884 moved the WCTU into support for the Prohibitionists. Anthony did not sever her relations with Willard but instead worked with her on issues they had in common. Anthony saw that the Prohibition party appealed to the most conservative tendencies in women with a platform that not only called for prohibition of the sale and consumption of alcoholic beverages but also promoted national laws to further restrict the right to divorce and favored other antifeminist measures. To Anthony, prohibition did not represent a right; it was not comparable to the Fourteenth and Fifteenth amendments. "The protection of the Negro is a *principle* while Prohibition is a method—a plan of dealing with the liquor question." Prohibition was a restrictive method, while citizenship was an enabling right.[41]

But women in the movement disagreed with Anthony when she accepted women for their work on woman's suffrage, even when she disagreed with their other positions. Matilda Joslyn Gage declared the WCTU "the great dangerous organization of the movement" and unsuccessfully tried to get Mrs. Stanton to work with her against it. Gage and Olympia Brown represented a group of women who feared that the Christian influence of the WCTU would begin to dominate their suffrage campaigns. In fact, as far as suffrage was concerned, Willard had only tried to harness the Christian women's energy behind suffrage.

Many reformers began to fear a growing "Catholic domination" in the country. The woman's suffrage workers saw a threat to the realization of their goals coming from the Catholic Church. They were particularly concerned about the Irish immigrants. They feared that the new male citizens would support and vote for the most conservative, restrictive measures relative to women. Then came a new influx of immigrants, primarily from southern and eastern Europe. Some woman's suffrage workers began to express growing anti-immigrant sentiments, because they feared that immigrant men (among them Italian and Polish Catholics and Russians and other Poles), with their traditional backgrounds, would oppose American women's demands for citizenship with suffrage.

Mrs. Stanton's work reflected this concern. By 1890, Stanton had launched a formidable attack against Christian theology, which she identified as a central cause of the social and political subordination of women. In preparing a *Woman's Bible,* she insisted that religions must be denounced "for their degrading teaching in regard to women."[42]

Anthony disagreed with Stanton. For Anthony, beliefs and attitudes would change only when behavior and actions were forced to change.

> You say "women must be emancipated from their superstitions before enfranchisement will be of any benefit," and I say just the reverse, that

women must be enfranchised before they can be emancipated from their superstitions. Women would be no more superstitious today than men, if they had been men's political and business equals and gone outside the four walls of home and the other four of the church into the great world, and come in contact with and discussed men and measures on the plane of this mundane sphere, instead of living in the air with Jesus and angels. So you will have to keep pegging away, saying, "Get rid of religious bigotry and then get political rights;" while I shall keep pegging away, saying "Get political rights first and religious bigotry will melt like dew before the morning sun;" and each will continue still to believe in and defend the other.[43]

Anthony's own religious training had been secularized. In her Quaker childhood she had not directly suffered under the weight of Christian dogma, except as it shaped her induction into the rigors of female piety. As an adult, her spirituality was closer to transcendentalism than to any Puritan theology. The question of religious domination did not compel her interest. But that had never stopped her before in addressing a woman's issue. Most importantly, she wanted concrete, behaviorial change and believed that attitudes would only change afterward. She was not particularly threatened herself by what others saw as a growing Catholic influence, and she did not believe that this influence could in any way threaten the Constitution's doctrine of the separation of church and state.

Gage was among those who were concerned with the issue of religion. But she was determined to prevent the unity between the National and the American. And she was not alone. Olympia Brown worried that the National-American would cease to campaign for a national constitutional amendment and would revert to the state-by-state approach of the American. Isabella Hooker took the position that "if we must bear to the end of our struggle, why not go separately." She believed that "our differences will be made manifest by an outside union—whereas few persons know how there came to be two societies & all can work with one or the other *according to preference.*"[44]

Stanton was perturbed that Anthony refused to connect the menacing threat of religious domination with the new conservative drift of the women's movement. She told Olympia Brown that "the National Association has been growing politic and conservative for some time. Lucy and Susan alike see suffrage only. They do not see woman's religious and social bondage. Neither do the young women in either association, hence they may as well combine for they have one mind and one purpose."[45] History has proven Anthony right on this point. A basically white Anglo-Saxon country would not allow Catholics to gain too much power, and the fear that the separation-of-church-and-state doctrine would be threatened was unfounded. But Stanton was right when she identified the increased conservatism of a suffrage only politics.

If Anthony was not radical enough on issues of religious domination for women like Stanton and Gage, she was not religious enough for many women of the WCTU, who had walked out of their 1884 meeting when Frances Willard introduced Anthony, because "she didn't believe in God." For her part, Frances Willard feared that the WCTU would be thrown overboard in the union between the National and American because Anthony had refused to support the Prohibition party.

Factionalizing started again. Gage organized a Liberal Woman Suffrage Association to keep their movment free from religious influences. Anthony thought that "would be just as ridiculous as a *Christian W.S.A.*" and assumed that nothing would come of it. "It cannot be that our women will be cajoled or deceived into such a foolish step." But Gage persisted and formed her organization. Anthony insisted that the National yield neither to Willard on one extreme nor to Gage on the other; but keeping its focus on suffrage as the center of woman's political rights, it must remain broad and open to both women and the ideas they represented. "I tell them I have worked 40 years to make the W.S. platform broad enough for Atheists and Agnostics to stand upon, and now if need be I will fight the next 40 to keep it Catholic enough to permit the straightest Orthodox religionist to speak or pray and count her beads upon."[46]

Factionalism is usually personalized, and there had been underlying personal tensions building for some time between Gage and Anthony. Now they began to surface and take the shape of political differences. Gage had apparently felt overshadowed by Anthony. When the women were closing their offices in Washington in 1877 following their protest of the Centennial Celebration of 1876, Susan was about to leave and turned to embrace Mrs. Gage, "But Mrs. Gage did not return my kiss—but turned her cheek."[47] Over the next few months, Mrs. Gage's irritability increased, and she openly complained to Susan that she felt overshadowed. Susan, who understood this problem well from her own experience with Mrs. Stanton, wrote to Mrs. Gage, "trying to sooth her suspicion that I have not always been just to her in bringing her to the front or trying to." Finally she admitted that she believed that Mrs. Gage "is a dear, good woman—but desperately misanthropic—distrusts everybody's loyalty to her & the truth."[48] At one point, Mrs. Gage had apparently pressed Rachel Foster about her place on the program of one convention. Anthony cautioned Rachel, "I fear she has been saying something sort—a—cross to you—about time of speaking. If she has never mind it—your young heart and shoulders must learn to bear the crotchets of all sorts of people, and not get broken or bent under them."[49]

Anthony refused to dwell on these personal antagonisms. When she was personally rebuffed, she acted as she did when she was politically attacked—she proceeded with her work. She was the only woman who had remained in the forefront of the movement consistently for over forty years, and her work, if not her charisma, earned her the authority to launch new campaigns or hold the reigns of the movement's strategy when she was under fire. What in moments of crisis appeared to many to have been autocratic behavior on her part was from her standpoint the action necessary to steer the movement through one precarious situation after another. Because of her long years of work, she was one of the few who gave the movement direction in the midst of the confusing controversies. Her clarity came from her commitment to her *people*. In that sense her charisma distinguished her decisions and positions from those who were only involved in a fully committed but more tangential fashion.

But women's personal insecurities and their feelings of being overshadowed by Anthony's compelling presence could not be abated by ignoring them. This was one of those times when Anthony was caught between the roles of a surrogate husband and a feminist leader. This time—like husbands often became for their wives over whom they unjustly held authority—Anthony became the focus of some women's personal rebellion. What confused the issue and accelerated personal antagonisms was that as they did with their husbands, some women began to rebel against Anthony without stepping back to look at their behavior reflectively. Therefore they did not distinguish between the sources of real male power over and against women and true leadership that carried a full weight of responsibility with it.

Anthony followed her own judgment on the question of unity. That opened her to attack and rebellion from other women in the movement, who, on the other hand, resented her authority but still expected her to carry the full responsibility for the movement. This time there seemed to be no path that would not hurt feelings and create jealousies from one side or the other.

Despite all the dissension and disagreement within the movement, the National and American Woman Suffrage associations merged in February 1890. The unification was largely due to the persistent efforts of Lucy Stone's daughter, Alice Stone Blackwell. However, the dissension continued when Gage charged that Anthony had brought the National to unity by undermining and manipulating its membership. With Olympia Brown and other women, she issued a statement asserting that at the 1889 National convention (which Gage did not attend) the National had agreed to merge with the American, not giving absent members the opportunity to voice their dissent (although Brown was in fact present at that convention).

When negotiations had first begun in 1888, Rachel Foster had forwarded to the American the names of the women from the National who would form the decision-making committee with women from the American. Included on that list were the names of Olympia Brown, Matilda Joslyn Gage, and Isabella Hooker, even though each had expressed disapproval of union. This committee met and before the opening of the 1890 convention drew up an agreement on union. Most of the issues had been agreed upon by the National in its 1889 meeting, and a new committee had been formed, which still included Olympia Brown but did not include Gage because of her absence from the 1889 meeting. Negotiations and final decisions on unity of the National and American were made first by the executive committees of each organization and then in a joint meeting. Gage protested the unification and she asserted that she had been intentionally dropped from the National's executive committee by Anthony's crafty maneuvering.

Accompanied by her two daughters, Elizabeth Cady Stanton joined Susan B. Anthony in Washington in February 1890 to celebrate Anthony's seventieth birthday and to attend the final meetings that were to unite the National and American. Lucy Stone was too ill to attend, but beforehand all three "pioneers had agreed that it would be best for unity that none of their names be put forward for the presidency of the National-American." But the "Nationals" insisted that either Anthony or Stanton be named president. Gage rumored that Anthony had maneuvered this union in order to make herself president of the National-American. That accusation changed Anthony's mind about the presidency. She was furious and told Rachel that "no one need calculate on filling Mrs. Stanton's place—this time—not even SBA who reports say is very anxious to supercede her old friend ECS!!"[50] The charge was particularly ironic considering that for forty years and until Stanton's death Anthony refused to ever accept an office that would place her above Mrs. Stanton.

Anthony convinced Mrs. Stanton to run for the presidency and threw her own political might behind the move. She prepared a firm statement, the contents of which were directed particularly toward Mrs. Gage. "I made her understand in my speech on Mrs. Stanton for Pres. that all of *her mean efforts* to persuade any members that I favored Union from ambition to supercede Mrs. Stanton were fully known to me."[51] Anthony was grave and earnest when she spoke to the joint meeting.

> I appeal to every woman who has any affection for the old National or for me not to vote for Susan B. Anthony for president. I stand in a delicate position. I have letters which accuse me of having favored the union solely for personal and selfish considerations, and of trying to put Mrs. Stanton out. Now what I have to say is, don't vote for any human being but Mrs. Stanton. There are other reasons why I wish her elected, but I have these personal ones: When the division was made twenty years ago, it was because our platform was too broad, because Mrs. Stanton was too radical; a more conservative organization was wanted. If we Nationals divide now and Mrs. Stanton is deposed from the presidency, we virtually degrade her. If you have any love for our old association, which from the beginning, has stood like a rock in regard to creeds and politics, demanding that every woman should be allowed to come upon our platform to plead for her freedom—if you have any faith in that grand principle—vote for Mrs. Stanton.[52]

Stanton was elected president and Anthony vice-president-at-large; the next day, February 18, 1890, the National-American met publicly for the first time. Anthony was deeply moved when Stanton gave her opening presidential address with her two daughters by her side. "Harriot came on to the stage & said a few words—in look & manner she showed herself worthy her mother & her mother's life-long friend & co-worker. It was a proud moment for me— & for all of us—of the old National—and ought to be to all who truly love the cause fully."[53]

Stanton's presidential speech spoke directly to the dangers, the narrowness, and the prejudices that had been creeping into suffrage agitation over the last decade. She reminded the women that femininity was not the honor they were to guard. "My friends, what is man's idea of womanly? It is to have a manner that pleases him, quiet, deferential, submissive, that approaches him as a subject does a master. He wants no self-assertion on our part, no defiance, no vehement arraigning of him as a robber and a criminal."

She cautioned against religious interests of groups like the WCTU. "I hope this convention will declare that the Woman Suffrage Association is opposed to all Union of Church and State and pledges itself as far as possible, to maintain the secular nature of our government." When she reasserted her position on divorce, she revealed how much the feminist analysis of the issue had regressed from their earlier position in her famous speech on that subject in 1860.

> The message I should like to go out from this convention is that there should be no further legislation on the questions of marriage and divorce until woman has a voice in the state and national governments. Surely here is a relation in which above all others there should be equality; a relation in which woman really has a deeper interest than man and if the laws favor either party it should be the wife and mother. Marriage is a mere incident in a man's life. He has business interests and ambitions in other directions but as a general thing it is all a life to woman where all her interest and ambitions center. And if the conditions of her surroundings there are discordant and degrading she is indeed most unfortunate and needs the protection of the laws to set her free rather than hold her in bondage. And yet it is proposed to have a national law restricting the right of divorce to a narrower basis . . . If liberal divorce laws for wives are what Canada was for the slaves, a door of escape from bondage, we had better consult the women before we close the avenues to freedom.

Now Stanton faced a different woman's movement than she had in 1860. There was a developing sentiment in society to restrict divorce to its narrowest possible basis. This forced Stanton to defend liberal divorce laws, which was actually a much weaker position than the one she had taken in 1860—that was, to make marriage a contract where divorce would become automatic if the contract were broken.

Stanton continued her speech and cautioned against exclusion from their platform: "We must manifest a broad catholic spirit for all shades of opinion in which we may differ and recognize the equal rights of all parties, sects and races, tribes and colors. Colored women, Indian women, Mormon women and women from every quarter of the globe have been heard in these Washington conventions and I trust they always will be."[54] Already there were sounds of discomfort in the auditorium. The Suffrage Association was heading in the exclusivist directions Stanton had warned against. It would be the price—a very high price—that Anthony would have to pay for the union she understood to be necessary if they were to build the mass base they needed to win the vote. Anthony, who was pragmatic and practical, was not fully attentive to all of the implications of unity— especially the extent to which the movement became connected to regressive trends in the society, virtually robbing it of its potential to redefine and reshape the meaning of womanhood, which was the very goal of Anthony's life.

Unity brought further ruptures. One week after the unification meeting, Gage opened a convention of the Woman's National Liberal Union. This was an organization she formed to uphold the principles of the National, which she saw as lost in the merger, and to promote the principles of liberalism and progressivism—particularly against the enemy of freedom, the Church. Gage kept this organization active and remained its president until her death in 1898. During those years she wrote an important condemnation of Christianity—particularly in terms of its promotion of the inferiority of women—entitled *Woman, Church and State.*

Stanton returned to Europe not long after the meetings that unified the National and the American. In effect, Anthony became president of the National-American. This appeared to confirm Gage's suspicions, although few others were worried. Most women knew that whether Anthony held office or not her leadership was generally uncontested.

By 1890, at the age of seventy, Susan B. Anthony was a serious and politically astute woman and had been so for some time. She and Stanton were among the very few women who had been with the movement through its forty years of historical transformation. In March of that year, she witnessed from the gallery of the House of Representatives the vote that admitted Wyoming to the Union. As a territory, back in 1869, Wyoming had granted women their suffrage. When it applied for statehood, Wyoming insisted on entering the Union with woman's suffrage. In forty years, this was the first major victory for woman's suffrage. As exciting as it was, it was a long time to struggle for women's political rights in one state. Campaigning had toughened Anthony over the years to the reality of the opposition to women and had forced her to sharpen her strategies accordingly.

Anthony's indignation was still high, but her political behavior was no longer militant. When she surveyed the political scene, she saw the practical impediments. When one woman proposed that suffrage associations throughout the country turn the women out to the polls to vote on every election day, Anthony responded, "My dear, it is impossible thus to persuade the women, after the Supreme Court of the United States has declared they have no right to vote under the National Constitution." But it was not the law that actually stood in Anthony's path. "Your suggestion means a revolution which women will not create against their own fathers, husbands, brothers and sons. A whole race of men under a foreign or tyrannical government, like the Cubans, may rise in rebellion, but for women thus to band themselves against the power enthroned in their own households is quite another matter."[55] This was the revolution Anthony herself had championed until she faced the fact that women would not unite behind it—a dilemma that no women's movement has ever successfully transcended.

Anthony continued her vigorous traveling schedule and took on tough campaigns for woman's suffrage in South Dakota and Kansas in the early 1890s, showing little evidence that advancing age would limit her mobility. Photographs from the 1890s reveal a woman with white hair and a face etched with the lines of age. But her body, her posture, and her carriage remained unusually young, strong, and erect.

Now more than ever Susan wanted a home of her own, and she wanted Mrs. Stanton to share it with her for their remaining years. For several years Susan had virtually lived between her family's house in Rochester and the Riggs House in Washington, where she was given a suite of rooms for her use. Since their sister's death, Mary had rented out rooms in the Rochester house and took in borders. When word spread among the suffrage women that Susan and Mary were thinking of taking possession of their house and renovating it for themselves, the Political Equality Club and several "nieces" put the house in proper order with Mary. They surprised Susan when she came home from one campaign in June of 1891 and found that "handsome rugs had been laid on the floor, lace curtains hung at the windows, easy chairs placed in the rooms, a large desk in Miss Mary's study, a fine oak table in the dining-room," along with a desk that Rachel sent for Aunt Susan, a set of china from Anna Howard Shaw (who was now living with Susan's niece Lucy Anthony), cutlery, and from her brother D. R. in Kansas came the linens.[56]

Mrs. Stanton wrote from England that she was delighted Susan was about to settle down. "My advice to you, Susan, is to keep some spot you can call your own; where you can live and die in peace and be cremated in your own oven if you desire."[57] House-keeping was a new experiment for Susan. She told her brother Merritt to tell friends to "visit sister Susan in her first attempt at a house all by herself alone!!" By "alone" she meant that she and her sister Mary were no longer boarders with her sister Guelma's family. Mary laughed at Susan's earnestness and was convinced that her sister would not succeed. "But at least," Susan said, "she seems happy to let me prove that I can do it." Most of all Susan felt, "I am going to take a lot of comfort being in my own house and entertaining my friends at my very own table."[58]

In creating a home, Mrs. Stanton was particularly on Susan's mind. Mrs. Stanton had separated from her husband many years before and was now a widow. Susan knew that she had to find a new home upon her return from England. For a long time Susan dreamed that they would share their remaining years together. Now she proposed to Mrs. Stanton that she come to Rochester and live with her. As was typical of her, Susan framed the proposal as a project. "This is the first time since 1850 that I have anchored myself to any particular spot, and in doing it my constant thought was that you would come here, where are the documents necessary to our work, and stay for as long, at least, as we must be together to put your writings into systematic shape to go down to posterity."[59] Susan reminded Mrs. Stanton that she had no writings of her own to go down to history, but that the joy of her life would to be to see to the publication of Mrs. Stanton's works.

But the fifty-year pattern of Mrs. Stanton and Susan's relationship could not be overcome. Susan as always wanted to be with Mrs. Stanton, and Mrs. Stanton continued to resist the idea and kept Susan at a safe distance. She still relied on her family to protect her from Susan. And this time her children in New York, Bob and Margaret outrightly rejected Susan's proposal for their mother. Instead, Mrs. Stanton took an apartment in New York City with Bob and Margaret, who did not hold the reverence for Aunt Susan that Theodore and Harriot far away in Europe did. Undoubtedly, this reflected Mrs. Stanton's conflict: One side of her was drawn like a magnet to Susan and the other allowed her family to make the decisions for her that she could not make for herself. Susan was saddened—how deeply we will never know. She had long ago ceased to express her personal pain and framed her joys as well as sorrows in terms of their movement. That, if anything, would have made Stanton's refusal to live with her an exceedingly painful decision to accept. The idea of spending their remaining years together and devoting her work to Mrs. Stanton's papers was one she had cherished. Susan wrote: "Well, I hope you will do and be as seemeth best unto yourself, still I can not help sending you this inner groan of my soul, lest you are not going to make it possible that the thing shall be done first which seems most important to me."[60] Now the possibility that they would fully share their lives was closed.

Mrs. Stanton was probably the more realistic of the two, as she knew that despite her intentions Susan would not likely remain fixed in one spot for any period of time, and she had every reason to believe that Susan would constantly be pushing her into new projects. But there was something else. Mrs. Stanton was a woman of her own self-determination, as she wonderfully revealed in her speech "The Solitude of Self" in 1892. If more eloquent in phrasing, it was close in sentiment to Anthony's speech "True Womanhood" of 1857; but it also reflected on old age. "In age, when the pleasures of youth are passed, children grown up, married and gone, the hurry and bustle of life in a measure over, when the hands are weary of active service, when the old arm chair and the fireside are chosen resorts, then men and women alike must fall back on their own resources." She called for "self-sovereignty." Recalling that we come into the world alone and go out the same way, she said that "there is a solitude which each and every one of us has always carried with him, more inaccessible than the ice-cold mountains, more profound than the midnight sea; the solitude of self. Our inner being which we call ourself, no eye nor touch of man or angel has ever pierced." This solitude, Stanton proclaimed, "only omniscience is permitted to enter."[61] This speech was an affirmation of her own life struggle. Elizabeth Cady Stanton had become a woman unto herself.

For Anthony, the solitude of self that Mrs. Stanton was just discovering had been her mainstay, the source of her fortitude for over forty years. It began to form in the early years of her career from her unbroken identity as a single woman. Mrs. Stanton had always been attracted by Susan's unmediated self-reliance. But Susan's ability to live her life without any of the traditional female dependencies threatened people close to her.[62]

"The Solitude of Self" was Mrs. Stanton's speech to the National-American convention in 1892. She had thought of not going to the meeting. But though she kept her friend at a safe distance from her, she continued to rely on Susan to push and prod her. "All the influences about me urge to rest rather than action," she wrote to Susan from her New York apartment shortly before the convention. Susan immediately recognized Mrs. Stanton's call for help. She worried that for Mrs. Stanton "inaction meant rust and decay." She went directly to New York to take her seventy-seven-year-old friend to the convention with her. After giving her speech, Mrs. Stanton resigned the presidency of the National-American and ceased to attend its conventions.

But Elizabeth Cady Stanton would forever be the driving heart and force of their movement to Susan, whose idea of the highest honor that could be given to any woman was this: "The title I claim for Mrs. Stanton is that of leader of women."[63]

12

A Grand Old Age

IN 1897 SUSAN. B. ANTHONY LOOKED BACK OVER A "HALF-century of woman's evolution" and recorded women's progress. Over-optimistically, she found that "the close of this nineteenth century finds every trade, vocation, and profession open to women, and every opportunity at their command for preparing themselves to follow these occupations. . . . Woman is no longer compelled to marry for support but may herself make her own home and earn her own financial independence. . . . With but few exceptions, the highest institutions of learning in the land are as freely opened to girls as to boys . . . this general advancement of women has come with marked improvement in household methods. . . . There has been a radical revolution in the legal status of women . . . the old common law has been annulled by legislative enactment."[1] What Susan B. Anthony identified as gains for women, when measured against women's previous condition, seemed to be enormous strides.

In these later years of her life, Anthony remembered the days when she, Stanton, and some others had been among the few women in the nation who had dared publicly to demand vital rights for their sex: property rights for married women; coeducation; opening of the professions, trades, and unions to women; equal pay; and, of course, suffrage. Over the last fifty years many states had modified their laws governing property rights for married women, but obtaining a divorce and winning custody of their children were still difficult procedures for women. Eighty percent of the colleges, universities, and professional schools admitted women, and women's participation in the labor force had significantly increased (although in industry, their working conditions were usually miserable and unhealthy with exploitive wages, and long working hours).

If in those past fifty years the condition of women had changed, American society in general had grown faster and had changed even more dramatically. The small mills of the 1820s that had turned into factory systems by mid-century were now overshadowed by the introduction of a corporate-industrial economy. Privately owned railroads stretched across the continent in a mass of interlinking networks. They became the first example of the modern corporation, quickly followed by the corporate empires of Andrew Carnegie in steel and John D. Rockefeller in oil.

Politics followed and favored economic change. The radical Republicans and abolitionists all but disappeared from the scene; by 1876, the federal troops in charge of overseeing reconstruction had been withdrawn from the South. The Republican party, which had held national power for thirty-five years of the second half of the century, became the champion of northern industrialist and corporate interests. The Democrats, still the party of the South, represented the large land-owning classes. By 1890, many claimed that it was difficult to distinguish between the two parties any longer.

With women's gains over the last half of the nineteenth century, Anthony was not unconscious of the giants steps taken in consolidating men's economic power. Her national work for woman's suffrage brought her face to face with the new economic realities.

> Nearly every money-making enterprise, large or small, is owned and conducted by men. The great monopolies—railroad, coal, oil, sugar, liquor, tobacco, ect.—have their agents and attorneys at Washington and at every State capital not only to secure laws in their favor, but to prevent the passage of any which would be inimical to their interests. In addition to the capitalists themselves the vast majority of their employees, being men, are voters, so that these corporations can put into the political scales the weight of both money and ballots.[2]

Remembering that "there is not one foot of advance ground upon which women stand to-day that has not been obtained through the hard-fought battles of other women," Anthony saw that "the department of politics has been slowest to give admission to women." Without their political rights, women were nonetheless in the "position of sovereigns instead of subjects," who had to "beg, petition and pray" for justice and equality.[3]

Because her focus was on political rights, Anthony had lost some of her radical perspective. When women's condition during this period is compared to the increasingly complex and rapidly expanding society—especially its corporate interests—women's advancement in the years 1850 to 1900 actually seems to have evolved at a snail's pace. Early and mid-century marital feudalism had so effectively retarded women's opportunities to move forward that the equality achieved by 1900 was not the impressive gain it would have been had it occurred in the 1850s. Each time the economy expanded, new openings were created at the top for white men, who as a class moved upward and outward economically. In turn, this expanded the base enough to leave room for some white women and black women and men to enter at the lower levels, where they filled the spaces abandoned by white men. Patriarchal domination remained a constant, but one that continually accommodated itself to other social and economic changes that had not seemed possible a generation or two before. This is the character of patriarchal power, which sustains itself over centuries by adapting its domination of women to changes in economic and social conditions. It can be likened to shifting sands that do not dislodge one who is standing in the sand; as the waves lap on the beach, the water simply reforms the sand around one's feet.

If it were true for white women that patriarchal domination shifted to accommodate to economic changes, then it was more poignantly the case for blacks, both men and women. The new corporate capitalism was built from and coexisted with the feudalistic economy of southern blacks. They were no longer enslaved but were barely able to survive their conditions in the South, where seventy-five percent of blacks labored in sharecropping or as tenant farmers at the beginning of the twentieth century. Sharecroppers did not receive wages but like feudalistic serfs they were required to turn over a part of their yield to the white landowners, to whom they were forever indebted for rent and farming equipment. Segregation build on "Jim Crow" laws kept the races apart in all aspects of life. Lynching became a favored form of white racist violence. By the end of the century, southern blacks were migrating en masse to the North only to find new and different forms of racism. Clearly, the gains that Anthony had enumerated in 1897 were scarcely felt by black women.

If domination had shifted into new modes and taken on new forms, many women were also moving in directions they had not before.

Jane Addams became the leading symbol and charismatic leader of women's reform with her work in Chicago. There she founded settlement houses and addressed the new problems of juvenile crime in the cities. Black women moved to the forefront of their cause; the journalist Ida Wells and the Women's Club reform leader Mary Church Terrell charted new paths. Black women, for the first time, were able to create their own social and political force. And by the end of the century, Susan B. Anthony had passed from being the leader of the movement for woman's rights to being the symbol of women's craving for emancipation.

The year 1895 was a milestone in the lives of both Susan B. Anthony and Elizabeth Cady Stanton; it marked their seventy-fifth and eightieth birthdays. Anthony was greeted with celebrations and honors from city to city when she crossed the country by train for the Woman's Congress in San Francisco. But the one that was held on February 15 in Washington, D.C., exemplified the ways that the women's movement had become Anthony's real family. Rachel Avery Foster "surprised and delighted me by the announcement that she had secured an $800 annuity for me . . . thus helping to lift me financially above the need of earning the necessary sum to meet my simple expense."[4] Rachel had secretly collected five thousand dollars from about two hundred contributors and had placed it in a trust fund. This guaranteed that Aunt Susan would be paid two hundred dollars every three months for the rest of her life. For the first time in her public career, Anthony had not only her own home but financial security. And for the first time, she could not (as she inevitably would try to) turn the money over to one of her campaigns.

For Susan, the celebration of all celebrations would be Mrs. Stanton's eightieth birthday that November. The National-American proposed that they sponsor the event, but Anthony said no because to do so would honor Mrs. Stanton only for her suffrage work. The younger suffragists did not agree. "Mrs. Stanton stands for suffrage above all else," they claimed. Even if they could no longer appreciate the broad base on which their movement had been founded almost a half-century before, Anthony saw to it that Stanton's radical politics were reflected in her birthday party.

She insisted, "Surely for all classes of women, liberal, orthodox, Jewish, Mormon, suffrage and anti-suffrage, native and foreign, black and white—to unite in paying a tribute of respect to the greatest woman reformer, philosopher and statesman of the century, will be the realization of Mrs. Stanton's most optimistic dream." Anthony refused to spearhead the event, for that would reduce it to a "mutual admiration affair," and she won out on the sponsorship matter. The National Woman's Council that had been organized at the 1888 International Council of Women sponsored the celebration.

While preparations were underway for Stanton's eightieth-birthday celebration, Anthony was on the road. Between January and July of 1895 she had been to Atlanta, Georgia, had toured through Kentucky, Tennessee, and Louisiana, then had returned to Washington, D.C., and finally home to Rochester. Then she traveled to California with stops in St. Louis, Denver, Cheyenne, Salt Lake City, and Reno. In California, she stopped in San Francisco, Palo Alto, Yosemite, San Jose, Los Angeles, Riverside, Pasadena, Pomona, San Diego and Santa Monica. On her way home to Rochester, she lectured in several cities across the country.

She traveled and worked as if she still had the stamina of a thirty-year-old woman. When she reached Rochester after this whirlwind, she was called to speak in Lakeside, Ohio. On July 25, she addressed a large audience. As she finished her speech, she "simply collapsed—the whole of me coming to a sudden standstill like a clap of thunder under a clear sky." She was taken to a friend's house and the next day summoned enough energy to take the train back to Rochester. She could not understand what had happened; she had been in good health and there had been no sign of illness.

When she got back home, she found that she could not get out of bed. Mary called the doctor and waited and worried. News that Susan B. Anthony had fainted after her lecture immediately hit the press. Reporters around her house waited with prepared obituaries in hand. One Chicago paper telegraphed its reporter: "50,000 words if still living, no limit, if dead."[5] Susan hung on. The doctor diagnosed nervous prostration, visited her regularly, and assigned a nurse to her. Mrs. Stanton wrote: "I never realized how desolate the world would be to me without you until I heard of your sudden illness" and urged Susan to stay home, rest, and "save your precious self."[6] A month later Susan told a friend that she would soon be rid of her doctor and nurse and that she was completely fed up with a month of "do-nothingness."[7]

On November 12, she was in the Metropolitan Opera House, "crowded from pit to dome" to honor her oldest and dearest friend.

Susan sat to the right of Mrs. Stanton, who had been led to a rose-covered throne. No one could have been more proud than Susan B. Anthony of the tribute to the woman she revered. Anthony went to the podium and read telegrams of congratulations and her own tribute, while Mrs. Stanton sat regally on her throne. She was almost blind and had difficulty standing for any length of time. Her speech was read for her, but from its tone and impact it was clear that age and physical infirmity had not diminished her radical spirit.

She exposed the ways that religion dominates women, and by raising this issue at this her eightieth-birthday celebration, she opened the most painful controversy of her and Anthony's old age—the *Woman's Bible* debate. Some years earlier, Stanton had formed a committee to assist her with the *Woman's Bible* and had asked Susan to participate. "No, I don't want my name on that Bible Committee," Susan had told her emphatically. The two old pioneers went their separate ways over the issue of religious domination. "You fight that battle and leave me to fight the secular—the political fellows." Anthony reminded Mrs. Stanton that "the *religious* part has *never been mine*—you know I won't take it up—so long as the men who hold me in durance vile—won't care a dime what the Bible says—all they care for is what the saloon says."[8] There is no denying that Susan was disappointed that Mrs. Stanton had chosen to focus her remaining years on questions of theology. In fact, she felt that Mrs. Stanton's Bible commentaries "are so entirely unlike her former self—so flippant & superficial." She confessed that she had always been proud of all of Mrs. Stanton's speeches, "But of her Bible Commentaries, I am not proud—either of their spirit or letter."[9]

Neither Stanton nor Anthony accepted the Bible as an inspirational work. Both saw it as a recording of history, many parts of which read as a history of patriarchy—of men's domination over women. Stanton challenged the Bible's interpretation of women with a powerful analysis of biblical texts.

However, Anthony argued, this interpretation did not confront such issues as the horrors of lynching in America, a racial brutality that would soon be extended to the new territories in the Atlantic and Pacific islands acquired by the United States after the Spanish-American War. These were the objective conditions of subjugation. "This barbarism does not grow out of ancient Jewish Bibles—but out of our own sordid meanness!!" She told Mrs. Stanton to "stop hitting poor old St. Paul—and give your heaviest raps on the head of every Nabob—man or woman—who does injustice to a human being—for the crime of color or sex!! . . . I do wish you could center your big brain on the crimes we, ourselves, as a people are responsible for—to charge *our* offenses to false books or false interpretations—is but a way of seeking a *refuge of lies.*"[10]

They argued and disagreed on this question for several years. But they agreed with Emerson that friendships should not be treated daintily, "but with roughest courage. When they are real, they are not glass threads of frostwork, but the solidest things we know." Anthony underlined this passage several times: "I hate, when I look for manly furtherance, or at least a manly resistance, to find a mush of concession. Better to be a nettle in the side of your friend than be his echo."[11]

The Woman's Bible was first published two weeks after Stanton's birthday celebration. In reaction, conservative women of the National-American at the annual convention two months later proposed a resolution to dissociate their organization from it:

> this association is non-sectarian, being composed of persons of all shades of religious opinions, and has no official connection with the so-called Woman's Bible, or any theological publications.[12]

Susan B. Anthony, in the chair as president of the association, was astounded and for a moment struck dumb. It was one thing to disagree with Mrs. Stanton over priorities but never would she consider that either Stanton or her critique of religion be censored. The feminist and radical writer Charlotte Perkins Gilman had the same concern. She immediately moved to amend the resolution by striking out everything after the word "opinions." The argument intensified and Anthony found that her most beloved "nieces"—Anna Shaw, Carrie Chapman Catt, and Rachel Avery Foster—were among the strongest supporters of the resolution.

As the women discussed the resolution, Susan thought back to all those times in the 1850s when she was asked to keep Ernestine Rose off their platform because of her avowed atheism. Then later, when Victoria Woodhull was on the scene, some prominent woman "wanted us to pass a resolution that we were not free-lovers."[13] But never had their movement censored thought. Now these young women who were "unborn when Mrs. Stanton called the first Woman's Rights convention" proposed to censure her. Anthony stepped down from her chair. She was eloquent in her anger.

> What you should do is to say to outsiders that a Christian has neither more nor less rights in our Association than an atheist. When our plat-

form becomes too narrow for people of all creeds and of no creeds, I myself shall not stand upon it. Many things have been said and one by our orthodox friends that I have felt to be extremely harmful to our cause; but I should no more consent to a resolution denouncing them than I shall consent to this. Who is to draw the line? Who can tell now whether Mrs. Stanton's commentaries may not prove a great help to woman's emancipation from old superstitions that have barred her way? Lucretia Mott at first thought Mrs. Stanton had injured the cause of all woman's other rights by insisting upon the demand for suffrage, but she had sense enough not to bring in a resolution against it. In 1860, when Mrs. Stanton made a speech before the New York Legislature in favor of a bill making drunkenness a cause for divorce, there was a general cry among the friends that she had killed the woman's cause. I shall be pained beyond expression if the delegates here are so narrow and illiberal as to adopt this resolution. You would better not begin resolving against individual action or you will find no limit. This year it is Mrs. Stanton; next year it may be me or one of yourselves who will be the victim.[14]

What had been second generation feminism now passed into a new stage—one even further removed from the political consciousness that originated the movement—reform feminism. Their values were reflected in this drastic and self-serving resolution. They meant to dissociate their middle-class propriety from anything controversial. With this resolution the suffragists pushed Susan to the point of questioning for the first time (at least the first time she records) her sustaining belief that political power in the hands of women would change and elevate the condition of politics in the country. "If we do not inspire in woman a broad and catholic spirit, they will fail, when enfranchised, to constitute that power for better government which we have always claimed." And the action of the National-American clearly shook her politics of building a mass-based movement around woman's suffrage as its primary issue. "You would better educate ten women into the practice of liberal principles than to organize ten thousand on a platform of intolerance and bigotry," she insisted.[15] What, after all, was a political movement of women if it pandered to public opinion as parties like the Republicans had been doing for decades? Without universal principles of justice and equality, the demand for suffrage was merely an appeal to self-interest. And now these reform-minded women seemed to be chiefly concerned with not alienating religious authorities and Christian women.

The members of the National-American adopted the resolution with a vote of fifty-three to forty-one, without modification or amendments. Anthony was heartbroken and thought of resigning the presidency of her own association. Mrs. Stanton was outraged and printed the resolution in the appendix of the next edition of the *Woman's Bible,* which had become an overnight best seller. Anthony castigated her nieces, "I see nothing but the beginning of a petty espionage, a revival of the Spanish inquisition," and she told them she was "sick at heart" over their violation of the right of individual judgment and for wronging Mrs. Stanton personally.[16]

"I visited Mrs. Stanton before coming home, and found her, as you may well understand, thoroughly indignant over the petty action of the convention," Susan told a friend. Mrs. Stanton insisted that Susan resign from the presidency of the National-American; it was, she believed, the least she could expect in support against being censured by them. For "three weeks of agony of soul, with scarcely a night of sleep," Susan deliberated and finally decided that she must remain in office as a duty to "try to reverse this miserable, narrow action."[17]

This was another one of those many times she was holding on in desperation to a slim hope. The National had been the center of her life for thirty years. Her own "statesmanship," if not her identity, was tied to this association, and she still had active years left in her. At the age of seventy-six, abandoning it must have seemed impossible to her.

What Anthony had underestimated was the impact of the new reform generation on woman's suffrage. Women's clubs had sprung up in city after city in the 1880s as a kind of spontaneous response to the needs of socially minded middle- and upper-class women. They were the first generation of fully educated college women in America, who when they left school, filled with ambition and energy, found that there was no place for them in a society unwilling to welcome women into professions.[18] Some of them went into teaching while others turned to reform work. The club women dedicated themselves to literary pursuits and a kind of civic good housekeeping.

These women's clubs refused to be associated with any political issues and avoided controversy. But Anthony saw that if she could get the support of the women's clubs, they could be a potentially significant force that would give legitimacy to woman's demand for suffrage. And typical of her strategy, since she had made suffrage the number-one feminist issue, she believed women would be forced to recognize their need for political rights by the fact that they were denied them. "My one source of gratification in the present club-engrossment of our women is that they cannot work far in any direction without finding themselves crippled in their efforts by the lack of political force. It is good to have woman's moral influence on the right side of every question, but it would be better if to this she could add political power, for then she would be able not only to crystallize moral sentiments into laws but to enforce these laws after they were enacted."[19]

To a certain extent she was right; for while many club women stayed away from controversy, some found their way into the suffrage movement. These reform feminists brought with them the values and the concern for propriety of the club women. They believed that as women they were on a par with men. However, at some level they knew they were not. As a result, they assumed an air of propriety and espoused a belief in traditional values that has often made women think they will be accepted as good, if not equal.

The club women were only part of the story. There was also the Remonstrants, an explicit antisuffragist organization which accused the suffragists of trying to destroy home and family. They argued that woman was not fit for political life (because, they believed, women had a constitution which by nature was too delicate to withstand its rigors). Next to the Remonstrants the suffragists' beliefs appeared extreme. Indeed, the club women provided the "acceptable" middle road.

This new generation of women yielded as much diversity and breadth of imagination among themselves as did their aged foremothers in their own day. The woman's movement would be undeniably affected by the radical and passionate mind of the feminist and writer Charlotte Perkins Gilman, one of the few who fought against the *Woman's Bible* resolution. Feminism of this period would forever carry the stamp of the sociologist and champion reformer Jane Addams. Addams is best known for the experiment she launched in social reform when she opened Chicago's Hull House, which, by the time Charlotte Perkins Gilman visited it in 1896, had become "at one and the same time an unemployment agency, a battered wives shelter, a day care center, a lending library, a savings bank, and a reformers meeting ground."[20] It has only recently been discovered that Addams was one of the pioneer sociologists of the University of Chicago, a group who became known as the "Chicago school."[21] Hull House provided the empirical base for social observation for the new, emerging discipline of American sociology.

Indeed, as Gilman found, Hull House was a center for anarchists, Marxists, socialists, and unionists, who co-mingled with the poor, the unemployed, immigrants, and others in crisis.

In contrast to Addams, Charlotte Perkins Gilman exposed the exploitation of woman's labor in her seminal work, *Women and Economics,* where she found that women's domestic labor "is neither given nor taken as a factor in economic exchange. It is held to be their duty as women to do this work; and their economic status bears no relation to their domestic labors unless an inverse one."[22] Marital feudalism remained entrenched in women's private lives, while family life had changed dramatically under industrialization. In fact, many family functions had become socialized into institutions of education, psychiatry, and social welfare. But Gilman advocated that housework also be professionalized in order to free women from it, whereas, Addams offered women programs to assist them with their household duties such as child-care centers. Of the two she was probably the more practical but inevitably more reformist also. Her approach followed the tendencies of reform and from it feminists began to emphasize social housekeeping. They increasingly justified their demand for women's political rights by showing how it would elevate the quality of housekeeping, maternity, and child care—the very conditions that dominated and subordinated women as a class.

Instead of challenging the domination of women in the home they began to argue that woman's private sphere would remain unchanged if women had the vote—contradicting the political goal women had envisioned in launching their movement. Citing the four states that had enfranchised women by 1902, Ida Harper argued that in those states there were examples of women who are "better, happier wives, mothers and housekeepers because they are more intelligent and live a broader life." In fact, Harper argued, it was through political rights that "their housekeeping qualities should extend to the municipality and their power of motherhood to the children of the whole nation."[23] Settlement houses, sanitary commissions, and purity crusades brought the values of their private, home-oriented morality into their new worldly roles, which did not collide with men's control of the public political world.

Women were being forced into a re-adaption to male domination to fit the changing times. In its final stages, the women's movement was adjusting to the changing forms of male domination rather than confronting them. Women like Carrie Chapman Catt, Anna Howard Shaw, and others of this new generation, would take the mantle from Anthony and Stanton and carry the women's movement into the twentieth century. Susan B. Anthony could have easily become an historical artifact, a symbol of the struggle of an earlier era. But her analysis of woman's suffrage, as an access to political power along with Stanton's and Gage's work against religious domination, were even more necessary to the women's movement than they had been twenty, thirty, or even forty years before if it was to retain any feminist vision.

By 1896, women were enfranchised in Wyoming and Colorado. Utah and then Idaho became the last states to adopt woman's suffrage during Susan B. Anthony's lifetime. Prior to winning the vote in Wyoming and Colorado, woman's suffrage again became embattled in New York and Kansas. But the political scene was changing. In the early 1890s, the Populists appeared on the political scene and won sweeping victories in midwestern states. They represented a grass-roots alliance of farmers and laborers, who supported an eight-hour working day; government ownership of the railroads, telegraph, and telephone; and a graduated income tax. The Populists represented a decidedly American sentiment. They intended to purify politics of its corruption, political machines, and bosses on the East Coast, and they relied on popular support from the people to build a new powerbase. But they also meant to purify American politics of foreign elements—especially the growing immigrant population. The nativist attitudes of the Populists became confused with the feminist opposition to immigrant men. These were men who brought with them the patriarchal religious values of Catholic Europe, which could be wielded as political power over women.

Anthony worried about immigrant men, whom she saw as an increasingly large class of new male voters who had been educated under "monarchical forms of government that do not understand our principles."[24] Stanton went further in her analysis. She claimed that "the danger is not in their landing and living in this country, but in their speedy appearance at the ballot box and their becoming an impoverished and ignorant balance of power in the hands of wily politicians." She believed that "we should welcome all hardy, common sense laborers, as we have plenty of room and work for them," but they should not be allowed to vote. Stanton insisted that if "popular objection to woman suffrage is that it would 'double the ignorant vote' " then "the patent answer to this is 'abolish the ignorant vote.' " She would deprive all uneducated women and men of the right to vote.[25] The concept of educated suffrage stemmed directly from Stanton's concern with religion, which was motivated in part by her concern with the Catholic tradition immigrant men brought with them.

Anthony disagreed on educated suffrage. Nevertheless, each year when she was en route to the National-American convention, she stopped by Mrs. Stanton's New York City apartment to visit and tried to coax her to go to the conventions with her. Mrs. Stanton rarely was able to leave home, so Susan usually carried her friend's latest speech to the convention. Even when she disagreed with their content, she delivered the speeches on educated suffrage on behalf of Mrs. Stanton.

Anthony's position had not changed. "I always have believed in universal suffrage." She remembered her own common origins and could not forget the time when her father had closed their home school after the panic of 1837 and her fears of what would become of her without an advanced education. Now she insisted that "while an education is highly desirable, yet a man may be unable to read but may attend political meetings, talk with his neighbors and form intelligent opinions."[26] She considered the idea of educated suffrage hypocritical and challenged those who "call it a 'mistake' giving to poor and uneducated men the right to vote; whereas, the greatest wrongs in our government are perpetrated by rich men, the wire-pulling agents of corporations and monopolies, in which the poor and ignorant have not part."[27]

When the Populists agreed to support woman's suffrage, Anthony was pleased but wanted to give them the most minimal response. "I would wave my handkerchief." But the Populists wanted more and asked that she go before the voters of Kansas and support their party. "I most certainly will," she responded unhesitantly. The Republicans charged her with disloyalty, and she fired back that "I belong to but one party under the shadow of the flag, and that is the party of idiots and criminals. I don't like my company."[28]

Woman's suffrage lost in Kansas, and Anthony returned home to Rochester to find reporters waiting for her to cover her "going over" to the Populists. "One would think I had committed the sin against the Holy Ghost in thanking the Populists for their good promise & saying I preferred them no matter what their financial vagaries— with justice to women, to the Republicans, no matter what their financial wisdom without justice to women," was all she had to say after closing the door to the last reporter.[29] What Anthony did not do, as she had on the issue of educated suffrage, was clarify that her support of the Populists was not an endorsement of their nativism. That was all the more dangerous given that the current generation of reform feminism was not guided by an egalitarian ideology.

Her next challenge was the collusion of the Republicans with the liquor dealers' corporations, which apparently used poor immigrant and working men against woman's suffrage in the 1896 California campaign. Anthony spent most of that year in California. She appealed for support of elite women—particularly Mrs. Leland Stanford, wife of the founder of the University of Palo Alto, and Mrs. William Randolph Hearst, wife of the head of the growing San Francisco-based newspaper empire. She also organized a canvass of every town in the entire state with a population of two hundred or more. The people's response was positive and enthusiastic. All these issues came to the surface in the Kansas campaign of 1894. In 1896 the national Republican party again refused to support woman's suffrage, and Anthony wrote to Stanton that she wished "that you were young and strong and free, and could fire off the planet such ineffable slush as is being slobbered over our cause."[30] The suffragists besieged the state party convention and managed to get a plank from state Republicans, Populists, and Prohibitionists—from all but the Democrats. By the fall of 1896, the women had secured state-party planks, petitioned and canvassed the state, won the support of some prominent women, and generally seemed to have public opinion on their side. Anthony did not want suffrage confused with temperance and convinced Frances Willard to move the national WCTU convention of 1896 from California to another state, so as to not "divert public thought from the enfranchisement of women to prohibition."[31]

The liquor dealers played a major role in the 1896 woman's suffrage campaign in California, which they entered only ten days before the November elections. The powerful Liquor Dealers' League appealed to business owners and shopkeepers to vote against the amendment that would enfranchise the women of California. Then they found another constituency. "The men in the slums of San Francisco were taken in squads and, with sample ballots, were taught how to put the cross against the suffrage amendment and assured that if it carried there never would be another glass of beer sold in the city." The suffragists decided they should try to distribute their literature to this newly recruited class of male voters but were told by a prominent editor that "most of them cannot read and if they could the whisky men would never allow a page of it to get into their hands."[32]

The Liquor Dealers' League was not solely responsible for the defeat of woman's suffrage in California. But its campaign, which brought to the election polls men from the slums, often drunk, some of whom were immigrants, pushed many suffragists into echoing many of the nativist sentiments of the Populists. Many of them began to speak more openly for suffrage restrictions, such as educated suffrage, which would prevent any other class of men from access to the ballot before women received it.

The platform for educated suffrage was an appeal to establish elitist laws, laws which would protect rights only for middle- and upper-class men. As such, the campaign for educated suffrage played into the hands of white, southern politicians, who were trying to disfranchise blacks—that is, black men. Throughout the decade of the 1890s, southern politicians systematically called state constitutional conventions for the purpose of nullifying the Fifteenth Amendment to the Constitution. And this created the next set of contradictions for the woman's suffrage movement. For Anthony, "colorphobia and sexphobia" were intricately interconnected in theory, in principle, and in practice, but not on the public platform. As far as she was concerned, it was the Republicans, the abolitionists, and black male leaders like Frederick Douglass who had forced the separation of race and sex in the struggle over the Fourteenth and Fifteenth amendments. It was they who had insisted on the "Negro's hour." In those years, when she and Stanton had looked for support, they learned that the natural allies of woman's rights did not reside outside their own class—women as a sex. They learned that even most of the individual men who were in sympathy with the cause of woman's rights bonded with other men of their own group—be it blacks, labor unions, or abolitionists—and were willing to sacrifice the political rights of women of their race in favor of their own rights.

In 1884 Frederick Douglass's wife of forty-four years died, and he married Helen Pitts, a white woman from Rochester. The press was inflamed by the controversial marriage and tried to get a comment from Anthony. "I have but one question," she told them, "that of equality between the sexes—that of the races has no place on our

platform." When Stanton was about to make a statement supporting Douglass's interracial marriage, Anthony warned her, "I do hope
you won't put your foot into the Douglass question, the intermarriage of races!" Then she went on, "Only to think of how Douglass
threw the principle of Equality of political rights to women—overboard—in '69—& all along—saying himself first & you after-
words! If there were no other reason—you should now let him carry
his own burden if he has voluntarily risked such."

For Anthony it was not a question of intermarriage. She argued
to Stanton that Douglass had shocked public sentiment and the
"general sense of propriety" by this new marriage, and "he may be
right & general feeling wrong, it doesn't matter to my point." Her
point was that his action had aroused public sentiment and if the
suffrage association became identified with it, the very fact of its
controversiality would turn away the attention of the woman's suffrage audiences from "the one question of woman—and her disfranchised." If there were to be public outrage and shock attached
to the woman question, let it come from their own issues on their
own platform.[33]

If Anthony refused to open the woman's suffrage movement to
any other issue, she still insisted that other movements include women.
In 1900, Anthony appealed to the National Negro Race Conference
to "include women of color" and to make it clear that "you are
asking political equality for all the race, and not for the male half
alone." She argued that when black men were given political rights,
"From that hour the colored wife owed service to a husband instead
of to a slave-owner, so that legally she simply exchanged a white
master for a colored one who controlled her earnings, her children
and her person."[34]

By the 1890s, black women had begun to organize on their own.
Despite the persistence of poverty and the semislavery conditions of
black life in America, many Blacks found their way to education
and the middle classes. Middle-class black women began to form
their own club movement, which was in many ways similar to the
white women's clubs. They also proposed to take the values of the
home and private morality into the world.[35] But the differences between the two movements were even more revealing than their similarities. Black women's clubs were necessarily concerned with the
poor and illiterate. Mary Church Terrell, a founder of this movement, saw black women as "bound by the ties of race and sex" to
this mission.[36]

In 1898 the Supreme Court upheld the Fifteenth Amendment to the Constitution, again guaranteeing *de jure,* if not *de facto,* equal protection to all races. Anthony noted how "the Southern States have by one device or another succeeded in excluding from the ballot-box very nearly the entire negro vote, openly and defiantly declaring the absolute supremacy of the white race, but there is not a suggestion on their part of allowing the citizens to whom they deny the right of suffrage to be counted out from the basis of representation." Anthony and Stanton agreed to attack the practice of counting all citizens—black and white—to determine the number of seats each state would have in the House of Representatives and then excluding women and black men from suffrage. In the 1899 meeting of the National-American, Anthony announced that "I think the time has come when this Association should make a most strenuous demand for an amendment to the Constitution of the United States forbidding any State thus to count disfranchised citizens."[37]

Stanton agreed. "If the Southern States that deny suffrage to negro men should find that it limited their power in Congress" by counting for the basis of representation only those citizens who vote, "they would see that the interests of the races lay in the same direction." And logically, "the same rule applied there in excluding all women from the basis of representation would reduce the number of their members of Congress by one-half."[38] But they never found the support from the new generation of suffragists to pursue these proposals.

Black women were not excluded from the National-American as they were from most of the white women's clubs. At the 1898 National-American meeting, when Mary Church Terrell asked, "As a colored woman, I hope this Association will include in the resolution the injustices various kinds of which colored people are victims," Anthony invited her to form her statement into a resolution, which was adopted.[39] But at best this represented an uneasy situation for black women, particularly in some local organizations that were more closed to addressing racial issues.

In the 1890s, when the National-American actively pursued suffrage in the southern states, any potential alliance between black and white women became even more problematic. The 1895 National-American convention held in Atlanta, Georgia encouraged southern women to join the movement; however, many of them and some northerners too still accepted the ideology of black racial inferiority. As racism was not a major issue of the woman's movement, their racial convictions and the interests of white power they supported were not challenged or condemned. If white women did not overtly express their racism, there was no conflict within the association. Although Anthony herself continued to speak and act against racism, she continued her separation of the issues of racial domination from suffrage as a political strategy on the association's platform. This provided an implicit acceptance of other women's racism, and it kept black feminists at the periphery of the woman suffrage movement.

At this same time, white women were again being politically set up against black women by white men who used the safety of white women as the pretext to try to disfranchise blacks in the south and to justify lynching black men. Lynching was a new type of random racial terrorism that was growing in the South. Lynching hysteria was fed by stories and myths of the rampant rape of white women, murder, and arson committed by black men. Many white southern politicians chivalrously built their cause against blacks on the need to protect the virtues of white womanhood. In other words, the same men who were not about to concede the ballot to any woman—educated or not were trying again to deny it to black men. Between 1890 and 1918, the year that women won the constitutional amendment for the vote, southerners on the House Judiciary Committee had kept the woman's suffrage amendment from coming to the floor of the House for a vote.[40] It was precisely their opposition that caused Anthony and the National-American to expand their movement into the South and that in turn brought a surge of racism into the woman's movement. In analyzing racial domination, it cannot be dissociated from the structural power base of white men which not only dominates women but makes them appear to hold the power to dominate Blacks.

In 1892, a black woman journalist exposed the more virulent and brutal side of white southern racism. Ida Wells had been born a slave during the Civil War. After the war, long after Lincoln's Emancipation Proclamation, she was sold from family to family several times. Later, when she had won her freedom and had entered journalism, she discovered that three male friends were lynched on March 9, 1892, by an angry Memphis mob, who proclaimed that they were acting to protect white southern womanhood. Wells not only exposed the lynching in her paper but also pointed out that

the actual offense of the black men had been that they were successful shopkeepers in Memphis whose competition seriously affected white business. Three months after she had exposed other
lynchings, Ida Wells's newspaper offices were mobbed and destroyed while she was away. By the fall, she became a journalist for
the *New York Age* and initiated a one-woman campaign against
lynching.

Anthony had followed Wells's reports on lynching. "No Pagan
or Barbarous Nation can suffer greater cruelties & outrages than
does this of ours," she commented one day while reading the newspapers. "The Negro lynchings are something blood curdling & the
myriads of wife murders pass almost unnoticed—though they blister one's own newspapers."[41] She was incensed that while Chris-
tians were lynching black men "because of the color their skin,"
they hypocritically condemned atrocities in Turkey. Anthony noted
more than once that "inconsistency is the jewel of the American
people."[42] And what, in Anthony's opinion, provoked lynching? "The
rule is that the poor creature's offense is simply some independent
refusal to be menials to a white woman [which] is termed an
insult."[43]

A few months after Anthony returned to Rochester from the 1895
National-American convention in Atlanta, Georgia, she attended one
of Ida Wells's lectures. She sat fuming while a Texan harassed Miss
Wells with hostile questions. Wells handled the antagonist with poise
and answered all his disruptive queries, until he asked, "If the negroes don't like it in the South why don't they leave and go North?"
Miss Anthony's old abolitionist blood boiled. With "flashing eyes
and ringing voice," she sprang to her feet and confronted him. "I
will tell you why; it is because they are treated no better in the
North than they are in the South." And she did not sit down until
she had supported her point with one example after another of
northern racial bigotry.

Immediately after the lecture Miss Anthony invited Miss Wells to
be a guest in her home. The next day, before Anthony left to see
her dressmaker for a fitting, she offered Miss Wells the services of
her stenographer for her correspondence and told her stenographer
to "please ask Miss Wells if she would like you to dictate her letters
and have them written on the type writer." The girl said nothing,
and Susan hurried out the door.

When she returned, "I found Mrs. Wells scribbling away." She
wondered why Miss Wells had not accepted her hospitality. "Couldn't

you dictate, let Anna type for you?" Miss Wells said nothing, and Susan understood. Her back stiffened. Lifting her black skirt, she marched upstairs where she found her "type writer." "You didn't understand me, did you, to ask Miss Wells?" The young girl responded, "I didn't choose to write for a colored woman, I engaged to work for you." Susan had had enough. "When I ask an employee to do a favor to a guest, I expect her to comply." The girl retorted, "It's alright for you Miss Anthony to treat Negroes as equals, but I refuse to take dictation from a colored woman." Anthony stood over the young woman and said, "Miss Wells is my guest and any insult to her is an insult to me. So if that is the way you feel about it, you needn't stay any more." The young woman sat motionless, and Anthony nudged her abruptly. "Come, get your bonnet and go." Later she noted in her diary, "So the little, fatherless & homeless girl of 20 left."[44]

It was during the California campaign of 1896 that Susan B. Anthony met Ida Harper, an Indiana reporter. Anthony liked her instantly and watched her skillfully handle the press in California and finally proposed that Mrs. Harper return to Rochester with her and write her biography. While she saw her biography as necessary to the history of the woman's movement, it would not be a big project, she assured Mrs. Harper. Of course, the author would "want everything she can get about me, but she will find there is precious little when she sits down."[45] Ida Harper agreed, on the condition that Anthony would stay home, not accept any speaking engagements or state campaigns, and be available to answer questions and clarify problems.

When they arrived in Rochester, Anthony showed Ida Harper into the attic, where Harper must have been aghast at what she saw.

> Ranged around the walls were trunks, boxes and bags of letters and other documents, dating back for a century and tied in bundles just as they had been put away from year to year. There were piles of legal papers, accounts, receipts and memoranda of every description, and the diaries and note-books of sixty years. The shelves were filled with congressional, convention and other reports; there were stacks of magazines and newspapers, large numbers of scrap-books and bushels of scraps waiting to be pasted.[46]

It was a researcher's dream. But for someone who had been convinced by Anthony that there was little there and the project would probably not take more than a year, the attic must have taken on nightmarish qualities.

Anthony hired stenographers, and Harper put them to work ironing out old letters, sorting them, and then classifying them. As soon as the letters were ready, they spent evenings pasting newspaper clipping into scrapbooks. By the time the papers were put into order, the attic had been transformed into an ideal place to work. Its two plain rooms had been sealed in natural wood; they were light and airy and lined with shelves on which papers had been arranged. It was a sunny spot at the top of the house, and the windows opened to the treetops. For hours in the afternoon, as one of her stenographers remembered, "Mrs. Harper and & Miss A. sit in the bay window, looking over old letters. Miss A. sits at one side of her table, straight in an old red tea-gown and a straight backed chair, while Mrs. Harper, plump and cushiony, jogs back and forth in her rocker and nibbles popcorn at intervals."[47]

The house at 17 Madison Street bustled with people and activity. There was the girl who took care of household chores, one or two stenographers assisting Anthony and Harper, who either labored over manuscript papers together or worked in their separate studies, and sister Mary, Susan's right hand and devoted supporter, who managed to keep the household together. For Susan, being at home meant keeping a regular schedule, which she missed during months of traveling with irregular schedules and living between trains and hotels. Now she was up at half past six or seven, taking her sponge bath in a tub of cold water. After that she gave herself a vigorous rubbing and then dressed in a casual and usually colorful tea-gown before coming down to breakfast at half past seven. She ate her oatmeal or dish of fruit and cream and drank coffee with her sister and the rest of the household, save Ida Harper, who did not get up until very late—perhaps at nine o'clock. By that time Susan was in her study and already had read the newspapers. As Harper recalled, "Each morning, as the postman arrives, Miss Anthony sits down at her desk and, going over the piles of letters, puts to one side those which can wait, dictates replies to those requiring the longest answers and, while they are being typewritten, plunges with her pen into the rest."[48]

After an afternoon of work on the biography and then dinner, she discussed the old days and reminisced with Mary and Ida Harper. Then it was back to her study, with her "big office-desk overflowing with papers, which have also flowed into baskets and boxes set about the floor,"[49] as one of her stenographers, Genevieve Hawley, described the scene. Often she would write until about ten o'clock in the evening. Then it was time for a brisk evening walk before going to bed.

She was strong and vigorous, still trim and alert. When she was asked if she found life tiresome at this age, she responded immediately, "Oh no! I don't want to die just as long as I can work. The minute I can't I want to go. I dread the thought of being enfeebled. I find the older I get the greater power I have to help the world. I am like a snowball—the further I am rolled, the more I gain. When my powers begin to lessen, I want to go. But, I'll have to take it as it comes."[50]

This energy outdistanced and exasperated her young stenographers. Genevieve Hawley found that "I can do her letters *good* enough; but I cannot do enough of them." At first she thought it was her own youth and lack of experience. Then she met one of Anthony's former stenographers, a veteran of thirteen years of experience in office work, who told her that working for Susan B. Anthony was harder than ordinary office work.[51]

After some months of this routine, Genevieve began to notice that "she grudges so much time spent on digging among dead things of the past when there is so much work waiting to be done."[52] Susan seemed almost depressed when they began to work on the post–Civil War period of her biography. "It seems to me that I never was so void on inventive thought of work in my life. The reason is, I am all swallowed up in the struggles of the past. I go along very well so long as the opposition was from our enemies—that is up to 1860. But now when we come to 1866–67–68–69—with the '*Negro's Hour*' cry, from our very best friends, the Train assistance, and the utter repudiation of me—then in 1870–71—the secession—then the Woodhull!!"[53]

Memories flooded back, and the whole of that difficult period came alive to her again but now with a different urgency. "I went through all the fire of charges of stealing, and of every other crime in the whole calendar, twenty-five years ago. . . . I never made a public denial of one of them through the years of bitterest kind of persecution, and believe I was greatly the gainer by working right on and ignoring them."[54] But now, at the age of seventy-seven, she was forced to go back through those painful years. She could remain silent no longer as she thought of how she would be remembered by history. Her biography must be a vindication. "I have this

PM been reading the letter of Blackwell & everybody at the Train episode—and they make me shiver clear to my fingers ends & toes too. Mrs. Harper & I are studying how to make the story true and not incriminate anybody."[55]

The vindication Anthony sought and Harper detailed in *The Life and Work of Susan B. Anthony* was so subtly stated that it has passed by the attention of most readers of these documents of women's history. But it did not go unnoticed by Henry Blackwell. As soon as the biography was published, he rushed to press with an edition of *The Woman's Journal,* which contained his own version of Anthony's role in the Train episode (which contrasted so dramatically with the version he had told to Isabella Hooker in 1870). He managed to get the New York State Woman's Suffrage Association, of which Susan's sister Mary was a member, to raise one hundred dollars to distribute this edition of the *Journal.* Anthony was infuriated with his manipulation. "Just to think of my sister working thus to send his falsehoods broadcast—it makes me ache to the very center of me."[56]

Anthony could not dwell in the past or even over her own need for vindication from it, because there was another emergency. In 1898, the United States annexed Hawaii and then from its victory in the Spanish-American War, it acquired the Philippines, Puerto Rico, and Guam. When their annexation was formalized, the United States denied some of these territories the right to choose their own governments or to form their own constitutions, as various states had been permitted to do before they had entered the Union. Anthony was enraged and ready to act against these first definitive signs of American imperialism.

She noted that in taking new territories, the United States government extended the area of disfranchisement in the country, as "today Congress itself assumes the prerogatives of making the laws for newly-acquired Territories." This was no different than the actions of the South in trying to disfranchise Negroes. It was an open declaration of the supremacy of the white race.

In the nineteenth century, America had spread across the continent and settled the country from coast to coast with a belief in its own superiority—its "Manifest Destiny." By the end of the century, expansionism extended beyond the borders of the United States and had become a form of imperialism. Winning new territories from the Spanish-American War made imperialism a fact of American politics. The United States began to establish itself as a world power. Now the belief in superiority embedded in the American self-definition, which for a century had subjugated anyone who was not a white, Anglo-Saxon, Protestant male, would be extended to other lands and what seemed then to be remote regions of the world. Rationalizing its own sense of its superiority over other peoples and now other lands, the American government justified its actions by proclaiming that it was bringing democracy, its republican form of government, to the "less-civilized" regions of the world.

In 1900, the United States formalized its annexation of Hawaii as a territory and extended to its people—that is, its men—the rights of citizenship. Anthony spoke forcefully to the National-American convention while Hawaii's annexation was being discussed in Congress. Her temper and tone were not essentially different than they had been forty years earlier in the months before the Civil War.

> I have been overflowing with wrath ever since the proposal was made to engraft our half-barbaric form of government on Hawaii and our other new possessions. I have been studying how to save, not them, but ourselves from the disgrace. This is the first time the United States has ever tried to foist upon a new people the exclusively masculine form of government. Our business should be to give this people the highest form which has been attained by us.[57]

Anthony measured the value of government by its political treatment of women, and she offered as her models the governments of the states of Wyoming and Colorado, which had enfranchised women. But she could not spark the suffragists to the same anger and indignation as she had over these new encroachments on other peoples. She was old, honored, and revered by them as a symbol of their cause but was no longer the leader whose ideas shaped their movement. In frustration she told one of the women, "I wonder if when I am under the sod—or cremated & floating in the air—I shall have to stir you and others up. How can you not be on fire—when the Senate Foreign & Territorial Comm. are considering the Hawaiian Commissions damnable proposition to restrict the right to vote & hold office to *male citizens?* . . . Do come into the living present and work to save us from any more barbarism of *male governments.*"[58]

With or without their support, Anthony issued vigorous protests. The bill to grant territorial status to Hawaii was on President

McKinley's desk when he received (but at least in terms of action doubtlessly ignored), Susan B. Anthony's protest against "the most outrageous piece of legislation ever turned out of the congressional mill." Rather than include the word "male" everywhere that the eligibility of voters was discussed in the bill, Anthony proposed that it would be more honorable to state outrightly that "no woman shall ever be allowed to vote or hold any office in the Hawaiian islands."[59]

Now, in the closing years of her life, her radical egalitarianism stood unshaken. "A race of men capable of enslaving any other race or class—is incapable of justice to themselves—ever," she argued. For her, the struggle still meant "to begin at the tap root of the disease culminating in general desecration of human rights—in blood shed & murder—in lynchings & outrages upon men and women of all races.[60]

It was men—as a class and through their exclusive access to political power—that committed these outrages against humanity. "All of our wars today are the result of a government *wholly masculine*. I do not believe any one of them would have been possible had the women of the United States and of England had their full and rightful share in deciding all questions that were at issue between the various nations. Man is the fighting half of the human family, and woman is the peace-making half."[61]

It was this political outlook that gave Anthony common ground with women from other countries. By May of 1899, when she embarked on her second trans-Atlantic voyage to attend the third convocation of the International Council of Women, she had become the international symbol of woman's rights. She called the first meeting of the International Council in 1888, and it held its second meeting in 1893, when the United States celebrated the four-hundredth anniversary of Columbus's discovery of America with the grand World's Columbian Exposition in Chicago. So that women would not be excluded from this World's Fair as they had been from the Centennial Celebration of the country in 1876, Anthony had spearheaded a drive to have women appointed to take part in the planning of the exposition. In concession Congress issued a mandate for a Board of Lady Managers, and as a result a World's Congress of Representative Women became a significant part of the exposition. With 528 delegates, 27 countries and 126 organizations were represented. Now six years later, the international women's movement reassembled in London. The meetings overflowed from the great building of Westminster to the town and church halls and to St. Martins. This time women came not only from Europe and America but also from China, India, Argentina, South Africa, Persia, and Palestine.

Susan B. Anthony opened the session and spoke at several of the meetings. Nearly eighty years old, with fifty of those years dedicated to the cause, she now embodied it. She was dined and honored by organizations and titled families during the meetings. Anthony was the "queen" of the meetings, but she was not content to hold their congress without recognition of their cause from the regina of England, Victoria herself. She told one of her hostesses, Lady Aberdeen, that if their congress was to meet in the United States, she would surely try to arrange an invitation for them to call upon the president. "Isn't it possible for us to secure some recognition from the Queen?"

Victoria invited the women of the congress to tea at Windsor Castle. To Anthony, "her gracious and kindly reception cannot have any other interpretation than approval of the aims of this International Congress of Women."[62] But Anthony was frustrated with Victoria's limitations. "However much I appreciate her splendid record I cannot but remember that in all matters connected with women she has been very conservative, never wholly yielding her assent to any innovation until it was already practically established." And then she pointed out how the Queen had appeared "wholly oblivious" to the three great works of English women: abolition of the Contagious Disease Acts, which had legalized prostitution and forced many girls into in garrison towns; obtaining property rights for married women; and the movement for woman's suffrage.[63]

When she returned to America in the summer of 1899, Susan went to Lake Geneva for a long visit with Mrs. Stanton at the home of Elizabeth Smith Miller. In these later years, when their visits were less frequent, they found time to spend together every summer at Mrs. Miller's home in the Finger Lakes. They sat on the porch overlooking the lake and cooled by the lake breeze and reminisced over old times. There were few "pioneers" left to remember the old days and recall why they had felt so keenly about issues that the younger generations clearly did not understand or see as important. But their time was getting short. Susan worried about Mrs. Stanton's blindness. "Though she may outlive me by years, this infirmity having come upon her makes me fear that her time may be shorter than mine."[64]

On Susan's mind was her own approaching eightieth birthday, the date she had set for resigning the presidency of the National-American—the action Mrs. Stanton had advocated when the association renounced the *Woman's Bible.* For that matter, Stanton had her own candidate in mind to promote as Anthony's possible successor, instead of one of Susan's "nieces"—Anna Howard Shaw, Carrie Chapman Catt, or Rachel Foster Avery, all of whom had voted to censor the *Woman's Bible* in 1895.

There was no getting around Anthony's determination that upon her retirement one of her "nieces" would take over the organization, regardless of any of their various plans to prematurely withdraw or retire. The question that remained was who would be chosen. The choice was between Anna Howard Shaw, the closest of Anthony's "nieces" and one of the most impassioned orators on woman's suffrage of the day, and Carrie Chapman Catt, who was not as close to Anthony personally but was the most effective organizer in the movement. Having spearheaded the campaign that won women the vote in Colorado, Catt had been appointed head of the association's organizing committee shortly after coming to the National-American. Catt decidely did not want to follow Anthony as President, and Shaw desperately wanted it. Her "highest ambition had been to succeed Miss Anthony, for no one who knew her as I did could underestimate the honor of being chosen by her to carry on her work."

Even with Mrs. Stanton's alternative choice, everyone knew that the decision would be Anthony's. Both Catt and Shaw recognized that whatever their personal desires or ambitions they must behave on this point as Anthony would—for the good of the cause, not from their personal needs or desires. Consequently, neither woman betrayed her own desires; instead, Shaw told "Aunt Susan" that Mrs. Catt was her only possible successor, "while simultaneously Mrs. Catt was pouring into Miss Anthony's other ear a series of impassioned tributes to me."[65]

By the time the convention opened, it was known that Anthony had decided on Catt as her successor. The vote was taken, and Carrie Chapman Catt was announced as the new president. The women cheered—for a moment—then there was a sudden hush, the deepest silence. Amidst the excitement of the moment in welcoming their new president, it was "as though all at once every one realized that she was witnessing the passing of Susan B. Anthony, their beloved leader."

In the awkwardness of the moment, when no one knew what to do next, Susan B. Anthony took Carrie Chapman Catt by the hand, brought her to the center of the stage, and with tears in her own eyes pronounced in a somewhat shaken voice, "In Mrs. Catt you have my ideal leader. I present you my successor." The hall was a tumult of emotion, filled with crying and applause and white handkerchiefs waving in the air. Tension rose until Rachel Foster Avery finally stepped forward and nominated Susan B. Anthony for the office of honorary president. The overwhelming acceptance of her motion revealed how much the suffragists were not willing to let go of their leader.

Then it was Mrs. Catt's turn to speak. "Miss Anthony will never have a successor." She was herself a movement, not only president of the association. Catt knew that "I shall not be its leader as Miss Anthony has been; I shall be only an officer of this association." In addition, she knew "that there was a general loyalty to her which could not be given to any younger worker."[66] Carrie Chapman Catt would, in fact, carry the woman's suffrage struggle to victory fourteen years after Susan B. Anthony's death, intermittently holding the office of president of the association during that time. Anna Howard Shaw, who had been vice president of the National-American since 1892, continued in that office until 1904.

Ida Harper remembered this historic 1900 convention and the schedule that the eighty-year-old Anthony followed. "She presided at three public sessions of the convention daily and at all the business meetings; held a day's conference and made a speech in Baltimore; conducted hearing before the Senate committee; addressed a parlor meeting and attended several dinners, and receptions; participated in her own great birthday festivities, afternoon and evening; and remained for nearly a week of executive committee meetings."[67] She let her girls know that she was glad to be back in Washington. She had disapproved of their decision to move the Natonal's meetings from one state to another as they had for five years. "One reason why so little has been done by Congress is because none of us has remained here to watch our employees in the capitol."[68]

To honor Susan B. Anthony on her eightieth birthday, President McKinley welcomed the National-American to a reception at the

White House. Whether or not he supported their cause, Susan, as a careful politician, knew that being received by the president of the United States would render a legitimacy to woman's suffrage that their movement needed. After a reception in the East Room of the White House, where Anthony stood to the right of President McKinley and presented each of the delegates of the National-American to him by name, she visited his wife, who was too ill to attend the reception. That evening Anthony walked into the convention with the huge bouquet of white lilies given to her by the First Lady, held them up before the delegates, and said, "Mrs. McKinley shakes hands with you all spiritually and sends you these lovely flowers."[69]

Honors and tearful greetings continued throughout the meetings and into the celebration of her birthday. In her farewell address, Anthony, in a somewhat shaken voice, summed up her life. "Once I was the most hated and reviled of women, now, it seems as if everybody loves me."[70] Against all odds, her charismatic force had insisted its way into the public consciousness. Her opposition had tried to repudiate her and to caricature her, and when she prevailed through it all, they turned to her with awe, often not understanding or accepting any more of her message than they had when they had tried to dismiss her.

Susan was finally exhausted, and the fatigue began to show. Although she was moved by all of the attention, "The one that had touched me most is a simple note which came from an old home of slavery, from a woman off whose hands and feet the shackles fell nearly forty years ago. That letter, my friends, contained eighty cents—one penny for every year. It was all this aged person had."[71] This, she knew, was not only a symbolic testimony to her stature, it represented her struggle.

When she returned to Rochester, Susan sat down at her desk each day and for weeks wrote personal notes in answer to the more than one thousand birthday letters, cables, and testimonies she had received. There were still many projects before her, and one that had been on her mind for several years was her long standing appeal to have women admitted to the University of Rochester. Founded in 1850, the university originally was more of a Baptist preparatory school for young men going on to the theological seminary. When the new president, David J. Hill, took over in 1879, he shifted its orientation to that of a liberal university. Almost immediately Susan took note, formed a committee of Rochester women, and demanded that the university become coeducational. Nearby Syracuse and Cornell had just begun admitting women. Hill preferred the plan that Harvard was adopting—to establish a separate coordinating college, to be called the Harvard Annex for Women (later Radcliffe). But in whatever form, Hill argued, coeducation was not financially possible for the university.

Ten years later, in 1891, when it became known that Hill was seeking support for the university from local industry, commerce, and the Rochester citizenry, Anthony pressed for her demand again. During one of Mrs. Stanton's visits to Rochester, she and Anthony entertained university officials, trustees, and two hundred local guests in Anthony's home to reassert women's demand for coeducation. By then the university had a full liberal-arts curriculum, specialization programs, elective courses, a new science faculty, and formal graduate study. It had all of the earmarks of the new university in the late nineteenth century. The women wanted their share and would not permit the University of Rochester to ignore the trend toward college education for women. In the midwestern states, women had been admitted to many colleges. In the East, where the exclusively male colleges were most entrenched, women's colleges (beginning with Vassar in 1860) began to open. In 1870, the public, tuition-free Female College opened in New York, which was later renamed Hunter. Then followed the opening of Wellesley and Smith in 1875 and Bryn Mawr in 1880. But by 1891, only 16 of the 158 women's colleges offered an education equivalent to that given at men's colleges or universities.[72] In 1900, 5,237 women graduated from institutions of higher education, compared to 22,173 men.

In Rochester, the university officials listened to Anthony and Stanton and seemed to agree in principle to their demand; but, they insisted, the women must raise the $200,000 that the officials claimed was needed for additional instructional facilities. The women protested, but the university held firm. Anthony decided upon another course. She convinced President Hill to admit a young woman, Helen Wilkinson, into the freshman class of that year, and Anthony paid her expenses. The new student was greeted with jeering and harassment. Curiously, the president betrayed the male fears that gripped the universities when they were on the verge of coeducation. Speaking in chapel, he told the male student body to "live like men and engage in all those exercises which will give you strength and muscle and steadiness of nerves."[73] However, the men seemed to survive the threatening female presence, and Helen Wilkinson remained in the university for two years, until she was forced to withdraw because of a serious illness, which took her life a year later. The university refused to admit any other women.

In 1898 the trustees agreed to lower their requirement to $100,000, undoubtedly assuming that the women could not raise it anyway. By the time Susan had returned to Rochester after her eightieth-birthday celebration, they had raised $40,000. Realizing that the women would not give up, the trustees again lowered the required amount to $50,000. By September 8, 1900, the deadline set by the university for receiving the full amount, the women still needed $8,000. Susan was notified on September 7 and spent the next day trying to raise it. First she appealed to her sister Mary, who gave her $2,000 that she had been holding for the girls after they were admitted to the University of Rochester; then "to stores, to offices, to factories they drove, Miss Anthony making her plea with all the eloquence and pathos she could command." Her expression was likened to that of Joan of Arc. That afternoon she appealed to their Unitarian minister Reverend Gannett, who, with his wife who was a close friend of Susan's, contributed $2,000. With a few more successful appeals, by late afternoon a very exhausted Susan B. Anthony appeared before the trustees of the University of Rochester and presented pledges for $8,000.

It was not enough! The trustees informed Anthony that they rejected the guarantee behind the last $2,000. Anthony was stunned. then summoning almost the last bit of strength left in her, she rose and stood before them in deadly seriousness and said quietly, "Well gentlemen, I may as well confess—I am the guarantor . . . I now pledge my life insurance for the $2,000."[74]

A few days later Anthony appeared again before the board of trustees and happily reported afterwards, "They let the girls in." She was overjoyed, but it was evident that she was not well. That morning she had awakened feeling very weak and could barely speak. After the trustees' meeting, she received friends and the press in her parlor. Mary stood nervously by and worried that her sister looked pale and said very little to the guests. Then in the bustle of activity among the jubilant crowd, Mary noticed that Susan had disappeared. She quietly went upstairs, slipped into her sister's bedroom, and found Susan unconscious on her bed. "A lesion of a small blood-vessel in the brain, a touch of apoplexy light as the pressure of a baby's finger," the doctor later told Mary.[75]

When Susan regained consciousness, she was left with some paralysis and was unable to speak for some time. Susan's doctor, a woman homeopathic physician, attended to her constantly for over a week. Slowly Susan began to recover. In mid-October, when she was well enough to go out for a ride, she asked to be taken first to the University of Rochester. "These are no longer forbidden grounds to the girls of our city," she could proudly observe. Genevieve Lull Hawley, who had become Susan's secretary, told her aunt that "the doctor promises her ultimate recovery; but she had very little strength yet . . . she has risen about nine, had her breakfast brought to her and gone to bed early. She walks about the neighborhood or drives out almost every afterday . . . reads papers and sees a few friends, but that is about all."[76] As the weeks went on, she noted that Anthony "still looks feeble, reads a little, sews a little, sleeps almost every afternoon."[77] The doctor warned her against further activity. The stroke had cut deeply into her vigor, and she would not fully regain her strength. Another stroke could fell her at any time. Above all, she must avoid crowds.

Ignoring all admonitions, in December Susan was in Madison Square Garden for the suffrage bazaar organized to raise money for the movement. She reported to Mary that "every day I feel more like myself."[78] But she never regained her old vigor and finally admitted, "I suppose at eighty-one we must naturally begin to feel a change come over us."[79]

13

"Failure Is Impossible"

"I CONJURE SUSAN TO STAY AT HOME; AS LONG AS SHE CAN walk up & down Madison Street there is no necessity for her gallivanting off to the ends of the earth." Mrs. Stanton, now blind, was still worried about Susan's overly active life. Especially since Susan's stroke, Mrs. Stanton thought she should be managed a bit and commanded her to "stay at home under Mary's wing!" Mrs. Stanton and sister Mary apparently succeeded for the moment; Mary reported to Mrs. Stanton that "Susan was not going to any conventions this winter, but would stay at home & rest." To this Mrs. Stanton replied, "A rational idea, we all sing in chorus 'A-MEN!'" But in reality, Susan's submission to this plan did not last long. Mrs. Stanton, confiding her frustrations with Susan to Ida Harper, gave a rare insight into Susan's drive by comparing her to Theodore Roosevelt. "The fact is, he is vain of seeming so strong and active and I am afraid there is a touch of the same feeling in Susan."[1]

Ida Harper had long since given up trying to hold Susan to her various promises to stay home and to help her, first with the biography, which was published in its first two volumes in 1898 and later with the fourth volume of the *History of Woman Suffrage*, which Susan had literally intimidated Ida Harper into writing. While Harper was finishing the second volume of the biography, Susan began to drop strong hints that she should undertake the next volume of the *History* with comments like, "I am placing carefully on these shelves the material which will be needed by someone in writing the *History*." Harper sensed the meaning behind Susan's seemingly offhanded comments. "I was overwhelmed with the consciousness that within the innermost recesses of her being was the intention that I should undertake this stupendous task." Harper resisted. To her surprise, Susan then dropped the subject for nearly a year, leaving her even more anxious about it.

Then one night, "Just as I was going to bed, Miss Anthony came into my room." She was direct. "When will you be ready to come here and begin work on the History?" Caught off-guard, Harper reeled around in surprise and then collapsed into the chair overcome with hopelessness. She stated her refusal and offered excuses, but Anthony brushed them aside as if they were inconsequential. Finally she thought she had found a way out. "If you will only let me off from this work, I'll come back here and get everything ready and plan it all and put things in such shape that anybody can do it." Susan drew herself up and, throwing her head back as she did when she had made up her mind, told Harper, "Think this over till morning, and if you decide that you will not undertake it, I'll burn up the material and that will be the end."

As soon as she uttered these words in the tension of the moment, Susan caught herself in the consequences of her own adamance. Her voice broke and her eyes filled with tears. Ida Harper was vanquished, "I'll do it Miss Anthony, I'll do it." Crying, she embraced and kissed this eighty-year-old woman who at once was her tyrant and her most beloved "Aunt."[2] There would be no mellowing of Susan B. Anthony in her final years.

As soon as Harper began to organize the work for the *History*, Anthony announced that she would probably be going to California. Harper was not surprised; she had learned to manage these frustrations. But Genevieve Hawley, who was young and as impressed as she was intimidated by Miss Anthony, was unable to handle her increasing crankiness and stubbornness. At one point, when the young Hawley approached Anthony about a raise in pay and Anthony refused, the secretary appealed to Ida Harper to play the intermediary. Harper had warned Genevieve, "You must stand up for your rights or you'll never get them."[3] Harper interceded but it did not help. "Nobody can convince her that you have not a comfortable income *outside* of your work. She has told me this again & again & refused to believe me when I said she was mistaken." Susan B. Anthony fought all of her life for the rights of women to their own economic independence; but evidently in her own home, particularly at this late point in her life, her other standard prevailed—that of feminism, dedicating one's life to the cause of women.

If she was sometimes short and impatient with those around her—

to all save her sister Mary, who was true family and the one to whom Susan was most indebted for keeping a home together for them in their old age—the demands made upon Susan every time she appeared in public were as unrelenting. By contrast, in the summer of 1901 Susan spent three and a half weeks in Providence, Rhode Island, with Sarah Jane Eddy. There she sat for her portrait—a grand oil painting that was a remembrance of Susan in her garnet velvet dress on her eightieth birthday, when a long line of children again came to her, each laying a rose in her lap. Susan's connections with the young artist went back to the 1850s, when she had met Eddy's grandfather, Francis Jackson, on her first trip to Boston and then had accepted the endowed fund he had given for the cause. When Eddy's own mother died in 1885, she bequeathed twenty-four thousand dollars to Susan for the cause. Susan had developed close ties with Francis Jackson's family over the years and during this visit to Providence relaxed into the comfort that comes from old friendships.

One day Susan went out with another friend to a lecture given by the president of Brown University. The moderator of the program spotted her in the audience, announced her presence, spoke of her long and wonderful work, and then asked her to come forward to speak. "I was so taken by surprise that I flatly refused." Her friend nudged her and whispered, "You must at least stand up and make your bow," which Susan did, but it was not enough. She was beckoned once again to the stage. "Finally I pulled off my bonnet and walked up and said a few words, but I was dreadfully upset, as I had felt that here was one place where I could go and not be dragged out."[4]

After her stroke, Susan never returned fully to her old self, and at her age she wanted some privacy. But she could not evade her public. She had lost a certain vitality, and now when she was called upon to speak, she made only brief statements. There were no long speeches any more. Then in February 1902, while she was visiting a niece in Philadelphia, she contracted pneumonia and was forced to remain there for three weeks. While she recuperated, she wrote to Mary every day and, according to Ida Harper, who was still confined at 17 Madison Street writing the *History*, "There was no end of directions in regard to sending suffrage literature to all points of the compass and seeing that every letter which came was answered." But above all Susan worried about Mary, who was confined at home recovering from a broken wrist. Susan had wanted so much to be there for Mary's seventy-fifth birthday. She sent instructions to another of her secretaries, Anna Dann, who was also living at 17 Madison Street: "Don't fail to do everything possible for Sister Mary; comb her hair and help her dress and look after her constantly. Do all you can to help Mrs. Harper in the work but let it be Sister Mary first and always."[5]

By the end of May, Susan was well enough to travel and set off from Philadelphia for some meetings and a week-long visit with Mrs. Stanton. It was the first time in over ten years that Susan had stayed in Mrs. Stanton's home, as there was never the space in the small New York apartment that there had been in her larger Tenafly home. Mrs. Stanton was now eighty-six years old, and her health was failing rapidly. But her agitation over and critique of religion had not slackened, and Susan noted that on that question, "We have grown a little apart since not so closely associated as of old."[6]

Mrs. Stanton was sometimes bitter over the attention Susan received. "If my suffrage coadjutors had ever treated me with the boundless generosity they have my friend Susan, I could have scattered my writings abundantly from Maine to Louisana." She did not finally begrudge Susan the recognition, for "she deserves all she has received." But at times she could not look beyond the jeweled pin of the American flag with stars only for the suffrage states or the precious silk woven for Susan by the enfranchised women of Utah. She irritably charged that while the suffragists had given Susan "thousands of dollars, jewels, laces, silks and satins," she had received only "criticism and denunciation for my radical ideas."[7]

In fact, in 1897 Susan had received a diamond pin from her nieces Lucy Anthony and Louise Mosher James and her adopted nieces Anna Howard Shaw and Rachel Foster Avery. On her eightieth birthday, suffragists bestowed her with more jewels she would never wear, fine china, and other refinements. These were more than tokens of affection; they were a recognition of a life that had forgone the comforts of home and family—small rewards for never having retreated from the hardships of the struggle for over fifty years. Stanton was correct that her radicalism in later years had unjustly brought her ridicule, but she was also indifferent to what it meant for Susan to have remained single and to have dedicated her life to the movement.

In June 1902, Susan stopped for another visit with Mrs. Stanton. When it was time to leave, they both knew that the end was near. Susan embraced Mrs. Stanton and began to weep, "Shall I see you again?" Mrs. Stanton was composed. "Oh, yes, if not here, then in the hereafter, if there is one, and if there isn't we shall never know it."[8] Susan promised to return in November to be with Mrs. Stanton for her eighty-seventh birthday.

Back in Rochester on a crisp autumn afternoon when the trees around the Anthony home were still full of glorious color and the leaves began to drop, Ida Harper walked into Susan's upstairs study and handed her a telegram that had just been delivered to the house. She opened it and read it and then let it fall in her lap. "Mother passed away at three o'clock" was the only message, signed Harriot Stanton Blatch. Susan sank into her chair in a "melancholy quiet" for the rest of the afternoon and gazed at Mrs. Stanton's portrait on the wall. She said nothing. The other women in the house, also saddened by the telegram, knew to leave her alone with her grief. They were angry that Mrs. Stanton's daughter had not directed the telegram to Ida Harper, who could have at least prepared Susan for this shock, but they kept their anger to themselves. Susan's grief was their absorbing concern. They knew that they could only begin to imagine what Mrs. Stanton had meant to Susan. By twilight, sister Mary finally slipped into the room and gently insisted that Susan come downstairs. Susan had lost track of the hours and had not noticed the reporters who swarmed around her house.

When she came downstairs she was more noticeably frail than ever. Mary and Ida Harper were worried about Susan. They made arrangements for her trip to New York the next day, while Susan sat without speaking except to try to answer the reporters' questions. Even Genevieve Hawley was aware of the deep pain behind her stoic silence. "What it means to her one can only guess; but she keeps all the shock and loneliness and heartache to herself, and hardly says anything." One reporter asked for a photo, and her secretary went to the attic with her. "To see poor Miss A. questioned over and over about her early times with her dead friend and climbing up to the attic to find a picture for the reporter, with her hands shaking so she could hardly lift the cards, was a piteous thing, though none of us would have dared tell her so."[9] Anthony was pained by the reporters' questions, for she wanted to say grand and wonderful things about Mrs. Stanton, but "I cannot express myself at all as I feel, I am too crushed to speak. If I had died first she would have found beautiful phrases to describe our friendship, but I cannot put it into words."[10]

Finally that evening after her sister helped her to bed, a reporter from the New York *Sun* telephoned, and Ida Harper was firm. "I would not call Miss Anthony out of bed tonight to give an interview to President Roosevelt," she said. Then with all the protectiveness she felt for the dear old lady, she gave the interview which would appear the next day under Anthony's name. It was all the reporter could get.[11] The next day Mary took Susan to the train and made her promise to wire as soon as she reached New York. For a woman who had spent most of her life "on the cars," this was the longest and loneliest journey of all.

When Susan arrived in New York she went directly to Mrs. Stanton's apartment. Still in shock, she was overcome by the absence. The unimaginable grief stunned her. "It was an awful hush— it seems impossible—that the voice is hushed—that I have longed to hear for 50 years—longed to get her opinion of things—before I knew exactly where I stood—It is all at sea—but the laws of nature are still going on—with the shadow or turning." The shock of losing her most beloved made life seem to stand still. It was as if she were suspended from daily reality, especially when she saw that life went on for others in its ordinary ways in the streets. Normal daily activity seemed incomprehensible to Susan in this moment of grief. "What a world it is—it goes right on & on—no matter who lives or who dies!!"[12]

Reporters continued to press Anthony for interviews. She tried to give them but speaking was difficult. The funeral was private, with only a few friends joining the family. Susan B. Anthony sat in an armchair near the casket, "looking with aching heart into the face which with the crown of beautiful, snowy hair was so grand in the majesty of death."[13] When the casket was closed and covered with flowers for the final services, one photo was chosen to rest upon it. It must have been Mrs. Stanton's wish to have her photo of Susan with her at the end.

Since she had begun writing the *History of Woman Suffrage* with Stanton, Anthony had held an abiding concern for passing their movement—the cause of woman's rights—on to future generations. But in 1903 at the age of eighty-three, that focus began to include the more personal act of preparing to hand down her possessions and passing on her life accomplishments to the next generation. But what were they? She had no savings; she had only a minimal income from her endowment and did not even have life insurance, since she had signed that over to the University of Rochester. And there were no beloved children or grandchildren to designate as heirs. In fact, Susan's most personal possession was her life's work; she had a movement to preserve and protect, a cause that she had to insure would continue. Now part of her attention was focused on how to close her life in a way that would benefit the progress of the cause.

As the great fundraiser of their movement, she worried that her death would leave the cause without money to continue. She began to think about raising a great fund to carry on woman's suffrage campaigns after her death. But each time she raised a large amount of money there were present exigencies that required it, such as financing the publication of the fourth volume of the *History* in 1903. Large or small, everything which could be turned toward the future of the movement received Anthony's attention. When she saw that her secretary, Genevieve Hawley, had made some pretty needle books for their suffrage bazaar, she gave her scraps of black silk brocade, which were left from a dress she had had made, and asked her to make some needle books from them. When Genevieve finished the needle books, Susan marveled at the delicate embroidery but would not let them be sold. Instead, she carefully tucked them away in a bureau drawer and gave Ida Harper instructions that "these are to be distributed after I'm gone. They will have more value then."[14]

The black silk brocade had been made up into what she called her "Utah dress."[15] The fabric, a gift of the women at the Utah Silk Commission on her eightieth birthday, delighted Susan because "the silk worms—the mulberry trees were raised by Mormon women—the coloring—the spinning, the weaving, everything was done by the Mormon women in Utah . . . it is a very beautiful silk."[16] Susan wrote to each woman who had been involved in preparing the silk for her; "My pleasure in the rich brocaded silk is quadrupled because it was made by women politically equal with men."[17] Statements like this left the door open for many to interpret Anthony's support of Mormon women as a concurrence with the Mormon practice of polygamy, which she responded to as "base slander."

There were other tasks involved in concluding her life, and one that weighed heavily upon Susan was the problem of what to do with the fifty years of papers accumulated in her attic and used for her biography and the fourth volume of the *History*. Mary, in particular, wanted to "regenerate the house from top to bottom." When six months had passed after the publication of the *History* and five years since her biography—"a reasonable length of time for its statements to be questioned"—Susan was forced to decide which papers could be destroyed.[18] She could not do it.

Every day she sat at a table with Ida Harper, who poured out a new pile of letters between them. Then they began to sort. Harper would suggest that certain letters were of no value, and Susan would insist, "They had better be saved." Harper finally rose from the table in frustration. "Now there is no use in my wasting time here for you are not going to allow this trash to be burned." Susan looked grave, "I can't overcome the habit of a lifetime." Finally, she gave up and walked away—the task was too much for her. "The only way for me is to wash my hands of the whole business."[19]

Everyone else in the house was relieved, especially Mary who took this abdication as *carte blanche* to start burning the papers. Susan's library, which consisted of the scrapbooks prepared for writing the biography, diaries, and correspondence, had already been sent to the Library of Congress in Washington, to be preserved there as "The Susan B. Anthony Collection."[20] Ida Harper finally selected what she deemed to be the valuable letters and autographs. Many of them were kept in private collections, but over the century most of those that were saved have gone to archives in libraries. "The family letters were laid aside for Miss Anthony's disposal; all of her own were preserved; Mrs. Stanton's—hundreds of them—were sent to her children; Lucy Stone's to Miss Blackwell." Then Mary went to work. "Every morning for weeks she slipped downstairs at daybreak, built a bonfire behind the woodhouse and stood over it with a big shovel."[21]

Mrs. Stanton had not been as organized as Susan in putting her own papers together. Ever since Susan had proposed that they do it together, the task had remained unfinished. Now Mrs. Stanton's son Theodore wrote to Susan that he wanted to bring his sister Harriot to Paris, and if Susan could come with Ida Harper, "Hattie and I could all take hold of the work and get out promptly a nice biography." Dear Susan "could take a good rest & the rest of us could pitch in."[22] Susan wanted to make the ocean voyage, but there was so much other work occupying her at home—and home no longer meant 17 Madison Street. In fact, she was traveling again and constantly speaking to clubs and going to receptions and dinners.

After the 1903 National-American convention in New Orleans, Susan visited Booker T. Washington at his Tuskegee Institute in Alabama. Accompanied by several suffragists and her sister Mary, she was given a tour of the buildings and grounds and shown the many programs in the new field of "industrial education" that Washington had organized for black students at his institute. Anthony had followed the progress of Tuskegee since Washington had founded it in 1881 as a school to prepare blacks for the changing economy which was shifting in the South from agriculture to industry.

For years Booker T. Washington had been accepted by many blacks and some whites—particularly President Theodore Roosevelt—as the spokesman of his race. But many other black groups, including black women's clubs, were ambivalent about him. They lauded his work in building racial pride but they rejected his accommodation to whites which was particularly evident in his refusal to forthrightly champion black political rights. Instead, he chose to work behind the scenes. As a confidant of President Theodore Roosevelt, he provided a way for blacks to gain access to appointments in government. But because Washington worked behind the scenes the appointments he won came through patronage and were not necessarily the result of political accomplishments. By the time Susan B. Anthony visited Tuskegee in 1903, a new militant voice—of a recent black Harvard Ph.D. named W. E. B. Du Bois—was emerging as a confrontational, civil rights-oriented response to Booker T. Washington's politics of accommodation.

Anthony, who always insisted on universal suffrage, did not agree with Washington when he adopted the position in support of limited voting rights, which represented a restrictive franchise. She rejected Washington's strategy of masking his political goals of full citizenship and integration behind an emphasis on harmonious relations and evidence of friendship between whites and Negroes.[23] On the other hand, Anthony warmly supported Washington's program for building racial pride, in which he educated blacks to become the living contradiction to the racist assumptions of white southern society. In the face of virulent southern racial hatred, he taught blacks that they "must substitute efficiency for the slipshod work of slavery days, responsibility for irresponsibility, knowledge for ignorance and superstition, accepted moral standards for the amorality of the slave quarters."[24]

Washington came dangerously close to blaming the victim. But he lived in the reality of southern racial hatred, and he became convinced that blacks had to disproved their inferiority; something that poor, uneducated whites never had to disprove. He believed that education, training, and gainful employment would protect blacks from the savage acts of racial bigotry. When he was attacked by

other black leaders, Anthony supported him and saw the attacks—
that were similar to those she herself had experienced many times—
as challenges to his effective leadership. "Women are so like the
negroes; that is they are so like any subject class. They fall apart
the minute one of their own number gets, by perseverance and work
elevated to a little higher position than themselves . . . look at
Booker T. Washington, negroes are fighting him, it is mainly because they are jealous of his prominence."[25] But it is also likely that
Anthony identified with Washington because she herself had by then
compromised her earlier radical politics.

Susan B. Anthony spoke to fifteen hundred young black women
and men that Sunday afternoon in the Tuskegee chapel. The school
paper reported that "the welcome accorded Miss Anthony was warm
and enthusiastic to the last degree, a sea of snowy handkerchiefs
greeted her with the Chautauqua salute when she arose to begin her
address." They found that she was a "delightful talker—strong, eloquent, witty and convincing," and they loved her reminiscences
over the old days of abolition and her comments on the wonderful
work of Tuskegee, upon which she "invoked the blessings of the
Almighty."[26] She promised that day to raise one hundred dollars
for a new broom factory they hoped to open at the institute.

In the audience that day was the thirty-three-year-old wife of the
treasurer of Tuskegee, who until she had married had been a teacher
there. Adella Hunt Logan had first been inspired to suffrage work
when she heard Susan B. Anthony speak in 1895 at her alma mater,
Atlanta University.[27] After that she became active in the woman's
suffrage movement, and two years later she asked her suffragist friends
if she could be placed on the program of the National-American.
Isabel Howland, one of the more active suffrage workers in the
NAWSA, was enthusiastic about the idea and consulted Anthony.
Anthony told her that regarding the celebration of the first woman's
rights convention in 1848, she "would be delighted to have a rep-
resentative of the colored race of the South speak at our Fiftieth
Anniversary." But that was not the end of the story.

Mary Church Terrell, who was an educator in Washington, D.C.,
and the organizer of the National Association of Colored Women
(the association of black woman's clubs), was already invited. She
was known for her dynamic public lecturing, and Anthony thought
that "with the training of Oberlin and Paris back of her, she ought
to be a good representative of the possibilities of her race. I only
hope she is not too light to stand for the colored people."[28] On the

other hand, Anthony, who wanted black women represented in their meeting, insisted on having the most refined, educated, and eloquent speakers on the woman's suffrage platform, a standard that she and Mrs. Stanton had imposed on all women speakers for several years. Anthony and Stanton had been critical of the speaking abilities among the younger generation of white suffrage workers. Over the years, Anthony had become keenly sensitive to the need to demonstrate racial pride, as Booker T. Washington had pointed out. At the same time, she increasingly responded to the antisuffragist Remonstrants' or "antis'" claims that women were physically, mentally, and emotionally incapable of public work by insisting that the woman's suffrage speakers embody the highest accomplishments of women. Anthony raised her standards for suffragists, and black women were additionally held to Booker T. Washington's standards of demonstrating racial pride. If she was defensive against anti-woman attitudes in the demands she made of white woman's suffrage speakers, she was even more so in those she made of black women, who carried the double burden of having to disprove both racial and sex inferiority before the public. But beyond that, her position reveals how much the conservative influence of reform that came after the merger of the National with the American, produced compromise and a defensive reaction in Anthony that she would not have dreamed of thirty or forty years earlier. When the National-American organized a meeting in the South, this question became one of paramount concern to Susan B. Anthony.

Therefore, when Adella Logan asked to be listed as a speaker at the 1898 National-American convention, Anthony, who did not know this young woman's abilities, straightforwardly explained her reservations to Isabel Howland.

> I remember Miss Logan's letter and was very much pleased with it and if I *knew* she was a splendid speaker and would just make every one of the full Anglo-Saxon women feel ashamed of their race, I would hold up both hands for her to come to Washington next February. I would not on any account bring on our platform a woman who had a ten-thousandth part of a drop of African blood in her veins, who should prove an inferior speaker either as to matter or manner, because it would so militate against the colored race. Of course we have women in our society, the Calys, Mrs. Young and lots of others who will come up from the south and the Congressmen and their wives in Washington who would be hopping mad if we brought colored women

on our platform. We have always had Frederick Douglass and our Mrs. Harper but to bring right from the South a woman who would almost be an ex-slave, would vex them more than either of these they are accustomed to seeing. So I want to leave it to your judgment, and knowledge, if you know she can write a speech strong in argument, beautiful in rhetoric, and can deliver it in a splendid fashion, then let me know and bring her to Washington.

But Susan did not merely leave it to the other women to decide. Instead she forcefully, if not heavy-handedly, reinforced her position to them. She continued:

You see I do not in the slightest shrink from having a colored woman on the platform, but I do very much shrink from having an incompetent one, so unless you really *know* that Miss Logan is one who would astonish the natives, just let her wait until she is more cultured and can do the colored race the greatest possible credit.[29]

Adella Logan was not invited to speak at the anniversary meeting, but she continued to campaign for woman's suffrage. She told Anthony at the time of the meeting, "We are trying to help a very needy class of women who are slow to believe that they might get any help from the ballot. Possibly they would not but surely as much as the illiterate man can get. I hope to see my daughter vote right here in the South."[30]

As a black woman with an intense commitment to racial justice and with a deep involvement in woman's suffrage campaigns, Adella Logan embodied the enigmatic position of black women lodged between the two movements of human rights. She represented the victims of the splits between those movements, and the concessions that Anthony, by the age of seventy-eight, had made to conservative reform—all of which intensified the dilemma of black women.

It was only within the work of the suffrage associations that Anthony took woman's political rights to be their sole issue. Outside of the National-American, she worked toward women's unity and emancipation in many fields. Particularly in her international work, she emphasized the broader range of woman's rights. Since their first International Council in 1888, the international women's rights movement had emphasized women's education and work over the political demand for woman's suffrage, because many women in European countries were not yet able to raise that demand. But by 1904, enough progress had been made toward women's rights in Europe that the time was right to form an international woman's suffrage association as part of the International Council meeting in Berlin. For two years, Carrie Chapman Catt had been preparing for this step, and Anthony eagerly awaited the Berlin meeting and the introduction of Catt's plan for an international woman's suffrage movement.

Making her first ocean voyage, Mary accompanied her eighty-four-year-old sister Susan to Europe. The journey invigorated Susan; she loved being at sea. "It is so green that you feel so safe when at sea—it seems like a house afloat."[31] Typically, she was up in the morning before anyone else and was soon moving about awakening Ida Harper, Anna Shaw, and niece Lucy for breakfast. Even on the coldest days she walked the deck, with Mary always at her side. Her legs bothered her "after walking round the deck once or twice. So I am glad to sit down & wrap up—and go into dream land. It is so queer that you feel so safe when at sea."[32]

The International Council was a grand success. When Catt's proposal for an international suffrage campaign was adopted, Susan told Anna Shaw that this was the climax of her career.[33] Mary was impressed with the grand meetings, and she noted that they took place "with apparently so little friction as might occur in an affair of less importance." She predicted that if the German women continued in this way, they would become the political equals of men "long before their American sisters will be thus honored." She attributed the success of the meeting and the progress of the cause of German women to the "more intelligent, not merely well to do, but wealthy people who have become interested and have made the whole thing so popular."[34]

There are always humble moments, even at the climax of a grand career. When the German suffragists held a mass public meeting during the congress, they asked Anthony to remain at her hotel, fearing that her presence would dominate their platform. When the meeting opened and Susan B. Anthony did not appear, the crowd was agitated. "The entire audience rose, men jumped in their chairs and the cheering continued without a break for 10 minutes." After the meeting Anna Shaw burst into Anthony's hotel room and found her sitting alone and very solemn, almost sad. Excited, Anna poured out the story of the event and told of how the crowd had called for "Susan B. Anthony." Susan sat there motionless trying to be stoic, but her "lips quivered and her brave old eyes filled with tears." This was one of the few times that Anna Shaw saw behind Susan's stoic presence. She realized that while Susan had dutifully remained in her room, "all the time the woman's heart longed for affection and recognition."[35]

Before the congress concluded, Augusta Victoria, the Queen Consort, received the women for a reception at her palace, and the city fathers of Berlin gave them a banquet that dazzled Mary. "It was, by far, the *biggest* thing of the kind that any of us ever witnessed—when the doors of the refreshment rooms were thrown open, the tables with decoration of American beauties & other flowers, the number, size of tables—the brilliant electric lighting, the magnificent granite pillars & beautiful mirrors was a sight for a modest American to see." When they found the lemonade tinged with wine, Susan and her sister, teetotalers since their Quaker youth, called for water while they dined on "fish, roast beef, boiled ham and tongue" with "strawberries, jellies and the sweets later."[36]

Susan and Mary traveled throughout Germany with Anna Shaw and Lucy Anthony, then went on to England for a month-long visit before leaving for home. This time their ocean voyage was overshadowed with the news that their brother D.R. in Kansas was very ill and not expected to live. Although Susan was exhausted from the trip, as soon as they arrived home she and Mary left almost immediately for Leavenworth. By the time they arrived they found D.R. improved, but he was very weak. Susan worried and waited. She had thought that her brothers and sister Mary would survive her. But four years before, J. Merritt had died suddenly. Susan had been crushed and wept for days on end.[37] Merritt was Susan's youngest brother who, like D.R., had gone to Kansas to fight pro-slavery forces during the controversy over whether Kansas would come into the Union as a slave or free state. Before the Civil War, Merritt had fought with John Brown and had then enlisted to fight with the North from 1861 to 1865. He settled in Kansas after the war, raised his family, and lived there the rest of his life. Now in 1904, it was evident that Susan would survive her only other brother, D.R. After ten days of visiting with him, Susan, herself very weak, conceded to the family decision that she must immediately return to Rochester and rest. But a month later, she received a telegram at home telling her and Mary that D.R. had died. The grief-stricken sisters again boarded a train for Kansas for his funeral. Daniel, who had been the editor of the Leavenworth paper and mayor of the city, had retired with a comfortable income. After taking care of his wife in his will, at Susan's request, he left five thousand dollars to the National-American Woman Suffrage Association. Unknown to Susan until the will was read, he left twelve hundred dollars to her and Mary to be paid annually for the rest of their lives.

In studying the life of Susan B. Anthony—following her from one trip to another, across the ocean and the continent several times, with hundreds of shorter trips and dozens of campaigns, too many to mention all of them in her biography—one comes to realize that the young girl who suffered severe homesickness at Deborah Moulson's academy had grown into a woman who lived on the road. Traveling to campaigns, meetings, and councils had become a way of life for Susan, which would end only with her death.

She surprised her friends again when she announced that she would attend the National-American convention scheduled for Portland, Oregon, in June of 1905. Even she admitted that "I never expected to go over the mountains again but this *Convention* has made me go. I have only missed one convention since the War and I missed *one before the war* . . . and I don't like to make a break."[38] She knew her time was short, but "I feel that it would be just as well if I reached the end on the cars or anywhere else as at home." Therefore, there was nothing to stop her when the California suffragists asked that she return to them once again as long as she was already on the West Coast. Sister Mary was with her, and now she would not travel anywhere without Anna Shaw. "I give myself over entirely to Miss Shaw. Wherever she goes I shall probably go."[39] So off they all went to California, where Susan with her friends visited first the northern part of the state: Shasta Springs, Red Bluffs, and Chico. They had a longer visit to San Francisco then went on to San Jose and finally Los Angeles with a visit to Venice. Having been on the West Coast since early June, they headed east on August 4.

In February of 1904, there had been a reception at the White House in honor of Anthony's eighty-fourth birthday. She had been unimpressed with the personal tribute paid to her by the politicians and the President. But the President's recognition of woman's suffrage—something consistently withheld—would have pleased her. During the reception, she approached Theodore Roosevelt, who was then running for his second term of office. "Now Mr. President, we don't intend to trouble you during the campaign, but after you are elected, look out for us."[40] True to her promise, two weeks after his reelection in 1905 she was at the White House for a private appointment with Roosevelt. Anthony had seen how Booker T. Washington had been able to influence Roosevelt during his first term in office. Roosevelt had come to rely on Washington for advice on Negro issues and for presidential appointments of blacks.

Anthony wanted the same attention for women and told Roosevelt so in her meeting with him. Would he mention woman's suffrage in his speeches? Yes, he would recognize women "as wives, as mothers, as wage-earners, but never with any reference to political rights." Would he put women on boards and commissions? Well, he would consider it. Would he see that suffrage was extended to the women of the Philippines, now going through the final annexation as a territory? "What! Give the franchise to those Oriental women!" Anthony argued this point to no avail. Finally, she leaned forward in her chair with a sense of urgency, and her voice was firm but intense as she laid her hand on his arm. "Mr. Roosevelt, this is my principal request—it is almost the last request I shall ever make of anybody." She appealed to a higher dignity. "Before you leave the presidential chair, recommend Congress to submit to the Legislatures a Constitutional Amendment which will enfranchise women, and thus take your place in history with Lincoln, the great emancipator."[41] Roosevelt did not respond to her either then or for the remainder of his term in office.

After her meeting with Roosevelt, while resting in Philadelphia with Anna Shaw and her niece Lucy, Susan decided on another visit— this time to President M. Carey Thomas of Bryn Mawr. President Thomas greeted them and gave them a tour of the campus. Having taken her doctoral degree in Switzerland twenty years before, President Thomas had turned her love of scholarship into a first-rate college for women. Taking hold of the school with the powerful force of her own magnetic and sometimes autocratic personality, she established an undergraduate program and a graduate school in one of the most demanding of academic curriculums, the German tradition of "mental discipline" in which she had studied.

After a tour of the college, Anthony and Anna Shaw sat down to dine with Thomas and her companion, Mary Garrett, a philanthropist and strong supporter of woman's suffrage. "Miss Thomas," Anthony began over lunch, "your buildings are beautiful; your new library is a marvel; but they are not the cause of our presence here." Thomas expected as much. "I know you have something on your mind. I am waiting for you to tell me what it is." Anthony had on her mind the upcoming February 1906 National-American convention. She explained that she wanted both Thomas and Garrett to "make our Baltimore convention a success," by arranging "a college night on the programme—a great college night, with the best college speakers ever brought together."[42] Anthony wanted the world to witness the advancement of woman. When these accomplishments were understood, women's political rights could no longer be denied. For that purpose, the women college leaders must be brought into the cause.

The strain of travel and political work, along with the worry of how to pass on her movement to others, was great on Anthony. Her heart was weak, and while she was with M. Carey Thomas, she fainted. "It seemed as if all the hold-together muscles just let go." She was confined to bed there for ten days. When she reached home in Rochester after Thanksgiving, she was deluged with get-well letters and Christmas gifts.

By February, she had regained some of her strength and so decided to attend the convention in Baltimore. In the face of a severe northern New York blizzard with drifting snow and icy winds blowing off Lake Ontario, Susan insisted on leaving for Baltimore. Mary was at her side in a closed carriage, which was found for the ride to the train station. Susan, wrapped in blankets, did not have the resistance to withstand the severe weather and developed a bad cold. By the time she reached Washington, neuralgia had settled in. Mary Garrett offered her Baltimore home for Susan's comfort. A physician was brought in from Johns Hopkins who ordered a trained nurse to constantly attend her. Mary and Anna Shaw asked that the nurse dress as a maid so that Susan would not realize the seriousness of her condition.

Anna Shaw, now president of the National-American, and other close "nieces," which included M. Carey Thomas and Mary Garrett, attended the convention and then joined Susan and Mary each day to apprise them of the progress of the meetings. At the end of the day, M. Carey Thomas and Mary Garrett were constantly with Susan. "As we sat at her feet day after day between the sessions of the convention listening to what she wanted us to do to help women and asking her questions, I realized that she was the *greatest person that I had ever met.*"[43] President Thomas was taken aback when she learned from Anna Shaw how few the resources were that sustained the cause and how dependent the movement was on voluntary contributions. In Quakerly fashion she said to

Mary Garrett, "I don't think that we have quite done our duty in this matter." In fact, the same thing was on Susan's mind as she lay in bed day after day. There must be a great fund for woman's suffrage; she could not leave this world without raising the money to sustain Anna Shaw and the movement and keep them advancing in the coming years.

Finally, after long discussions with Anthony, Thomas and Garrett announced to the business committee of the National-American that they would raise sixty thousand dollars to be paid to the cause at a rate of twelve thousand dollars a year for five years.[44] And they kept their word. Susan was weak, but now she was at peace. This had finally settled one of her remaining concerns in passing on the movement to the younger generation.

A woman doctor, nurses, sister Mary, loving couples of women— Anna Shaw still living and working with niece Lucy Anthony, M. Carey Thomas and Mary Garrett—formed Susan's world now, a kind of private realization of the dreams for the true woman, the beckoning of an epoch of single women that Susan had so much believed would transform the world.

Susan struggled from her bed to attend the college-night program of the National-American, having missed all the other sessions. Finally, the meetings in Washington concluded with a celebration of her eighty-sixth birthday. Even the train ride from Baltimore was unbearable for Susan. When she arrived, she told her friends to "take me to my room quickly, I have been suffering the most excruciating torture ever since we left Baltimore."[45] She mustered what little strength she had left and appeared for the birthday celebration as if she had completely recovered.

From the Capitol congressmen had sent greetings to her, which were read at length along with a note from President Roosevelt. They were personal messages, all of them. But Anthony was not flattered, "When will men do something besides extend congratulations? I would rather President Roosevelt say one word to Congress in favor of amending the Constitution to give women suffrage than to praise me endlessly."

Soon it would be time for her closing remarks. It had been a lovely but solemn evening. Despite the presence she maintained throughout the evening, her suffering and weakness showed through. It was not a jubilant affair, and Susan knew that she was dying. Standing close to Anna Shaw, with her hand on Shaw's shoulder, she encouraged the women to carry on the struggle and finally, almost interrupting herself, she looked into the distance for a brief moment and concluded her short talk by emphatically declaring, "Failure is impossible!" She never spoke another word in public.

Sister Mary was with Susan at every moment as was the nurse Thomas had brought from Johns Hopkins. Both accompanied Susan in the train back to Rochester. She arrived home early in the morning of February 17, but she was too weak even to climb the stairs to her bed until late that day. She never came down again. She fell into double pneumonia, and two nurses were there to attend to her constantly. Susan was ready to die just as she had said she would be when she could no longer work. She recovered from the pneumonia, but her heart was weak. Her woman doctor revealed that she had had valvular heart trouble for six years.

Susan's niece Lucy came and spent hours reading her the letters that arrived each day, and Mary was constantly at her sister's bedside. There was unfinished business on Susan's mind. On March 7, without announcing that she was coming, Anna Shaw arrived. Mary was relieved. "Oh, Anna Shaw." She fondly embraced the woman who had become her sister's closest companion since Susan had retired from the presidency of the National-American. "We have been wanting you all day! Early this morning Sister Susan said she must see you and talk with you. She insisted so much that I should write you that I finally did so and about an hour ago mailed the letter."[46] Anna started up the stairs, but Mary cautioned that Susan was sleeping. Anna Shaw waited and went to Susan the first thing the next morning after the doctor had left her room.

Then began a series of long conversations, Anna sitting next to Susan's bed with Susan holding her hands. Susan had made out a will to dispose of some of the money she had received in recent years. Now she meant to "revoke every other money gift which I have made in previous letters of request to my executors"—all must go to the fund for the cause. In her final years, Susan actually had a small income from the annuity Rachel Foster Avery had arranged for her and from the stipulations of D.R.'s will. At that time, she had a total of $2,308.48 in the bank and in securities. Then there were two $500 governments bonds, five shares of stock at $165 each, and three lots in Kansas, left to her by her brothers. All, Susan directed, was to go to the memorial fund for the National-American, which was administered by M. Carey Thomas.

Then Susan spent hours reminiscing over the "happy, happy times we have traveled about together," even though the work was often hard and wearying. Only once in these days did she express sadness in her life. "Just think of it, Anna, I have been striving for over sixty years for a little bit of justice no bigger than that, and yet I must die without obtaining it. Oh, it seems so cruel!" Anna tried to be encouraging and hopeful, trying to convince her that she would get well; but Susan knew she was close to death. It did not worry her. "I wish I could live on, but I cannot . . . my poor old body is worn out." She looked intently into Anna's eyes; there was something more. "Before I go I want you to give me a promise: Promise me that you will keep the presidency of the association as long as you are well enough to do the work."

Holding Susan's hand in hers, Anna was hesitant. "How can I promise that. I can keep it only as long as others wish me to keep it."

Susan was firm. "Promise to make them wish you to keep it."

"But if the time comes when I believe that some one else can do better work in the presidency than I, then let me feel at liberty to resign it."

"No, no, you cannot be the judge of that. Promise me you will remain until the friends you most trust tell you it is time to withdraw, or make you understand that it is time. Promise me that."

Anna promised, and Susan gave her final instructions: "No matter what is done or is not done, how you are criticized or misunderstood, or what efforts are made to block your path, remember that the only fear you need have is the fear of not standing by the thing you believe to be right. Take your stand and hold it: then let come what will, and receive the blows like a good soldier."

Anna was overcome. Susan did not want to leave her standing alone. "Anna, if there is a continuance of life beyond, and if I have any conscious knowledge of this world and of what you are doing. I shall not be far away from you; and in times of need I will help you all I can."

During the last two days, Mary sat next to Susan's bed watching and comforting. Anna knelt at her bedside holding her hand. Neither relaxed the vigil. Susan, on the verge of unconsciousness, began to utter names. They were the names of the women in her life— some who had gone over the river, some unknown to anyone in the room, others loyal suffragists. "They all seemed to file past her dying eyes that day in an endless, shadowy review, and as they went by she spoke to each of them." She came back to consciousness, her cheek on Anna's hand. "They are still passing before me—face after face, hundreds and hundreds of them . . . I know how hard they have worked. I know the sacrifices they have made."[47]

There was one more thing. Susan fully regained consciousness and became restless while she looked into Anna's eyes with a certain intensity. Anna knew. "Do you want me to repeat my promise?" Susan lightly shook her head and Anna promised again. "As I did so she raised my hand to her lips and kissed it" and passed into unconsciousness. For thirty hours Susan lay unconscious, gripping Anna's hand and reaching after it if Anna slipped away for a moment. Mary sat near her sister's bed in her own agony watching and waiting. At 12:40 A.M. on Tuesday, March 13, 1906 Susan B. Anthony died.

Epilogue

TWELVE WOMEN DRESSED IN WHITE FORMED A GUARD AROUND her casket and kept a vigil there, while ten thousand mourners passed by. She was dressed in her traditional black silk with the jeweled pin of an American flag on her breast. Four tiny diamonds were the only stars—for the suffrage states. Mary, pressing her handkerchief hard to her lips, sat silently and carried her grief stoically as her sister would have. She sat this way until at the funeral an old, poor black woman, leaning on a crutch, came in and upon seeing Susan's body sobbed aloud. Mary could endure no longer, and the "tears streamed down her cheeks and it seemed as if her heart would break."

After the mourners passed by, the doors of the Central Presbyterian Church were closed, the pin removed from Susan's gown and given to Anna Howard Shaw, and the simple Quaker casket was closed. The doors were reopened for the twenty-five hundred people who attended the funeral, while several hundred stood outside in the blustery March storm. The honor bearers, women students from the University of Rochester, dressed in their black academic gowns complete with their mortarboards, carried the flowers sent to Susan's house and led the family and closest friends in the funeral procession behind the casket.

Reverend Anna Howard Shaw spoke the final words.

There is no death for such as she. There are no last words of love. The ages to come will revere her name. Unnumbered generations of the children of men shall rise up to call her blessed. That which seems

death to our unseeing eyes is to her translation. Her work will not be
finished, nor will her last word be spoken, while there remains a wrong
to be righted or a fettered life to be freed in all the earth. You do well
to strew her bier with palms of victory and to crown her with unfading
laurel, for never did more victorious hero enter into rest.

On Women's Biography

IN 1897, WHILE ELIZABETH CADY STANTON WAS PREPARING HER memoirs, she wrote Susan B. Anthony:

> Dear Susan, I do think in this earlier part of your life there should be some mysterious or undefined references to some faint suffering love affair. If your sisters can glean any facts in that line from your true inwardness, nothing could be more agreeable to me than to weave a sentimental chapter entitled, for insistence "The Romance of Susan B. Anthony's Younger Days." How all the daily papers would jump at that![1]

Stanton had a reason for wanting to create a new image of her best friend. During their time, Anthony and women like her—women who refused to be dependent on men and who committed themselves to their own sex through the women's rights movement— were portrayed by Henry James in *The Bostonians* as fanatically driven, unfulfilled, incomplete women. Freud offered the world a clinical diagnosis to explain single women who lived as Anthony did; their choice was labeled sexual repression or sublimation of sex into work. And by the turn of the century, the woman who refused to be dominated was seen by sexologists as cold and hard. In Anthony's case, her passionate charisma was reduced to evidence of rigid authoritarianism.

This letter, typical of Stanton's humor, also reflected her submission to romantic essentialism. She knew that an account of her best friend's love life would have justified Anthony's work and her political life. Late in her own life, even Anthony herself succumbed to presenting to the public an identity which was not actually her own. Several times when questioned by reporters on the subject of her love life, she said that she had been in love many times, and then quickly restored her story to her own reality by turning it into a political statement, saying that marriage without equality was inconceivable to her, and that she had never met an equal to marry. But in the process to prove that she was normal and not sick or aberrant, she would overstate the being-in-love-several-times story (which was actually a relatively insignificant reality in her life). Whether or not this gave her ego satisfaction, it was something she eventually understood as necessary to get people to listen to and take seriously her political demands.

Patriarchal society will not accept any woman who refuses to be dominated. If she persists thus, it rewrites her history and reshapes her character, punitively twisting her will, bending her image, and distorting her identity until her defiance appears as a deformity— an aberration of nature. But over time it has proven impossible to completely suppress the reality of the lives of independent, self-defined women such as Susan B. Anthony. They periodically re-emerge from behind the historical deformation of their lives to defy patriarchy once again. In traditional history, a life like Anthony's seems to be an anomaly; but to feminists, the anomaly suggests that this kind of life story has more to say about all women. In feminist research, the anomaly—the "rupture of history"—is often the point where we begin to look for women's reality. It is there that we comprehend the fuller extent of what patriarchy has distorted or excluded in its domination of women.[2]

Like any other oppressed group, women live in the contradiction of actively and creatively constructing their own identity while the male-dominated society imposes a reductive, biologized identity upon them thus making them merely products of drives and instincts. To the extent that women's lives do not fit the traditional female definitions, all women are misfits.

For the past two decades the study of women's history and feminist theory has generated new research and insights that have begun to correct masculinized history. We have now reached a critical juncture where history and theory require grounding in women's realities. Women's biography is emerging as a new genre, which can challenge the very structure and categories of the history men have jealously guarded as their own.

Historical sociologists are beginning to un-think the dualisms in which macro has been disconnected from the micro and the individual has been dissociated from theories of society. And French philosopher Paul Ricoeur has criticized top-down history for replacing "the subjects of action with entities that are anonymous" and for making history a science that studies nations, societies, social classes, or mentalities.[3] Feminist historians have broken ground by demonstrating the discontinuity between women's history and traditional historical periodization.[4] By unpeopling history and sociology, and disconnecting daily life and subjective reality from the epochs, periods, and major social categories, grand history and macro-sociology have remained the strongholds of patriarchal thought. These disciplines are concerned with the history of the great wars, the grand philosophical traditions, the stories of great men, and the origins of theories. In reaction to male control of history women have recaptured a history of women—a new social history "from the bottom up." But the social history of women has not yet seriously impinged on or forced a reformulation of periodization and grand political and economic theories.

Biography requires that we be true to our subject, that we not only re-create the phenomenology of daily life to uncover the subjectivity of the self but that we locate our subject in her own historical context and that requires reperiodization. Thus biography can render the constructed divisions that separate social history from grand history, divorce theory from reality, macro from micro, into false categorizations.[5] The theory of women's biography I am developing since completing Susan B. Anthony's life story moves in a progression from the phenomenology of daily life to the structure of history. This theory is meant to force the anomalies and the distortions and eclipses of masculinized history into a new clarity. This is the beginning of a new study but I have chosen to develop some of the ideas here as they have been motivated by this study of Anthony's life.

History is key to the structuring of human subjectivity as it offers a past from which we can locate ourselves in time, culture, and community. When women are defined in terms of essentialist roles that are drawn from instinctual or biological mandates, they are confined to a personal past and known only through private existence.

I am posing a very clear opposition between imposed essentialist determinism that defines the female and the active social construction of herself in the world. I am intentionally situating these as polar opposites to create ideal types that crystallize the fullest reality of each end of the spectrum of identity, realizing that all that is between them is more complicated and confused than the oppositions themselves represent.

Discovering the Acting Subject

Feminists are looking at history with a new eye—the eye of woman from her own historical group—the collective base of networks from which women come to be known as acting subjects of history. By history we mean subjective history. Our documents are women's lives: their letters, diaries, testimony, experiences, and interactions.

Subjective history begins with the life story. This is what Ricoeur refers to as a return to the narrative. He argues that "history cannot . . . sever every connection with narrative without losing its historical character."[6] However, the narrative or life history must begin by garnering the facts and re-creating the objective conditions of an individual's life. That is where I began with Susan B. Anthony's life. I began by reading all of her diaries, papers, and letters, and even many of the books in her personal library, which is now in the Library of Congress. I followed her through exciting events and, likewise, lived through the mundane day-to-day routine, the repetitiveness that was reflected in many letters and diaries. Then as I read the statements from the woman's rights movement, their conference calls and documents, articles from newspapers that covered their actions and Anthony's appearance in one city after another, she became more present to me, despite the century difference in our lives. I read her favorite novels, the ones most popular with women of her day, especially novelists and poets like Charlotte Brontë and Elizabeth Barrett Browning. I finally perceived from her reading of these novels what inspired her and what in them reflected her own life to her. This brought her even closer to me. Then I visited the villages and cities where she lived, spending afternoons walking down country roads and into city backyards to see what she saw. And while I was writing about her political work and sometimes finding her too distant from me, I even stood up, set up something like a lectern on my work table, and read some of her speeches aloud, as if they were being presented to audiences. I finally got a feel for her, a sense of who she was that went far beyond a studied analysis of her life. This was a different way of knowing that made her very present to me.

But to this point of the research, biographical study is only descriptive and is not yet connected to human subjectivity—that is, the self, the life force. The research has established the historical context from which biography grows from narrative into interpretation. Anthony would have remained a distant object, a model with whom I identified but did not know, until I went one step further and began to interpret the facts of her life by deriving the actual meaning she attributed to those facts. The research into her papers and documents allowed me to reconstruct the objective conditions of situations in Anthony's life. From them I was able to interpret the meanings that she attributed to her interactions both with herself and with others.

When we engage in this kind of interpretation with our subject when writing a biography, we necessarily interact with that individual. We begin to know our subject the way we know others in our lives. From that kind of knowing, we hope to be able to approximate how our subject knew herself and others in her life. As Anthony interpreted the words and gestures of those in her life, I found that the more fully I approximated her meaning in interpreting her words and actions, the more fully she became a subject to me because I was involved with her. As I began to understand Anthony's interactions with others, such as her family, her friends, and her foes and colleagues, I came to know her in a way that actually developed into a relationship with her over time. She was no longer the object of my study, she had become a subject to me.

But how can one be sure of their interpretation of the meaning of the "other," when the "other" is not present to verify it? Sociologists usually rely on large numbers of subjects to reveal the patterns of social behavior because they can be interpreted as representative. It is different with biography. As I progressed in my involvement with Anthony, I began to find myself almost automatically predicting her response or her course of action in particular situations; from the information in her letters or other documents, she would verify my interpretation. This is what sociologists call saturation when studying collective life histories; it is that point which one reaches when a certain predictability intervenes and is verified.[7]

By this time, the relationship with the subject has passed beyond the basic level of interpretation just described. Instead, as we do with close friends, we assume a subjective connection even before systematically interpreting an action or trying to find the meaning of a phrase. Regarding our friends we can be prompted to say, "I know she would not do that" or "That isn't like her" or "She's just like that." We presume something because our interactions have taken us in closer, into a deeper level of knowing, that of subject to subject—intersubjectivity. And this is how I came to know Susan B. Anthony. At first there was an initial attraction and an interest in getting to know her better. It was not an instant knowledge or liking but one that developed over time and created closeness. For in involving ourselves in women's lives and touching their subjectivity, we begin to know what will ring true for them. This gave me a truly objective and dialectical point of reference to challenge the traditional historical interpretation of Anthony's life.

I summarized this dynamic of subjective interaction in a 1986 paper I delivered in Paris. "We are concerned here with the subjectivity of self as the self comes to be known to itself through interaction with others and with oneself where the interaction involves interpreting and internalizing the meaning of the other who then does not remain an object but becomes a subject to the self, a subject as the subjectivity in the interaction emerges and is internalized by the other. This is not only the basis for interpreting biography, but it forms the core of social life, it creates the connections among individuals, the means by which we are located in the social world. One's subjectivity, however, can never be fully or completely comprehended or interpreted by the other; nor should we want to for it is in the fullness of my own subjectivity that I am the 'me' who is distinguished from others, this is where we know the unique in ourselves."[8]

Finding and revealing a woman's subjectivity should not be confused with identifying with her. Many biographers today talk about their identification with their subject to the extent that it is sometimes assumed that to write a biography is to write one's autobiography. I disagree. It is true that women like Susan B. Anthony and Elizabeth Cady Stanton remain important models for women of today. Many women have identified with them, likened our struggle to theirs, and have taken courage from their spirited lives. But the biographer must take a further step to transcend personal identification with her subject. As the biographer of Susan B. Anthony, if I identified with her, finding my life in her biography, I would have falsely equated us. Ultimately, identification is not an equation at all but a kind of heroine worship; it is an objectification of the other— a refusal of subjectivity. Instead of identification, I came to share a dialectical relationship with Anthony that continually revealed more to me about how she knew herself and from herself how she knew and interacted with others. Surprisingly, I came to know more of myself through my interaction with her. Subjectivity, the necessary but sufficient condition of women's biography, can only be understood in an historical context—that which reveals the acting subject in movement over time.

Probably the most important impact of essentialist determinism in the (de)formation of human subjectivity is in how it shapes temporality. To define women by their sexuality and reproductivity is to remove them from the progression of history. In contrast to the historical understanding women as acting subjects of history, through essentialism women are universalized by sexual relations and/or motherhood.

Without a concrete location in history, there is no social cohesion to bind woman to woman. Likewise without a group identity, women are made more vulnerable to being ahistorical. This is where essentialism enters and makes women socially atomized. Woman, alone with her husband, lover, or family is isolated her from the social realities that would bond her with her sex. Essentialism as such constitutes an effort to annihilate women's subjectivity. It is a lie about one's self. It is a lie about women, because it rests on the assumption that one's self is unrelated to other similar selves. To not be able to identify oneself with a "we" is to not take one's group or oneself as subjects of history.

Susan B. Anthony's biography is the story of a single woman who constructed her life course by surpassing the impositions of biological determinisms on her identity, while the social rejection she experienced for nonidentity with woman's role revealed the regulatory force it held over women as a class. Because she was single and therefore able to sustain an unbroken identity with her sex her biography reveals that when woman is married and therefore not able to be a woman unto herself she is isolated from other women and must construct her primary identity through her husband and her family. Marriage and any form of relationship which causes women to shift their identity from themselves separates women from each other, denies them their identity with their own sex—their class of women—and therefore denies them a true "we." For Anthony, being single—that is, a woman unto herself—no longer meant being alone and separate. Her life story reveals that for her being single meant affirming her identity as a woman with women. In other words, she did not have to become unsingle. She did not have to change her name, her legal status, or shift her needs and identity from herself and her woman's world to a mate, as did her married sisters. For Susan B. Anthony, being single meant that she identified with a woman's "we." Because she was not married she was able to live in, with, and through her own group—women. This unbroken identity eventually led her to the center of the women's movement, where her political identification with her own group was built not only in reaction to being oppressed but also from the independence of women coming together out of their own strength. In this way, women transcend the alienation of the self, which becomes locked into essentialist meanings, by actively pursuing their own lives in a social context that does not prohibit group identification. The social construction of self that refuses to be determined by natural, in-evitable roles provides the beginning point for exploring who women are as a class, and that will ultimately direct us to locate women in a valid historical context.

Not being particularly interested in marriage and ultimately re-fusing the role of the old maid, Anthony faced the world with few models before her. At that moment she began to make choices. Even though she was not sure what she would do or where it would take her, she discovered a new sense of the future that opened up before her. Her seemingly ordinary choices, such as deciding to spend more time working for temperance reform than in her garden which she loved, were relentlessly moving her into directions women had not taken before.

Unmarked by ceremony, gifts, and congratulations, the choice to be single is usually found in small acts, seemingly insignificant de-cisions that move one in immediately imperceptible ways away from marriage—sometimes even before one has rejected marriage per se. It may not be so much a reaction against marriage more than it is a disinterest in this social institution. Being single involves no dra-matic breaks, no severing or disruption of one's identity.

Making choices moved Susan out of her cousin's family. It broke her away from women's private sphere. But when I followed her from the private sphere to the public world, it became apparent that merely having an independent will and income was not enough to prepare her for the world outside of the home and teaching.

True womanhood—with its personal, moralistic piety—was seen as not only appropriate for women's morality but for rearing chil-dren (which is why teaching was so compatible with women's private sphere). Women had internalized the Puritan morality that caused them to understand the character of morality as individual, self searching, signified by the transgression of God's will, rectified by a personal piety that led to righteousness over private behaviors. Women monitored themselves, each other, and their children.

Confined to an individual level, this moralistic piety became for many women a way of not knowing the world outside the family—their private sphere. When Anthony began her political work, she interacted in a different historical context. Her moral piety shifted while her moral percepts did not.

This change from home to society, from private moralistic piety to public, group-oriented moral analysis of issues in ethical terms fit for public discourse was not only a personal shift for Susan B. Anthony. Her individual experience at this time was mirrored by the women's movement in general. I agree with the feminist historians who credit the women who participated in temperance reform work in the 1840s with the real beginnings of the nineteenth-century American women's rights movement. But further distinctions must be made between the two moments of women's protest. The first phase associated with early temperance work was preconscious feminism. Temperance reform focused on individuals and on personal solutions to private behavior that would remain private. The reformers thought neither of changing society nor of analyzing the problem beyond its individual manifestations. Their approach was: If liquor makes men drunk and drunk men are abusive then take the liquor away from them. Women could speak in public but from a personal morality meant only for the private sphere. In many ways, this assured their opponents that their threats were ultimately harmless. With the Declaration of Sentiments, written by Elizabeth Cady Stanton and adopted at the 1848 Seneca Falls convention, that privatized morality was transformed into political issues that confronted the civil and legal structures that supported patriarchal domination of women.

Personal transformation of morality involves restructuring women's subjectivity. In 1852, as president of Anthony's newly formed Woman's State Temperance Society, Stanton declared: "Let no woman remain in the relation of wife with a confirmed drunkard. Let no drunkard be the father of her children. . . . Let us petition our State government so to modify the laws affecting marriage and the custody of children, that the drunkard shall have no claims on wife or child." When Anthony's morality was transformed to the public sphere, she reversed social causality. She showed that it was not alcohol that threatens women and the family, but the structure of marriage that made women vulnerable to drunken husbands.

Her new analysis reflected a shift in emphasis to society, group behavior, institutions, and political meanings. Her private righteousness over personal transgression became externalized to a civil responsibility and an egalitarian ethic fit for confronting social issues in the public world. Anthony learned that it was not women's private, moralistic piety that allowed women to influence the world as the guardians of its morality. It was actually the reverse: The public sphere controlled by men, defined the limits and shaped the possibilities of the private. As Anthony's subjectivity reformed around her egalitarian ethics, her political work took on clear definition. A violation of the moral code was no longer wrong because it offended some vague precepts of propriety or ideas of personal sinfulness, but because it violated human beings' civil and political rights. Further, that violation was found not only in individual acts, it was systematized into institutions like marriage and slavery and legalized by the courts and governments. Transformation from internalized piety to moral and ethical positions taken in the public world was a struggle in political consciousness, a story of the reformulation of subjectivity that became necessary once Anthony began to make choices that took her outside the home and teaching.

What I am developing here is a theory of women's subjectivity and political consciousness which identifies development as transformation and not merely a progression from one stage to another. Political consciousness is consciousness of domination and it requires *un*learning what one has been taught in order to not know that one and one's group are the objects of domination. Under domination morality is internalized and shapes the self so that it will not conflict with or challenge power. In the nineteenth century, that meant adhering to a morality that was not meant to go beyond the private sphere. To take moral and ethical positions over their demands for legal and political rights, women and their movement had to transform their morality into an ethical responsibility that would reflect both their analysis of collective domination and the moral bases for their proposed remedies. In Anthony's case, this meant abandoning the piety of true womanhood for a morality based on radical egalitarianism.

The effect on Anthony was pronounced and it reveals how political consciousness shapes subjectivity. Consciousness of domination produced awareness of the possibilities which would surpass it. As Anthony's public work opened new futures to her with many unknowns before her, her life began to reveal what had happened to women like her married sisters whose lives were defined by impossibilities rather than opportunities. Marriage revealed what women cannot, must not, should not and ultimately will not do. Anthony transformed the objective reality of an old maid's life into a new reality for herself, which surpassed the previous definition of women,[9] and the future opened before her. By transforming personal piety into civil responsibility, she began to connect her experience of choice and possibility to all women and to the objective conditions that block their future, as well as the conditions that transcend their immanence, which domination makes impossible.[10] This revealing knowledge of the self and the other is *political consciousness*.

The fulcrum between the individual and history is the social group. In 1949, Simone de Beauvoir noted that except in feminist gatherings, women do not say "we." By contrast, "Proletarians say 'We'; Negroes also. Regarding themselves as subjects, they transform the bourgeois, the whites, into 'others.' But women do not say we."[11] Women will not enter history one by one; that is not the nature of power and domination. Whether or not any one woman overtly identifies with women as her group, women exist as a class by virtue of their collective relations to male power. To claim their own history, women must be located in their own historical group.

How then do women form their own group identity? What is involved in restructuring subjectivity from being unsingle to identification with oneself and with women. Determinisms are overcome through choice. Making choices and projecting from the past onto a new activity means realizing not only what one *can* do but what one *must* do. This continually reveals new possibilities—new becoming.[12] Again Anthony's life is illustrative. As I indicated (in this biography)—the decision to remain single—is socially (that is, politically) interpreted as an inevitability or nonchoice. Deciding to marry is given the appearance of a dramatic decision marked by legal announcements, civil and religious ceremonies, change of residence, and for the woman change of social status. In other words, marriage appears to be the institution that is socially constructed and chosen—therefore not at all inevitable. Yet it is the legitimized social location that encloses women in atemporal, universalized roles of sexuality and motherhood, the active context in which domination is internalized and inevitability becomes subjectively structured in dissociation from woman's group identity. The ontological loneliness of being unsingle, when identity is formed around and through someone other than one's self, is the consequence of women breaking their identity from their *subjective we*.

In opposition to this world view of woman stands woman's dream to be a woman unto herself. To be a woman whose identity and life are shaped through her ideas, her actions, and her own projects. The desire to live with another and, contradictorily, to be a woman unto oneself is more of a dilemma for many late twentieth-century women than it was for their sisters a century before. Some women attempt to approximate that dream by finding "a room of one's own." Others realize some of what it means to be woman unto oneself when their children are grown and gone, and they are no longer with their mate. Tragically, some women never touch these possibilities. Indeed, in our times, it is the intention of right-wing antifeminism to insure that women never will.

Biography as History

From examining women's lives, we can redefine the meaning of being a woman and discover what masculine history has suppressed: how women make history and therefore who women are. Thus, women's biography must be a new reading of history, which demands the rewriting of all history. But that is not enough. Women's lives have either been hidden behind the portrayals of them as wives, mothers, and lovers; or, when women cannot be defined through essentialist images, their lives have been viciously distorted, as in the case of Susan B. Anthony.

Too often biographies of women have short changed their subjects by assuming that the fullness of woman's subjectivity is equatable with their personal lives, where intimate relations with husbands, lovers, and children often usurp the search for interaction and subjectivity that we discover when we find the diverse and significant ways women act in their own historical circumstances. The emerging genre of women's biography must be based on a search for women's subjectivity, where the subject becomes known to us through her actions and her history.

History becomes a dynamic active force revealed in the present, acting on the future. Therefore this concept of women's biography cannot be concerned with "placing women in history," as if history is an already formed reality and all we need to do is make a slot in it for women.

Here we must distinguish between the interpretation necessary in women's biography from that in biographies of men. Generally men's life stories reflect the known society and accepted renditions of history. Consequently traditional historical periodization provides a valid base for interpreting men's lives because it highlights and reveals them. But women's biography must break through the essentialisms that have a grasp on their identities and give them their place in society. In lifting women's biography from its imbeddedness in essentialism, women's history can be found through biographical interpretation which enters into the historical complexity and multidimensionality of women's lives that has been made all the more complex by their exclusion from history. If women's biography is written from an approach that begins with their roles as mothers and sexual partners where a history of childbearing and motherhood is simply added on, the result is that women's lives are not treated as if they are multidimensional at all. They remain detached from the grand epochs and periods of history.

In writing the biography of Susan B. Anthony, I was able to discover her as an acting subject by exploring the choices she made— the large and small ones, as well as the significant and insignificant ones. Choice is action; it reveals human engagement with the world and others around us. It is the social plane where one interacts from intentionality with received reality. Making choices moves the individual from receiving reality to acting upon it and thus translating received reality into her life. Choice has to do with the future; it is constantly renewed forward motion toward something. The future and how a woman interacts with it are shaped by and requires projecting from the past.

These distinctions are critical to understanding how women internalize domination, because the ability to conceptualize the future, and the history from which the future is projected, are crucial to experiencing and learning who we are and what we can become. If woman is limited to a personal past, which detaches her from identification with her group, and if history has excluded or diminished the representation of her group in its story, her subjectivity becomes structured by a past and therefore toward a future that is confined by these limits. A confined and limited future diminishes possibility and that in turn will effect how far a woman thinks she can go in acting for and from herself. In that case, when a women projects beyond her personal life, she faces only a history of the "other." *He* is historical, and he understands her as a timeless universal. Her subjectivity, confined to the personal, is limited, defined, and deformed by a temporality and universalization which have been *her* base for formulating her future. In contrast, women's biography that is engaged with the subjects in her multidimensionality restores a history to women that breaks their atemporality.

Therefore, women's biography can no longer be confined to the story of women's private lives. Nor can women be satisfied only with a rich, new social history of everyday life, even though these accounts have given us histories of the hidden realities of housework, motherhood, and of women's networks. It takes women organized on their own behalf to reclaim all that men have appropriated for themselves—particularly the grand periods, major epochs, and eras of their history. Women's history will be a comprehensive reality when not only are the stories of individual women and the histories of women's daily lives recorded but when feminism forces a rewriting of all history. Through biography we will come to know who woman is and what she can be—even by facing what she has been denied, not permitted, or forbidden to own of herself and the world. Recapturing biography for women is to insist on having it all for our subject, for her class, for ourselves.

Notes

Abbreviations Used in the Notes

THE FOLLOWING ARCHIVES HOLDING ORIGINAL SUSAN B. ANTHONY manuscript papers were consulted and are referred to in the Notes in an abbreviated form.

B	Bancroft Library
BPL	Boston Public Library
C	Cornell University Library
HL	Huntington Library
LC	Library of Congress
MHS	Massachusetts Historical Society
NYPL	New York Public Library
RHS	Rochester Historical Society
RPL	Rochester Public Library
RMSC	Rochester Museum & Science Center
R	Rutgers University, Douglass Library
SL	Schlesinger Library on the History of Women in America, Radcliffe
SFHS	Seneca Falls Historical Society
SSC	Sophia Smith Collection, Smith College
SD	Stowe-Day Foundation
URL	University of Rochester Library
V	Vassar

Prologue

1. Anna Howard Shaw, *The Story of a Pioneer* (New York: Harper, 1915), 208.

2. Elizabeth Cady Stanton, Susan B. Anthony, Matilda Joselyn Gage, *The History of Woman Suffrage* (New York: Fowler & Wells, 1881), vol. 1, 391–96.

3. Ibid.

1. The Rise of a Common Woman

1. Thomas Woody, *Early Quaker Education in Pennsylvania* (New York: Columbia University Press, 1929. Reprint. Arno, 1969), 19.

2. Ida Harper, *The Life and Work of Susan B. Anthony,* vol. 1, (Indianapolis: Bowen-Merrill, 1910), 10.

3. Blackstone cited in Mary Beard, *Woman as a Force in History* (New York: Collier Books, 1946), 89.

4. For a discussion and definition of feudal relations, see F. L. Ganshof, *Feudalism.* Translated from the French by Philip Gierson. (London: Longmans, 1959), 66–85.

5. Linda Kerber, *Women of the Republic: Intellect & Ideology in Revolutionary America* (Chapel Hill: University of North Carolina Press, 1980), 119.

6. William Buchan, M.D., *Domestic Medicine or the Prevention and Cure of Disease* (Exeter, J. B. Williams, 1828), inscribed by Susan B. Anthony, 1902, LC.

7. Phillippe Aries, *Centuries of Childhood.* Translated by R. Baldick. (New York: Vintage, 1962). Aries establishes the nineteenth century as the "age of the child" and the early twentieth century as the "age of adolescence." Bernard Wishy, *The Child and the Republic* (Philadelphia: University of Pennsylvania Press, 1968). Wishy identifies the American characteristics associated with the advent of childhood in the nineteenth century. As women's work in the home was being reshaped by industrialization in the public economy and much of women's productive work, such as spinning and weaving, was now done in mills, women's work as child rearers took on new heightened and romanticized meaning. Carl Degler, *At Odds: Women and the Family in America from the Revolution to the Present* (New York: Oxford University Press, 1980), 68. Degler points out that by 1820, "large numbers of advice books on child-rearing came off the presses in Britain and the United States." Of course, the new emphasis on childhood and its spontaneity and naturalness made play a more significant pastime of children than it had been in previous eras. Instead of children assisting mothers with chores, family life moved toward mothers supervising children's play.

8. Anthony Benezet, *The Pennsylvania Spelling Book* (Philadelphia, 1779).

9. Susan Strasser, *Never Done, A History of American Housework* (New York: Pantheon, 1982), 14–16.

10. Ibid., 105. As the century progressed and industrialization advanced, feminists were active in revolutionizing housework to ease the conditions for women. See Dolores Hayden, *The Grand Domestic Revolution* (Cambridge, Mass.: MIT Press, 1981). But as Strasser found, new tasks replaced the older ones, keeping women in the home burdened with a labor that had no monetary value attached to it.

11. Katharine Anthony, *Susan B. Anthony: Her Personal History and Her Era* (New York: Doubleday, 1954), 25.

12. Because women's labor was not regulated by the contractual terms that characterized the capitalist mode of production, married women were forced to rely on their husband's beneficence in providing for family needs. For discussion of the domestic mode of production, see Christine Delphy, "The Main Enemy," in her *Close to Home* (Amherst: University of Massachusetts Press, 1984).

13. Edith Abbott, *Women in Industry* (New York: Appleton, 1910), 102. As Gerda Lerner points out in "The Lady and the Mill Girl: Changes in the Status of Women in the Age of Jackson" in her *The Majority Finds Its Past* (New York: Oxford University Press, 1979), 15–30, the "lady" was differentiated from the working girl. Women working outside the home were condemned for their lack of femininity.

14. Capitalism actually continued an exploitation already begun under patriarchal domination, where women's labor in the home was without set hours or monetary value, creating the conditions for long working hours and low wages in the labor force. An important theoretical assumption of this biography is that until women's labor was removed from the home and private domination to the public work force, exploitation of women in both the public and private spheres was bound to remain unobserved and unchallenged.

15. See Thomas Dublin, *Women at Work* (New York: Columbia University Press, 1979), 66, and Philip Foner, *Women and the American Labor Movement: From Colonial Times to The Eve of World War I* (New York: Free Press, 1979), 25.

16. Ida Harper, vol. 1, 19.

17. Ida Harper, vol. 1, 22.

18. Ibid., 23

19. Carroll Smith-Rosenberg and Charles Rosenberg, "The Female Animal: Medical and Biological Views of Woman and Her Role in Nineteenth-Century America." *Journal of American History* 15 (September 1973): 340.

20. Reginald Charles McGrane, *The Panic of 1837* (Chicago: University of Chicago Press, 1924. Reprint. 1965).

21. Daniel Anthony to brother, June, September 1837, Susan B. Anthony Papers, SL.

22. Daniel Anthony to Guelma, November 9, 1837, RMSC.

23. William Penn, letter to wife and children. "Tracts on Moral and Religious Subjects," 1822, in Woody, *Early Quaker Education in Pennsylvania,* 29.

24. Daniel Anthony to Guelma, October 20, 1837, Susan B. Anthony Papers, SL.

25. Ida Harper, vol. 1, 25.

26. Ibid., 24.

27. Poem, "Home," January 17, 1834, Susan B. Anthony Memorial, URL.

28. Susan B. Anthony Diary, 1837, SL.

29. Daniel Anthony to daughters, November 29, 1837, RMSC.

30. S.B.A. to parents, December 9, 1837, Susan B. Anthony Papers, SL.

31. Susan B. Anthony Diary, January 4, 1838, Susan B. Anthony Papers, SL.

32. Ibid. Here "friends" is used in the Quaker sense to mean family members as well as childhood playmates.

33. S.B.A. to parents, December 31, 1837, Susan B. Anthony Papers, SL.

34. Susan B. Anthony Diary, February 8, 1838, SL.

35. Ibid., January 18, 1838, SL.

36. Ibid., February 12, 1838.

37. Ibid., July 11, 1838.

38. Ida Harper, vol. 1, 30–31.

39. Susan B. Anthony Diary, March 24, 1838, SL.

40. Ibid., February 10, 1838.

41. Keith Melder, *Beginnings of Sisterhood: The American Woman's Rights Movement 1800–1850* (New York: Schocken, 1977). Melder identified the ambiguous values of female seminary education, which emphasized the virtues of woman's private sphere, but he found that "for many young women whose minds were first challenged by these institutions, the experience was one of liberation." (p. 23).

42. S.B.A. to Mary, July 7, 1839, SL.

43. Susan B. Anthony Diary, February 6, 1838, SL.

44. Ida Harper, vol. 1, 35.

45. Susan B. Anthony Diary, January 26, 1838, SL.

46. Ibid., February 3, 1839.

47. Ibid., May 7, 1838.

48. Remington to S.B.A., March 8, 1846, SL.

49. Susan B. Anthony Notes, no date, RPL.

50. Susan B. Anthony Diary, March 17, 1839, SL.

2. To Marry or Not to Be a Wife

1. S.B.A. to parents, June 25, 1839, Susan B. Anthony Papers, SL.

2. S.B.A. to sister, June 15, 1839, Susan B. Anthony Papers, SL.

3. S.B.A. Diary, June 27, 1839, Susan B. Anthony Papers, SL.

4. S.B.A. to sister, June 15, 1839, Susan B. Anthony Papers, SL.

5. S.B.A. to Aaron, August 28, 1839, Susan B. Anthony Papers, SL.

6. Aaron to S.B.A., July 25, 1839, Susan B. Anthony Papers, SL.

7. Ibid., August 5 , 1839.

8. S.B.A. to Aaron, August 10, 1839 and S.B.A. to sisters, June 15, 1839, Susan B. Anthony Papers, SL.

9. Guelma and Aaron to S.B.A., July 28, 1839, Susan B. Anthony Papers, SL in note from Aaron at end of letter.

10. Guelma and Aaron to S.B.A., July 21, 1839, note added by Aaron, Susan B. Anthony Papers, SL.

11. S.B.A. to sisters, June 15, 1839, Susan B. Anthony Papers, SL.

12. Carroll Smith-Rosenberg, "The Female World of Love and Ritual: Relations Between Women in Nineteenth Century America," *Signs*, 1, No. 1 (1975)ı 1 29. Smith-Rosenberg identifies women's intimate relations with each other as a separate structured framework, which represented a significant part of women's lives. See also Nancy Cott, *Bonds of Womanhood* (New Haven, Conn.: Yale University Press, 1977). Cott points out how women's peer relations held primacy in their emotional and affective life. According to her, by the 1830s women's sphere of life became a subculture that led to the development of women's consciousness of themselves as a group—a prerequisite for the birth of a woman's rights movement.

13. S.B.A. to Aaron, July 21, 1839, Susan B. Anthony Papers, SL.

14. Ibid., August 18, 1839.

15. Ibid., August 28, 1839.

16. Ibid., August 18, 1839.

17. Susan B. Anthony Diary, June 10, 1839.

18. Ida Harper, *The Life and Work of Susan B. Anthony*, vol. 1, 38, 46.

19. Susan B. Anthony Diary, April 28, 1839, Susan B. Anthony Papers, SL.

20. Newspaper clipping citing letter of May 21, 1881, from S.B.A. to "Dear Friend," HL.

21. Elizabeth Cady Stanton, *Eighty Years and More: Reminiscences 1815–1897*, 1898. Reprint. (New York: Schocken, 1971), 172.

22. S.B.A. to Aaron, June 14, 1839, Susan B. Anthony Papers, SL.

23. See Ann Firor Scott, "The Ever Widening Circle: The Diffusion of Feminist Values from the Troy Female Seminary 1822–1872," *History of Education Quarterly* (Spring 1979): 3–25. See also David Allmendinger, Jr., "Mount Holyoke Students Encounter the Need for Life-Planning 1837–1850," *History of Education Quarterly* (Spring 1979): 40–41.

24. Susan B. Anthony Diary, July 27, 1839, SL.

25. S.B.A. to parents, June 25, 1839, Susan B. Anthony Papers, SL.

26. Susan B. Anthony Diary, July 19, 1839, SL.

27. Ibid.

28. Ibid., July 19, 1839.

29. S.B.A. to Aaron, August 10, 1839, Susan B. Anthony Papers, SL.

30. Susan B. Anthony Diary, June 15, 1839, SL.

31. A. F. Dickenson to "Respected Niece," July 12, 1839, Susan B. Anthony Papers, SL.

32. S.B.A. to Aaron, July 14, 1839, Susan B. Anthony Papers, SL.

33. Susan B. Anthony Diary, May 1839, SL.

34. Ibid., June 22, 1839.

35. S.B.A. to parents, June 25, 1839, Susan B. Anthony Papers, SL.

36. Susan B. Anthony Diary, June 22, 1839, SL.

37. Daniel Anthony to brother, September 7, 1845, SL.

38. S.B.A. to father, mother, sister, and brother, May 24, 1846, Susan B. Anthony Papers, SL.

39. Caroline to S.B.A., February 7, 1846, Susan B. Anthony Papers, SL.

40. S.B.A. to "Dear Friends at the Cottage," August 12, 1846, Susan B. Anthony Papers, SL.

41. S.B.A. to parents, May 3, 1846, Susan B. Anthony Papers, SL.

42. S.B.A. to brothers and sisters, May 11, 1846, Susan B. Anthony Papers, SL.

43. Ida Harper, vol. 1, 50.

44. S.B.A. to "Dear Friends at the Cottage," August 12, 1846, Susan B. Anthony Papers, SL.

45. S.B.A. to brother and sister, April 15, 1846, Susan B. Anthony Papers, SL.

46. S.B.A. to mother, February 7, 1847, Susan B. Anthony Papers, SL.

47. S.B.A. to brother and sister, May 11, 1846, Susan B. Anthony Papers, SL.

48. Reported by S.B.A. to brother and sister, April 15, 1846, Susan B. Anthony Papers, SL.

49. S.B.A. to father, mother, brother, and sister, May 24, 1846, Susan B. Anthony Papers, SL.

50. S.B.A. to mother, December 27, 1846, Susan B. Anthony Papers, SL.

51. S.B.A. to parents, May 3, 1846, Susan B. Anthony Papers, SL.

52. S.B.A. to Mary, June 18, 1846, Susan B. Anthony Papers, SL.

53. S.B.A. to parents, February 20, 1849, Susan B. Anthony Papers, SL.

54. S.B.A. to mother, July 11, 1848, Susan B. Anthony Papers, SL.

55. Ibid., October 15, 1848.

56. As marriage moved away from contractual agreements between families to romantic relations between partners, there was a new emphasis on an individual's personal feelings. A preoccupation with one's feelings and desires was also made possible for women like Anthony by the new freedom from the constant concern with work and household chores that had previously marked women's lives.

57. S.B.A. to mother, October 15, 1848, Susan B. Anthony Papers, SL.

58. Ibid., October 10, 1848.

59. S.B.A. to parents, May 28, 1848, Susan B. Anthony Papers, SL.

60. Ibid.

61. S.B.A. to mother, October 31, 1848, Susan B. Anthony, SL.

62. Ibid., October 15, 1848.

63. Ida Harper, vol. 1, 53.

64. Ibid., 54.

65. S.B.A. to mother, March 7, 1849, Susan B. Anthony Papers, SL.

66. This discussion of the role of reflection in political consciousness was developed by Jurgen Habermas in *Knowledge and Human Interests* (Boston: Beacon, 1968). He identifies emancipatory power of reflection, where in this kind of self-reflection the subject, in this case Anthony, has the opportunity to consider herself in relation to her life and its connection to history. "The experience of reflection articulates itself substantially in the concept of self-formative process" (p. 197). Habermas goes on further to define self-reflection as "at once intuitive and emancipative, comprehensive and liberating from dogmatic dependence" (p. 208).

Because reflection is a fully conscious process whereby one comes to know oneself in relation to history—and therefore domination—it is the base for political consciousness, which is then not developmental over the life span but rather critical as it relies on reason to dispel dogma. But to identify the emancipatory character of consciousness does not reveal the quality of that consciousness, which is a particularly important question in the study of the social origins of a women's movement. On this point Hannah Arendt discusses compassion in political revolution in *On Revolution* (New York: Penguin, 1977). Compassion is personal identification with the suffering of others of one's group that arouses revolutionary passion in the suffering of the oppressed.

67. Ida Harper, vol. 1, 54.

68. S.B.A. in a letter to D. R. Anthony, June 11, 1848, HL.

69. S.B.A. to brother, December 19, 1848, Susan B. Anthony, SL.

70. Ibid.

71. Ibid.

72. Harper, Vol. I, 52.

73. S.B.A. to mother, March 7, 1849, Susan B. Anthony Papers, SL.

74. Undated fragment of letter from S.B.A. to mother, Susan B. Anthony Papers, SL.

75. S.B.A. to parents, April 17, 1849, Susan B. Anthony Papers, SL.

76. S.B.A. to mother, March 7, 1849, Susan B. Anthony Papers, SL.

77. S.B.A. to brother, May 11, 1849, Susan B. Anthony Papers, SL.

78. S.B.A. to Sister Hannah, May 14, 1849, Susan B. Anthony Papers, SL.

79. Ibid.

80. S.B.A. to Brother and Sister McLean, May 14, 1849, Susan B. Anthony Papers, SL.

3. *"Woman Must Take to Her Soul a Purpose"*

1. Susan B. Anthony, "The Status of Woman, Past, Present, and Future," *The Arena* (May 1897): 902.
2. Daniel Anthony to S.B.A., February 8, 1849, Susan B. Anthony Papers, SL.
3. Ibid.
4. Susan B. Anthony, "The Status of Woman, Past, Present, and Future," *The Arena* (May 1897): 902.
5. Lee Chambers Schiller, "The Single Woman: Family and Vocation among Nineteenth Century Reformers," in *Woman's Being, Woman's Place*, edited by Mary Kelley (Boston: G. K. Hall, 1979), 334–50.
6. Susan B. Anthony, "The Status of Woman, Past, Present, and Future," *The Arena* (May 1897): 903.
7. Ibid.: 902.
8. S.B.A. notes presumably written for Harper's biography, no date, RPL.
9. Blake McKelvey, *Rochester, the Flower City, 1855–1890* (Cambridge, Mass.: Harvard University Press, 1949)
10. Ida Harper, *The Life and Work of Susan B. Anthony*, vol. 1, 159–60.
11. Susan B. Anthony Scrapbooks, 1851, item dated February 21, LC.
12. Abigail Bush recounted to S.B.A., April 14, 1898, Gannett Papers, URL.
13. Susan B. Anthony, and Ida Harper, *History of Woman Suffrage*, vol. 1, 457.
14. Ibid., 459.
15. Susan B. Anthony Scrapbook, October 27, 1902, LC. Stylistically, I have adopted "Susan and Mrs. Stanton," for their interactions, "Susan" for all her other personal interactions, and "Anthony" for her public work.
16. *History of Woman Suffrage*, vol. 1, 459.
17. Anthony and Stanton became a great couple of the nineteenth century without ever dichotomizing or prioritizing their individual virtues and different abilities. The attempt to elevate Stanton over Anthony is a recent product of historical interpretation, which has rigidly dichotomized their relationship.
18. Ida Harper, vol. 1, 65.
19. S.B.A. "address first delivered at Batavia, New York, in company with Emily Clark," May 1852, LC.
20. Ida Harper, vol. 1, 69–70.

21. E.C.S. to S.B.A., 1852, V.

22. *History of Woman Suffrage,* vol. 1, 60.

23. E.C.S. to S.B.A., 1852, V.

24. E.C.S. to S.B.A., April 2, 1852, Theodore Stanton and Harriot Stanton Blatch, *Elizabeth Cady Stanton As Revealed in Her Letters, Diary, and Reminiscenses,* vol. 2, 41.

25. E.C.S. to S.B.A., 1852, V.

26. E.C.S. to S.B.A., April 2, 1852, Theodore Stanton and Harriot Stanton Blatch, vol. 2, 41.

27. Elizabeth Cady Stanton, *Eighty Years and More: Reminiscences 1815– 1897,* Reprinted. (New York: Schocken, 1971), 201.

28. Ida Harper, vol. 1, 67.

29. Ibid., 66.

30. S.B.A. address first delivered at Batavia, New York, in company with Emily Clark, May 1852, LC.

31. Ian R. Tyrrell, *Sobering Up: From Temperance to Prohibition in Antebellum America, 1800–1860* (Westport, Conn.: Greenwood Press, 1979), 253.

32. Susan B. Anthony, "Woman's Half Century of Evolution," *North American Review* (December 1902): 806.

33. S.B.A. "address first delivered at Batavia, New York, in company with Emily Clark," May 1852, LC.

34. Ida Harper, vol. 1, 84.

35. *History of Woman Suffrage,* vol. 1, 459.

36. Ibid., 460.

37. Harper, vol. 1, 113.

38. Ida Harper, vol. 1, 72.

39. Alexis de Tocqueville, *Democracy in America,* vol. 2 (New York: Vintage, 1945), 104–18.

40. Ida Harper, vol. 1, 54.

41. Barrington Moore, *Injustice: The Social Bases of Obedience and Revolt* (White Plains, N.Y.: M. E. Sharpe, 1978), 482. Moore identifies "social and cultural space" as the one prerequisite of social and moral transformation that underlies all other changes. "A society with social and cultural space provides more or less protected enclaves within which dissatisfied or oppressed groups have some room to develop distinctive social arrangements, cultural traditions, and explanation of the world around them" (p. 482). This "social space" has often been identified as women's culture in reference to feminist movements. Carroll Smith-Rosenberg in *Feminist Studies* 6 (Spring 1980), has identified women's culture as having "its own autonomous values, identities, symbolic systems, and modes of communication" (p. 58). She extended her earlier analysis of female rituals and networks to elaborate the effects of women's culture. "If one can assume that cosmological and symbolic systems develop in relation to social structure, then

women, with less power will frequently develop their own *veltanschau-ugen*" (p. 61).

42. *History of Woman Suffrage,* vol. 1, 458.

43. E.C.S. to S.B.A., June 20, 1853, Theodore Stanton and Harriot Stanton Blatch, vol. 2, 51.

44. Ida Harper, vol. 1, 101–102.

45. *History of Woman Suffrage,* vol. 1, 547. As S.B.A. was the only one of the authors present at this meeting, I attribute this statement to Anthony.

46. Ibid., 567.

47. Ibid., 567–68.

48. Susan B. Anthony Scrapbooks, 1853. Letter from S.B.A. to *New York Daily Tribune,* August, LC.

49. This and the preceding quotations from Ida Harper, vol. 1, 99.

50. Susan B. Anthony Scrapbook, 1853, LC.

51. E.C.S. to S.B.A., March 13, 1853, Elizabeth Cady Stanton Papers, LC.

52. Susan B. Anthony Diary. S.B.A. Rochester, 1854, SL.

53. Susan B. Anthony Diary. S.B.A. Rochester, 1854, reflection on the year 1853, SL. Personal reflection, which Habermas (*Knowledge and Human Interest*) would call self-reflection, such as Anthony engaged in over her mother's life, was extended to the collective condition of womankind when she began to confront it in the reality of women's daily lives.

54. S.B.A. to E.C.S., November 11, 1853, Elizabeth Cady Stanton Papers, LC.

55. This quote and preding summary from *History of Woman Suffrage,* vol. 1, 458.

56. E.C.S. to S.B.A., December 1, 1853, Theodore Stanton and Harriot Stanton Blatch, 54–55.

57. *History of Woman Suffrage,* vol. 1, 604.

58. Ibid., 462.

59. Ida Harper, vol. 1, 115.

60. Lucy Stone, *The Woman's Journal,* no date, published in Boston, SL.

61. Blake McKelvey, *Rochester: The Water-power City, 1812–1854* (Cambridge, Mass: Harvard University Press, 1945), 349.

62. Ida Harper, vol. 1, 116.

63. Ibid.

64. E.C.S. to S.B.A., February 19, 1854, Elizabeth Cady Stanton, LC.

65. Ida Harper, vol. 1, 117.

66. S.B.A. to Elizabeth Oakes Smith, September 18, 1854, URL.

67. Elizabeth Oakes Smith, *Bertha and Lily: or the Parsonage of Beech Glen, A Romance* (New York: J. C. Derby, 1854), 26.

68. Ibid.

4. A Passion for Justice

1. Susan B. Anthony and Ida Harper, *History of Woman Suffrage,* vol. 1, 100.

2. Ibid.

3. Susan B. Anthony Diary, March 29, 1854, Susan B. Anthony Papers, SL.

4. S.B.A. to *Liberator,* April 1854, Susan B. Anthony Scrapbooks, 1854, LC.

5. Dialogue drawn from Susan B. Anthony, April 3, 1854, SL.

6. Harriet Beecher Stowe, *Uncle Tom's Cabin,* 1851. Reprint. (New York: Bantam, 1981), xviii.

7. Ibid., 48.

8. This and following quote from Susan B. Anthony Diary, March 30, 1854, SL.

9. Ibid., April 9, 1854.

10. Ibid., April 14, 1854.

11. From material compiled and edited by Una Winter for "Susan B. Anthony and the Woman Suffrage Movement—Susan B. Anthony Lectures and Reminiscences," 1940, copy in Sophia Smith Collection.

12. *History of Woman Suffrage,* vol. 1, 460–61.

13. Carolina Cowles Richards, *Village Life in America* (New York, 1913).

14. Susan B. Anthony Diary, December 29, 1854, SL.

15. Ida Harper, *The Life and Work of Susan B. Anthony,* vol. 1, 127–28.

16. Susan B. Anthony Diary, January 5, 1855, SL.

17. Ida Harper, vol. 1, 126.

18. Susan B. Anthony Scrapbook, 1855, LC.

19. Ibid., 1857.

20. Ibid., 1855.

21. S.B.A. to Martha Coffin Wright, July 6, 1856, SSC.

22. Elizabeth Cady Stanton, *Eighty Years and More.* Reprint. (New York: Schocken, 1971), 170.

23. Susan B. Anthony Diary, May 6, 1873, LC.

24. Ida Harper, vol. 1, 119–20.

25. Ibid., 134–35.

26. Ibid., 135.

27. Ibid., 131.

28. Ida Harper, vol. 1, 131.

29. Cited in Walter M. Merrill, *Against Wind and Tide: A Biography of William Lloyd Garrison* (Cambridge, Mass.: Harvard University Press, 1963), 93.

30. Ida Harper, vol. 1, 132.

31. S.B.A. to Samuel May, 1855, HL.

32. Ida Harper, vol. 1, 133.

33. Ibid., 137.

34. Ibid., 148.

35. Ibid.

36. There are widely different scholarly interpretations of the causes of the women's movement, each interpretation producing a very different analysis of the significance of that movement. The thesis of this biography is that the woman's rights movement and Susan B. Anthony's political leadership were formed through a transformation into political consciousness when women's rights advocates in general, and Anthony in particular, confronted the objective conditions of domination that framed their own and other woman's lives. In contrast, for example, Blanche Glassman Hersh, in *The Slavery of Sex: Feminist-Abolitionists in America* (Urbana: University of Illinois Press, 1978), identifies women's antislavery work as a premovement, "which led directly to the first attempts to organize for woman's rights in the 1840s and 1850s and provided "the basis for feminist ideology" (p. 6). In the assumption of a direct causality between the two movements, the objective conditions and social forces in women's lives that shaped their movement are overlooked, and the dialectical interactive effects of each movement on the other are discounted. Further, while recognizing that the woman's rights movement was secular and focused on pragmatic reform, this analysis fails to account for the feminist-abolitionists forming a movement based upon civil responsibility and public morality. Seeing feminism as derivative from other movements reduces feminist theory and politics to a mere set of ideas, an idealist approach, which is disconnected from women's material conditions. Ellen DuBois, in *Feminism and Suffrage: The Emergence of an Independent Women's Rights Movement in America, 1848–1869* (Ithaca, N.Y.: Cornell University Press, 1978) rejects the causality that attributes feminism to abolition. But she finds that, "Abolitionism provided them with a way to escape clerical authority, an egalitarian ideology, and a theory of social change, all of which permitted the leaders to transform the insights into oppression of women which they shared with many of their contemporaries into the beginnings of the woman's rights movement" (p. 32). This derivationist approach has been extended into analysis of the twentieth-century women's movement with Sarah Evans's thesis in *Personal Politics* (New York: Vintage, 1979, which asserts that in the 1960s the women's liberation movement was born from the civil rights and new-left movements.

37. Ida Harper, vol. 1, 153.

38. Ibid., 156.

39. Ibid., 162.

40. Ibid., 157.

41. Ibid., 156.
42. Ibid., 157.
43. Ibid., 158.

5. The Woman's Enlightenment

1. S.B.A. speech, "True Womanhood," 1857, SL. Harper dates this speech at 1859 from a diary entry for that year, in Ida Harper, *The Life and Work of Susan B. Anthony,* vol. 1, 172.

2. Elinor Rice Hays, *Lucy Stone: One of America's First and Greatest Feminists* (New York: Tower, 1961), 137.

3. Ida Harper, vol. 1, 177–78.

4. Ibid., 142.

5. Ibid., 139.

6. Ibid., 130.

7. Ibid., 135–36.

8. S.B.A. to Martha Coffin Wright, January 20, 1856, SSC.

9. Ida Harper, vol. 1, 162.

10. S.B.A. to Martha Wright, June 6, 1856, SSC.

11. Ida Harper, vol. 1, 162.

12. Ibid., 142.

13. E.C.S. to S.B.A., July 20, 1857, R.

14. Ida Harper, vol. 1, 171.

15. Ibid.

16. Mrs. Gaskell, *The Life of Charlotte Brontë* (New York: Penguin, 1975), 308.

17. Sandra Gilbert and Susan Gubar, *The Madwoman in the Attic: The Woman Writer and Nineteenth Century Literary Imagination* (New Haven Conn.: Yale University Press, 1979), 342.

18. Charlotte Brontë, *Jane Eyre,* 1848. Reprint. (New York: Bantam, 1981), 240.

19. S.B.A. speech, "True Womanhood," 1857, SL.

20. Aurora Leigh's self-won independence and autonomy and her female sensitivity and literary sensibility have been celebrated in feminist literary criticism, Ellen Moers, *Literary Women.* (New York: Oxford University Press, 1963.) In her introduction to the 1978 Women's Press edition of *Aurora Leigh,* Cora Kaplan identifies the congruence of Barrett Browning's feminist perspective in this work with the utopian socialists of the period. And she faults them both with denying "self-generating consciousness" in the working classes. She consequently sees Aurora Leigh as a female version of bourgeois ideology (p. 35). Barrett Browning's approach to marriage in *Aurora Leigh* attacks, not nineteenth-century capitalism, but the marital feudalism that defined women's lives in the nineteenth century. This suggests that classical historical periodization of economic transfor-

mation does not establish the historical framework within which women's lives in biography or fiction can be interpreted.

21. S.B.A. to E.C.S., September 29, 1857, Elizabeth Cady Stanton Papers, LC.

22. Inscription in S.B.A.'s personal copy of *Aurora Leigh,* LC.

23. Elizabeth Barrett Browning, *Aurora Leigh* (London: Women's Press, 1978), 88.

24. S.B.A. speech, "True Womanhood," 1857, SL.

25. Ibid.

26. S.B.A. speech, "True Womanhood," 1857, SL.

27. Fernand Braudel effectively argued that different modes of exploitation—slavery, feudalism, and capitalism—historically "exist side by side and indeed complement one another." These structural inequalities create historical regression and time-lags from which capitalism—the latest economic model—benefits due to its reliance on hierarchies. Fernand Braudel, *The Perspectives of the World, Civilization & Capitalism, 15th–18th Centuries,* vol. 3, translated from French by Sian Reynolds. (New York: Harper & Row, 1979). On the character of the Enlightenment, see Peter Gay, *The Enlightenment, An Interpretation: The Science of Freedom* (New York: Norton, 1969), 3.

28. Peter Gay, *The Enlightenment, An Interpretation: The Rise of Modern Paganism* (New York: Norton, 1966), 3.

29. See Claire Goldberg Moses, *French Feminism in the 19th Century* (Albany: State University of New York Press, 1984); Andree Michel et Genevieve Texier, *La Condition de la française d'aujourd'hui* (Paris: Editions Gonthier, 1964), 71–91 and "Histoire de la conditions de la Francais dans le mariage"; Jane Abray, "Feminism in the French Revolution," *American Historical Review,* (February 1975): 43–62; Scott H. Lytle: "The Second Sex (September 1793)," *Journal of Modern Historical Review* (1955): 14–26.

30. Irene A. Brown, "Domesticity, Feminism, and Friendship: Female Aristrocratic Culture and Marriage in England, 1660–1760," *Journal of Family History,* (Winter 1982): 406–24.

31. E.C.S. to S.B.A., January 1856, V.

32. S.B.A. to E.C.S, May 26, 1856, R.

33. E.C.S. and S.B.A., "Educating the Sexes Together," 1856, LC.

34. S.B.A. to E.C.S., September 27, 1857, LC.

35. E.C.S. to S.B.A., July 4, 1858, R.

36. Susan B. Anthony and Ida Harper, *History of Woman Suffrage,* vol. 1, 70.

37. Christine Delphy, "The Main Enemy," in her *Close to Home* (Amherst: University of Massachusetts Press, 1984), finds that unlike the labor of the husband who is exploited in the capitalist mode of production, the wife's labor is controlled by a domestic mode of production where wives'

work is not specified and arbitrarily determined by their husband's requirements. Their work in unpaid, no specific hours are set, the contract is one of lifetime indebtedness, and support does not depend on women's labor, but on the husband's good will. Delphy concludes that "since the benefits wives receive have no relationship to the services which they provide, it is impossible for married women to improve their standard of living by improving their services" (p. 70)—a condition which prevails still today.

38. Ida Harper, vol. 1, 147.

39. S.B.A. to E.C.S., September 27, 1857, Elizabeth Cady Stanton Papers, LC, also excerpts of this letter put together as the complete letter in Stanton and Blatch typescripts, R.

40. E.C.S. to S.B.A., August 1857, V.

41. E.C.S. to S.B.A., July 4, 1858, R.

42. Ida Harper, vol. 1, 142.

43. Barrett Browning, *Aurora Leigh,* 389.

44. *History of Woman Suffrage,* vol. 1, 678.

45. Ibid., 678–79.

46. Sylvia Pankhurst, *The Suffrage Movement* (London: Virago, 1977), 48.

47. *History of Woman Suffrage,* vol. 1, 707.

48. Ibid., 482.

49. Ibid., 716.

50. See Alice Rossi, ed., *Essays on Sex Equality by John Stuart Mill* (Chicago: University of Chicago Press, 1970) for her discussion of Harriet Taylor as the formative influence on Mill's essay.

51. John Stuart Mill, *On the Subjection of Women* (New York: Fawcett, 1971), 63.

52. Richard Evans, *The Feminists: Women's Emancipation Movements in Europe, American & Australia 1840–1920* (New York: Barnes & Noble, 1977). Evans uses Mill to identify feminism with nineteenth-century liberalism. "Mill's book was influential because it summed up the feminist case in a way that linked it firmly to the political theory of liberal individualism" (p. 19). Richard Krouse in "Patriarchal Liberalism and Beyond: From John Stuart Mill to Harriet Taylor," in Jean Elshtain, ed., *The Family in Political Thought* (Amherst: University of Massachusetts Press, 1982), 145–72, traces liberalism and contract theory through Mill's essay and finds that Mill evaded the question of marriage/divorce. As Mill himself explained, the feminist issue was not "what marriage ought to be, but . . . what woman ought to be." Both Evans and Krouse miss the challenge to the idea that feminist theory was essentially liberal by accepting Mill's evasion of the marriage/divorce question. Krouse is identified with the position of nineteenth century liberals when he asserts that Harriet Taylor's view of divorce—to be granted on the request of the parties—is "morally

disturbing" and that it was to Mill's credit that his views were "more measured and complex" than Taylor's solution—to immediately abolish the law of marriage (p. 165).

53. *History of Woman Suffrage,* vol. 1, 724.

54. *Ibid.,* 733.

55. E.C.S. to S.B.A., June 14, 1860, Theodore Stanton and Harriot Stanton Blatch.

56. E.C.S. to Martha Wright, June 2, 1860, Theodore Stanton and Harriot Stanton Blatch.

57. *History of Woman Suffrage,* vol. 1, 735.

58. E.C.S. to S.B.A., June 14, 1860, Theodore Stanton and Harriot Stanton Blatch.

59. Wendell Phillips to S.B.A., June 5, 1860, URL.

60. Irving H. Barlett, *Wendell Phillips, Brahmin Radical* (Boston: Beacon, 1961).

61. E.C.S. to Garrison, May 22, 1860, BPL.

62. S.B.A. to Garrison in letter of E.C.S. to Garrison, May 22, 1860, BPL.

63. While it has been generally assumed that the woman's rights movement suffered an internal split in 1868–69 due to different and opposing political strategies for suffrage, one important thesis of this biography is that this split was actually initiated by the abolitionist men as early as 1860 over the issue of divorce.

64. E.C.S. to S.B.A., June 14, 1860, Theodore Stanton and Harriot Stanton Blatch.

65. Ida Harper, vol. 1, 197.

66. Ibid., 200–202.

67. Ibid., 203, from letter to Garrison.

68. Ibid., 203–204.

69. E.C.S. to S.B.A., June 14, 1860, Theodore Stanton and Harriot Stanton Blatch, 82.

70. Ida Harper, vol. 1, 204.

71. S.B.A. to E.C.S., probably February 1861, V.

72. Ibid., February 27, 1862.

6. Which Slaves' Emancipation?

1. S.B.A. speech, "No Government," SL.

2. *The Post Standard,* Syracuse, N.Y. (February 4, 1940): 18.

3. Ida Harper, *The Life and Work of Susan B. Anthony,* vol. 1, 212. See 207–12 for descriptions of other meetings.

4. S.B.A. to Martha Wright, May 28, 1861, Garrison papers, SSC.

5. Susan B. Anthony and Ida Harper, *History of Woman Suffrage,* vol. 1, 748–49.

6. Elizabeth Cady Stanton, *Eighty Years and More: Reminiscenses 1815– 1897.* Reprint. (New York: Schocken, 1971), 254.

7. *History of Woman Suffrage* vol. 1, 746–47.

8. S.B.A. to Lydia Mott, *History of Woman Suffrage,* vol. 1, 748.

9. Albie Sachs and Joan Hoff-Wilson, *Sexism and the Law (New York: The Free Press, 1978), 78.* For history of divorce, see Nancy F. Cott, "Eighteenth Century Family and Social Life Revealed in Massachusetts Divorce Records" in Nancy Cott and Elizabeth Pleck, eds., *A Heritage of Her Own* (New York: Simon & Schuster, 1979), 107–35. Linda Kerber, in *Women of the Republic: Intellect & Ideology in Revolutionary America* (Chapel Hill: University of North Carolina Press, 1980), points out that where divorce was available in eighteenth-century colonial America, the "divorce petitioner was a woman whose husband had deserted her, usually leaving her economically troubled, if not desperate" (p. 162). Kerber found that outside of New England where some states had divorce statutes, although the case had to be desperate to apply them, divorce was only possible through a private bill passed by the legislature. "A divorce remained nearly as difficult to obtain in the new republic as it had been in the colonies" (pp. 183–84).

10. "Lincoln-Douglas: Debates on the Slavery Question" in *Lincoln and the Coming of the Civil War,* edited by Norton Garfinkle (Lexington, Mass.: Heath, 1959), 14. Originally published in *Collected Works of Abraham Lincoln,* vol. 3, edited by Roy Basler. (New Jersey: Rutgers University Press, 1953).

11. S.B.A. speech, "The Civil War and Slaves" 1862, SL.

12. S.B.A. speech, "Fourth of July Address," Framingham, Mass., 1862, SL.

13. Stephen B. Oates, *Our Fiery Trail: Abraham Lincoln, John Brown, and the Civil War Era* (Amherst: University of Massachusetts Press, 1979), 83.

14. *History of Woman Suffrage,* vol. 2, 57.

15. Stone cited in Elinor Rice Hays, *Lucy Stone: One of America's First and Greatest Feminists* (New York: Tower, 1961) 197; Anthony cited in *History of Woman Suffrage,* vol. 2, 61.

16. *History of Woman Suffrage,* vol. 2, 68.

17. Ida Harper, vol. 1, 234.

18. Stephen B. Oates, 82.

19. Katharine Anthony, *Susan B. Anthony, Her Personal History and Her Era* (New York: Doubleday, 1954). Anthony employs a Freudian analysis to explain S.B.A.'s relationship to her father, suggesting a deep Oedipal identification; after identifying Daniel Anthony as an abolitionist, she asserts that Susan was the "inheritor of his drives, his 'ideas,' his genius, and

his dreams" (p. 42). Yet there is no evidence that Daniel was an active abolitionist or that Susan had anything other than the normal affection of a daughter for her father.

20. Ida Harper, vol. 1, 224.

21. Ibid., 231.

22. Ibid., 232.

23. Ibid.

24. Elizabeth Cady Stanton, *Eighty Years and More*. Reprint. (New York: Schocken, 1971), 164.

25. S.B.A. to E.C.S., about February 1861, V.

26. Ida Harper, vol. 1, 220.

27. S.B.A. to Martha Wright, April 22, 1863, R.

28. Max Weber in H. H. Gerth and C. Wright Mills, eds., *From Max Weber: Essays in Sociology* (New York: Oxford University Press, 1946), 246.

29. Ibid., 248.

30. Ida Harper, vol. 1, 234.

31. Ibid., 158.

32. Ibid., 241.

33. Ibid., 242.

34. S.B.A. Diary, July 4, 1865, LC.

35. Ibid., July 1, 1865.

36. Ibid., July 23, 1865.

37. S.B.A. to E.C.S., April 19, 1865, LC.

38. Ida Harper, vol. 1, 244.

39. Howard Jay Graham, "The Conspiracy Theory of the Fourteenth Amendment," in *Reconstruction, An Anthology of Revisionist Writings,* edited by Kenneth Stampp and Leon F. Litwak (Baton Rouge: Louisiana State University Press, 1969), 107–8.

40. E.C.S. to S.B.A., August 11, 1865, Theodore Stanton and Harriot Stanton Blatch.

41. Ida Harper, vol. 1, 245.

42. E.C.S. to Phillips, May 25, 1865, Theodore Stanton and Harriot Stanton Blatch, 104–5.

43. Kenneth Stampp, *The Era of Reconstruction, 1865–1877* (New York: Knopf, 1965), 85.

44. Cited in Peter N. Carroll and David W. Noble, eds., *The Free and the Unfree: A New History of the United States* (New York: Penguin, 1977), 223.

45. Ibid., 282–83.

46. Stampp, in *The Era of Reconstruction,* points out that it was with the help of the Negro male vote that General Grant, the Republican party's nominee, was elected president.

47. *History of Woman Suffrage,* vol. 2, 168.

48. Ibid., 154.

49. S.B.A. to Dall, December 26, 1865, MHS.

50. Call for the Eleventh National Woman's Rights Convention, April 1866, URL.

51. Ida Harper, vol. 1, 260.

52. S.B.A. to friend Studwell, August 20, 1866, URL.

53. Lucretia Mott to S.B.A., November 18, 1866, HL.

54. Ida Harper, vol. 1, 261.

55. Ibid., 268.

7. The Male Betrayal

1. Susan B. Anthony and Ida Harper, *History of Woman Suffrage,* vol. 2, 193, 194, 225.

2. Ibid., 224.

3. Ida Harper, *The Life and Work of Susan B. Anthony,* vol. 1, 275.

4. *History of Woman Suffrage,* vol. 2, 238.

5. Ibid., 236.

6. Erik S. Lunde, *Horace Greeley* (Boston: Twayne, 1981).

7. *History of Woman Suffrage,* vol. 2, 315.

8. Ida Harper, vol. 1., 278.

9. *History of Woman Suffrage,* vol. 2, 287.

10. Ida Harper, vol. 1, 280.

11. *History of Woman Suffrage,* vol. 2, 288.

12. Ibid., 283.

13. Ibid., 286.

14. Isabella Beecher Hooker to Susan Howard, January 2, 1870, written from notes she took during her meeting with Blackwell in December 1869, Document 98/E5-10, SD. Ellen DuBois is among the historians who blamed Susan B. Anthony for "violating twenty years of woman's rights history." (See *Feminism and Suffrage,* (p. 95), when in fact this was a Republican party scheme. Although as a plot it was unknown to Anthony, as general agent representing the American Equal Rights Association, she worked in concert with Blackwell and others.

15. Henry Blackwell, *The Woman's Journal,* Boston, March 11, 1899, RL.

16. Elizabeth Cady Stanton, *Eighty Years and More: Reminiscences 1815–1897.* Reprint. (New York: Schocken, 1971), 247.

17. Ida Harper, vol. 1, 288.

18. *Weekly Monitor,* Fort Scott, Kans., October 26, 1867, Susan B. Anthony Scrapbooks, LC.

19. Ida Harper, vol. 1, 290.

20. W. L. Garrison to A. H . Love, December 18, 1867, BPL.

21. Elizabeth Cady Stanton, *Eighty Years and More*, 255.

22. George Francis Train to S.B.A., *The Revolution*, January 7, 1869.

23. Kenneth Stampp, *The Era of Reconstruction, 1865–1877* (New York: Knopf, 1965), 92.

24. Ibid., 93.

25. Ida Harper, vol. 1, 300.

26. Alice Stone Blackwell, *Lucy Stone: Pioneer of Women's Rights* (Boston: Little, Brown, 1930), 209.

27. S.B.A. to Mr. Higginson, May 20, 1868, BPL.

28. S.B.A. to Dall, June 30, 1866, MHS.

29. *History of Woman Suffrage*, vol. 2, 323.

30. Ibid., 318.

31. Ibid., 330, 332.

32. Eugene Genovese, *Roll, Jordan Roll: The World the Slaves Made* (New York: Pantheon, 1974), 73.

33. Ibid., 146.

34. This and preceding quotes drawn from *History of Woman Suffrage* vol. 2, 380–81.

35. Ida Harper, vol. 1, 323–24.

36. Ibid.

37. S.B.A. to editors, August 24, 1898, URL; S.B.A. to Rachel Foster Avery, May 14, 1897, URL. In contrast to Anthony's account of her response to Frederick Douglass, Stanton had insisted that the following account of it be printed in the *History of Woman Suffrage* and makes Anthony sound racist compared to her original statement: "The old anti-slavery school say woman must stand back and wait until the negroes shall be recognized. But we say, if you will not give the whole loaf of suffrage to the entire people, give it to the most intelligent first. If intelligence, justice and morality are to have precedence in the Government, let the question of woman be brought up first and that of the negro last. While I was canvassing the State with petitions and had them filled with names for our cause to the legislature, a man dared to say to me that the freedom of women was a theory and not a practical thing. When Mr. Douglass mentioned the black man first and the woman last, if he had noticed he would have seen that it was the men that clapped and not the women. There is not the woman born who desires to eat the bread of dependence, no matter whether it be from the hand of father, husband, or brother; for any one who does so eat her bread places herself in the power of the person from whom she takes it. Mr. Douglas talks of the wrongs of the negro; but with all that he today suffers, he would not exchange his sex and take the place of Elizabeth Cady Stanton" (*HWS*, vol. 2 383).

38. *History of Woman Suffrage* vol. 2, 400.

8. *Reformers versus Radicals*

1. S.B.A. to Dall, June 30, 1866, MHS.

2. Milton Rugoff, *The Beechers: An American Family in the Nineteenth Century* (New York: Harper & Row, 1981), 419.

3. See Carroll Smith-Rosenberg, "The Hysterical Woman: Sex Roles and Role Conflict in 19th-Century America," *Social Research* 39, no. 4 (Winter 1972): 652–58 and Ann Douglass Wood, "Fashionable Diseases: Women's Complaints and Their Treatment is Nineteenth-Centry America" in *Cleo's Consciousness Raised,* edited by Mary Hartman and Lois Banner (New York: Harper Colophon Books, 1974), 1–22.

4. Isbella Hooker to Caroline Severance, August 27, 1869, SD.

5. E.C.S. to Paulina Wright Davis, July or August 1869, SD.

6. Isabella Hooker to Severance, August 27, 1869, SD.

7. William Lloyd Garrison to wife, October 29, 1869, BPL.

8. William Lloyd Garrison to Isabella Hooker, November 12, 1869. SD.

9. See William Lloyd Garrison to Johnson, November 14, 1869, BPL.

10. *The Revolution,* October 28, 1869.

11. *The Revolution,* October 28, 1869.

12. Ibid.

13. S.B.A. to T. W. Higginson, May 20, 1868, BPL.

14. Isabella Hooker to Mary Livermore, November 15, 1869, SD.

15. Isabella Hooker to Henry Blackwell, December 3, 1869, SD.

16. S.B.A. to Isabella Hooker, November 3, 1869, SD.

17. S.B.A. to T. W. Higginson, May 20, 1868, BPL.

18. *The Roundout Freeman,* February 1, 1870, Susan B. Anthony Scrapbooks, 1870, LC.

19. Susan B. Anthony Scrapbooks, 1869, LC.

20. *New York World,* November 27, 1869, Susan B. Anthony Scrapbooks, 1869, LC.

21. Ibid.

22. *Cleveland Daily Leader,* November 25, 1869, Susan B. Anthony Scrapbooks, 1869, LC.

23. *The Revolution,* October 28, 1869.

24. Isabella Hooker to Henry Blackwell, December 3, 1869, SD.

25. S.B.A. to Isabella Hooker, December 1869, SD.

26. Ibid., December 17, 1869.

27. Ibid., March 21, 1870, Bloomington, Indiana.

28. *The Revolution,* June 17, 1869.

29. Alice Stone Blackwell, *Lucy Stone, Pioneer Woman Suffragist* (Boston: Little, Brown, 1930), 213.

30. Ida Harper, vol. 1, 347.

31. Ibid.

32. S.B.A. to Isabella Hooker, March 21, 1870. SD.

33. Anne Firor Scott and Andrew Scott in *One Half the People: The Fight for Women Suffrage* (Philadelphia: Lippincott, 1975) point to the deep ideological differences between the moderates and radicals. With rapid social change affecting women's lives, moderates like Stone and Blackwell did not want to arouse the fear that political power in the hands of women would destroy woman's place in the home. "Stanton and Anthony were willing to attack this ideology head-on" (p. 17). Ellen DuBois, in *Feminism and Suffrage: The Emergence of an Independent Women's Movement in America 1848–1869* (Ithaca, N.Y.: Cornell University Press, 1978), argues that the split "advanced the women suffrage movement as a whole by providing it with a much firmer basis for sustained growth and with a sustained political program, which it had always lacked" (p. 164).

34. *The Revolution*, March 19, 1868.

35. Ibid., September 1868.

36. Ibid., November 5, 1868.

37. Philip S. Foner, *Women and the American Labor Movement: From Colonial Times to the Eve of World War I.* (New York: The Free Press, 1979), 133.

38. *The Revolution*, October 8, 1868.

39. Philip S. Foner, p. 145.

40. *New York World*, August 18, 1869, as cited in Israel Kugler, *From Ladies to Women: The Organized Struggle for Woman's Rights in the Reconstruction Era* (New York: Greenwood Press, 1987) 142–3.

41. *The Revolution*, September 9, 1869.

42. Philip Foner, in *Women and the American Labor Movement*, implies that the split was a consequence of Anthony's middle-class privilege and orientation. He argues that the split in women's labor organizing was class based and that the "suffragists' alliance with the women typesetters was part of a general conflict emerging between middle-class and wage-earning women in the Working Women's Association" (p. 151). Objectively, it would be difficult to identify Anthony as middle class, either in terms of her income and material advantages at that moment or in terms of the status of her parents from whom she had been independent for nearly thirty years. As Anthony and Stanton were in Foner's view the principle middle-class suffragists associated with the Working Women's Association, it seems here that his imposition of superficial class divisions rather obscures the feminist position that for women advances and rights in labor and in unions were intricately connected to political power. The men could easily afford to sever labor from politics at this time, as they already held

political rights. By dissociating political power from labor rights, Israel Kluger, in "The Trade Union Career of Susan B. Anthony," *Labor History* 2 (Winter 1961), attributed only personal motivation to Anthony's action during the strike, instead of seeing that as a feminist and a leader of her people she refused to separate one right or power from another. Kluger concluded that her behavior was opportunistic and her cause monomaniacal (p. 100) for political ends.

43. *The Revolution,* 1869, bound ed., 357. SSC.
44. Ibid.
45. Ida Harper, vol. 1, 343.
46. A Chicago paper, in Susan B. Anthony Scrapbooks, 1869, LC.
47. From the *Cincinnati Gazette,* as reported in *The Revolution,* November 18, 1869.
48. S.B.A. to Isabella Hooker, January 12, 1870, SD.
49. Ida Harper, vol. 1, 354–55.
50. Ibid., 356.
51. Ibid., 301–02, (taken from the *Cincinnati Commercial*).
52. Ibid., 356.
53. Ibid., 362.
54. Susan B. Anthony Diary, June 20, 1870, LC.
55. Susan B. Anthony Scrapbooks, 1870, LC.
56. Ibid.
57. Ibid.

9. The Vagaries of Love

1. Catharine Beecher to E.C.S., May 16, 1870, HL.
2. See William Leach, *True Love and Perfect Union: The Feminist Reform of Sex and Society* (New York: Basic Books, 1980), especially Chap. 5, "The Vindication of Love," for a discussion of the "feminist's" critique of romantic and sentimental love and their assertion of what Leach identifies as "rational love," which "fostered harmonious sexual relations based on equivalent experience and growth" (p. 125).
3. Nellie Bly interview, *Woman's Journal,* February 22, 1895.
4. Altina Laura Waller, *The Beecher-Tilton Adultery Scandal: Family, Religion, and Politics in Brooklyn, 1865–1875.* Dissertation, University of Massachusetts, 1980.
5. Elizabeth Tilton to Theodore Tilton, January 31, 1868, cited in Waller, *The Incredible Saga of Victoria C. Woodhull* (New York: Putnam, 1967), 80.
6. Cited in Johanna Johnston, *Mrs. Satan, The Incredible Saga of Victoria C. Woodhull* (New York: G. P. Putnam, 1967), 133.
7. S.B.A. to M.C.W., May 30, 1871, SSC.

8. Ida Harper, *The Life and Work of Susan B. Anthony,* vol. 1, 394–95.

9. *Ibid.*

10. Ironically, scholarly discussion of romantic love and ideology reveals that both liberal and Marxist thinkers seem to agree on the interpretation of causes of the family's transformation during this period. Marxist historian Eli Zaretsky, in *Capitalism, the Family and Personal Life* (New York: Harper & Row, 1976), argued that proletarianization of labor created a new form of family life—one that separated from the sphere of goods production. Noting that the productive functions of the family were socialized (i.e., subsumed into the capitalist mode of production) and that the family sphere became the focus of personal life, Zaretsky implies that capitalism has freed women from physical labor in the home, and that housework is not productive in the Marxian sense, he charges that this gave women a diminished role in the family. Extended child care and emotional support to husband and family are seen to supplant productivity. Likewise, liberal Christopher Lasch, in *A Haven in a Heartless World* (New York: Basic Books, 1977), found the family to be "an emotional refuge in a cold and competitive society" (p. 6). In this work he describes the separation of work and leisure as synonymous with the separation between public and private spheres. Here both Marxist and liberals ignore the facts: 1) many women labored in the public world and then came home to the labor of the domestic mode of production, which now included emotional services; 2) woman's labor in the home was productive and there was no "refuge" for her from her experience of alienation under domination; and 3) women were not just passive victims of the romantic love ideology. Women established a significant resistance to it, particularly the feminists.

11. S.B.A. to M.C.W., May 30, 1871, SSC.

12. S.B.A. to friend, August 20, 1869, V.

13. Nellie Bly interview, in *Woman's Journal,* February 22, 1895.

14. This and preceding quote, Ida Harper, vol. 1, 463.

15. Cited in Johnston, 86.

16. Elizabeth Cady Stanton, Susan B. Anthony, and Matilda Joslyn Gage, *History of Woman Suffrage,* vol. 2, 443.

17. Cited in Johnston, 87.

18. *History of Woman Suffrage,* vol. 2, 445.

19. Cited in Johnston, 89.

20. *History of Woman Suffrage,* vol. 2, 464.

21. Isabella Hooker to S.B.A., March 11, 1871, SD.

22. S.B.A. to Mrs. Wright, March 21, 1871, SD.

23. *Ibid.*

24. S.B.A. to Hooker, January 21, 1871, of ND 1871, SD.

25. S.B.A. to Hooker, January 21, 1871, and April 22, 1871, SD.

26. Ibid., March 5, 1871.

27. Cited in Johnston, 102.

28. Ida Harper, vol. 1, 379.

29. S.B.A. to Hooker, June 1871, SD.

30. S.B.A. to E.C.S., May 29, 1872, SD.

31. Ida Harper, vol. 1, 388.

32. Susan B. Anthony Diary, July 9, 1871, LC.

33. Elizabeth Cady Stanton, *Eighty Years and More: Reminiscences 1815–1897*. Reprint. (New York: Schocken, 1971), 288.

34. Ida Harper, vol. 1, 391.

35. Susan B. Anthony Diary, July 12, 1871, LC.

36. Ibid., July 13, 1871.

37. Ibid., July 15, 1871.

38. Ida Harper, vol. 1, 392.

39. Susan B. Anthony Diary, August 18, 1871, LC.

40. Ida Harper, vol. 1, 396.

41. S.B.A. to M.C.W., 1871, Garrison Papers, SSC.

42. Ida Harper, vol. 1, 393 and Elizabeth Cady Stanton, *Eighty Years and More*, 292–93.

43. Ida Harper, vol. 1, 394.

44. Susan B. Anthony Diary, January 1, 1872, LC.

45. S.B.A. to E.C.S., September 10, 1871, SD.

46. S.B.A. to Hooker, February 6, 1871, and March 5, 1871, SD.

47. Susan B. Anthony Diary, May 10, 1872, SL.

48. Ida Harper, vol. 1, 413.

49. Elizabeth Cady Stanton, *Eighty Years and More*, 166.

50. S.B.A. to Hooker, May 19, 1872, SD.

51. *Ibid.*

52. Ida Harper, vol. 1, 413.

53. S.B.A. to M.C.W., May 17, 1872, SD.

54. S.B.A. to Hooker, April 22, 1871, SD.

55. Ibid., June 24, 1872.

56. Ibid., June 19, 1872.

57. Ibid., August 7, 1872.

58. S.B.A. to M.C.W., May 17, 1872, SSC.

59. S.B.A. to Hooker, June 24, 1872, SD.

10. Convicted of Being a Woman

1. S.B.A. to E.C.S., November 5, 1872, HL.

2. Ida Harper, *The Life and Work of Susan B. Anthony*, vol. 1, 423.

3. Ibid., 427.

4. This and preceding dialogues drawn from statement of Inspector E. T. Marsh, November 4, 1922, Bergen, N.Y., SSC.

5. Ida Harper, vol. 1, 426. Elizabeth Cady Stanton, Susan B. Anthony,

and Matilda Joslyn Gage, *History of Woman Suffrage,* vol. 2, 628 records the arrest date as Thanksgiving day, November 28. But Harper, vol. 1, 426 dates the arrest on Nov. 18. I have accepted the Nov. 28 arrest date as a letter on the arrest from Anthony's attorney was sent on November 27. Preliminary examination was held the next day on November 29.

6. S.B.A. to M.C.W., January 1, 1873, SSC.

7. This and preceding dialogue drawn from Ida Harper, vol. 1, 427, 433.

8. Susan B. Anthony Diary, March 4, 1873, LC.

9. Woodhull to S.B.A., January 2, 1873, HL.

10. Ida Harper, vol. 1, 462.

11. S.B.A. to M.C.W., January 1, 1873, SSC.

12. Susan B. Anthony Diary, March 11, 1873, LC.

13. S.B.A. speech, "Constitutional Argument," 1872, in Ida Harper, vol. 2, 977–92.

14. Susan B. Anthony Diary, June 19, 1873, LC.

15. Ida Harper, vol. 1, 439–41.

16. S.B.A. to Hooker, September 12, 1873, SD.

17. Susan B. Anthony Diary, October 1, 1873, LC.

18. S.B.A. to Hooker, September 8, 1873, SD.

19. S.B.A. to mother, in Ida Harper, vol. 1, 447.

20. Susan B. Anthony Diary, November 20, 1873, LC.

21. *Ibid.*

22. S.B.A. to Harbert, February 26, 1875, HL.

23. S.B.A. to Lizzie Boynton, December 23, 1876, HL.

24. Susan B. Anthony Diary, January 27, 1874 and February 19, 1874, LC.

25. S.B.A. speech, "Homes of Single Women," SL.

26. Ibid., July 8, 1877, LC.

27. S.B.A. to Hooker, April 21, 1873, SD.

28. S.B.A. to "Dear Sir," January 12, 1875, V.

29. Hooker to Blackwell, quoting from Blackwell, November 22, 1873, SD.

30. S.B.A. to Hooker, October 13, 1873, SD.

31. Susan B. Anthony Diary, October 20, 1873, LC.

32. Ibid., November 2, 1876.

33. S.B.A. to Gage, October 21, 1875, LC.

34. S.B.A. to "Dear Friends," August 20, 1869, V.

35. Frederick Engels, "Introduction" to Karl Marx, *The Class Struggle in France* (New York: International Publishers), London, March 6, 1895.

36. S.B.A. to Henry Blackwell in Ida Harper, I, p. 419.

37. Ida Harper, vol. 1, 420.

38. S.B.A. to M.C.W., June 13, 1872, SSC.

39. Ida Harper, vol. 1, 419.

40. Ibid., 420.

41. Interview with J. Sheldon Fisher, Rochester, N.Y., July, 1981.

42. *Minor* v. *Happerset* (U.S. Reports), 21 Wallace 162 (1875).

43. S.B.A. to Hooker, from Tenafly, January 20, 1875, SD.

44. S.B.A. to Ellen Wright Garrison, Tenafly, January 22, 1895, SSC.

45. S.B.A. to Gage, January 19, 1876, LC.

46. *History of Woman Suffrage,* vol. 3, 2.

47. Ibid., 33.

48. Ibid., 20.

49. Elizabeth Cady Stanton, *Eighty Years and More: Reminiscences 1815–1897.* Reprint. (New York: Schocken, 1971), 309.

50. Susan B. Anthony Diary, June 15, 1876, LC.

51. Elizabeth Cady Stanton, *Eighty Years and More,* 311.

52. Ibid., 309. In a private letter from Stanton to Isabella Hooker dated July 5, 1876, SD. Stanton stated, "Regarding who wrote it. Mrs. Gage & Susan & Mrs. Spencer all made suggestions and points for the Declaration & I put it together in my language. Then each one criticized and improved. A splendid work has been accomplished here." Note Stanton's commitment to representing the collective nature of their work rather than her own particular gift in writing and expression.

53. *History of Woman Suffrage,* vol. 3, 29.

54. Ibid., 30.

55. S.B.A. to Caroline Dall, August 5, 1876, MHS.

56. Lucy Stone, letter, August 30, 1876, HL.

57. Ida Harper, vol. 1, 481.

58. Susan B. Anthony Diary, September 22, 1876, LC.

59. Ibid., September 4, 1876, SD.

60. S.B.A. to Hooker, September 4, 1876, SD.

61. Ibid.

62. S.B.A. to Eugene Mosher, October 4, 1877, URL.

63. Ida Harper, vol. 1, 488–89.

64. Ibid.

11. *The Unity of Women—At What Cost?*

1. S.B.A. to Rachel Foster, June 9, 1887, URL.

2. Drawn from letter, S.B.A. to Sarah Jane Eddy, December 31, 1888, HL.

3. Drawn from letter, S.B.A. to Rachel Foster, April 5, 1882, URL.

4. Ida Harper, *The Life and Work of Susan B. Anthony,* vol. 2, 553.

5. Susan B. Anthony and Ida Harper, *History of Woman Suffrage,* vol. 3, 931.

6. Ibid., Chap. 56, "Great Britain," by Ashurst Biggs, 867.

7. S.B.A. to sister, October 27, 1883, in Ida Harper, vol. 2, 576.

8. S.B.A. to brother D.R., April 1, 1883, in Ida Harper, vol. 2, 557.

9. S.B.A. to Rachel, October 1, 1883, in Ida Harper, vol. 2, 573.

10. Edith Thomas, *The Women Incendiaries,* translated by James and Starr Atkenson (New York: George Braziller, 1966). Claire Goldberg Moses, *French Feminism in the 19th Century* (Albany: State University of New York Press, 1984), Chaps. 8 and 9. Moses (p. 233) emphasizes the point that while the Republicans and their commitments to equality enlarged the social space for feminism, the feminist movement had a strong impact on the Republicans, which in turn brought the feminists new education and divorce laws. As Moses points out, this reverses the thesis of Richard Evans, in *The Feminists, Women's Emancipation Movements in Europe, America and Australia, 1840–1920* (New York: Barnes & Noble, 1977), which attributed the reform in divorce and women's education solely to Republican anticlericalism (p. 128).

11. Richard Evans, *The Feminists, Women's Emancipation Movements in Europe, America and Australia, 1840–1920,* (New York: Barnes & Noble, 1977), 127.

12. S.B.A. to Mrs. Spofford, May 20, 1883, in Ida Harper, vol. 2, 562.

13. Claire Goldberg Moses, 207–9.

14. S.B.A. to Mrs. Spofford, May 15, 1883, in Ida Harper, vol. 2, 562.

15. S.B.A. to brother D.R., May 11, 1883, in Ida Harper, vol. 2, 560.

16. Susan B. Anthony Diary, May 29, 1883, LC.

17. Ida Harper, vol. 2, 667.

18. Ida Harper, vol. 2, 589–90.

19. E.C.S. to S.B.A., March 10, 1887, URL.

20. *History of Woman Suffrage,* vol. 4, 125–26.

21. S.B.A. to nieces Julia and Lucy E., March 26, 1887, URL.

22. Ida Harper, vol. 2, 635.

23. S.B.A. to Elizabeth Smith Miller, January 26, 1888, NYPL.

24. Susan B. Anthony Diary, February 1 to February 16, 1888, LC.

25. Elizabeth Cady Stanton, *Eighty Years and More: Reminiscences 1815–1897.* Reprint. (New York: Schocken, 1971), 413.

26. Ida Harper, vol. 2, 667.

27. Ibid., 668.

28. *History of Woman Suffrage,* vol. 4, 133–34.

29. S.B.A. to Harbert, February 16, 1885, HL.

30. Ibid., July 7, 1880, HL.

31. Alice Stone Blackwell, *Lucy Stone, Pioneer of Women's Rights.* (Boston: Little, Brown, 1930), 229.

32. Ida Harper, vol. 2, 627.

33. S.B.A. to Rachel Foster, December 28, 1887, URL.

34. Ida Harper, vol. 2, 629.

35. S.B.A. to Rachel, January 15, 1887, URL.

36. S.B.A. to Rachel Foster, June 24, 1887, URL.

37. S.B.A. to Miriam Alice, June 24, 1887, URL.

38. Anna Howard Shaw, *The Story of a Pioneer* (New York: Harper Brothers, 1915), 189–91.

39. Ruth Bordin, *Woman and Temperance, The Quest for Power and Liberty, 1873–1900* (Philadelphia: Temple University Press, 1981), Chap. 6, 95–116.

40. S.B.A. to Willard, March 19, 1882, HL.

41. S.B.A. to Mrs. Coonley, June 22, 1892, URL.

42. Elizabeth Cady Stanton, *Eighty Years and More,* 381.

43. Ida Harper, vol. 2, 857.

44. Hooker to Garrison, Jr., January 14, 1889, SSC.

45. E.C.S. to Olympia Brown, May 8, 1888, SL.

46. S.B.A. to Ellen Wright Osborne, February 5, 1890, SS.

47. Susan B. Anthony Diary, January 21, 1877, LC.

48. Ibid., March 21, 1877.

49. S.B.A. to Rachel, May 18, 1881, LC.

50. Ibid., December 21, 1889.

51. Susan B. Anthony Diary, February 17, 1890, LC.

52. Ida Harper, vol. 2, 631.

53. Susan B. Anthony Diary, February 18, 1890, LC.

54. E. C. Stanton, "Address to the Founding Convention of the National American Woman Suffrage Association," February 1890, Elizabeth Cady Stanton Papers, LC.

55. Ida Harper, vol. 2, 918.

56. Ibid., 707.

57. Ibid.

58. S.B.A. to Merritt, July 8, 1891, LC.

59. Ida Harper, vol. 2, 712.

60. Ibid.

61. Elizabeth Cady Stanton, "The Solitude of Self" in *Elizabeth Cady Stanton, Susan B. Anthony: Correspondence, Speeches,* edited by Ellen Dubois (New York: Schocken, 1981), 248–54.

62. When the life history of Susan B. Anthony is studied through her interaction with Elizabeth Cady Stanton, one encounters a dynamic relationship which grows and changes dialectically as they change individually and in relation to each other. This continually presented to them new facets of their involvement with each other in the context of a stability coming from years of knowing each other. The stability of their relationship is found in their early understanding that neither required or necessarily desired from the other perfect agreement—something that was possible as a force in sustaining their relationship because they were each in their own and different ways self-determined women. Therefore, their relationship took on the power of their political vision of the "new true woman." This analysis does not have to be imposed on their lives or relationship, as it is

easily drawn from a multitude of their letters, speeches, diaries, and testimonies over forty-five years. It is difficult to find evidence or analysis to support the thesis of Elizabeth Griffiths in *In Her Own Right, The Life of Elizabeth Cady Stanton* (New York: Oxford University Press, 1984), in which she asserts that by this later period of their lives, the Stanton-Anthony bond was weakened to the extent that "each woman pursued a separate course" (p. 214). This suggests that *if* they had politically disagreed on priorities, their relationship would have terminated. It also assumes the questionable thesis that Stanton did not become a "self-sovereign," especially in relationship to Anthony until the last years of her life. This thesis only works if one sees Stanton as submissive to Anthony's dictates and domination—a popular view of Anthony but one that denies the full subjectivity of each of these women.

63. Susan B. Anthony, "Woman's Half-Century of Evolution," *North American Review*, December 1902, 800.

12. A Grand Old Age

1. Susan B. Anthony, "The Status of Woman, Past, Present, and Future," *The Arena* (May 1897): 904–05.
2. SBA to the American Unitarian Association, May 24, 1900, RPL.
3. Susan B. Anthony, pp. 904–905.
4. S.B.A. to Mrs. Selbey, April 4, 1895, URL.
5. Ida Harper, *The Life and Work of Susan B. Anthony*, vol. 2, 841.
6. Ibid., 842.
7. S.B.A. to Clara Colby, August 26, 1895, HL.
8. S.B.A. to E.C.S., July 24, 1895, HL.
9. S.B.A. to Mrs. Colby, December 18, 1895, HL.
10. S.B.A. to E.C.S., December 2, 1898, typed copy, HL.
11. Emerson's essay "Friendship," Ralph Waldo Emerson, *Essays* (Boston: Phillips, Sampson, & Co., 1854), S.B.A's copy, 184, 191, LC.
12. Elizabeth Cady Stanton, *The Woman's Bible*, Reprint. (Seattle: Coalition Task Force on Women and Religion, 1974), Appendix, 215.
13. Ibid.
14. Ibid., 216.
15. Ibid., 217.
16. Ida Harper, vol. 2, 853–54.
17. Ibid., 855.
18. See William O'Neill, *Everyone Was Brave: The Rise and Fall of Feminism in America* (Chicago: Quadrangle, 1969).
19. Ida Harper, vol. 3, 1198.
20. Mary A. Hill, *Charlotte Perkins Gilman: The Making of a Radical Feminist* (Philadelphia: Temple University Press, 1980), 273.

21. Mary Jo Deegan, *Jane Addams and the Men of the Chicago School: 1892–1918* (New Jersey: Transaction Books, 1986).

22. Charlotte Perkins Gilman, *Women and Economics, 1898*. Reprint. (New York: Harper Torchbook 1966), 15.

23. Susan B. Anthony and Ida Harper, Introduction, *History of Woman Suffrage,* vol. 4, xxxi.

24. Susan B. Anthony, cited in Alan P. Grimes, *The Puritan Ethic and Woman Suffrage* (New York: Oxford University Press, 1967), 87.

25. *History of Woman Suffrage,* vol. 4, 316–17.

26. Ida Harper, vol. 2, 899.

27. Ibid., vol. 2, 922.

28. Ibid., vol. 2, 789.

29. Susan B. Anthony Diary, June 23, 1894, LC; Ida Harper, vol. 2, 880.

30. Harper, vol. 2, 880.

31. S.B.A. to Ellen Clark Sargent and Sarah B. Cooper, January 23, 1896, C.

32. Ida Harper, vol. 2, 887.

33. S.B.A. to E.C.S., January 27, 1884, URL.

34. S.B.A. to National Negro Race Conference, July 12, 1900, RPL.

35. Paula Giddings, *When and Where I Enter: The Impact of Black Women on Race and Sex in America* (New York: Bantam, 1985), 95–98.

36. Cited in Ibid., 97.

37. *History of Woman Suffrage,* vol. 4, 325–26.

38. Ibid., 376.

39. Mary Church Terrell, *A Colored Woman in a White World,* 1940. Reprint. (New York: Arno Press, 1980), 143.

40. Bettina Apthekar, *Woman's Legacy: Essays on Race, Sex, and Class in American History* (Amherst: University of Massachusetts Press, 1982), 59.

41. S.B.A. to Mrs. Colby, August 26, 1895, HL.

42. *History of Woman Suffrage,* vol. 4, 240.

43. S.B.A. to Clara Colby, 1895, HL.

44. Susan B. Anthony Diary, April 9, 1895, LC. *Crusade for Justice: The Autobiography of Ida B. Wells,* edited by Alfreda M. Duster (Chicago: University of Chicago Press, 1970), 228–29.

45. Ida Harper, vol. 2, 909.

46. Ibid.

47. Ibid.

48. Ibid., 935.

49. Genevieve Lull Hawley to Auntie, March 12, 1897, URL.

50. Nellie Bly, *Woman's Journal,* 1895.

51. G.L.H. to Auntie, March 21, 1897, URL.

52. Ibid., May 28, 1897, URL.

53. S.B.A. to Rachel, May 14, 1897, URL.

54. Ida Harper, vol. 2, 897.

55. S.B.A. to Rachel, May 14, 1897, URL.

56. S.B.A. to Elizabeth Smith Miller, March 21, 1899, NYPL.

57. *History of Woman Suffrage,* vol. 4, 33.

58. S.B.A. to Mrs. Colby, December 17, 1898, HL.

59. Rochester dispatch to Associated Press, published in *Boston Transcript,* April 30, 1900, URL.

60. S.B.A. to Elizabeth Smith Miller, August 22, 1900, NYPL.

61. S.B.A. to Mary McHenry Keith, July 25, 1900, B.

62. Ida Harper, vol. 3, 1157.

63. Ibid.

64. S.B.A. to Mrs. Colby, December 14, 1898, HL.

65. Anna Howard Shaw, *Story of a Pioneer* (New York: Harper, 1915), 284.

66. *History of Woman Suffrage,* vol. 4, 388.

67. Ida Harper, vol. 3, 1165.

68. Ibid., 1167.

69. Ibid., 1169, 1273.

70. Ibid., 1173.

71. Ibid., 1138.

72. Phyllis Stock, *Better Than Rubies: A History of Women's Education* (New York: Putnam, 1978), 192.

73. Arthur J. May, *University of Rochester, 1850–1962* (Rochester, University of Rochester, 1977), 118. See G. J. Barker-Benfield, *The Horrors of the Half-Known Life: Male Attitudes Toward Women and Sexuality in Nineteenth Century America* (New York: Harper, 1976), Chap. 15, "The Spermatic Economy and Proto-Sublimation." Barker-Benfield elaborates the patterns by which men came to believe they needed to divert the temptation to express themselves sexually in order to concentrate their energies on higher goals.

74. Ida Harper, vol. 3, 1223–24, and May, 119–21.

75. Ida Harper, vol 3, 1225.

76. G.L.H. to Auntie, November 4, 1900, URL.

77. Ibid., November 25, 1900.

78. G.L.H. to Auntie, December 9, 1900, URL.

79. S.B.A. to Mrs. Spofford, December 28, 1900, RPL.

13. *"Failure Is Impossible"*

1. E.C.S. to Harper, September 30, 1902, HL.

2. Ida Harper, *The Life and Work of Susan B. Anthony,* vol. 3, 1211–13.

3. Harper to Genevieve Lull Hawley, January 11, 1901, URL.

4. Ida Harper, vol. 3, 1242.

5. Ibid., 1250.

6. Ibid., 1255.

7. E.C.S. to E. B. Harbert, July 25, 1901, HL.

8. Ida Harper, vol. 3, 1256.

9. G.L.H. to Auntie, October 26, 1902, URL.

10. Ida Harper, vol. 3, 1263.

11. G.L.H. to Auntie, October 26, 1902, URL.

12. S.B.A. to Harper, October 28, 1902, HL.

13. Ida Harper, vol. 3, 1264.

14. Harper to Hawley, August 18, 1902, URL.

15. This dress has been preserved and is on display at the Susan B. Anthony home, a national historical monument in Rochester, New York.

16. S.B.A. to Hawley, April 25, 1901, URL.

17. Ida Harper, vol. 3, 1202.

18. Ibid., 1256.

19. Ibid., 1296–97.

20. Ibid., 1283.

21. Ibid., 1296–97.

22. Theodore Stanton to S.B.A., June 9, 1903, HL. Amy Dykeman in " 'To Pour Forth From My Own Experience': Two Versions of Elizabeth Cady Stanton," *Journal of Rutgers University Libraries* 64 (June 1982): 1–16 details the ongoing problem for scholars with Theodore Stanton and Harriot Stanton Blatch's collection of their mother's papers. Comparing transcribed typescripts of letters held by the Douglass Library at Rutgers University and others at Vassar with those published in the Stanton and Blatch edition of *Elizabeth Cady Stanton as Revealed in Her Letters, Diary, and Reminiscences* (New York: Harper, 1922), it is evident that they omitted some letters and sometimes even synthesized two or three separate letters written at different times into one. That Stanton's children were trying to elevate their mother's reputation was evident in their exclusion of several letters from Susan B. Anthony, and in Harriot's frequent repetition of the phrase that it was her mother who converted Susan B. Anthony to woman's rights. Without Anthony's hand to guide them in their work, they clearly went far beyond the role of editors. As Dykeman pointed out, "The real tragedy, though, is the erroneous transcription or omission of passages in the letters that deal with Stanton's views on major issues of her day. Patterns emerge when the Douglass copies are compared, to the published version: Stanton's views on marriage and divorce, her notes for her speeches and articles, her domestic duties, men, black male suffrage, and her health are often deleted . . . many of Stanton's references to personal acquaintances, especially Susan B. Anthony, are suppressed" (Amy Dykeman p. 10). In the research and study for this biography of Susan B.

Anthony (1987) all available typescripts, originals, and the Stanton and Blatch edition were cross-checked for the most accurate representation of thoughts and ideas.

23. August Meier in Robert C. Twombly, *Blacks in White America Since 1865: Issues and Interpretations* (New York: McKay, 1971), 85, 87, and 94.

24. Spencer, 51.

25. S.B.A. to Elizabeth Boynton Harbert, June 24, 1903, HL.

26. *The Tuskegee Student,* April 4, 1903.

27. Adele Logan Alexander, "How I Discovered My Grandmother . . . ," *Ms. Magazine* (November 1983): 29.

28. S.B.A. to Rachel, December 31, 1897, URL.

29. S.B.A. to Isabel Howland, October 5, 1897, URL.

30. Adella Logan to S.B.A., January 24, 1898, URL.

31. S.B.A. to Anna Dann, May 28, 1904, RPL.

32. Ibid., May 1904, HL.

33. Anna Howard Shaw, *The Story of a Pioneer* (New York: Harper, 1915), 209.

34. Mary Anthony to friends at Home, June 19, 1904, RPL.

35. Anna Howard Shaw, 210.

36. Mary Anthony to friends at Home, June 19, 1904, RPL.

37. Ida Harper, vol. 3, 1218.

38. S.B.A. to Cousin Jessie, June 12, 1905, HL.

39. S.B.A. to Ellen Clark Sargent, 1905, HL.

40. Ida Harper, vol. 3, 1307.

41. Ibid., 1375–76.

42. Anna Howard Shaw, 221–22.

43. M. Carey Thomas tribute to Susan B. Anthony, SSC.

44. Ida Harper, vol. 3, 1399–1400; Anna Howard Shaw, 225.

45. Ida Harper, vol. 3, 1402.

46. Ibid., 1418.

47. This and preceding dialogue drawn from Anna Howard Shaw, 234.

Postscript: On Women's Biography

1. Theodore Stanton and Harriot Stanton Blatch, *Elizabeth Cady Stanton As Revealed in Her Letters, Diary, and Reminiscences,* vol. 1 (New York: Harper, 1922).

2. "Culture et pouvoir des femmes: Essai d'historiographie," Centre des recherches historique, *Annales* (Mars-avril, no. 2):290.

3. Paul Ricoeur. *Time and Narrative, vol. 1,* translated by Kathleen McLaughlin and David Pellauer (Chicago: University of Chicago Press, 1984), 177.

4. Joan Kelly, "The Social Relation of the Sexes: Methodological Im-

plications of Women's History," in *Women, History and Theory* (Chicago: University of Chicago Press, 1984).

5. See Jean-Paul Sartre, *The Family Idiot: Gustave Flaubert, 1821–1857, vol. 1,* translated from the French by Carol Cosman (Chicago: University of Chicago Press, 1981) for both biography and method which approaches the unity of these dichotomies.

6. Paul Ricoeur, 177.

7. Herbert Blumer, "Introduction to the Transaction Edition," *Critique of Research in the Social Sciences, An Appraisal of Thomas and Zaniescki's The Polish Peasant in Europe and America* (New Brunswick: Transaction, 1975). See xxx–xxxiii for a discussion of representativeness in life-history methodology. See also Daniel Bertaux, "L'approche biographique, sa validite methodologique, ses potentialitiés," *Cahiers internationaux de sociolgie* 69 (1980): 206–8 for a discussion of saturation in biographical methodology.

8. Kathleen Barry, "The Method of Biography in Feminist Research," paper developed and presented at Centre Nationale de la Recherche Scientifique, Laboratoire d'Anthropologie Sociale, Paris, 1986. This concept of the fundamental dynamics of interaction is drawn from Herbert Blumer's concept of symbolic interaction based on the work of George Herbert Mead. See Herbert Blumer, *Symbolic Interactionism: Perspective and Methods* (Englewood Cliffs: Prentice-Hall, 1969 ; and George Herbert Mead, *Mind, Self and Society from the Standpoint of a Social Behaviorist* (Chicago: University of Chicago Press, 1934, 1967). While finding symbolic interaction an important explication of subjectivity in interaction, this paper explores the intersections of interaction with social structure and history.

9. Sartre's concept of "the negation of the negation" is useful here. See *Search for a Method,* where he shows that "defined by the negation of the refused reality in the name of the reality to be produced, it remains the captive of the action which it clarifies, and disappears along with it," (p. 92) and that "only the project, as a mediation between two moments of objectivity can account for history; that is for human creativity" (p. 99) (New York: Knopf, 1963, Vintage, 1968).

10. See Simone de Beauvoir, *The Second Sex,* where she equates immanence with stagnation, "the brutish life of subjection to given conditions," translated from the French by H. M. Parshley (New York: Bantam, 1953), xxviii.

11. Simone de Beauvoir, *The Second Sex,* xviii.

12. Jean Paul Sartre, *The Search for a Method,* 85–100.

Bibliography

Primary Sources

Abbott, Edith. *Women in Industry*. New York: Appleton, 1910.

Anthony, Susan B. "The Status of Woman, Past, Present, and Future." *The Arena* (May 1897):901–903.

———. "Woman's Half Century of Evolution." *North American Review* (December 1902):800–810.

Anthony, Susan B., and Harper, Ida. *History of Woman Suffrage*. Vol. 4. Rochester: Susan B. Anthony, 1903.

Barrett Browning, Elizabeth. *Aurora Leigh*. 1856. Reprint. London: Women's Press, 1978.

Brontë, Charlotte. *Jane Eyre*. 1848. Reprint. New York: Bantam, 1981.

Dall, Caroline. *The College, the Market, and the Court*. Boston: Memorial Edition, 1914.

Emerson, Ralph Waldo. *Essays*. Boston: Phillips, Sampson & Company, 1854.

Fuller, Margaret. *Women in the Nineteenth Century*. 1845. Reprint. New York: W. W. Norton, 1971.

Gage, Matilda Joslyn. *Woman, Church and State*. Reprint. Boston: Persephone, 1980.

Gaskell, Mrs. *The Life of Charlotte Brontë*. Reprint. New York: Penguin, 1975.

Gilman, Charlotte Perkins. *Women and Economics*. 1898. Reprint. New York: Harper Torchbook, 1966.

Harper, Ida. *The Life and Work of Susan B. Anthony*. 3 vols. Indianapolis: Bowen-Merrill, 1899, 1908.

Hawthorne, Nathaniel. *The American Notebooks*. Edited by Randall Stewart. New Haven, Conn.: Yale University Press, 1932.
——. *The Scarlet Letter*. 1850. Reprint. New York: Airmont, 1962.
Shaw, Anna Howard. *The Story of a Pioneer*. New York: Harper & Row, 1915.
Smith, Elizabeth Oakes. *Bertha and Lily: or the Parsonage of Beech Glen, a Romance*. New York: J. C. Derby, 1854.
Stanton, Elizabeth Cady. *Eighty Years and More: Reminiscences 1815–1897*. 1898. Reprint. New York: Schocken, 1971.
——. *The Woman's Bible*. 1898. Reprint. Seattle: Coalition Task Force on Women and Religion, 1974.
Stanton, Elizabeth Cady, Anthony, Susan B., and Gage, Matilda Joselyn. *History of Woman Suffrage*. Vol. 1. New York: Fowler & Wells, 1881. Vol. 2. Rochester: Susan B. Anthony, 1881. Vol. 3. Rochester: Susan B. Anthony, 1886.
Stanton, Theodore, and Blatch, Harriot Stanton, eds. *Elizabeth Cady Stanton as Revealed in Her Letters, Diary, and Reminiscences*. 2 vols. New York: Harper, 1922.
Terrell, Mary Church. *A Colored Woman in a White World*. 1940. Reprint. New York: Arno Press, 1980.
Wells, Ida B. *Crusade for Justice: The Autobiography of Ida B. Wells*. Edited by Alfreda M. Duster. rev ed. Chicago: University of Chicago Press, 1970.
Wollstonecraft, Mary. *Vindication of the Rights of Woman*. 1790. Reprint. New York: W. W. Norton, 1967.

Secondary Literature

Abray, Jane. "Feminism in the French Revolution." *American Historical Review* (February 1975):43–62.
Alexander, Adele Logan. "How I Discovered My Grandmother." *Ms.* (November 1983):29.
Anthony, Katharine. *Susan B. Anthony: Her Personal History and Her Era*. New York: Doubleday, 1954.
Aptheker, Bettina. *Women's Legacy, Essays on Race, Class and Sex*. Amherst: University of Massachusetts, 1982.
Arendt, Hannah. *On Revolution*. Middlesex, England: Penguin, 1963.
Aries, Phillippe. *Centuries of Childhood*. Translated by Robert Baldick. New York: Vintage, 1962.
Bacon, Margaret H. *As the Way Opens: The Story of Quaker Women in America*. Richmond, Va.: Friends United Press, 1980.
——. *Valiant Friend: The Life of Lucretia Mott*. New York: Walker, 1980.

ⁿner, Lois. *Elizabeth Cady Stanton: A Radical for Woman's Rights.* Boston: Little, Brown, 1980.

——. *The Horrors of the Half-Known Life: Male Attitudes Toward Women and Sexuality in Nineteenth Century America.* New York: Harper, 1976.

Bartlett, Irving H. *Wendell Phillips, Brahmin Radical.* Boston: Beacon, 1961.

Beard, Mary. *Woman as a Force in History.* New York: Collier Books, 1946.

Becker, Carl L. *The Heavenly City of the Eighteenth-Century Philosophes.* New Haven, Conn.: Yale University Press, 1975.

Bendix, Reinhard. *Max Weber: An Intellectual Portrait.* Garden City, N.Y.: Doubleday, 1960.

Blackwell, Alice Stone. *Lucy Stone: Pioneer of Women's Rights.* Boston: Little, Brown, 1930.

Bordin, Ruth. *Woman and Temperance, The Quest for Power and Liberty, 1873–1900.* Philadelphia: Temple University Press, 1981.

Braudel, Fernand. *The Perspectives of the World, Civilization & Capitalism, 15th-18th Centuries.* Vol. 3. Translated from the French by Sian Reynolds. New York: Harper & Row, 1979.

Brinton, Howard. *Quaker Education in Theory and Practice.* Wallingford, Pa.: Pendle Hill Pamphlets, 1940.

Brown, Irene A. "Domesticity, Feminism, and Friendship: Female Aristocratic Culture and Marriage in England, 1660–1760." *Journal of Family History* (Winter 1982):406–24.

——. "Friendship and Spiritual Time in the Didactic Enlightenment." Unpublished paper.

Buhle, Mary Jo and Paul. *A Concise History of Woman Suffrage.* Urbana: University of Illinois Press, 1978.

Bury, J. B. *The Idea of Progress, An Inquiry Into Its Growth and Origin.* New York: Dover, 1960.

Bushman, Claudia L. *Mormon Sisters: Women in Early Utah.* Salt Lake City: Olympus, 1976.

Chafetz, Janet and Dworkin, Anthony. *Female Revolt: Women's Movements in World Historical Perspective.* New Jersey: Rowman & Allanheld, 1986.

Chambers-Schiller, Lee. *Liberty, a Better Husband.* New Haven, Conn.: Yale University Press, 1984.

——. "The Single Woman: Family and Vocation Among Nineteenth Century Reformers." In *Women's Being, Woman's Place,* edited by Mary Kelley. Boston: G. K. Hall,.1979.

Clarkson, Thomas. *A Portraiture of Quakerism.* London: Longman, Hurst, Rees, Orme, 1806.

Clifford, Geraldine J. "'Daughters into Teachers': Demographic Influences on the Transformation of Teaching into 'Women's Work.'" Paper prepared for Radcliffe Research Scholars Colloquium Series, Spring 1982.

Conrad, Susan. *Perish the Thought: Intellectual Women in Romantic America, 1830–1860*. Secaucus, N.J.: Citadel Press, 1976.

Conway, Jill. "Perspectives in the History of Women's Education in the United States." *History of Education Quarterly* (Spring 1976):1–7.

———. "Women Reformers and American Culture, 1870–1930." *Journal of Social History* 5, no. 2 (Winter 1971):164–77.

Cott, Nancy. *Bonds of Womanhood*. New Haven, Conn.: Yale University Press, 1977.

———. "Eighteenth Century Family and Social Life Revealed in Massachusetts Divorce Records." In *A Heritage of Her Own*, edited by Nancy Cott and Elizabeth Pleck. New York: Simon & Schuster, 1979.

Davis, Angela. *Women, Race and Class*. New York: Random House, 1981.

Davis, David Brion, ed. *Ante-Bellum Reform*. New York: Harper & Row, 1969.

Deegan, Mary Jo. *Jane Addams and the Men of the Chicago School: 1892–1918*. New Jersey: Transaction, 1986.

Degler, Carl. *At Odds: Women and the Family in America from the Revolution to the Present*. New York: Oxford University Press, 1980.

Delphy, Christine. *Close to Home*. Amherst: University of Massachusetts Press, 1984.

Doherty, Robert W. *The Hicksite Separation*. New Brunswick, N.J.: Rutgers University Press, 1967.

Donald, David. *The Politics of Reconstruction 1863–1867*. Baton Rouge: Louisiana State University Press, 1965.

Douglas, Ann. *The Feminization of American Culture*. New York: Avon, 1977.

Douglass, Frederick. *The Life and Times of Frederick Douglass*. 1892. Reprint. New York: Macmillan Collier, 1962.

Drake, Thomas E. *Quakers and Slavery in America*. New Haven, Conn.: Yale University Press, 1965.

Dublin, Thomas. *Women at Work*. New York: Columbia University Press, 1979.

Dubois, Ellen Carol. *Feminism and Suffrage: The Emergance of an Independent Women's Movement in America 1848–1869*. Ithaca, N.Y.: Cornell University Press, 1978.

———, ed. *Elizabeth Cady Stanton and Susan B. Anthony, Correspondence, Writing, Speeches*. New York: Schocken, 1981.

Dunn, Mary Maples. "Women of the Light." In *Women of America, A History*, edited by Carol Ruth Berken and Mary Beth Norton. Boston: Houghton Mifflin, 1979.

Dykeman, Amy. "'To Pour Forth from My Own Experience': Two Versions of Elizabeth Cady Stanton." *Journal of Rutgers University Libraries* 64 (June 1982):1–16.

Engels, Frederick. "Introduction." London, March 6, 1895, to Karl Marx.

In *The Civil War in France*. New York: International Publishers, n.d.

Epstein, Barbara Leslie. *The Politics of Domesticity: Women, Evangelicalism and Temperance in Nineteenth Century America*. Middletown, Conn.: Wesleyan University Press, 1981.

Euston, Barbara. "Feminism and the Contemporary Family." In *A Heritage of Her Own*, edited by Nancy Cott and Elizabeth Pleck. New York: Simon & Schuster, 1979.

Evans, Richard. *The Feminists, Women's Emancipation Movements in Europe, America and Australia, 1840–1920*. New York: Barnes & Noble, 1977.

Evans, Sarah. *Personal Politics*. New York: Vintage, 1979.

Faderman, Lillian. *Surpassing the Love of Men*. New York: William Morrow, 1981.

Flexner, Eleanor. *Century of Struggle*. New York: Atheneum, 1968.

Foner, Eric. *Free Soil, Free Labor, Free Men: The Ideology of the Republican Party Before the Civil War*. New York: Oxford, 1970.

Foner, Phillip. *Frederick Douglass: A Biography*. New York: Citadel Press, 1964.

——. *Women and the American Labor Movement; From Colonial Times to the Eve of World War I*. New York: The Free Press, 1979.

Fornell, Earl Wesley. *The Unhappy Mediums. Spiritualism and the Life of Margaret Fox*. Austin: University of Texas, 1964.

Frost, Jerry. "As the Twig is Bent: Quaker Ideas of Childhood." *Quaker History* 60 (1971):68–87.

Ganshof, F. L. *Feudalism*. Translated from the French by Philip Grierson. London: Longmans, 1952.

Garfinkle, Norton, ed. *Lincoln and the Coming of the Civil War*. Lexington, Mass.: Heath, 1959.

Gay, Peter. *The Enlightenment, An Interpretation: The Rise of Modern Pragmatism*. New York: W. W. Norton, 1977.

——. *The Enlightenment, An Interpretation: The Science of Freedom*. New York: W. W. Norton, 1969.

Genevose, Eugene. *Roll, Jordan Roll: The World the Slaves Made*. New York: Pantheon, 1974.

Giddings, Paula. *When and Where I Enter: The Impact of Black Women on Race and Sex in America*. New York: Bantam, 1985.

Gilbert, Sandra, and Gubar, Susan. *The Madwoman in the Attic: The Woman Writer and Nineteenth Century Literary Imagination*. New Haven, Conn.: Yale University Press, 1979.

Grimes, Alan P. *The Puritan Ethic and Woman Suffrage*. New York: Oxford University Press, 1967.

Gutman, Herbert. *Work, Culture and Society in Industrializing America*. New York: Vintage, 1977.

Harplen, Delores. *The Grand Domestic Revolution.* Cambridge, Mass.: MIT Press 1982.

Hartmann, Heidi. "The Unhappy Marriage of Marxism and Feminism: Towards a More Progressive Union." In *Women and Revolution,* edited by Lydia Sargent. Boston: South End Press, 1981.

Hays, Elinor Rice. *Lucy Stone: One of America's First and Greatest Feminists.* New York: Tower, 1961.

Hersh, Blanche Glassman. *The Slavery of Sex: Feminist-Abolitionists in America.* Urbana: University of Illinois Press, 1978.

Hewitt, Nancy. *Women's Activism and Social Change: Rochester 1822–1872.* Ithaca, N.Y.: Cornell University Press, 1984.

Hill, Mary A. *Charlotte Perkins Gilman: The Making of a Radical Feminist, 1860–1896.* Philadelphia: Temple University Press, 1980.

Hoff-Wilson, Joan. "The Illusion of Change: Women in the American Revolution." In *The American Revolution: Exploration in the History of American Radicalism,* edited by Alfred Young. De Kalb: Northern Illinois University Press, 1976.

Horkheimer, Max, and Adorno, Theodor W. *Dialectic of Enlightenment.* New York: Continuum, 1982.

Hufton, Olwen. "Women in Revolution 1789–1796." *Past and Present* (1971):148–66.

Hymowitz, Carol, and Weissman, Michaele. *A History of Women in America.* New York: Bantam, 1978.

Johnston, Johanna. *Mrs. Satan: The Incredible Saga of Victoria C. Woodhull.* New York: G. P. Putnam, 1967.

Josephson, Hannah. *The Golden Threads: New England's Mill Girls and Magnates.* New York: Duell, Sloan & Pearce, 1949.

Kelly-Godal, Joan. "The Social Relations of the Sexes: Methodological Implications of Women's History." *Signs* (Summer 1976):809–23.

Kerber, Linda. *Women of the Republic: Intellect & Ideology in Revolutionary America.* Chapel Hill: University of North Carolina Press, 1980.

Kluger, Israel. "The Trade Union Career of Susan B. Anthony." *Labor History* 2 (1961):90–100.

——. *From Ladies to Women: The Organized Struggle for Woman's Rights in the Reconstruction Era.* Westport, Conn.: Greenwood Press, 1987.

Koehler, Lyle. *A Search for Power: The "Weaker Sex" in Seventeenth Century New England.* Urbana: University of Illinois Press, 1980.

Kraditor, Aileen. *The Ideas of the Woman Suffrage Movement 1899–1920.* New York: Doubleday Anchor, 1965.

——. *Means and Ends in American Abolitionism.* New York: Pantheon, 1967.

Krouse, Richard. "Patriarchal Liberalism and Beyond, From John Stuart Mill to Harriot Taylor." In *The Family in Political Thought,* edited by

Jean Elshtain. Amherst: University of Massachusetts Press, 1982.

Lacy, Dan. *The Abolitionists*. New York: McGraw-Hill, 1978.

Lasch, Christopher. *A Haven in a Heartless World*. New York: Basic Books, 1977.

Laslett, Peter. *The World We Have Lost*. London: Methuen, 1968.

Leach, William. *True Love and Perfect Union: The Feminist Reform of Sex and Society*. New York: Basic Books, 1980.

Lerner, Gerda. *The Female Experience, An American Documentary*. Indianapolis: Bobbs-Merrill, 1977.

——. *The Grimke Sisters from South Carolina*. New York: Schocken, 1971.

——. *The Majority Finds Its Past*. New York: Oxford University Press, 1979.

Lockridge, Kenneth. *Literacy in Colonial New England*. New York: W. W. Norton, 1974.

Lunde, Erik S. *Horace Greeley*. Boston: Twayne, 1981.

Lutz, Alma. *Created Equal: A Biography of Elizabeth Cady Stanton, 1815–1902*. New York: John Day, 1940.

——. *Emma Willard, Pioneer Educator of Women*. Boston: Beacon, 1964.

——. "Susan B. Anthony and John Brown." *Rochester History* 15 (July 1953).

——. *Susan B. Anthony: Rebel, Crusader, Humanitarian*. Boston: Beacon, 1959.

Lytle, Scott H. "The Second Sex: September 1793." *Journal of Modern Historical Review* (1955):14–26.

McClellan, Elisabeth. *Historic Dress in America 1607–1870*. 1904. Reprint. New York: Arno Press, 1977.

McGrane, Reginald Charles. *The Panic of 1837*. 1924. Reprint. Chicago: University of Chicago Press, 1965.

McKelvey, Blake. *Rochester, the Water-Power City, 1812–1854*. Cambridge, Mass.: Harvard University Press, 1945.

——. *Rochester, the Flower City, 1855–1890*. Cambridge, Mass.: Harvard University Press, 1949.

——. *Rochester, the Quest for Quality, 1890–1925*. Cambridge, Mass.: Harvard University Press, 1956.

——. "Susan B. Anthony." *Rochester History* 7, no. 2 (April 1945):1–24.

McLoughlin, William G. *The Meaning of Henry Ward Beecher, An Essay on the Shifting Values of Mid-Victorian America, 1840–1870*. New York: Alfred A. Knopf, 1970.

May, Arthur J. *University of Rochester, 1850–1962*. Rochester: University of Rochester Press, 1977.

Melder, Keith. *Beginnings of Sisterhood: The American Woman's Rights Movement 1800–1850*. New York: Schocken, 1977.

Merrill, Walter M. *Against Wind and Tide: A Biography of William Lloyd Garrison*. Cambridge, Mass.: Harvard University Press, 1963.

Michel, Andree, and Texier, Genevieve. *La Condition de la française d'aujourd'hui*. Paris: Editions Gonthier, 1964.

Millett, Kate. *Sexual Politics*. New York: Doubleday, 1970.

Moers, Ellen. *Literary Women*. New York: Oxford University Press, 1963.

Moore, Barrington, Jr. *Injustice: The Social Bases of Obedience and Revolt*. White Plains, N.Y.: M. E. Sharpe, 1978.

Moses, Claire Goldberg. *French Feminism in the 19th Century*. Albany: State University of New York Press, 1984.

Nevaskar, Balwant. *Capitalists Without Capitalism*. Westport, Conn.: Greenwood Press, 1971.

Newcomer, Mabel. *A Century of Higher Education for American Women*. New York: Harper & Brothers, 1959.

Oates, Stephen B. *Our Fiery Trial: Abraham Lincoln, John Brown and the Civil War Era*. Amherst: University of Massachusetts Press, 1979.

Pankhurst, Sylvia. *The Suffrage Movement*. London: Virago, 1977.

Pease, William. "The Gannetts of Rochester: Highlights in a Liberal Career." *Rochester History* 17 no. 4 (October 1955):1–24.

Riegel, Robert E. "Patterns of Nineteenth Century Feminism." In *The Woman Question in History*, edited by Barbara Welter. Hinsdale, Ill.: Dryden Press, 1971.

Rossi, Alice S., ed. *Essays on Sex Equality by John Stuart Mill*. Chicago: University of Chicago Press, 1970.

Rowbotham, Sheila. *Hidden from History*. New York: Vintage, 1973.

Rugoff, Milton. *The Beechers: An American Family in the Nineteenth Century*. New York: Harper & Row, 1981.

Ryan, Mary. "Femininity and Capitalism in Antebellum America." In *Capitalist Patriarchy and the Case for Socialist Feminism*, edited by Z. Eisenstein. New York: Monthly Review Press, 1979.

———. *Womanhood in America: From Colonial Times to the Present*. New York: New Viewpoints, 1975.

Sachs, Abie, and Wilson, Joan Hoff. *Sexism and the Law*. New York: The Free Press, 1978.

Schneider, Herbert. *A History of American Philosophy*. New York: Columbia University Press, 1963.

———. *The Puritan Mind*. Ann Arbor: University of Michigan Press, 1958.

Scott, Anne Firor. "The Ever Widening Circle: The Diffusion of Feminist Values from the Troy Female Seminary 1822–1872." *History of Education Quarterly* (Spring 1979):3–25.

———. *The Southern Lady: From Pedestal to Politics 1830–1930*. Chicago: University of Chicago Press, 1970.

Scott, Anne Firor, and Scott, Andrew MacKay. *One Half the People: The Fight for Woman Suffrage*. Chicago: University of Illinois Press, 1975.

Shahar, Shulamith. *The Fourth Estate: A History of Women in the Middle Ages*. Translated by Chaya Galai. New York: Methuem, 1983.

Shaplen, Robert. *Free Love and Heavenly Sinners: The Story of the Great Henry Ward Beecher Scandal.* New York: Alfred A. Knopf, 1954.

Simms, Henry H. *A Decade of Sectional Controversy, 1851–1861.* 1942. Reprint. Westport, Conn.: Greenwood Press, 1978.

Sklar, Kathryn Kish. *Catharine Beecher: A Study in American Domesticity.* New York: W. W. Norton, 1973.

——. "The Founding of Mount Holyoke College." In *Women of America. A History,* edited by Carol Berkin and Mary Beth Norton. Boston: Houghton Mifflin, 1979.

Smith, Daniel Scott. "Parental Power and Marriage Patterns: An Analysis of Historical Trends in Hingham, Massachusetts." In *The American Family in Social-Historical Perspective.* New York: St. Martin's Press, 1978.

Smith-Rosenberg, Carroll. "Beauty, the Beast and the Militant Woman: A Case Study in Sex Roles and Social Stress in Jacksonian America." *American Quarterly* 23 no. 4 (October 1971): 562–84.

——. "The Female World of Love and Ritual: Relations Between Women in Nineteenth Century America." *Signs* I, no. 1 (1975):1–29.

——. "The Hysterical Woman: Sex Roles and Role conflict in 19th-Century America." *Social Research* 39 no. 4 (Winter 1972):652–58.

Smith-Rosenberg, Carroll, and Rosenberg, Charles. "The Female Animal: Medical and Biological Views of Woman and Her Role in Nineteenth Century America." *Journal of American History* 15, no. 2 (September 1973): 332–56.

Stampp, Kenneth. *The Era of Reconstruction, 1865–1877.* New York: Alfred A. Knopf, 1965.

Stampp, Kenneth, and Litwak, Leon F., eds. *Reconstruction: An Anthology of Revisionist Writings.* Baton Rouge: Louisiana State University Press, 1969.

Stock, Phyllis. *Better Than Rubies, A History of Women's Education.* New York: Putnam, 1978.

Stow, Sarah. *History of Mount Holyoke.* South Hadley, Mass.: Mount Holyoke Seminary, 1887.

Stowe, Harriet Beecher. *Uncle Tom's Cabin.* 1851. Reprint. New York: Bantam, 1981.

Strasser, Susan. *Never Done, A History of American Housework.* New York: Pantheon, 1982.

Suhl, Yuri. *Ernestine L. Rose and the Battle for Human Rights.* New York: Reynal, 1959.

Thomas, Edith. *The Women Incendiaries.* Translated by James and Starr Atkinson. New York: George Braziller, 1966.

Tilly, Louise, and Scott, Joan. *Women, Work and Family.* New York: Holt, Rinehart and Winston, 1978.

Twombly, Robert C. *Blacks in White America since 1865, Issues and Inter-*

pretation. New York: McKay, 1971.

Tyrrell, Ian. *Sobering Up: From Temperance to Prohibition in Antebellum America, 1800–1860.* Westport, Conn.: Greenwood Press, 1979.

Ulrich, Laurel Thatcher. *Good Wives: Image and Reality in the Lives of Women in Northern New England 1650–1750.* New York: Alfred A. Knopf, 1982.

Unger, Samuel. *A History of the National Woman's Christian Temperance Union.* Ph.D. dissertation. Ohio State University, 1933.

Waller, Altina Laura. *The Beecher-Tilton Adultery Scandal: Family, Religion, and Politics in Brooklyn, 1865–1875.* Dissertation, University of Massachusetts, 1980.

——. *Reverend Beecher and Mrs. Tilton: Sex and Class in Victorian America.* Amherst: University of Massachusetts Press, 1982.

Weber, Max. "The Sociology of Charismatic Authority." Translated and reprinted in *From Max Weber: Essays in Sociology,* edited by H. H. Gerth and C. Wright Mills. New York: Oxford University Press, 1969.

Welter, Barbara. "Cult of True Womanhood—1820–1860." *American Quarterly* 18, 2:1 (Summer 1966): 151–74.

——. *Dimity Convictions: The American Woman in the Nineteenth Century.* Athens: Ohio University Press, 1976.

Wertenberger, Thomas Jefferson. *The Puritan Oligarchy, the Founding of American Civilization.* London: Scribner, 1947.

Wheeler, Leslie, ed. *Loving Warriors: Selected Letters of Lucy Stone and Henry Blackwell, 1853–1893.* New York: Dial, 1981.

Willner, Ann Ruth. *The Spellbinders, Charismatic Political Leadership.* New Haven, Conn.: Yale University Press, 1984.

Winthrop, John. *The History of New England.* Edited by James Savage. Boston: 1894.

Wishy, Bernard. *The Child and the Republic.* Philadelphia: University of Pennsylvania Press, 1968.

Wood, Ann Douglass. "Fashionable Diseases: Women's Complaints and Their Treatment in Nineteenth-Century America." In *Cleo's Consciousness Raised,* edited by Mary Hartman and Lois Banner, 1–22. New York: Harper Colophon, 1974.

Woodward, C. Vann. "John Brown's Raid and the Abandonment of Nonviolence." In *Abolitionists: Reformers or Fanatics?* New York: Holt, Rinehart and Winston, 1965.

Woody, Thomas. *Early Quaker Education in Pennsylvania.* New York: Columbia, 1920. Reprint. New York: Arno, 1969.

——. *A History of Women's Education in the United States.* New York: Science Press, 1929.

Zaretsky, Eli. *Capitalism, the Family and Personal Life.* New York: Harper & Row, 1976.

Selected Bibliography
On Women's Biography

Barry, Kathleen. "The Method of Biography in Feminist Research." Paper presented to Laboratoire d'anthropologie sociale, CNRS, Paris, Fall 1986.

de Beauvoir, Simone. *The Second Sex*. Translated from the French by H. M. Parshley. 1949. Reprint. New York: Bantam, 1953.

Becker, Howard. 1970. "The Life History and the Scientific Mosaic." In *Sociological Work*. Hawthorne, N.Y.: Aldine, 1970.

Bertaux, Daniel. "L 'approche biographique, sa validité méthodologique, ses potentialités." *Cahiers internationaux de sociologie* 69 (1980).

Bloch, Marc. *Feudal Society*. Chicago: University of Chicago Press, 1970.

Blumer, Herbert. "An Appraisal of Thomas and Znaniecki's 'The Polish Peasant in Europe and America.'" Reprint with new introduction of 1939. New Brunswick, N.J.: Transaction Books, 1979.

——. *Symbolic Interactionism: Perspective and Methods*. Englewood Cliffs: Prentice-Hall, 1969.

Braudel, Fernand. *Écrits sur l'histoire*. Paris: Flamarion, 1969.

Buck-Morss, Susan. *The Origin of the Negative Dialectic*. New York: The Free Press, 1977.

"Culture et pouvoir des femmes: essai d'historiographie." Centre de recherches historiques. *Annales* 2 (Mars–Avril 1986).

Duby, Georges. *Medieval Marriage*. Translated by Elborg Forster. Baltimore: Johns Hopkins University Press, 1978.

Ferrarotti, Franco. "Biography and the Social Sciences." *Social Research* 50 (1983).

Foucault, Michel. *The Use of Pleasure, the History of Sexuality*. Vol. 2. Translated by Robert Hurley. New York: Random House, 1985.

Kelly, Joan. *Women, History and Theory*. Chicago: University of Chicago Press, 1984.

Mead, George Herbert. *Mind, Self and Society from the Standpoint of a Social Behaviorist*. Chicago: University of Chicago Press, 1934, 1967.

Ricoeur, Paul. *Time and Narrative*. Vol. 1. Translated by Kathleen McLaughlin and David Pellauer. Chicago: University of Chicago Press, 1984.

Sartre, Jean-Paul. *The Family Idiot: Gustave Flaubert, 1821–1857*. Vol. 1. Translated from the French by Carol Cosman. Chicago: University of Chicago Press, 1981.

——. *Search for a Method*. Translated by Hazel H. Barnes. New York: Knopf, 1963; Vintage, 1968.

Stinchcombe, Arthur L. *Theoretical Methods in Social History*. New York: Academic Press, 1978.

Index